From Sources
A Guide to Resear

Michael Hogan
David Reinheimer

HEINLE & HEINLE
— ★ —™
THOMSON LEARNING

For more information, contact Heinle & Heinle Publishers Cambridge, MA 02142, or electronically at
http://www.thomson.com

Thomson Learning Europe
Berkshire House 168-173
High Holborn
London, WC1V 7AA, England

Thomson Learning Editores
Campos Eliseos 385, Piso 7
Col. Polanco
11560 México D.F. México

Thomas Nelson Australia
102 Dodds Street
South Melbourne 3205
Victoria, Australia

Thomson Learning Asia
221 Henderson Road
#05-10 Henderson Building
Singapore 0315

Nelson Canada
1120 Birchmount Road
Scarborough, Ontario
Canada M1K 5G4

Thomson Learning Japan
Hirakawacho Kyowa Building, 3F
2-2-1 Hirakawacho
Chiyoda-ku, Tokyo 102, Japan

Thomson Learning GmbH
Königswinterer Strasse 418
53227 Bonn, Germany

Thomson Learning Southern Africa
Building 18, Constantia Park
240 Old Pretoria Road
Halfway House, 1685 South Africa

ISBN 1-413-09663-8

The Adaptable Courseware Program consists of products and additions to existing Heinle & Heinle
Publishing Company products that are produced from camera-ready copy. Peer review, class testing, and
accuracy are primarily the responsibility of the author(s).

WRITING THE RESEARCHED PAPER

DETERMINE PURPOSE AND TOPIC

Create an Interest Inventory

Choose a Topic

Determine Purpose and Audience

Draft a Project Proposal

BUILD A BIBLIOGRAPHY

Locate Sources in Your Library

Use Online Sources

Build a Working Bibliography

Annotate Your Bibliographic Sources

GATHER INFORMATION

Skim Your Sources

Read Useful Passages

Collect Notes

Conduct Interviews

Conduct Surveys

VALIDATE EVIDENCE

Consult a Variety of Sources

Keep a Reflective Journal

Compare Evidence in Your Sources

DISCOVER CONNECTIONS AND CONTEXTS

Draw Connections Between Facts

Determine the Background of Your Topic

Determine the Context of Your Topic

CRITIQUE YOUR SOURCES

Read Critically:

- Identify the claim of the thesis
- Determine the structure of the document
- Note the sources of the information
- Determine the accuracy of the information
- Determine the author's attitude
- Discover fallacies
- Determine the Relative Significance of the Source

DRAW INFERENCES

Look for Inferences:

- Compare evidence to your "mental models"
- Compare evidence to familiar information
- Look for connections between evidence

Present Inferences

- The syllogism
- The Toulmin model
- The Rogerian argument

ARRANGE YOUR PRESENTATION

Outline Your Project

Create a Title

Introduce the Topic

Present the Thesis

Structure the Discussion

Blend Quotations, Paraphrases, and Summaries

Conclude Your Essay

CHECK YOUR MANUSCRIPT

The Cover/Title Page

Page Format and Pagination

Writing Conventions

Citation Format

Bibliographical Format

is

**Harcourt
College Publishers**

A Harcourt Higher Learning Company

Now you will find Harcourt Brace's
distinguished innovation, leadership, and
support under a different name . . . a new
brand that continues our unsurpassed
quality, service, and commitment to
education.

We are combining the strengths of our
college imprints into one worldwide
brand: Harcourt

Our mission is to make learning
accessible to anyone, anywhere,
anytime—reinforcing our commitment
to lifelong learning.

We are now Harcourt College Publishers.
Ask for us by name.

One Company
"Where Learning
Comes to Life."

www.harcourtcollege.com
www.harcourt.com

For Beverly for knowing and
Charles Augustus and Leah Vashti,
who saw the future.

For Nikki and Fred, the reasons why.

PREFACE

TO THE INSTRUCTOR

Our goal in writing this text is to emphasize the process of research beyond the mechanical concerns of locating and collecting information. We want to support you in your efforts to help students look beyond the notes they collect. We want students to think about whether their sources are reliable, how their various sources present the "facts," and how the "facts" connect to a larger perspective through background or context. Ultimately, of course, we want students to create original responses without falling into fallacies and cliché. We aim to accomplish these goals in several ways, beginning with the design of the book.

Critical reading, critical thinking, and critical writing support the processes in *From Sources to Purpose* by which students improve their skills in conducting research and writing the researched essay. The title itself, *From Sources to Purpose*, embodies these processes, moving the students from the sources they read to their purpose in a researched essay. As the subtitle, *A Guide to Researched Writing*, indicates, the text takes students from selecting a topic, consulting sources, and making judgments about them to creating a researched paper that reflects original thinking.

The text can be used in programs offering a second semester freshman composition course or those offering only a single composition course. It may also be used across the curricula in departments that offer or require a course in critical reading, thinking, and writing. In addition, the text is appropriate for a high school advanced placement or college prep course.

The Design

The thirteen chapters of the text are divided into four parts. You can lead your students through the chapters to show them that research is more than finding tidbits of information on a topic and then stitching their notes together. Done well, researched writing displays originality and ownership.

Part I: Setting the Stage

"Setting the Stage" looks at where the students have been and where they will go in this course.

Chapter 1, "Reviewing Basic Writing Principles," reminds students that the skills they learned in their first writing course apply to this course and to all academic and professional writing.

Chapter 2, "Determining Purpose and Choosing a Topic," shows students how to create an interest inventory and choose a research topic. Then students draw up a project proposal that explains their purpose (to describe, define, learn, explain, analyze cause, recommend, evaluate, assert a position, or evaluate) and identifies the audience.

Chapter 3, "Creating and Presenting Meaning," shows how researched writing is a partnership between the facts in sources and the original perspective that writers create from seeing how those facts are significant. Just like using sources properly, creating meaning is a way students can claim ownership of researched writing.

Part II: Using Sources

Because all major assignments in this text are research based, we provide basic information on locating and using resources early in the course.

Chapter 4, "Building a Bibliography," addresses how to identify kinds of resources and locate them. Students create a "working bibliography," and they keep a reflective journal as they conduct their research in order to qualify the value of each source and respond to it.

In Chapter 5, "Using Sources in Your Writing," students learn about using source material; making decisions about whether to quote, paraphrase, or summarize; and how to blend source material into their own writing. Two styles for citing sources are introduced: Modern Language Association (MLA) and American Psychological Association (APA).

Part III: Reading Sources Critically

Part III introduces critical reading skills needed to work with sources. As students conduct their research, they discover that sources report information in different ways: omitting facts, disagreeing with each other, and sometimes even misreporting information.

The first step in researching, then, is to get the facts straight—the focus of Chapter 6, "Validating Evidence." In discussing the limitations of consulting only a few sources, we hope we lay to rest the question asked of all writing teachers: "How many sources do I have to have?" At the end of the chapter, students write the first of four intermediate papers. In the validation paper, students evaluate the reliability of some of their sources.

Chapter 7, "Discovering Connections and Context," stresses the importance of developing a larger perspective on a topic. By making connections between facts and discovering the context or background of their topic, students take another step in the process of creating meaning. At the end of this chapter, students focus on one aspect of their research topic and write a short paper looking at the connections and contexts among facts.

Chapter 8, "Critiquing Sources," teaches students to determine the reliability of a source by reading actively and critically. Just as students earlier validated the facts of their topics, now they validate authors' credibility, reasoning, and perspective on a subject. At the end of this chapter, students use the new techniques they have learned to critique an article pertaining to their research topic.

Finally, in Chapter 9, "Drawing Inferences," we take a closer look at the process of creating meaning introduced in Chapter 3. Students learn to create meaning by drawing inferences and conclusions based on verified evidence. They also learn different ways to organize those conclusions: the classical syllogism, the Toulmin model of argument, and Rogerian argumentation. At the end of Chapter 9, students write a short paper to practice drawing inferences from evidence they have gathered about their research topic.

Part IV: Writing To Your Purpose

Up to this point, students have used critical reading and thinking skills to write short papers that show their understanding of the processes of research. In Part Four the issue turns to effectively presenting the final project to the audience.

Chapter 10, "Citing Your Sources—MLA Style" and Chapter 11, "Citing Your Sources—APA Style," present MLA format and APA format for citing sources and preparing a bibliography.

Chapter 12, "Arranging Your Presentation," provides information on outlining, introductions, conclusions, and titles.

Finally, Chapter 13, "Managing Your Presentation," covers the mechanics of researched writing. Two fully annotated researched essays, one in MLA format and one in APA format, illustrate the techniques.

The Anthology of Student Writing illustrates nine different purposes in a variety of subject areas. Each model is complete, with full documentation. The introduction to each paper explains the student writer's choice of topic.

Finally, we include a troubleshooting appendix that covers common grammar, spelling, punctuation, and mechanics problems.

Features

Unlike other texts that focus on "the research paper," *From Sources to Purpose: A Guide to Researched Writing* emphasizes process throughout, as evidenced by its title—it is a guide to researched writing.

- Instruction leads students step-by-step through the processes of researched writing.
- Students apply critical reading and thinking skills as they validate sources, discover connections and contexts in sources, critique sources, and draw inferences.
- Throughout, we stress the importance of ownership in writing.
- Each chapter is organized the same way:
  —a definition of the chapter's goal,
  —techniques for achieving the chapter's goal,
  —professional writing models,
  —student writing models,
  —a writing assignment.
- The text follows two students through every phase of the project, from interest inventory and project proposal to finished product (one uses MLA style, and the other uses APA).
- As students work on their major project, they use their own sources to write four short intermediate papers.
  - Concepts are developed through graphics and high interest essays and articles
  - Students keep a reflective journal to evaluate and interact with their sources.
- Both the Toulmin model of argument and the Rogerian are presented.

- Instruction is clear and reader-friendly.
  - Chapter 1 reviews basic writing principles, and the text concludes with an appendix of troubleshooting writing problems.
  - The Anthology of Student Writing provides fully documented MLA researched papers for each purpose: to describe, define, learn, explain, analyze cause, recommend, evaluate, assert a position, and evaluate.

TO THE STUDENT

Why do research? Perhaps the word *research* conjures a painful task of searching out dusty old books on a boring topic you didn't even choose. We'd like to change your mind. Research is basically an activity of acquiring information, literally an act of reading. In a sense, reading any article or book is a type of research. When your instructor asks you to write a researched essay, you merely carry your reading into another dimension: selecting and recording information and then writing about it.

This kind of research is more formal, but by no means is it confined to high school or college English classes. Many corporations maintain specialized libraries so that their employees can conduct research on their current projects. Thus, in your professional life, you will often be involved in research to keep abreast in your field and to succeed in your professional goals.

From Sources to Purpose will help you learn how to read sources and how to think about them. Specific goals include

- learning about the subject,
- expanding your vision of the subject by making connections and discovering the context of your topic,
- reading critically and analyzing how sources are written: their organization,
- development, and logic.

In the second stage of research, you must make some decisions about your sources. The decisions include

- whether to quote, paraphrase, or summarize;
- how to blend quotations, paraphrasings, and summaries into your text;
- how to assimilate the information and create original ideas or perspectives.

The last stage is the writing of the paper, which itself contains three tasks:

- creating the first draft,
- revising subsequent drafts,
- polishing the final draft.

Ultimately, the driving force of your paper is your need to communicate. This is what we identify as your *purpose*. You read your sources with the goal of knowing your subject thoroughly and making sound decisions about selecting and integrating information in your paper. The decisions you make will be determined in part by your purpose.

From Sources to Purpose is divided into four parts that lead you progressively through four stages of creating researched writing. As you move from one stage to the next, you will be asked to complete four interim assignments that use the new techniques you are learning. As you complete these assignments, you should see that you control the process of research and writing. Instead of not knowing where to begin and how to proceed, you can start with familiar material and then move through the stages of finding a topic, researching the sources, and writing the final project.

To help you to understand the set of assignments for your semester's project, we have included the papers of two students as models, one in MLA format and one in APA format. Tobi Raney, an athlete herself, chose as her project topic the role of athletics in developing female self-esteem. And Julie McDowell chose the safety of aspartame as her topic because of her mother's concern about her consumption of soft drinks sweetened with aspartame. (You will soon see that their reasons for choosing these topics lay the foundations of the works that follow.) As you follow these two students' papers through each phase of the project, you will see how they understood each assignment and how they brought each to successful completion. Seeing their work will give you reassurance that you can master the goal of each assignment and the techniques necessary to write a successful paper.

To help you learn from your sources, we encourage you to keep a reflective journal. In your reflective journal, you record information from your sources and then interact with that information by commenting on it, questioning the issues and claims made, and drawing inferences based on connections you make between the recorded information, your comments, and your questions. Your connections and inferences give you *ownership* of your researched writing. No longer is your researched essay a collection of what others have to say on the subject. Rather, your researched writing has become your original contribution to the general discussion about your topic. Your relationship with your audience is meaningful and purposeful because *you* are sharing *your* insights about your topic.

As you work through this book and through the research process, you should also see that researched writing is the same task no matter in what course it is assigned. As you approach all the researched writing assignments during your college career, you will be able not only to complete them with skill and confidence, but also to learn from them by developing your own perspective on a wide variety of subjects.

We present this text to you as a means for developing your reading, thinking, and writing skills in research. The sequence of the chapters should empower you to take charge of any research project you initiate, whether in your education or in your professional lives. And in controlling your research and your writing, you will control your career.

ACKNOWLEDGMENTS

A text is never the product of the author or authors alone. Others must be willing to participate in the project, or it would never progress beyond the conception stage. Most important in the forming of this textbook are the En140 composition students who, by their acceptance of the goals set forth for them and their participation in class activities and the assignments, pointed the way to the eventual design of this text and the refinement of the assignments. Their shared discoveries about research resources revealed what others following them should look for in resource materials and how they should look at the information. Without the many dedicated students, this book could never have been a possibility. We wish a special thanks to Lisa Rendlemann, whose affirmation of the goals of the assignments made it clear that a text might be possible, and to Nichole Buehrle, whose work we used in part. We also extend a special acknowledgment to all those students who willingly released their papers for consideration of inclusion in this text. Their graciousness and enthusiasm cannot be fully expressed here. We especially recognize those students whose work was selected for inclusion. They willingly made extra efforts to produce quality manuscripts. In particular, we thank Tobi Raney and Julie McDowell for their dedication and good spirit in producing a complete set of manuscripts that embody the goals of each assignment and serve as models for other students.

A special note of thanks is due our colleague Jacob Gaskins who graciously proofed the first incarnation of the prospectus and the sample chapters. Also Helen Robbins of Lyon College, who contributed her list of "blending" words and phrases, making our work a little easier.

We also wish to thank the following teachers who class-tested the book and made suggestions for improvements: Mary Pyron, Patti Miinch, Michelle Slinkard, Drew Mebane, Wendy Taliaferro, Betsy Baker, Christopher Worth, and Jane Koppenaal. Furthermore, we express special appreciation to our department chair, Dr. Carol Scates, who approved of our project and gave encouragement.

We are grateful to the following reviewers, who gave encouragement and necessary suggestions for the improvement of the sample chapters and preface: Frank Fennel, Bernard Quetchenbach, Marjorie Ginsberg, Corri Wells, Laura Bates, Linda Brender, and Cindy Moore.

And finally, we sincerely thank the staff at Harcourt for giving us the opportunity to take this book from concept to reality, especially Julie McBurney, who saw its possibilities, and Harriett Prentiss, who tirelessly edited and instructed and encouraged us.

CONTENTS

PART ONE

Setting the Stage   1

CHAPTER 1

Reviewing Basic Writing Principles   3

DEFINITION: WRITING WITH PURPOSE AND OWNERSHIP   4
TECHNIQUES: BASIC WRITING PRINCIPLES   5
Prewriting Activities   6
Limiting the Topic   8
Formulating the Thesis Statement   9
Supporting the Thesis Statement   10
Structuring the Body   11
Using Transitions for Coherence   11
Revising for Unity and Development   12
Editing for Grammar, Spelling, Punctuation, and Mechanics   13
Proofreading the Final Draft   14
Finding a Research Topic   15
BASIC WRITING PRINCIPLES: PROFESSIONAL WRITING   16
Speech for a High School Graduate, Roger Rosenblatt   16
BASIC WRITING PRINCIPLES: STUDENT WRITING   19
What Does a College Education Mean to Me? Mary Walker   19
WRITING ASSIGNMENT: RESEARCHED WRITING PROJECT   23

CHAPTER 2

Determining Purpose and Choosing A Topic   25

DEFINITION: PURPOSE IN WRITING   26
TECHNIQUES: CHOOSING A PURPOSE   27
Describe   27
Define   28
Learn   28
Recommend   28
Explain   28
Analyze Cause   28
Evaluate   29
Persuade   29
Assert a Position   30

TECHNIQUES: CHOOSING A TOPIC   31

    Purpose, Topic, Ownership   32

    Creating the Interest Inventory   33

    The Interest Inventory: Student Writing   34

    Interest Inventory, Tobi Raney   34

    Interest Inventory, Julie McDowell   35

    Drafting the Project Proposal   37

    Project Proposal: Topic and Purpose   37

    The Project Proposal: Student Writing   38

    Project Proposal, Tobi Raney   38

    Project Proposal, Julie McDowell   39

WRITING ASSIGNMENT: THE PROJECT PROPOSAL   41

CHAPTER 3
Creating and Presenting Meaning   42

DEFINITION: MEANING AND EVIDENCE   43

TECHNIQUES: CREATING MEANING   46

    The Mysterious Case of E.P., Steven Levingston   46

    The 11-year-old Debunker, Jessica Gorman   52

TECHNIQUES: PRESENTING MEANING   54

    Present Sensory Perceptions   55

    Provide Examples   55

    Provide Illustrations   56

    Draw Comparisons   56

    Draw Contrasts   56

    Draw Connections   57

CREATING AND PRESENTING MEANING: PROFESSIONAL
WRITING   57

    The River as Book and as Picture, Mark Twain   57

CREATING AND PRESENTING MEANING: STUDENT WRITING   60

    The Mysterious Journey, Rachel Beam   61

WRITING ASSIGNMENT: CREATING AND PRESENTING
MEANING   64

PART TWO
Using Sources   67

CHAPTER 4
Building A Bibliography   69

DEFINITION: BIBLIOGRAPHY   70

    Kinds of Sources   71

TECHNIQUES: LEARNING YOUR LIBRARY   74

    The Stacks   75

    The Reference Collection   75

    Periodicals   76

    Online Sources   76

Catalogues   76
Learning the Library   76
TECHNIQUES: BUILDING BIBLIOGRAPHIES   77,
MLA style   77
APA style   82
TECHNIQUES: BUILDING A WORKING BIBLIOGRAPHY   86
Locating Sources in the Library   87
Locating Sources on the Internet   96
BUILDING A WORKING BIBLIOGRAPHY: STUDENT WRITING   96
Working Bibliography, Tobi Raney   97
Working Bibliography, Julie McDowell   99
WRITING ASSIGNMENT: THE WORKING BIBLIOGRAPHY   102
TECHNIQUES: BUILDING AN ANNOTATED BIBLIOGRAPHY   103
Previewing Sources   103
Writing Annotations   104
BUILDING AN ANNOTATED BIBLIOGRAPHY: PROFESSIONAL
WRITING   105
From *Jazz, Black Music in the United States: An Annotated Bibliography of
Selected Reference and Research Materials,* Samuel A. Floyd, Jr. and
Marsha J. Reisser   105
WRITING ASSIGNMENT: ANNOTATED BIBLIOGRAPHY   108

CHAPTER 5
Using Sources In Your Writing   *109*

DEFINITION: PLAGIARISM   109
TECHNIQUES: USING SOURCES IN YOUR WRITING   110
Gathering Information   111
Quoting Your Sources   113
Paraphrasing Your Sources   116
Summarizing Your Sources   118
TECHNIQUES: BLENDING YOUR WRITING AND YOUR
SOURCES   119
The Introduction   120
The Source Material   122
The Commentary   125
TECHNIQUES: CITING YOUR SOURCES   125
Citing Your Sources (MLA Style)   126
Citing Your Sources (APA Style)   129
USING SOURCES IN YOUR WRITING: PROFESSIONAL WRITING   134
From *The Alphabetic Labyrinth*, Johanna Drucker   134
From *Why People Believe Weird Things*, Michael Shermer   136
WRITING ASSIGNMENT: USING SOURCES IN YOUR WRITING   137

PART THREE

Reading Sources Critically   139

CHAPTER 6

Validating Evidence   141

DEFINITION: VALIDATION   143
TECHNIQUES: VALIDATING YOUR EVIDENCE   145
    Consult a Variety of Sources   145
    Keep a Reflective Journal   146
    Reflective Journal, Mary Stone   147
    Compare the Evidence in Your Sources   151
TECHNIQUES: WRITING THE VALIDATION PAPER   152
    Limit the Scope of the Topic   153
    Limit the Focus of the Topic   153
    Select Either the Inductive or Deductive Scheme   154
    Determine the Most Effective Arrangement   154
    Use Formal Citation of Sources   155
VALIDATING YOUR EVIDENCE: PROFESSIONAL WRITING   156
    A Chronology of Soviet Media Coverage, compiled by
        Alexander Amerisov   156
    The U.S. Media's Slant, William A. Dorman and Daniel Hirsch   162
VALIDATING YOUR EVIDENCE: STUDENT WRITING   170
    Defining Self-Esteem, Tobi Raney   170
    Too Much of a Sweet Thing? Julie McDowell   175
WRITING ASSIGNMENT: THE VALIDATION PAPER   181

CHAPTER 7

Discovering Connections and Contexts   183

DEFINITION: CONNECTION AND CONTEXT   184
TECHNIQUES: MAKING CONNECTIONS   185
    The New Adolf Hitler? Timothy Garton Ash   186
    Nervous Habits Often Reflect a Developmental Need (Abstract), Barbara
        F. Meltz   191
TECHNIQUES: DISCOVERING CONTEXT   193
    "Adam and Eve," *And Adam Knew Eve: A Dictionary of Sex in the Bible*,
        Ronald L. Ecker   194
    Taking Connections Out of Context   197
    "Quote taken out of context" says Microsoft, Aardvark News   197
    *The true story behind the Jonestown massacre including connections to the
        Kennedy and King assassinations*, Heavenly Deceptor   198
    From *Teenage Lincoln Sculptor*, Ethel Yari   199
    Storm over a Vietnam Memorial, Wolf von Eckhardt   206
DISCOVERING CONNECTIONS AND CONTEXTS: PROFESSIONAL
    WRITING   209
    From Muhammad Ali to Grandma Rose, Polly Shulman   209
    Dubious Influences, Richard Stengel   216

DISCOVERING CONNECTIONS AND CONTEXTS: STUDENT WRITING   219

From Corsets to Converse, Tobi Raney   219

Passing the Sugar Bowl, Julie McDowell   224

WRITING ASSIGNMENT: DISCOVERING CONNECTIONS AND CONTEXT   229

CHAPTER 8
Critiquing Sources   230

DEFINITION: CRITIQUE   231

TECHNIQUES: CRITIQUING SOURCES   232

Reading Critically: Encountering the Source   233

TECHNIQUES: DETECTING FALLACIES   236

Animals Have No Rights: Go Ahead and Lick That Frog, Rush H. Limbaugh III   241

CRITIQUING SOURCES: PROFESSIONAL WRITING   250

Ancient Astronauts and Erich von Däniken's Chariots of the Gods, Robert Todd Carroll   250

A Detailed Critique of the Time *Article: "On a Screen Near You: Cyberporn" (DeWitt, 7/3/95)*, Donna L. Hoffman and Thomas P. Novak   253

CRITIQUING SOURCES: STUDENT WRITING   258

Leslie Schenkman Kaplan: Her Problem Unsolved, Tobi Raney   259

Self-esteem Is Not Our National Wonder Drug, Leslie Schenkman Kaplan   264

"Pro and Con": Equal Representation, Julie McDowell   272

Aspartame: Pro and Con, Beatrice Trum Hunter and the FDA   274

WRITING ASSIGNMENT: CRITIQUING SOURCES   282

CHAPTER 9
Drawing Inferences   284

DEFINITION: INFERENCE   284

From *The Adventure of the Blue Carbuncle*, Sir Arthur Conan Doyle   285

TECHNIQUES: DRAWING INFERENCES   288

TECHNIQUES: PRESENTING INFERENCES AS ARGUMENT   290

The Syllogism   290

The Toulmin Model   292

Rogerian Argumentation   295

The Case of the Shroud, Joe Nickell   296

Archeologist Claims Proof Turin Shroud Wrapped Christ, Reuters   301

DRAWING INFERENCES: PROFESSIONAL WRITING   303

Taking a Stand, Pamela Grim   304

The Baby Who Stopped Eating, Robert Marion   311

DRAWING INFERENCES: STUDENT WRITING   319

Which Came First? Connecting Success and Self-Esteem, Tobi Raney   320

Considering the Past, Julie McDowell   322

WRITING ASSIGNMENT: DRAWING INFERENCES   323

PART FOUR

Writing To Your Purpose 325

CHAPTER 10
Citing Your Sources—MLA Style 327

THE MLA-STYLE WORKS CITED LIST 327
Books 328
Articles 330
Other Copyrighted Sources 332
Non-copyrighted Sources 333
Electronic Sources 333
MLA-STYLE PARENTHETICAL CITATIONS 335

CHAPTER 11
Citing Your Sources—APA Style 336

THE APA STYLE REFERENCES LIST 336
Books 337
Articles 339
Other Copyrighted Sources 340
Electronic Sources 340
APA STYLE PARENTHETICAL CITATIONS 341

CHAPTER 12
Arranging Your Presentation 343

DEFINITION: ARRANGEMENT 343
TECHNIQUES: OUTLINING YOUR PROJECT 343
The Formal Outline 344
Jumping for Joy, Formal Outline, Tobi Raney 344
The Sentence Outline 345
No Sugar-Coated Solution in Aspartame's Immediate Future, Sentence
Outline, Julie McDowell 346
TECHNIQUES: CREATING A TITLE 347
Sentences and Phrases as Titles 348
Questions as Titles 348
Single Words as Titles 348
TECHNIQUES: LEADING INTO YOUR THESIS 349
Using a Scene as a Lead 349
Using an Anecdote as a Lead 350
Using an Allusion as a Lead 350
Using Description/Definition as a Lead 351
Using Connections as a Lead 351
Leads to be Careful About 351
TECHNIQUES: CONCLUDING YOUR ESSAY 352
Using Definition as a Conclusion 353
Using Summary as a Conclusion 353
Using a Question as a Conclusion 354

Using Results as a Conclusion   354
Using Solutions as a Conclusion   354
Using Advice as a Conclusion   355
Using a Quotation as a Conclusion   355
Conclusions to be Careful About   355
TECHNIQUES: INCLUDING GRAPHICS AND APPENDICES   356
Presenting Graphics   356
Including Appendices   357

CHAPTER 13
Managing Your Presentation   359

TECHNIQUES: THE COVER/TITLE PAGE   359
The Cover Page   360
The Title Page   361
MANAGING THE PRESENTATION: STUDENT WRITING   362
Jumping for Joy, Tobi Raney   363
No Sugar-Coated Solution in Aspartame's Immediate Future, Julie
McDowell   376

SOME FINAL WORDS   390
AN ANTHOLOGY OF STUDENT WRITING   393

DESCRIBE   395
Crime on Campus, Matthew Maurer   396
DEFINE   401
Unwanted War, Justin Lankheit   401
LEARN   406
Agricultural Diversity in the Show Me State, Brian Hulshof   406
EXPLAIN   410
The True Predicament in Student Government Elections,
Amanda Rainey   411
ANALYZE CAUSE   418
Whose Life Is It, Anyway? Mary Stone   418
RECOMMEND   424
An Assessment of General Studies 101: Problems and Suggested Solutions,
Kim Schlosser   424
EVALUATE   432
Cremation or Burial: What Is Right for You? Melissa Thomas   432
ASSERT A POSITION   438
The Meaning of Education, Andrew Wright   438
PERSUADE   443
A Misinterpretation of Values, Amy Crow   443

APPENDIX
Troubleshooting Your Writing   449

1: TROUBLESHOOTING SENTENCES   452
1.1: Clauses   452
1.2: Phrases   455

1.3: Sentence Fragments   456

1.4: Comma Splices   457

1.5: Run-on or Fused Sentences   458

2: TROUBLESHOOTING GRAMMAR   459

2.1: Although/However/Though—Are They Interchangeable?   459

2.2: Are:—When a Colon Can't Be Used   459

2.3: As or Because—Which Should You Use?   460

2.4: Between—Which Case Does It Call for?   460

2.5: Dangling Modifier—Making Connections   460

2.6: Different From/Different Than—What's the Difference?   460

2.7: False Coordination—Joining Unequal Forms   461

2.8: Free-Standing Dates or Times—What Do They Modify?   461

2.9: Free-Standing Demonstrative Pronouns—What Do They Refer To?   462

2.10: Hopefully—A Cliché   462

2.11: Its/It's—Why They Are Not Identical   462

2.12: Myself / I—Why Aren't These Pronouns Equivalent?   463

2.13: Only—Where Should It Go?   463

2.14: Subject-Verb Agreement—Keep Them Matched   463

2.15: To Try And—No Coordination After *Try*   464

2.16: Used to/Supposed to—Troubles with a Silent *d*   464

2.17: Who/Which/That—Which Pronoun Should You Use?   465

3: TROUBLESHOOTING SPELLING AND USAGE   465

3.1: Frequently Confused Words   465

3.2: Other Usage Problems   467

4: TROUBLESHOOTING PUNCTUATION   468

4.1: Using a Comma in Coordination   468

4.2: Using a Comma after an Introductory Element   468

4.3: Using Commas in a Series   468

4.4: Using Commas with Coordinate Adjectives   469

4.5: Using Commas with Nonrestrictive Clauses   469

4.6: Using Commas with Conjunctive Adverbs   469

4.7: Commas, Periods, and Quotation Marks   470

4.8: Question Marks and Quotation Marks   470

5: TROUBLESHOOTING MECHANICS   470

5.1: Capitals   470

5.2: Italics   471

5.3: Abbreviations   471

5.4: Numbers   471

5.5: Hyphens   472

5.6: Brackets   472

6: TROUBLESHOOTING STYLE   472

6.1: Parallelism   473

6.2: Well, Yes, No   473

6.3: Contractions   473

6.4: Elevated Language   473

6.5: Redundancies   474

6.6: Clichés   475

7: FALSE RULES   476

7.1: Do Not Start a Sentence with *and* or *but*   476

7.2: Do Not End a Sentence with a Preposition   476

7.3: Sentences Should Have No Fewer than Ten Words and No More than Twenty-one Words   477

CREDITS 478

INDEX 480

PART ONE

Setting the Stage

Setting the stage means putting things into order so that you can carry out a task, in this case researched writing on a topic of your choice. Thus Part One begins with a review of basic writing principles and techniques to assure you that you can rely on skills that you have learned in previous writing courses. The first chapter basically addresses the question, "What do I know about writing?" Because you will select your own research topic, Chapter 2 asks you to create an interest inventory that will help you identify topics you are interested in. After reviewing your list, you are ready to write a Project Proposal on one of the topics for approval by your instructor. In this proposal, you identify your interest in the topic, your purpose, and the audience for your researched writing. In this chapter, you first encounter the work of two students, Tobi Raney and Julie McDowell, which will serve as models throughout this book. Chapter 3, "Creating and Presenting Meaning," presents the final component of "setting the stage" by showing how you can create ownership of your topic by determining the significance of the facts you have collected in your research.

Chapter 1   Reviewing Basic Writing Principles

Chapter 2   Determining Purpose and Choosing a Topic

Chapter 3   Creating and Presenting Meaning

Reviewing Basic Writing Principles

Poor Calvin! All he wanted to do was make something special for his Mom on Mother's Day.

Poor Calvin's mom! What she woke up to on Mother's Day was Calvin's demand for a bigger allowance and a hot breakfast. Think about how your Mom would react to getting this card on Mother's Day.

Calvin shows us what happens when we lose sight of our audience's identity and our purpose for writing: the message Calvin intended to get across to his mother was not the message Calvin's mother saw when she read her card. If this kind of misunderstanding happens to us as writers, then we have failed to complete our basic task: to effectively communicate a message to our audience. This chapter reviews some basic writing principles that Calvin should have kept in mind—and that we must always keep in mind whenever we write.

DEFINITION: WRITING WITH PURPOSE AND OWNERSHIP

> **Writing with Purpose:** Writing that attempts to achieve a specific goal for a certain audience.

Just as Calvin illustrates, we write to accomplish specific goals. Whether we are asking a parent for a bigger allowance, writing a required paper for a professor, or submitting a report to a boss, we have a purpose in mind. We want Mom or Dad to understand our tight budget and open the wallet a little wider; we want the professor to give the paper a passing grade; we want the raise or the promotion that the boss's approval will bring.

In college, you usually write because of course requirements. In this case, the audience is usually the instructor, although some assignments specify a different audience. For most assignments, however, you are writing to the professor, and that situation seems somewhat artificial and not very connected to "real life." But think about it: in the workplace, supervisors often assign writing tasks; these assignments just don't seem to be writing tasks because they don't always look like "papers" or "essays." But filling out request forms, writing evaluations, and preparing reports are all writing tasks. And the audience for these tasks is usually the very person who assigned the project—the supervisor.

The similarity between these two situations goes only so far. Yes, the person who assigned the task is the audience for the writing, but other elements of the writing situation will differ. A college essay, for instance, requires a different kind of writing than does an employee evaluation. One difference is that, when writing college essays, you are often given more choices about your purpose, your topic, and your content, whereas an employee evaluation usually involves a specific format focused on a predetermined purpose. Another difference is that, with every writing task, your audience has different expectations. The professor reading your essay is looking for your understanding of the subject matter and your skill as a writer, whereas your supervisor is looking for useful, accessible information.

Despite these differences in situation, the process in each case is largely the same. In both situations, you should

- Follow basic writing principles.

- Determine the purpose of the writing.
- Write to an audience.
- Claim ownership of the writing.

These four characteristics are true any time you write anything to anybody. So, before discussing the special kind of writing we call "researched writing," let's take a look (perhaps a second look for some of you) at how every writing task should be approached.

As writers, when we move from one writing task and from one course to the next, we often "close the door" on what we have learned in order to make room for the next writing unit. We've all done it: as soon as we walk out of the final exam, we forget everything we studied the night before because, after all, the class is over, and we don't need to know that information anymore. Or so we think.

When we move on to our next class, however, we are often faced with a new situation that we think requires a set of skills or ways of thinking that we have not yet acquired. Indeed, at the beginning of a writing class, students sometimes say, "I have never written this kind of paper before." Perhaps they have never been given this exact assignment, but they have written papers, and the writing skills they used to write papers in an earlier class can be applied to the assignment at hand.

So, whether you are responding to assignments in a composition course, writing papers in other disciplines, or writing reports at work, some basic principles of writing always apply. The writing principles that you learned and applied in your high school English class or your first college writing course can be carried forward into other writing situations. When your American history professor asks you to write an analysis of the Battle of Gettysburg, you can go back to the fundamental writing process to get you started on what may be an unfamiliar assignment. The same holds true when you write a memo asking your supervisor if you can attend the housewares convention that is coming to your city: you can use what you have learned about audience, purpose, organization, and development to convince your supervisor to see things your way.

TECHNIQUES: BASIC WRITING PRINCIPLES

A quick review of basic writing techniques and principles should reassure you of your ability as you face any new writing task.

- Prepare with prewriting activities, including brainstorming, freewriting, journaling, and outlining.
- Limit your topic.
- Formulate a thesis statement.
- Support the thesis statement.
- Structure the body of your paper logically.
- Use transitions to make your writing coherent.
- Revise, checking for unity and development.
- Edit for grammar, capitalization, spelling, and punctuation.
- Proofread the final draft.

See? You are familiar with these basic elements of writing. The writing you will do in this course will be research-based—that is, you will use outside sources as part of your writing—but you will use the principles you have already learned, starting with gathering ideas and ending with proofreading.

As you read this chapter, remember that the order in which writing principles and writing tasks are discussed is not necessarily the order in which you will do them when you sit down to write. You've probably heard that writing is a "recursive" process; this means that writers go backward and forward through this list of tasks, skip over some steps, and do two or three of them at the same time. Nonetheless, in order to talk about them, the tasks must be separated and placed in some kind of order. How you put these tasks to use is something you will have to work out when you actually start writing.

Prewriting Activities

Whether you select a topic or write on an assigned topic, you can use certain strategies to "kick-start" the writing process. Although there are many ways to generate ideas, a few of the more common methods include the following:

- brainstorming
- freewriting
- outlining

The important thing to remember about prewriting is that it is a unique process: every writer thinks a little bit differently, so writers all use slightly different methods of generating ideas. You should experiment with different prewriting methods to find the one that works best for you.

If your instructor assigns a paper on the value of a college education, you will certainly be familiar with general information from your experience. If your boss asks for a report on how to increase efficiency in shipping, you can draw on your immediate experience in the shipping department. In either case you can brainstorm, jotting down information that you already know as it comes to your mind. Of course, you probably won't remember everything you know about your topic in one brainstorming session, so you should plan on repeating this task a couple of times.

Here's one student's brainstorming list:

College Education

*2 or 4 years	*social skills
*better job	
*higher salary	
not necessary	
major	
minor	
technology	
*liberal	

As you look at this list or at the results of your brainstorming, you may notice that they're not very organized. Brainstorming lists are random because you write things down as they occur to you. As you look at a brainstormed list, however, you will notice that some pieces of information go together. Putting the related pieces of information together in groups creates clusters of information (which the student marked with asterisks in the previous list). Identifying the relationships between information clusters allows you to begin organizing your ideas into an essay.

Another strategy for jump-starting your thinking on your topic is freewriting. When you freewrite, you try to establish a clear channel from your mind to your hand and record your thoughts as they occur to you. If you're using a pen or pencil and a piece of paper, you should never stop writing—even if your mind is blank, keep your hand moving until you come up with a new idea. If you're using a computer, turn your monitor off and just type nonstop. In this way, without worrying about what's on the screen, you will relax and ideas will seem to just come to you.

Here's an example of freewriting on the value of a college education. The student wrote this freewriting exercise on a computer with the monitor turned off, so she would not worry about making errors. The focus in freewriting is on ideas, not on correctness.

I personally enjoy studying alot. To me going to college is an incredible valuable experience. the most important 'ingredient" in getting a good education is motivation. inorder to be motivated enough one should have good instructors and high tech equipment like computer based libraries and an access to different sources instructional materials like videos books, etc. as for instructors, they should always excite their students and make them think all the time. one can get a good education, if one realizes that the best motivation in college is their desire to know, their independence and researches on topics, and a clear idea which field that would their career would be in. College education b is also a good experience of meeting new people of your age and adjusting to the worlds of adults. College is the place where one starts taking responsibility for time and sometimes money the two most important things in a big world. College education is a piece of information the whole life of a student will be built on after high school and before work.

Outlining can also help you generate new ideas. When you write an outline, you often gain a new perspective on your ideas, which sparks new thoughts. Outlines can also help you see gaps in your ideas, places where you need to come up with more information about your topic. During prewriting, you do not need to write a formal outline. Prewriting is for your benefit, so use the kind of outline that helps you the most. Some instructors assign a formal outline as part of a final draft. A detailed discussion of this kind of outline appears in Chapter 12.

Thinking is unique to each writer. You don't think the way the writer on your left does, and that writer doesn't think the same way the writer on your right does. In order to generate ideas for a paper, you have to find the way you think most effectively. What you must do is try different ways to generate ideas to find out which method works best for you. Perhaps it's one of the ways listed here; perhaps it's a combination of two or more of these methods; perhaps it's a method that is completely unique to you. What is important is not how you came up with the ideas, but that you have ideas to use in your paper.

EXERCISE 1-1

Experiment with the prewriting methods discussed in this chapter to find a method that works well for you. Choose two or three of the topics that follow and prewrite on them. For each topic, use a different method of prewriting (brainstorming, freewriting, or outlining).

- career plans
- buying a car
- your home town
- dining at restaurants
- a movie you recently saw or a book you recently read
- a topic of your choice

Limiting the Topic

Obviously, you cannot cover all that could be said about a subject in which you are interested. Most assignments don't allow you the space. By limiting the scope of your topic, you give direction to your thinking and your writing. In general, you can limit your topic in three ways:

- by space
- by time
- by kind

For example, perhaps you are interested in writing about the issue of children assuming adult roles or activities too quickly. The topic is too big to cover in one paper because the "adultification" of children happens in many different ways, such as the introduction to real guns when a child is only five; racing mini-sized four-wheelers and motorcycles in competition;

exposure to alcohol, drugs, or sexual activities before puberty; or the pressure to do well in school as early as kindergarten so the child can later be admitted to a prestigious university. In order to make this broad topic manageable, you could limit it by space or location and discuss how children in suburbs are affected. Or you could limit it by time and talk about growing awareness of this issue during the 1990s. Or you could limit your topic by kind and discuss the impact of academic pressure on very young children. In fact, you could involve all three subjects and discuss how suburban children were affected by increased academic pressure during the 1990s.

The more you restrict or limit the topic, the more detailed your writing will be—just be sure not to limit your topic too much. If your topic is too narrow, then you won't have enough to say about your topic. For instance, how young Sarah Johnson was affected by parental pressure to learn her colors on February 3, 1995, would be too narrow for an essay topic. It might work well for a paragraph, but the idea is not broad enough to warrant discussion in an entire paper.

Effectively limiting your topic, however, makes your writing more detailed. And the more detailed your report, the more memorable it will be. Details show your ideas to your readers in a clear and vivid way that general statements cannot. Furthermore, more details offer more support for your thesis. Finally, if you limit the topic in a way that means something to you, then you will be able to approach the subject with originality and authority.

EXERCISE 1–2

Limit the general topics listed that follow. First, limit the topics by time. Second, limit them by space. Third, limit them by kind.

1. Animals

   - Limited by time: _____
   - Limited by space: _____
   - Limited by kind: _____

2. Books
3. Elections
4. Learning
5. Camping

Formulating the Thesis Statement

Once you have a limited topic, you need to formulate a thesis statement. An effective thesis presents the limited topic of your essay (determined by focusing your topic) and announces your claim about the topic (what you have to say about your topic). Focusing on a particular claim or comment about your limited topic, as a product of your prewriting activities and reading, gives your writing purpose and direction. The claim or comment that you focus on determines how you present and interpret the content of your paper.

Formulating a thesis statement allows you to claim ownership of your writing. If you have a thesis statement that is personally meaningful, then you will have something you want to say about that topic. The ownership and personal interest you express in your thesis statement will keep your readers interested in your paper.

Thus, your thesis statement shows your readers how you think about or understand your subject. Your thesis should consist of two parts: (1) the limited topic and (2) the claim that you are presenting about that topic. "This paper is about the effects of too much academic pressure on small children" would not be an effective thesis because it presents only the topic. Likewise, "Small children lose their interest in learning" would be ineffective because it contains only the claim. An effective thesis must include both: "Too much academic pressure on small children causes them to lose interest in learning."

EXERCISE 1–3

In a few sentences, explain why you think each of the following statements would or would not work as the thesis for a three- to five-page essay.

- "Star Wars" is a science fiction movie.
- This paper will tell you which restaurant is the best.
- Shopping on the Internet is an easy and economical method of buying a car.
- What you like to do and what you do well should determine what you choose as a career.
- My hometown is Cape Girardeau, Missouri.

EXERCISE 1–4

Choose three of the topics you limited in Exercise 1–2, and write an effective thesis that expresses a focused claim for each topic.

Supporting the Thesis Statement

Once you have formulated a thesis statement, you must support it in the body of your essay. Each body paragraph consists of two parts: (1) a topic sentence that makes a specific point about your thesis and (2) concrete evidence that explains, demonstrates, or verifies this point.

To develop the body paragraphs, ask the questions you think your reader might have about your thesis statement. Then answer those questions.

If your reader needs to know, *What* is it?

◆ Your support should include *definitions, comparisons, contrasts,* or *descriptions.*

If your reader needs to know, *How* did it happen? or *How* is it done?

♦ Your support should discuss *process.*

If your reader needs to know, *Why* did it happen?

♦ Your support should explain *causes, effects,* and *consequences.*

By asking about what kind of information your reader needs to understand your thesis statement, you will come up with a method of development that fits your thesis.

Structuring The Body

Whether your general purpose is to inform or to argue, most of your papers will be arranged *deductively,* with your thesis coming at the end of your introduction and the support following. In deductive writing, you present general ideas first and then follow up with specific details.

The following are some common arrangements for organizing the body of your essay:

- *ascending order:* present less important ideas, then more important ideas
- *descending order:* present more important ideas, then less important ideas
- *chronological order:* describe events in the order they happen in time
- *causal order:* explain causes then effects, or effects then causes
- *spatial order:* describe an object from one end to the other (e.g., top to bottom, left to right, inside to outside)
- *point-counterpoint:* support one idea, then a contrasting idea

EXERCISE 1–5

Look again at the thesis statements you formulated in Exercise 1–4. What questions would your readers want answered? To answer their questions, what kinds of information do you need to provide? How can you arrange your ideas?

Using Transitions for Coherence

As you arrange the ideas in your paper, you are placing those ideas in relationship to each other. To make those relationships clear to your reader, you use transitions between your ideas. Transitions are the glue that makes your paper coherent—a unified whole. Imagine a brick wall. If the bricks are merely stacked on top of each other, you can see that it's a wall, but a single push will knock it over. When you add the mortar between the bricks, all of the bricks are joined together in a single, strong wall. Transitions (like those listed in Table 1–1) are the mortar of writing.

TABLE 1-1

Word(s)	Relationship
rather than, than, whether	These words show relationships of **choice**.
if even, if, provided that, unless	These words show relationships of **condition**.
although, even though, though, whereas	These words show relationships of **contrast**.
where, wherever	These words show relationships of **location**.
as, because, since	These words show relationships of **reason** or **cause**.
in order that, so, so that, that	These words show relationships of **result** or **effect**.
after, before, once, since, until, when, whenever, while	These words show relationships of **time**.

EXERCISE 1-6

Use transitions to connect the ideas and sentences in the following paragraph. You may also need to revise some sentences.

With a loud crack, the baseball shot off the bat toward right field. The hitter sprinted toward first base. The ball skidded on the wet grass in the outfield, shooting past the running outfielder toward the corner of the park. The runner made a wide turn around first base. He ran toward second base. The outfielder finally caught up to the ball. He picked the ball up. He threw the ball toward the infield. The runner was on his way to third base. The ball was caught by the second baseman. The second baseman threw the ball to third base. The runner slid headfirst toward the bag. The third basemen caught the ball. The runner's slide created a huge cloud of dust. The third baseman tagged the runner. The umpire could not see if the runner was out.

Revising for Unity and Development

When you are writing a first draft, your main concern is to get something onto the paper or the computer screen. You know that writing is a process, so you know that you will come back to your first draft to see what you need to revise and improve. When revising a draft, check for two characteristics: unity and development.

When you check for unity, you are ensuring that your essay discusses only one idea—the idea in your thesis statement. You might find information that, although interesting, does not talk about any part of your thesis. If you find sentences that are off the topic, the solution is to delete them.

When you revise, also check for development. Do you provide enough information in your essay for your reader to fully understand your perspective on the topic? Do you need to say more about one idea or another? At this point, you should go back to prewriting to generate the additional ideas necessary, draft the new sections of your essay, arrange them, and give them coherence with the rest of the essay.

At the same time that you are checking for adequate development, ask if you are giving your audience information that they probably already have. If so, delete the unnecessary information.

It's a good idea to use peer review when you revise. In peer review, your peers—other writers in your class, for example—read your draft and identify areas you should look at as you revise. You are always writing for an audience, and peer review gives your audience a chance to evaluate your draft. In many ways, it's like test-driving a car because your audience gets to try out your paper before the final draft.

Here are the questions to ask your peer reviewers:

- What is your overall impression of the essay?
- Which parts of the essay are successful?
- Which parts of the essay need more work?
- Does the paper have unity and coherence?
- Are there any grammatical problems?

When you get your reviewers' comments back, read them closely. Make sure you understand why the reviewers suggested what they did, so that you know how to revise your essay. If you don't understand their comments, then ask them for more explanation. Ultimately, though, it is your paper. You don't have to do everything your reviewers suggest.

Editing for Grammar, Spelling, Punctuation, and Mechanics

As you are drafting and revising, you will probably be editing your writing as you go. In addition, many writers use the spell checkers and grammar checkers on their computers. If you do use these computer tools, however, remember that the computer can only do so much by itself. It will not find every mistake, and it will, in fact, skip over some errors. One of the authors of this book once had a student turn in an essay that had the word "dose" every time it should have read "does." The spell checker didn't catch this error because "dose" is a word. You must edit your paper by hand to check for spelling and grammar errors. Don't forget that your name, not the computer's, goes on your essay.

It is sometimes difficult to find errors in an essay, especially if you have been working with it for a long time. The more familiar you become with a piece of writing, the more you tend to skim over it without really seeing it. Here are some techniques you can use to minimize this familiarity:

- Let your paper sit for a while (a minimum of 24 hours is good).
- Read your paper out loud.
- Ask someone else to read the paper out loud to you.
- Read the paper backwards: start at the end, and go backwards word by word or sentence by sentence.
- If you are editing on a computer, change the font of your paper.

EXERCISE 1–7

Edit the following passage, relying on standard conventions of written English for punctuation, grammar, and spelling.

> The holiday season is such a busy time of the year. Not only is families preparing four Christmas, Hanukah, Kwanzaa New Year's and other Holidays, but there are also more sports going on than your usual remote control can handle. Professional hockey and basket ball are in full swing, in fact, their will be two basketball games on Christmas Day. The end of the Pro football season is also going on, as the teams tried to get into the play offs. That determine who will play in the super bowl. There are tournaments for colledge basketball. And, of course, there are important college football bowl games for going on for almost two weeks.

Proofreading the Final Draft

Proofreading is the absolutely final step in writing an essay. By now, your writing should be unified, fully developed, and free of spelling and grammatical errors. Before you turn in your paper, however, make sure that it looks right. Have you followed the format required by your instructor? For instance, are your margins large enough? Are there inadvertent typing errors? Has your printer printed two pages on one sheet of paper or perhaps skipped a page?

Appearance is important in writing. A clean copy of your essay shows your readers that you pay attention to the little things when you write, which will lead them to believe that you pay attention to the little things when you think. In other words, a clean, properly proofread essay adds to your credibility as a writer. A sloppy paper full of easily fixed errors, on the other hand, greatly diminishes your credibility in the eyes of your readers before they have even read a single word.

Finding a Research Topic

You must keep one idea in mind every time you write: *you* are the writer. It is your essay. You should do what works best for you. You may develop your own methods of prewriting; you may decide not to make some corrections the grammar checker suggests. You own your essay and should do what it takes to make it yours. It is especially important to remember this concept as you start looking around for a topic for the research project for this course.

As you search for the research topic that will be the basis for all of the major writing assignments in this course, keep in mind that there is no single, "perfect" topic. Your choice of a research topic should be directed by three considerations: (1) your audience, (2) your purpose, and (3) whether you feel ownership of the topic.

You own a topic when you want to know more about it. Perhaps you already have some knowledge of or experience with the topic but want to know more; or maybe you just learned of an issue and you're curious to know more. Either way, your curiosity forms the basis of your ownership. If you have no curiosity about your topic, it will show in your writing, and your readers will not be interested in it either.

In some courses, you may be assigned topics, but your instructors are unlikely to impose a claim or point of view for you to pursue. Thus, you should find some aspect of the assigned topic about which you are curious in order to establish your ownership of the essay.

Your purpose and your audience are closely related: you can't have one without the other. Your purpose is why you are writing the essay: what do you hope to do for your audience? At the most general level, you may write to inform, persuade, express, or entertain. As you will discover in the next chapter, however, several more specific purposes fall under these general categories. Keep your purpose in mind as you write because it affects the way you present the information in your essay.

Be careful not to confuse techniques of development (such as illustration, process analysis, comparison/contrast, etc.) with purpose. Those techniques give shape to the content of your essay, whereas your purpose is focused on your audience. The techniques for developing your essay are tools to use in achieving your purpose, ways to show your audience what you want them to know, believe, or do as a result of reading your essay.

EXERCISE 1–8

Using prewriting techniques, generate essay topics that you find interesting. Choose the prewriting method (brainstorming, freewriting, outlining, or a combination of these methods) with which you feel most comfortable. Write down every topic that comes to your mind. You will be choosing from these topics for your researched writing project in this class, so it's better to have many to choose from than only a few that don't seem as interesting.

BASIC WRITING PRINCIPLES: PROFESSIONAL WRITING

Roger Rosenblatt, a columnist for *Time* magazine, wrote an essay for each of his children upon their graduation from high school. The essay that follows was written for his oldest child. Because we do not have Roger's prewriting or drafts, we cannot examine his writing process; however, we can see the results of many of the basic writing principles reviewed in this chapter, as indicated by the annotations.

The title announces the topic—a common event in the spring.

Speech for a High School Graduate,
Roger Rosenblatt

The lead rejects common graduation openings and sets up the pattern of responding to examples that structures the body of the essay.

Others will exhort you to take risks, to be yourself, never to look back or lose your faith. Not I. If the truth be told, I do not want you to take risks. Oh, maybe a selected few to preserve your self-esteem, but not the killing kind of risk, nothing netless. As for being yourself, that's fine, as long as you are happy with yourself. Otherwise, be someone else. You'll find your way; most everyone does. Never to look back? I'd say look back quite often. If you don't look back, you won't know it was you who smashed the china. Never to lose faith? Of course you will. People lose their faith.

Having rejected the usual graduation clichés, Rosenblatt indirectly establishes the thesis.

So what truth can I give you, my college-boy-to-be, on your way out? You'd think I would be able to produce *something.* Words are supposed to spill from writers' minds like shrimp, especially on momentous occasions like graduations, weddings, funerals; we do it all.

Instead, I reach in my desk for some verbal pocket watch to wrap up for you in tissue paper, and come up blank. Too dazed or polite, you stare at my face the way Telemachus must have stared on the beach at Ithaca, searching for Ulysses among the sailors.

Telemachus is the son of Ulysses in Homer's *Odyssey.* He has been waiting a decade for his father to return from the Trojan War.

The metaphor of the pocket watch shows Rosenblatt's frustration at having no ready-made words to share.

The topic sentence introduces wishes as the first of five examples that structure the body of the essay.

Should I offer you wishes? Poets have done that for their children from time to time. In *Frost at Midnight* Coleridge wishes

Continued

The first example of a wish comes from the poet Samuel Taylor Coleridge.

his son Hartley a life surrounded by nature. I could wish the same for you, though I have less trust in nature's benevolence.

Still, Mary McCarthy said something interesting in an interview recently, that "our perception of the world and our values stem absolutely from the possibility of some reasonably true perception of nature—which is gradually disappearing and will soon become impossible." That could be so. Myself, I like watching the ocean.

The transition "still" shows Rosenblatt affirming the value of Coleridge's wish.

Yeats wished for his girl a sense of ceremony and tradition in *A Prayer for My Daughter*. I'd repeat that wish for you, as long as you did not turn into a snob, like Yeats. In *This Side of the Truth*, Dylan Thomas, probably hoping to protect himself, wished that his son Llewelyn would hold all judgments in abeyance. "Each truth," he wrote, "each lie, dies in unjudging love." That I will not wish for you. Have your love and your judgment too.

Rosenblatt offers more examples to develop the topic.

The topic sentence introduces aphorisms (or wise sayings) as the second example of a gift for his son.

If not wishes, how about aphorisms? Everyone can use an aphorism. I wish I could remember one, something especially Delphic or brilliant from *The Consolation of Philosophy*, the *Bhagavad Gita*, the Koran. Charlie Chan said: "Evidence like nose on anteater." Does that count? Russians are better at such things. Once in my earshot Lillian Hellman observed: "A crazy person is crazy all the time." I have frequently found that valuable, particularly when in the company of a crazy person who is, for the moment, lucid. Confucius said: "Filial piety is the constant requirement of Heaven." That seems to me an excellent aphorism.

Two examples are provided to develop the topic sentence.

In this paragraph, advice is offered as a third possible gift, and the topic is developed with several examples.

What would you say to purely tactical advice? Over the years I picked up several emotional maneuvers that might serve you well as contingency plans. When lonely, for example, read murder mysteries; I find them soothing. When angry, choose solitude. When lovesick, do push ups, run a mile or two, or step out with the boys; I don't know why that helps, but it does. When bored, see the movie *Bringing Up Baby*. When in despair, dress to the nines. I often wear a

Continued

white shirt to work when I want to pit elegance against the fates. You might try that. (Do you own a white shirt?) When glum, call home.

Or should I present you with a parable? You've probably heard the ones about the good Samaritan and the Prodigal Son. No matter. Neither parable applies to you. You were born a good Samaritan and prodigality has never been one of your problems. Frankly, I do not know a work of moral fiction that could improve your character, for it has always seemed to your mother and me (admittedly prejudiced but not blind) that your character never needed much improving. I have not known anyone more fair minded, more considerate, more able to swallow disappointment. Not from me did you get these things. Why should I expect to give you something now?

Parables are the fourth topic. The author rejects this choice, however.

Unless, as in the old days, you would like a story. This is a true one (I swear to it), about a father and a son in a playground twelve years ago, in the spring, around noon. The boy was five. He had a basketball, which he dribbled off his toes half the time, and which he kept shooting at the hoop underhand, both hands, straining to reach the rim. The father sat on a bench and watched. The boy kept at it. Then some bigger boys sauntered over, snatched the ball away and shot around, leaving the five-year-old watching too. Gearing up for the rescue, the father asked his son if he wanted him to retrieve the ball. The boy said, "No. I think I can handle it." Which he did, simply by standing among the others patiently, occasionally catching the ball and passing it to one of them, until one of them eventually passed it to him. That's all there is to that story. The five-year-old continued to play ball, and his father sat in the sun. Goodbye, my boy.

A story is the last option Rosenblatt considers; this topic is developed by illustration rather than by example.

The story about his son becomes a metaphor for the graduation speech: Rosenblatt has discovered that his son, having graduated, no longer requires help from his father.

READING QUESTIONS

1. *Why does Rosenblatt reject the openings normally used for graduation speeches?*
2. *Why is Rosenblatt not satisfied with the options of wishes, aphorisms, advice, or parables?*

3. *Who is Rosenblatt's audience? Although the essay is written for his son, is his son the only audience for the speech?*
4. *What is Rosenblatt's purpose for writing this speech?*
5. *How does Rosenblatt's purpose and audience affect the speech?*

BASIC WRITING PRINCIPLES: STUDENT WRITING

This student essay shows the writing process in its entirety, from prewriting to final draft. This essay was originally written as a timed, in-class assignment, and then revised as a later assignment. The one revision presented here is not the final draft, and the student writer identified further areas for revision through peer review and conferencing with the instructor. She developed more support and edited for word choice and grammar. As you read the revised draft, think of yourself as a peer reviewer: what suggestions for revision would you give the writer?

What Does a College Education Mean to Me? Mary Walker

Mary prewrote this essay by composing a brief brainstorming list and then choosing the ideas she would write about, indicating her choices by an asterisk. This list is the same brainstorming list you saw earlier in this chapter. Because this essay was written under a time limit, her prewriting is a little more general than it ought to be. When you prewrite, don't limit yourself to generating only general ideas; also come up with the specific ideas and concrete evidence that you will use as support. The more you figure out during prewriting, the easier it will be for you to write a successful essay.

Prewriting

College Education

*2 or 4 years   *social skills
*better job
*higher salary
not necessary
major
minor
technology
*liberal

What is the one thing you can do at any point in your life that will almost inevitably ensure you of a better lifestyle in the future? Getting a college education.

A college education is a factor in getting a good job today, but inevitably, it will be the defining factor for a better job, higher salary and a better lifestyle.

The 2-4 years that you spend there will help you in numerous ways; from helping you to get a better job w/ better pay, to helping you to expand your mind and social skills.

After generating ideas, Mary began to focus her topic by drafting some working thesis statements. The first try, as you will see, ended up as the opening to her essay. The second effort, she decided, would work better as the topic sentence of a paragraph. Her third try finally expressed her perspective on the issue.

First draft

What is the one thing you can attain at any point in your life that will almost inevitably ensure you of a better lifestyle in the future? A college education. The 2-4 years that you spend there will help you in numerous ways, from helping you to get a better job with a higher salary, to helping you expand your mind and social skills.

A college education is a factor in getting a good job today, but inevitably, it will become the defining factor for a better job, a higher salary, and a better lifestyle. The better and/or higher paying the job, the more likely it is that you will have to have a higher education (a college education). And with that better job and higher salary, no doubt, you will be able to afford those things that were financially unattainable to you prior to this education.

Better jobs and higher salary, although more frequently than not, are not the only reasons to attend college. There's also the liberalization (opening) of the mind and the increased social skills you attain while there

Continued

which can help to better your lifestyle in the future. Many employers take notice of your social skills when you're applying for a job and sometimes they do take notice of the activities that you take part in while attending school. From this, many employers will judge your character. The liberalization of your mind (which happens a lot to sheltered people while at college) will help you to except the fact that not everyone is the same and that not everyone will agree with you. It (college education) is the experience that jettisons many young men and ladies into the roles of men and women. It's a coming of age of sorts.

It's a vast and diverse world that we live in and 8 out of 10 times, you're not taught how to get through life both practically and logically in high school. College is the place where logical knowledge of books and the practical knowledge of real life and the real world meets even the most sheltered of us and produces the divers and well-rounded human being.

This draft consists largely of general ideas, with only a few concrete facts as support. Part of the reason for this lack of specificity is the general nature of Mary's prewriting. Another reason is that she chooses words such as "numerous" and "factor," which are not very concrete. When she revised the essay, however, she noticed that development was necessary and added additional support. In addition, classmates told her during a peer review workshop that there was a unity problem she would need to address in revision. She also edited the draft as she revised.

Revised draft

What's the one thing you can attain at any point in your life that will almost inevitably ensure you of a better lifestyle in the future? A college education. The 2-4 years that you spend there will help you in numerous ways, from helping you to get a better job with a higher salary to helping you to expand your mind and social skills.

Continued

A college education is one of many factors in getting a good job today, but inevitably, it will become the defining factor for a better job, a higher salary and a better lifestyle. The better and/or higher paying the job, the more likely it is that you will have to have a college education. Along with that better job, as a doctor or lawyer for example, and that

Mary develops this paragraph by adding concrete details as examples.

higher salary in the six figure range, no doubt you will be able to afford those things such as a Dodge Viper or a seven bedroom mansion that were unattainable to you prior to this education.

The better job and higher salary, although more frequently than not, aren't the only reasons to attend college. In

The beginning of this paragraph was edited to make sentences more direct.

addition to those things, there's also the liberalization or freeing of the mind and the increased social skills you receive while attending college that will also help to better your lifestyle in the future. In fact, many employers take notice of your social skills when you are applying for a job, and sometimes, they also take notice of the activities that you were involved in at school. As a result of looking at these social skills, many employers will judge your character.

Mary reorganized these paragraphs to maintain unity in each of them.

The liberalization of the mind that happens to a lot of sheltered people while at college will help you to accept the fact that not everyone is the same and that not everyone will agree with you. Nevertheless, college is the experience that pushes many young men and ladies into roles of real men and women. It's a coming of age of sorts.

It's a vast and diverse world that we live in and 8 out of 10 times you're not taught how to get through life both logically and practically in high school. College is the place where logical knowledge of books and practical knowledge of real life and the real world meets even the most sheltered of us and produces the diverse and well-rounded human being.

READING QUESTIONS

1. *Mary revised her first draft to improve the essay's development. Can you see any areas in the second draft that might need additional development? Are there passages that require less development?*
2. *Consider the essay's unity. What revisions can you suggest to ensure that all of the information in the essay is connected to the essay's claim?*
3. *Take a look at each paragraph individually. Does any paragraph need to be reorganized or revised to improve unity?*
4. *Does the writing in the essay seem coherent to you? Pick a paragraph that you think needs better coherence and revise it to include appropriate transitions.*
5. *Take a close look at the writing for punctuation, grammar, and spelling. Pick a different paragraph and edit the writing to conform to standard conventions.*

WRITING ASSIGNMENT: RESEARCHED WRITING PROJECT

Your major assignment is to produce a researched writing project that is documented and formatted according to the style requested by your instructor. This book will help you by demonstrating the process involved in researched writing: generating a topic for your project, establishing evidence from credible sources, and creating your own perspective on the evidence.

Researched Writing Project Assignments

1. **Interest Inventory** (Chapter 2): The interest inventory is a method of finding researched writing topics that you can own and be interested in. It will also help you find a purpose for your researched writing project.
2. **Project Proposal** (Chapter 2): The project proposal is a detailed description of your researched writing project. It helps you identify your limited topic, your purpose for writing, and your ownership of your topic.
3. **Validation Paper** (Chapter 6)*: The validation paper is your first interaction with your sources. In this paper, you establish the accuracy of the information you will use in your project.
4. **Connections/Context Paper** (Chapter 7)*: The connections/context paper builds on the validation paper. In this paper, you will draw connections between the evidence you have validated and explain those connections by discovering the context of your evidence.
5. **Critiquing Paper** (Chapter 8)*: In the critiquing paper, you take a closer look at your sources. You will evaluate the credibility of your sources to determine which sources are the most effective to cite in your final project.
6. **Inferencing Paper** (Chapter 9)*: In the inferencing paper, you draw original conclusions from the information presented by your

sources. These conclusions will form some of the material used to support the thesis in your final project.

7. **Final Presentation** (Chapter 13)*: The final draft of your researched writing project.

---

* For the validation paper, the connections/context paper, the critiquing paper, the inferencing paper, and the final presentation, you will be using sources in your writing. Therefore, you will need to document those sources according to the format assigned by your instructor. (A brief introduction to citation and documentation in MLA and APA formats is given in Part II of this book). Later chapters include a full and detailed discussion of citation in MLA style (Chapter 10) and APA style (Chapter 11).

CHAPTER 2

Determining Purpose and Choosing a Topic

Maria—

left early for class — going out with Jeff tonight — can I borrow your gray sweater?

Me — your favorite roommate ∸

Which came first, the chicken or the egg? Many people might reply, "The chicken," because they misunderstand evolution. A common misunderstanding of evolution is that it is aimed at the end product; in other words, a bird needs to fly, so evolution provides wings; however, evolution is not aimed at the end product, but rather the steps that lead up to the product. Which came first, the chicken or the egg? Evolution, properly understood, answers, "The egg."

Dear Sir or Madam:

I recently purchased your company's product called The Amazing Veg-o-Masher. This product does not operate as advertised; rather than mashing potatoes and other vegetables neatly and without effort, it liquefies them. Last night's dinner was not accompanied by silky smooth mashed potatoes, but by potato soup! Because your product does not work the way it is supposed to, your company should issue me a full refund of $39.95, plus tax.

TO: Mr. Johnson, Chief Financial Officer
FROM: Bill Smith, Purchasing
RE: Widget Contract

Having compared the bids we received for the widget contract, I recommend that we accept the offer from AAA Manufacturing. Although their price is not the lowest of the seven bidders, the quality of their widget is by far the highest.

All writing has a purpose. In the first example, Maria's roommate is trying to gather information. In the second example, the writer is defining the term "evolution." The third writer hopes to persuade the maker of the "Veg-o-Masher" to refund her money. In the last example, Bill is recommending a course of action to his supervisor. Regardless of the kind of writing or the audience, writers always have some goal or purpose in mind.

Purpose in writing is partially determined by the audience and partially determined by the content of the writing, as explained in Chapter 1. In turn, purpose can help focus the topic of an essay. This chapter takes a much closer look at purpose in writing and at several different purposes for writing. Then, the chapter shows how choosing a purpose will help you find a topic for your research project.

DEFINITION: PURPOSE IN WRITING

Purpose: The goal a writer hopes to achieve in a piece of writing.

The word *purpose* is rooted in the Latin *proponere*, meaning to "propose" or to "put forward," both of which suggest a goal, an intention, or an objective. Purpose gives writers direction, defining what they seek to accomplish. Furthermore, it gives the writer a relationship with the audience: in a sense, purpose is the contract the writer makes with the reader.

One way to look at writing is to see it as a triangle.

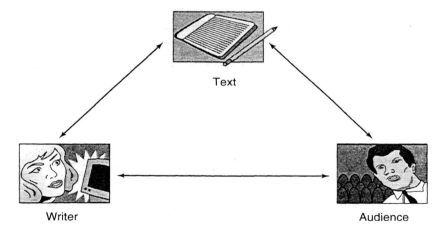

The writer, for instance you, stands at one corner of this triangle; the text you write stands at another; and the audience for whom you write stands at the third. Each of these three elements is equally important and necessary for effective writing. The relationship between any two points of the triangle is defined by purpose.

As a writer, for example, your purpose helps to focus your topic. If your topic is the pollution of ground water, then an essay whose purpose is to identify the causes will be very different from an essay that proposes solutions. Likewise, your purpose is the basis of the relationship between you and your audience. Different purposes lead you to different writing roles. For example, if you are identifying causes of ground water pollution, then you would probably adopt the role of an expert writing to a nonexpert; if your purpose is to assert a position, then you might adopt the role of one expert presenting your beliefs to an audience of other experts.

Your audience may be external, such as classmates, your instructor, or your boss; it may also be internal when you write for yourself as a "learning writer." An external audience comes to your paper with its own purpose. For instance, the audience may read your paper to acquire information, which means that it has certain expectations regarding your role as a writer and the nature of your writing. If the audience's purpose is to learn facts, then it is looking for a writer who is an expert on the issue and an essay whose purpose is likely to describe, define, or explain.

TECHNIQUES: CHOOSING A PURPOSE

When determining your purpose, you must keep in mind the three corners of the writing triangle. First, look at the evidence you have gathered and the meaning you have drawn from it (the text). Second, ask yourself: What do I want my writing to do to or for my audience (the writer)? Third, consider what your readers may have in mind when they read your essay (the audience).

Purpose is a matter of choice; again, remember that this is your essay. Even when a professor or supervisor assigns a purpose for your writing, you always make some decisions about the purpose. You make adjustments as you refine your understanding of the subject and what you are asked to do. Keep in mind that choosing a purpose is a fluid process. As time, place, subject matter, relationship to audience, and your knowledge of the subject change, so may your purpose.

9 Purposes In Writing
1. Describe
2. Define
3. Learn
4. Recommend
5. Explain
6. Analyze cause
7. Evaluate
8. Persuade
9. Assert a position

Once you realize that you choose the purpose of your writing, which largely determines how you will write an essay, you feel that you have control over your writing, and the task becomes more enjoyable. No longer is the situation one in which someone else makes you do something—now you decide for yourself what you are going to do.

Describe

When your purpose is to describe, you provide the details or essential characteristics of your subject. For example, you might describe "slash-and-gash" films by writing about this kind of movie's standard components: a remote location, an evil or supernatural killer, a bunch of naïve teenagers, and several bloody deaths.

Define

When your purpose is to define, you show that your subject fits in a particular category and how it is distinct from all other objects in the same category. In description, you discuss your subject in its own terms; in definition, you compare and contrast your subject with other, similar objects. For instance, in order to define a university as a distinct member of the category of postsecondary schools, you might show how a university is different from a liberal arts college, a community college, and a technical school.

Learn

Learning is a purpose that focuses more on yourself as the audience than on an external audience. All writing is a process of discovery, but you may choose to assemble information specifically to extend your storehouse of knowledge. You can write with learning as your ultimate purpose or as a step in drafting a paper with a different purpose. For instance, writing about what the term "rights" signifies under the Constitution and the Bill of Rights could be an essay by itself, or it could be a step in writing an essay that describes or defines "human rights" or "animal rights."

Recommend

If your purpose is to recommend, then you advise your audience to adopt a certain course of action. This recommendation must be based on evidence. Often, the evidence is based on an analysis of the present situation, why it is a problem, and why it needs to be changed. You want to convince your audience to take action on your issue. You might, for instance, recommend that your city council revise street addresses because too many street numbers are out of sequence (which causes problems for police, fire departments, delivery people, and citizens hunting for addresses).

Explain

If you are trying to clarify some aspect of an issue, then your purpose is to explain. You might be trying to clear up a misunderstanding, to present new information to your audience, or to show a new way to understand your issue. The subject of an explanation paper might be how the topography and climate of your state control the types of crops planted, how teenagers use slang, or how to shop for and purchase a new car.

Analyze Cause

If your purpose is to analyze a cause, then your paper should answer the question "why?" with a "because." A paper that analyzes cause might address the reasons for the present lower teen pregnancy rate or the effect of the Internet on education.

Unfortunately, analyzing cause is not quite as simple as saying, "This happened because of that." Very rarely is there a single cause for any given effect. Usually, several causes contribute to produce an effect, and you must distinguish between major and minor causes as well as immediate and remote causes.

Take, for instance, an overweight smoker who dies from a heart attack. Both the smoking and the weight probably contributed to the person's death, but one of those causes probably contributed more. If the person smoked three packs a day but was only twenty or thirty pounds overweight (rather than eighty or one hundred), then smoking would probably be the major cause of the person's death.

In this same scenario, neither smoking nor being overweight is the immediate cause of the person's death. Both the weight and smoking caused the heart attack, and the heart attack caused death. Therefore, the heart attack is the immediate cause of death, and smoking and being overweight are remote causes.

Evaluate

When your purpose is to evaluate, you judge the value of the topic according to specific criteria (note the relationship between the words "value" and "*evalu*ate"). Evaluation usually involves other purposes, such as defining the criteria by which you evaluate your subject and describing the subject as you evaluate it. Writing that evaluates is all around you: restaurant, movie, and book reviews all have evaluation as their purpose.

Evaluation can be found in other places as well. On the job, you evaluate procedures, products, performance, and recommendations. In your personal life, you might evaluate products for your homes, automobiles, medical options, and even churches and their congregations when you move to a new city. When you face surgery, insurance companies may require a second doctor's evaluation regarding the necessity of the procedure. And, you might evaluate alternative and traditional treatments before selecting the treatment that you, rather than the doctor, decide is best for you.

Persuade

Many of the purposes in writing involve some degree of persuasion because you are indirectly trying to convince your audience that your perspective on an issue is valid. In these cases, persuasion is not your main purpose. There are times, however, when you may want to choose persuasion as your main purpose. When you choose this focus, you will use logic and evidence to convince the audience to consider or accept a proposed idea.

Although you might think that persuasion must take the form of "this is *the* right answer," persuasion is often most successful when you try to convince readers simply to consider the validity of an idea or belief they do not currently hold. Persuasive essays can make an assertion about almost any topic: you could argue that some organized sports demand unrealistic levels of performance from young children, or that the city should consider building a skateboarding park, or that multiple choice examinations might not be the best way to test a student's knowledge.

Assert a Position

When your purpose is to assert a position, you explain where you stand on a certain issue. You are not trying so much to persuade your audience to consider adopting your position as you are trying to inform your audience what your position is and why you have taken this particular stance on the issue. In this kind of paper, you might explain your belief that all high school graduates—whether male or female—should perform one year of military or public service before going to college or beginning a career. You would not attempt to convince your audience to agree with you (if you did, your purpose would be to persuade); rather, you would explain why you believe what you believe.

EXERCISE 2–1

Identify possible purposes for the following paper topics.

1. Soccer is the new American pastime. (audience is experts)
2. Why there is a pet overpopulation problem. (audience is non-experts)
3. The importance of recycling. (audience is non-experts)
4. The scheduling of classes in the morning. (audience is experts)
5. How to play bridge. (audience is you)
6. How to play bridge. (audience is non-experts)
7. The best-tasting diet soda. (audience is experts)
8. How college football determines a national champion. (audience is non-experts)
9. The people in your home town. (audience is non-experts)
10. The need for a new elementary school in town. (audience is non-experts)

Although you can choose your purpose in writing from many options, writing with sources is often assigned as a persuasive "research paper." This practice does not mean, however, that you must use your sources strictly to persuade or argue. If you limit your choices of purpose to persuasion, then you may be greatly limiting your ability to create your own original meaning from your evidence. A more constructive way to think about assignments involving outside sources is to consider them as "researched writing." This term puts your writing and its purpose—which is not necessarily persuasive—at center stage. In researched writing, you choose a purpose that suits your subject and the meaning that you create from the evidence you gather.

Researched writing is the basic mode in most professional and workplace writing. If you look at some examples of professional writing, you'll see that persuasion is not always the main purpose of the professional or academic writer. Consider the field of economics. Table 2–1 lists the breakdown of feature articles and their purposes in the March/April 1998 issue of *Banking Strategies*.

TABLE 2-1

Title	Topic	Purpose
"Hedging the Bet"	The contrast between a banking corporation and its CEO in methods of market expansion	EXPLAIN
"Lifting the Veil on Tech Spending"	An analysis of tech spending to determine its profitability	ANALYZE CAUSE
"Payoff Deferred"	An analysis of the innovation in online banking	DESCRIBE
"Treading Cautiously"	Utility companies' caution in embracing electronic billing	ASSERT POSITION
"Network-Centric Banking"	An exploration of options in the face of Internet incursions in payments franchising	EVALUATE
"The Smart Card Disconnection"	The lack of smart card compatibility between European and American banks	EXPLAIN

No academic discipline or professional field can claim exclusive rights to any given purpose. In fact, a writer's purpose changes with specific topics and the nature of the audience.

EXERCISE 2-2

Using a recent issue of a magazine, journal, or other periodical, make a list of the feature articles, their topics, and the writer's purpose. Write a brief analysis of how the purposes of the articles are affected by the audience of the periodical.

TECHNIQUES: CHOOSING A TOPIC

How do you choose an interesting topic? You began the process of choosing a topic in Chapter 1. The exercise that asked you to use prewriting to generate interesting topics indirectly asked you to come up with topics that are connected to you and your experience. If you had trouble coming up with some possible topics, here a few examples of categories and more specific topics that might give you new areas to think about:

- Issues at your school or university:
  - plagiarism
  - parking
  - courses
- Medical issues you have had to deal with personally or within your family:
  - sleep disorders
  - diabetes
  - eating disorders

- Community concerns
  - crime.
  - taxes
  - a new public park project
- Federal mandates
  - acts or titles that affect school athletes, such as Title IX
  - the effects of Family Educational Rights and Privacy Act (FERPA) on student and parent relationships
  - affirmative action
- Hobbies
  - collecting something
  - reading
  - playing video games
- Entertainment
  - sports
  - movies
  - overlooked aspects (such as how a dirt racing track is constructed)
- Issues that define you at your age
  - becoming educated
  - preparing for a career
  - understanding what a university is
- Job experiences
  - observing managerial styles
  - customer relations
  - manufacturing processes

This list is only representative of the kinds of topics available to you for purposeful writing. It is by no means exhaustive because your life is rich in experience and knowledge. In addition, any one of these possible topics could be approached in different ways depending on the purpose you choose and your individual experience with the issue. For example, a commuter writing a paper on student parking would probably have a different point of view from a student who also works in the university department of public safety.

Purpose, Topic, Ownership

Choosing your purpose is a first step in claiming ownership of your writing. Yet, it is extremely difficult to separate purpose from topic from writer from audience. The relationships of these elements are so close as to be almost indistinguishable. You can't have a topic without a purpose, nor can you have a purpose without a topic. Sometimes, you may choose a topic because of your interest in it and decide what you want to do with it after reading many sources about it. But other times, you might decide that you want to expand your knowledge and not merely argue a point or state a position. In this case, you have decided on the purpose before seeking the topic.

If choosing a purpose is a first step toward ownership in a researched writing assignment, then choosing a topic follows closely. A danger lies in choosing a topic simply because it is heavily publicized in the media at the moment. Quite often, writers define the assignment as something outside of themselves, as though someone were sitting there with a bunch of cards in hand, saying, "Pick a topic—any topic." In this situation, the writer often ends up with a "Top 40" topic that is significant only because the topic is current: abortion, cloning, euthanasia, capital punishment, teenage drinking, teenage sex, violence in the schools, gun control, drafting females, sex in the military, hazing in fraternities and sororities, television violence, legalization of marijuana, and so on. Although the writer might have some acquaintance with any one or several of these issues, the readers of the essay have likely been overloaded with information about these topics in popular magazines, news magazines, newspapers, and nightly television news. Watching a program on TV about a certain topic does not in itself grant ownership.

You should also beware of topics that are so general as to be obvious in intention. For example, not long ago a student approached his instructor about writing on the value of physical exercise. Who could argue with that point? But this student planned to enter law enforcement as a career, so the instructor and the student talked about how police officers are often depicted in TV programs and movies as doughnut munchers riding around in squad cars. The conversation moved on to the physiques of some local law enforcement officers who appear in regional TV news programs, often displaying a waist girth that might slow them down when in pursuit of a suspected felon. Seeing that he could draw a connection between physical training and career officers, the student understood that his topic offered both ownership (it was closely connected to his own experience) and purpose (he could analyze cause).

Another student wanted to write about the destruction of the rainforests—a noble concern, but an issue about which she knew very little and which would therefore make her totally dependent on secondary sources. She had no more ownership of the topic than any average, well-informed person would have, so her instructor asked her to examine what her position about rainforests might indicate about her own value system. She shared that she had a "liberal" point of view. When she was reminded that she was living in a conservative region, she was able to see that examining the tension of being "liberal" among "conservatives" might be a productive topic to investigate. She could touch on ecological concerns as part of her purpose to explain the differences in "liberal" and "conservative" value systems. She would, like the law enforcement student, choose a purpose and thus have ownership of the topic.

Creating the Interest Inventory

The relationship between topic and purpose is symbiotic—you can't have one without the other. To help you choose the subject and purpose of your researched writing, draw up an interest inventory, a list of issues or topics that interest you and are connected to your individual experience.

The Interest Inventory: Student Writing

Following are two sample interest inventories written by two former students of the authors. Throughout the rest of the book, you will follow Tobi Raney and Julie McDowell as they complete the same researched writing project that you are working on. The work of these two students will guide you through your own project. We start with the interest inventory.

You will notice that Julie's format is somewhat different from Tobi's, but a rigid format is not the issue here. What is important is that you find several issues in which you are personally interested that you can use for a researched essay.

Interest Inventory, Tobi Raney

Note how Tobi defines a possible topic in terms of purpose.

Issue: Our responsibilities as humans to the next generation.

I might discuss divorce, stay-at-home parents, family values as the family's job before it's the government's job. Even those without kids have responsibilities. . . . Analyze cause (? of juvenile violence/broken homes/teenage pregnancy?)

At this point, there is no need to settle on a single topic—list related ideas as possible topics.

Reason for Interest: I'm a conservative who comes from a strong family. It seems to me that the general population seems to be becoming more selfish—especially in the family.

Possible Purpose: *Assert a Position* (Why, if at all possible, parents should stay together and parents, not day cares, should raise kids.)

At this point, you don't even need a definite purpose, but you should have an idea of possibilities.

Issue: Homosexuality

Reason for Interest: I love debates about this topic!

Possible Purpose: *Describe.* Trace the history of homosexuality and/or society's views of it.

Issue: Evolution

Reason for Interest: I believe evolution, whether fact or not, points to a Supreme Being. I might trace the history of theories explaining the beginning of the universe.

Possible Purpose: *Assert a Position.*

In the first list, Tobi uses the "Issue" heading to limit her topic; in others, the topic is limited under "Reason for Interest." It is more important that you limit your topic than that you worry about where you did it.

Continued

Issue: Makeup

Reason for Interest: I was reading a quiz that asked why I wore makeup and it sparked my interest. Why do women (and men) wear makeup?

Possible Purpose: *Learn*

Issue: Sports

Reason for Interest: I've done sports all my life. I'm interested in the history of track or volleyball; the history of uniforms in sports; the evolution of women's role in sports; characteristics of good coaches; etc.

Possible Purpose: *Learn*

Interest Inventory, Julie McDowell

Immediately, we can see that Tobi and Julie have different thinking, learning, and writing styles. What is different in the way these two students approached this assignment?

Methamphetamine in Southeast Missouri. Methamphetamine has become a very common problem in our region. Not only is it illegal, its manufacture is extremely dangerous. While receiving my hometown newspaper when I was at school, I noticed that there was at least one arrest every week. Most of the "cookers" have very little knowledge of chemistry, yet they are working with highly reactive chemicals—especially anhydrous ammonia. This is the aspect I would like to focus on, rather than the debate over whether or not it should or should not be illegal.

Julie uses a different format than does Tobi. Remember that content, not format, is what is important here.

Prayer as a healing therapy. Prayer is probably about as old as mankind. It has been attributed to finding lost items, giving thanks, and also for healing those who are sick or injured. I think it is a very intriguing subject and would produce interesting findings. I could possibly research the use of prayer throughout history and evaluate its benefits related to healing.

What is different about this proposal of Julie's? Why is this topic the strongest she has suggested so far?

Mosquitoes. With summer come these tiny but irritating insects. These bloodsuckers are responsible for causing itching welts on the bodies of

Continued

their victims. I have always attracted many more bites than my friends and family members. This has led me to wonder what it is about some people that attract more mosquitoes than others. Is it a special body chemical? Is it certain lotions and perfumes? Why doesn't bug spray help these people?

Birth Order. It has been documented that children who are the oldest in their family are generally more bossy and are perfectionists. As the oldest, I do fit many of the characteristics listed for my place in the birth order. I do not know much about this topic, but find it very interesting. I would like to analyze whether birth order determines personality and behavior, or rather, do we conform to these stereotypes.

Aspartame. This ingredient, found in most sugar-free foods, has long been a topic of controversy. Past studies have linked it to causing cancer and multiple sclerosis. For years I have been an avid consumer of diet drinks and sugar-free products. My mother has expressed concern about me having too much aspartame. I would like to learn more about this ingredient, how it affects the body, and whether there should be cause to worry about dangerous effects.

READING QUESTIONS

1. *Of the five topics each student gives, which do you think seems to give the writer the most ownership? Which topics seem to be "Top 40" topics?*
2. *Thinking as a reader, which topic do you think would be the basis for the most interesting project? Why? Compare your findings with the findings of other classmates.*

EXERCISE 2–3

Using your prewriting exercise from Chapter 1 as a starting point, create your own inventory list. Make a list of five topics that are of personal importance to you. For each topic, you should

- List an issue.
- Explain its importance to you.

• Identify the possible purpose you would seek to accomplish in researching this issue.

Working in pairs, use the following role-playing exercise to develop your interest inventories (you may want to look back at the section describing the instructor-student discussions). One of the pair should play the role of the instructor and interview the other to refine and develop the interest inventory. Remember, you are trying to help your partner to determine a topic that is of interest to him or her (not you) and that will stimulate and interest their (not your) reader.

Drafting the Project Proposal

The next step is to draft a project proposal. The project proposal is a formal statement about your ownership of the topic, your purpose for addressing the topic, and your plans for completing the researched writing project. The project proposal is important for four reasons. First, it establishes a plan for your researched writing project. Second, it makes you enter into a contract with yourself regarding the project's topic and purpose. Third, it introduces your topic to your instructor and shows the commitment you have made to the topic. Fourth, it also allows your instructor to guide you in the researched writing process.

An outline of the project proposal follows.

Project Proposal: Topic and Purpose

1. **Identify the topic:** (this statement names the general topic you have selected)
2. **Explain how you intend to limit the scope of the topic:** (limiting the scope of the topic confines it to a certain field so that you do not have to cover the entire topic)
3. **Identify your ownership of the topic:** (ownership establishes the reason for your interest in the topic)
4. **Identify the purpose:** (review the purposes for writing section and specify your purpose for this project)
5. **Explain the significance of your project:** (this explanation may address the benefit to the audience, action the paper might lead to, or your own understanding of the subject)
6. **Identify your intended audience:** (the audience might be yourself as a learner, a specifically targeted audience, or even different groups or readers; for example, Tobi Raney targets three audiences: young adult females, coaches, and parents)
7. **Identify questions for your instructor:** (asking your instructor questions about issues you have not resolved creates a collaborative relationship between you and your instructor and saves both of you time when you hold a conference about your project proposal)

The Project Proposal: Student Writing

Having chosen one of their possible topics, Tobi and Julie then wrote a topic proposal that included questions for their teacher conferences.

Project Proposal, Tobi Raney

Identify the topic: My topic will be self-esteem.

It is important to place limits on your topic: how can you make your project manageable, given the time constraints of your class, the space restraints (number of pages) of your assignment, and the information restraints of available resources?

Explain how you intend to limit the scope of the topic: I will limit my topic to the self-esteem of adolescent and young adult females in popular high school and college sports—volleyball, basketball, track, soccer, swimming, softball, etc. I will use athletics as an example to explain what self-esteem is and how a healthy self-image is gained in some women.

Identify your ownership of the topic: I have played sports ever since elementary school. My parents had to force me at first, but now I can't imagine my life without athletics. The commitment required by sports has taught me discipline, kept me out of trouble, boosted my confidence, taught me leadership, helped me make friends, and improved my body image considerably. I am also interested in learning if the self-esteem increase takes place only for successful athletes or for all participants.

Here is where you explain how your topic connects to your personal experiences and interests.

Identify the purpose: I would like to *define* self-esteem and *evaluate* the merit of athletic participation. I will attempt to determine how significantly sports affect young women's self-esteem.

Another way of making your project interesting for both you and the reader is to consider the consequences of your project. Rather than looking at this project as simply a way to pass a course, think about what else you can do with the results outside of class.

Explain the significance of your project: I hope the findings of my research will encourage several groups of people. I would like to encourage those who have never given athletics a chance to see if it profits them the way it has so many others. Those already

Continued

involved should recognize in my paper the benefits they reap from taking part in recreational activities. Coaches will see what appeals to and inspires young women and may be able to use this information to improve the quality of their instruction. Also, the average person may understand a little more why we athletes act a little fanatical sometimes.

Identify your intended audience: The audience of these papers will be primarily, but not exclusively, young adult females, coaches, and parents.

Because you should be using personal experience in your researched writing, you will have to use first-person pronouns.

Identify questions for your instructor: How do I document myself as a source? Can I use "I," "my," and "me" in my paper? What exactly are we writing about in our verifying the sources paper? Should evaluating the value of participation or defining *self-esteem* be my main purpose? Is it all right to have two?

At this stage in the researched writing process, it is not a problem to have more than one purpose. Eventually, you ought to focus on one purpose as your main objective in writing.

Project Proposal, Julie McDowell

Identify the topic: My topic will be aspartame—an ingredient commonly found in sugar-free foods.

Explain how you intend to limit the scope of the topic: I will limit my topic to the use of aspartame in sugar-free foods and the effects it has on the body, as well as the controversies it has created.

Identify your ownership of the topic: I consume sugar-free foods nearly every day, from soft drinks and candy to cereals. My mother has expressed concern that I am taking in too much of the ingredient, as

Continued

she has read several articles about it being linked to causing multiple sclerosis and cancer.

Identify the purpose: My purposes will likely be to learn what aspartame is, and to discover what it does to the body. I will try to determine if there is a need to worry about it having the ability to cause disease.

Explain the significance of your project: As consumers, we should educate ourselves about ingredients that have the potential to cause harm to our bodies. I intend to be able to present the reader—whether or not he or she uses products that contain aspartame—with a thorough account of how aspartame affects our bodies. Thus, after reading these findings, one could decide for himself/herself if he or she would benefit or be harmed by the sweetener.

Identify your intended audience: The audience of this paper will be all consumers of aspartame, especially those—like dieters and diabetics—who consume large amounts of it.

Identify questions for your instructor: Do you have any other suggestions for primary or secondary sources? Am I on the right track to limiting the scope of my topic? Should I limit my intended audience more?

WRITING ASSIGNMENT: THE PROJECT PROPOSAL

Use the following form to develop a project proposal. Each entry is explained in the previous project proposal section.

The Researched Writing Project Proposal

Name _____   Instructor _____

Section _____

1. Identify Your General Topic: _____
   _____

2. Identify Your Limited Topic: _____
   _____

3. Identify Your Ownership: _____
   _____

4. Identify Your Purpose: _____
   _____

5. Identify the Significance of Your Project: _____
   _____

6. Identify Your Intended Audience: _____
   _____

7. Identify Questions for Your Instructor: _____
   _____

CHAPTER 3

Creating and Presenting Meaning

Researched writing incorporates information from sources outside of your personal experience. To complete a researched writing project, you must gather information, draw meaning from that information, determine your purpose as a writer, discover the connections among several pieces of information, place the information into a context, determine which sources are acceptable for use in your writing, determine the best way to incorporate those sources into your writing, and make sure that your paper follows a proper format.

Whew! I bet you're as tired from reading that sentence as I am from writing it. When you look at the process of researched writing all at once, it seems like an impossibly complicated and time-consuming process. Like any major project, however, when you take researched writing one step at a time, it becomes much more manageable—it can even become easy, and dare I say it, fun.

The first part of this book is called "Setting the Stage" because the chapters all discuss important ideas you need to know about before you get very far into your researched writing project. The first chapter reviewed basic writing principles that apply to any kind of writing. The second chapter helped you determine a purpose and choose a topic for your researched writing project. This chapter examines how to create meaning from several pieces of information.

Everyone creates meaning every day whether speaking or writing. Here's a letter that describes one citizen's perceptions of a local government:

> It is time to vote for younger members of the City Council. Even when the will of the people has been made known, the City Council manages to subvert the issue. For example, the people wanted a tornado early

Continued

42

warning siren system. The council selected the bid of the makers of the puniest sirens, which could hardly be heard a block away, because the council did not really want an early warning system at all. Another example is the riverboat casino the people voted for. The council selected the bid of a gambling group that was about to go bankrupt. We still have no casino, but eighty miles to the south, where the citizens voted later than we did, another town is getting rich from its casino. And finally, when the council needs to build new streets to newly developed areas, it always puts in the narrowest streets possible to save money. Yet anyone could foresee that the increased traffic would demand four-lane streets, not two-lane streets. The result? We taxpayers end up spending money for street upgrades. We need to stop electing old politicians who have no vision and elect younger council members who can respond to the will of the people.

This paragraph is an example of a writer creating meaning from facts and information. The writer takes several pieces of information (the actions of the City Council) and draws a general conclusion (younger council members need to be elected).

This chapter defines some essential terms and then discusses the process of creating meaning, including several dangers to be aware of. Then, the chapter discusses the equally important skill of effectively presenting meaning to readers.

DEFINITION: MEANING AND EVIDENCE

Evidence: the body of information or material that forms the foundation of any writing.

The root of the word *evidence* is the Latin *videre,* which means literally "to see." In researched writing, evidence consists of the details and the factual information, which allow us to see the issue set before us.

Without details or factual data, writers are limited to generalities—they can only talk around the subject. Generalities give only limited and superficial information. Details, examples, comparisons, and facts add depth and breadth to a piece of writing. Details help the readers picture what the writer is saying, making the writing more powerful and persuasive. Read the following paragraphs for an example. Which of these paragraphs do you find more interesting?

Baseball is an exciting sport. When somebody hits a home run or strikes out a batter, everybody in the stadium cheers. A stolen base can be exciting, too.

Baseball is an exciting sport. When Mark McGwire or Sammy Sosa steps into the batter's box, your heart starts to beat a little faster. If they get ahold of a pitch and hit it over the fence, everyone in the stadium jumps to their feet at the same time and roars with enthusiasm. When David Cone pitched a perfect game against the Montreal Expos, you could hear the excitement in the voice of the announcer when he said, "He popped him up—and it's playable!" Meanwhile, Cone's teammates were also excited, jumping up off the bench and swarming over him in a big pig pile on the infield.

> **Meaning:** the significance or implications that the writer draws from the evidence.

The second paragraph clearly contains both specific details and general statements. The specific details are the facts; the general statement "Baseball is an exciting sport" is the *meaning* of all of those details. When you, as a writer, see a general idea that connects several pieces of evidence together, you are *creating* meaning: you are producing something new, unique, and original—your own vision of the facts.

As a reader, you are probably aware that specific details grab your attention and interest. It is often hard to remember a general idea by itself, but when specific details support that general idea (as in the second baseball paragraph), you are better able to picture the issue. Details are simply more effective than generalities alone. This principle does not mean, however, that interesting writing is simply a collection of specific details. Good writing needs both details and the general statements a writer draws from them, both facts and meaning. Alone, details are like a country without a leader—a chaotic and disordered mob with no purpose. Alone, generalities are like a leader without a country—full of ideas with no connection to anything concrete. Thus, details and generalities are symbiotic—they are interdependent.

Gathering a full and diverse body of details benefits both the writer and the readers. For the writer, a greater body of specific information affords a larger perspective and diminishes the possibility of quick, easy, and often incorrect associations. If you have only two pieces of information, you might draw an obvious conclusion. For example, say that you see Bill Jones driving a new Ferrari and you know that Bill's father is wealthy; you might conclude from this evidence that Bill's father bought the Ferrari. But add the information that Bill just received a promotion, and your conclusion may change. The greater the amount of information available to you, the more accurate your conclusions may be.

EXERCISE 3-1

Practice drawing conclusions in this exercise. Using the clues provided in the descriptions that follow, determine each person's occupation.

1. This person's clothes are damp with sweat and his face is bright red. He smells like beer and he has white powder on his hands. What does he do?
2. This woman has a measuring tape in her hand and a pencil behind her ear. She has a bruise on her thumb and works outside. What's her line of work?

EXERCISE 3-2

The comic strips that follow lack dialogue. Make a list of details that you observe in each frame: who is present, what they are doing, their facial expressions, etc. Using that list as evidence, create meaning from the situation and write dialogue that presents that meaning. Compare your dialogue with that of a classmate or two. Consider then what influences may have affected you and your classmates when you created your unique perspectives on the evidence.

HI AND LOIS

BLONDIE

BEETLE BAILEY

TECHNIQUES: CREATING MEANING

USE CAUTION
Creating meaning from evidence can easily go wrong. The following factors influence your ability to create meaning:
1. Your knowledge of the issue.
2. Your attitudes and predispositions toward the issue.
3. Your willingness to pay attention to all of the evidence.
4. Your methods of collecting evidence.

Because you create meaning from your unique, personal perspective, you must be aware of how your perspective can shape meaning. Several factors influence your perspective on the evidence, some of which you can control and some of which you cannot. First, what you know about an issue and what your intellectual world view is willing to accept can limit the meaning that you create. Second, how you feel about an issue before you look at the facts can cause you to choose an interpretation that is not supported by the facts. Third, how thorough you are in looking at all of the information determines how accurately you interpret the information. Finally, the methods you use to collect evidence can limit the information you use to create meaning.

The letter about the City Council at the beginning of this chapter shows what happens when a writer does not pay attention to all of the evidence. The issues the letter-writer mentions—the early warning system, the casino, and the new streets—are not as simple as the writer implies. In order to support the meaning created in the letter—that younger council members are needed—the writer has chosen to ignore part of the evidence. Note that the letter contains mostly general statements with very few specific details.

How information is collected can also affect the process of creating meaning. NASA regularly sends spacecraft on fly-bys of other planets to gather information about those other worlds. In early spacecraft fly-bys, photographs taken of a mountain range on Mars revealed what some people thought was a profile of a face, which they argued could have been created only by creatures of advanced intelligence. But a 1998 fly-by photograph taken by more precise equipment debunked this interpretation. The 1998 photo showed that the features were only randomly arranged cliffs, peaks, and talus slopes. In this case, the methods by which the information was gathered affected the meaning people created from the photographs.

The following article presents a real-life example of how knowledge, attitude, and methods can affect the meaning one doctor created from a body of information.

The Mysterious Case of E.P.

Steven Levingston

On a spring day in 1995, Dr. R. Michael Benitez was reviewing patient charts in his office at the University of Maryland Medical Center in Baltimore when the phone rang. Dr. Joseph Costa, the chief resident, was

---

Continued

on the line with a request. He wondered if Benitez would solve a medical mystery and present his findings at an upcoming conference.

Dr. Benitez was already a veteran of three clinico-pathological conferences (or CPCs). As before, he'd be given a complex case, and he would have to deliver a diagnosis in front of an auditorium full of medical colleagues and students. These lessons were not without pressure: the entire University of Maryland medical community would be judging Benitez and the ingenuity of his investigation. The doctor's clinical expertise would be in the spotlight.

"Sure," he replied. "I'd be happy to do it." With that, he trotted down the hall to Dr. Costa's office to pick up the case.

"Just give it your best shot," his colleague said.

Scanning the skimpy 1 1/2-page protocol on the patient, identified only as "E.P.," the 34-year-old cardiologist and assistant professor immediately noticed something strange. Where were the lab results? He wondered. What about a CAT scan? A chest X-ray?

Later, Dr. Benitez read through the report again. He learned that a middle-aged man was found unconscious on a Baltimore street one afternoon in October. He was taken to a local hospital, where he remained unresponsive until three the next morning. He then awoke trembling, delirious and hallucinating. He sweated profusely, and his heartbeat fluctuated. This condition lasted 28 hours.

Dr. Benitez noticed that the man's raving suddenly ceased and that he became tranquil and clearheaded, though his stomach hurt and he had a headache. Moreover, the patient had no idea he'd been in the hospital for three days and couldn't recall what had landed him there.

That evening the patient relapsed. The protocol mentioned that the man had entered the hospital with no smell of alcohol on his breath, and that when his doctor tried to use alcohol as a treatment, the patient refused even a drop. He drank a little water, but with difficulty. His mind was clouded, his breathing shallow, and again he became delirious. After

Continued

a number of hours in this state, he died.

The report revealed a few more meager clues: six months of sobriety preceded by alcohol abuse; possible past drug abuse and depression; cholera prior to hospitalization. Wow, Dr. Benitez thought, what's going on here?

With only a few weeks to find the answers, the doctor plunged in, poring over medical journals. On a pad of paper he jotted down delirium; relapse; fluctuating pulse and breathing; death. These four clues, he decided, pointed him toward the solution of the mystery.

Then he flipped back to the protocol. Trauma? The report stated that there was no evidence of it, so Dr. Benitez crossed trauma off his list. Alcohol withdrawal? The patient hadn't smelled of alcohol and claimed he'd abstained for months. Moreover, it would be highly unusual, Benitez reasoned, for a patient suffering from alcohol withdrawal to recover briefly, then relapse and die.

The medical gumshoe decided to research infectious diseases as a possible cause for relapsing symptoms. Yellow fever and malaria were among them. But that's crazy, he decided. No one gets these diseases around here, and the report did not mention foreign travel.

Scanning his CD-ROM medical encyclopedia for yellow-fever references, he found that a scourge had killed more than 4000 people in Philadelphia in the late 18th century. Suddenly his investigation took new shape. Had E.P. perhaps lived in the late 1700s or early 1800s? Maybe that was why there were no lab results or CAT scans.

After a careful look, though, Dr. Benitez had to scratch yellow fever and malaria off his shrinking list of possible deadly illnesses; neither one of them entirely fit the patient's symptoms.

Still baffled by the bizarre case, he read the patient's medical history again. There's something I haven't picked up on, he fretted. Then inspiration struck. One small detail in the protocol now emerged as a possible key to the mystery: the patient's vehement refusal to drink

Continued

alcohol, and his difficulty swallowing water. What would cause such a reaction to liquids?

The obvious answer was rabies. But that seemed strange. The case history indicated nothing about the patient foaming at the mouth. Wasn't that common? Dr. Benitez didn't know. Rabies is extremely rare. He'd never seen a case of it in his career.

He riffled through the pages of *Principles and Practice of Infectious Diseases*. The more Dr. Benitez studied the disease, the more it seemed to fit the patient's symptoms. Encephalitic rabies can cause confusion, hallucinations and wide variations in heart rates and respiration. These can be interrupted by intervals of lucidity. It is almost always lethal, with its intense course lasting an average of four days. And rabies can induce spasms in the muscles of the larynx and pharynx that make drinking nearly impossible.

Rabies, he read, is usually caused by exposure, through a bite or open wound, to the saliva of a rabid animal. It is often not recognized because patients may exhibit common ailments such as headaches and cramps. He also found out that the Hollywood version of patients foaming at the mouth is largely just that—the stuff of movies.

But why didn't the patient's case history refer to any encounter with a rabid animal? Again, Dr. Benitez pored over the medical literature. Rabies victims, he found out, often have no sign of exposure because the disease's incubation can take a year or longer. Many victims don't recall having a run-in with a sick animal.

As days passed, Dr. Benitez became more and more convinced of his diagnosis. But was he willing to go out on a limb with it?

One evening, a colleague asked him if he knew who the patient was. He didn't. He'd focused so intensely on the medical questions that the initials *E.P.* meant nothing to him. Dr. Benitez again reread the protocol, this time with a new eye. The patient was described as a writer: E.P., writer, Baltimore.

Continued

Suddenly bells clanged in Benitez's head. "Hear the loud alarum bells—Brazen bells! What a tale of terror, now their turbulency tells!" He thought of nights as a child reading "The Pit and the Pendulum" and other frightening tales.

Of course! The patient was Edgar Allan Poe, poet and author, master of the macabre, inventor of the modern detective story, creator of one of the world's best-known poems, "The Raven."

Dr. Benitez rushed to the public library and pulled out a stack of books on Poe. He learned that Poe's life was brief and tragic. Born on January 19, 1809, Poe was orphaned at age three. He married his cousin Virginia Clemm who died an agonizing death from tuberculosis. His stories, such as "The Premature Burial," may reflect his own gloom, induced partly by heavy drinking and partly by a troubled yet brilliant mind.

Benitez read the often romanticized accounts of Poe's last days. He had been found at a Baltimore tavern filthy, his raven-black hair unkempt, his clothes crumpled and soiled.

Muttering incoherently, he was taken to Washington College Hospital. When he awakened from his stupor, he raved at phantoms on the wall and cried out that someone should "blow out his brains with a pistol." He slipped in and out of delirium for several days. Finally, after lying still for a moment, Poe moved his head a little, muttered, "Lord, help my poor little soul" and then died.

While some of the details varied from one biographical account to another, the general picture that emerged of Poe's final suffering and death was consistent with what Benitez had read in the protocol. But nowhere was it recorded that Poe succumbed to rabies. The judgment of history was that on October 7, 1849, he died of alcoholism.

A few days later, Dr. Benitez stepped up to the lectern at the CPC, ready to present his theory. Carefully, he took the audience through his reasoning, proposing and rejecting a variety of ailments. Then it was time

Continued

to risk his conclusion. As he built his case for rabies, the crowd listened attentively.

Finally, Dr. Benitez revealed the patient as Edgar Allan Poe. When he finished, the room erupted in a rousing ovation.

Newspaper articles followed, proclaiming the new diagnosis. Though some scholars refuse to part with the romantic notion of Poe as the troubled, drunken writer, others found Dr. Benitez's reasoning persuasive. Poe "had all the features of encephalitic rabies," says Dr. Henry Wilde, an infectious-disease expert who frequently treats rabies.

"Dr. Benitez's ignorance of his patient's identity for most of his inquiry adds to his credibility," says Jeff Jerome, curator of the Edgar Allan Poe House and Museum in Baltimore. "This is the first time a modern doctor has looked at Poe's death without preconceived notions of the role of alcohol and drugs."

After reaching the diagnosis, Dr. Benitez wanted to see the hospital room where Poe had died. But a friend working at the medical facility, now called Church Home and Hospital, told Benitez that what is thought to have been Poe's death chamber, up a creaky spiral staircase, was now only a wall. The master of suspense had vanished almost without leaving a trace.

Almost, but not quite. For Dr. Benitez's research may have shed new light on Edgar Allan Poe's final mystery.

READING QUESTIONS

1. *Creating meaning begins with facts. What facts does Dr. Benitez have to create meaning with?*
2. *When Dr. Benitez first looks at his facts, he notices something "strange." What is the strange thing he notices? How do the methods used to collect the facts affect Dr. Benitez's ability to create meaning from the facts? How would the facts have been different if modern methods had been used to collect them?*
3. *How does Dr. Benitez's knowledge of rabies affect his ability to draw a conclusion from the evidence? How does his lack of knowledge concerning the patient's identity help him?*

4. *At two points in this article, Dr. Benitez ignores crucial evidence. What is the evidence that he ignores? How and when does he correct his mistake? How does the evidence, once he pays attention to it, change his investigation?*
5. *At what points in the article does Dr. Benitez reveal preconceived attitudes toward the evidence? What are those attitudes? How do the attitudes help or hinder his investigation?*

You can have all the evidence in the world, but if you do not use it correctly, you will have difficulty drawing accurate conclusions. Dr. Benitez's story is a great example of how to correctly use evidence. First, you must be aware of the context and background of the evidence, such as the yellow fever outbreak in Philadelphia and the long incubation period for rabies. Second, you must not let what you want to see or know blind you to what the evidence might mean, as is the case with the doctors who had "preconceived notions" about the connections between drugs and alcohol and Poe's death, or the scholars who do not accept Dr. Benitez's diagnosis because it is not "romantic" enough for them.

Ignoring evidence when it doesn't fit your meaning is perhaps the hardest danger to avoid when dealing with evidence. Early in his research, Dr. Benitez investigated yellow fever and malaria as possible causes of death. This conclusion didn't fit all of the facts; Dr. Benitez could have ignored the evidence that didn't fit, but he probably would have been very embarrassed when he gave the wrong diagnosis at the CPC. Instead, he realized he had the wrong answer, paid attention to all of the evidence, and ended up finding a cause of death that fit all of the facts he had.

In the following article, an eleven-year-old girl creates meaning from facts that she has gathered. A group of people, therapeutic touch practitioners, are unwilling to see all of the evidence and disagree with the girl's conclusion.

The 11-year-old Debunker

Jessica Gorman

On April 1 [1998], 11-year-old Emily Rosa of Loveland, Colorado, published a paper in the *Journal of the American Medical Association*, and it was no April Fool's joke. The seventh grader's study—which was coauthored by nurse Linda Rosa, Emily's mother—found no scientific basis for an alternative healing technique called therapeutic touch, which is practiced by tens of thousands of health-care professionals.

Continued

Practitioners of therapeutic touch say they can treat everything from infant colic to arthritis, Alzheimer's disease to cancer, by moving their hands over a person's body without directly touching it. During the process, the practitioners say, they feel and correct the patient's "energy field."

Emily was only nine when she decided to test the therapeutic value of touch. It began as a fourth-grade science project. In 1996 and 1997, Emily recruited 21 therapeutic-touch practitioners to determine whether they could detect a human energy field. The experiments were designed so that each test subject, seated at a table across from Emily, stretched out his or her arms, palms up. A large screen ran across the table and hid Emily from view. Emily tossed a coin to decide whether to hold her hand over a subject's left or right hand. If subjects could in fact feel her energy field, Emily reasoned, they should reliably tell her over which of their hands her own hand hovered.

But the test subjects did no better than chance, identifying the correct hand only 47 percent of the time in the 1996 experiment and just 41 percent of the time in the 1997 experiment.

Critics contend that either Emily's experiment or her energy field was flawed. Emily says practitioners have described an energy field as feeling "like peanut butter, and it's gooey, or soft like marshmallows, Jell-O." None of Emily's subjects complained about her field during the experiment, she says. But after she told the results, some said "they couldn't feel my energy field because of my age, or it flew away with the air conditioner." The biggest complaints, however, came after Emily published her study in one of the nation's leading medical journals.

READING QUESTIONS

1. *What evidence does Emily gather about the therapeutic touch practitioners? What meaning does she create from the evidence?*
2. *How does Emily gather her evidence? Does the method used to gather evidence affect what evidence she gathered? How?*

3. *What two objections do Emily's critics raise? Are they valid objections? Why or why not?*
4. *The therapeutic touch practitioners were not willing to accept Emily's conclusions. Which of the four dangers in creating meaning listed earlier in this chapter prevent the practitioners from agreeing with Emily? Explain why you think so.*

All writing, whether researched or otherwise, involves gathering as much evidence as possible and creating meaning from that information. As you create meaning, you have to be aware of the following:

- what you know about your issue as you begin your research
- any preconceived attitudes you might have about the issue
- the methods used to collect the facts (both by yourself and by your sources)
- all of the evidence, even if it forces you to change your conclusions

As you go through the different chapters in this book, you will be coming back to these ideas repeatedly.

TECHNIQUES: PRESENTING MEANING

When you present your meaning in writing, you must balance general statements of meaning with specific references to the detailed information you uncover in your research. You must also decide which evidence to include because you will likely not be using every fact that you uncover.

When a writer has difficulty handling details, it's usually because of one of two problems. The first problem is too much detail: having been told that details are important in developing the paper, the writer includes every detail to be found, making little distinction between what is necessary and what is not. Moreover, the writer has trouble drawing connections among the many pieces of evidence, so the readers end up drowning in a sea of facts, unable to find any solid conclusions to support them. The writer can easily solve this problem by selecting only those details that are clearly connected to his or her conclusions, and among that relevant evidence, presenting only those details that most effectively support his or her perspective.

The other problem a writer might have in presenting detailed evidence is quite the opposite—rather than including too much detail, the writer does not use enough. Having been told that details are necessary to a strong paper, the writer provides just enough information to satisfy that requirement and to show knowledge of the subject. Insufficient detail makes the writing appear superficial, however, and the conclusions seem forced, vague, and not clearly supported. In this case, readers are forced to skim along the surface of the essay, lacking the details that would have provided depth and greater understanding. To understand the writer's perspective on the issue, readers must imagine additional details that might support the thesis. This task shifts ownership of the essay from the writer to the readers.

In both cases, the writer has given up control of the writing. Rather than providing readers with both meaning and evidence, he or she offers only one or the other and demands that the readers do the work of connecting evidence and meaning. In other words, the writer has required the readers to do the writer's job. But the readers may not agree to do the writer's job, preferring instead to stop reading.

So, what should you do to avoid these problems in your own writing? How do you achieve the proper balance of detail and conclusion, of evidence and meaning? How do you maintain control of your perspective on an issue? Slow down. Don't rush the job. Gather all the material you can, and then choose the most relevant and effective supporting material. In making those choices, always remember your audience. As Chapter 1 suggested, you should ask yourself what your readers need to know (in other words, are they asking what, how, or why about your topic). Base your choices on your readers' needs.

> **TECHNIQUES FOR PRESENTING YOUR PERSPECTIVE**
> Present sensory perceptions
> Provide examples
> Provide illustrations
> Draw comparisons
> Draw contrasts
> Draw connections

The following techniques are particularly effective in presenting meaning. Keep them in mind as you gather information. Because you will likely not be using all of the information you gather about a topic, you need to think ahead. When you are gathering information, ask yourself: Will this fact be useful in presenting my meaning? Which technique can this fact be used for?

Present Sensory Perceptions

You encounter objects in the world through your five senses (i.e., sight, hearing, touch, taste, and smell). By using sensory perception in your writing, you help your readers encounter the objects you describe in the same way you did when you first encountered them. Most likely, you will depend on the sense of sight more than the other four senses when you present meaning because readers often want a "picture" of what you are presenting. Humans depend heavily on the visual sense, which is one reason why the expression "I see" is a synonym for "I understand."

Although using visual detail helps your readers to see and understand your writing, presenting perceptions from the other four senses can be helpful as well. If you are describing a siren, for instance, you might write about the quickly alternating highs and lows of an ambulance's siren or the slower, less urgent siren of a police car. Smells can be very powerful as well: describing the musty, dusty scent some books have can be an effective way to show your readers that a book has been sitting on a shelf for a long time.

Provide Examples

Examples, like sensory details, provide "pictures" of your ideas for your readers to see. An example is like a display or a snapshot of an idea—a quick representation. Like sensory details, examples should be detailed and concrete; otherwise, your snapshot is "fuzzy," out of focus, and ineffective. If you are discussing academic success, for example, you might provide the following example: "Doing well in school is a type of academic success." Your readers now have a snapshot of your idea, but it is very unclear and out of focus. Here's a better choice:

> Academic success might be defined by a student's record at college. Many people think that my brother Joe is a successful student because he earned a 4.0 GPA at the University of Missouri and graduated with honors.

Adding specific and concrete details to your examples brings the "snapshot" into focus, making it easier for your readers to understand your ideas.

Provide Illustrations

Illustrations are more extensive than examples; they can be anecdotal (like stories) or explanatory. In order to provide effective illustrations, you may find yourself employing many of the techniques listed here—an example may be presented through sensory detail and then illustrated by drawing comparisons, contrasts, and other connections.

Draw Comparisons

The three previous techniques help you clearly present details to your readers. Your perspective on an issue, however, includes both detailed information and general statements of meaning. Drawing comparisons and contrasts can help you explain to your readers the meaning you have created from the information.

When you draw comparisons, you are showing similarities between separate items of information. When you show the similarities between pieces of evidence, you begin to put them into groups, which is an important way of making meaning.

Drawing comparisons by using metaphors and similes can also help you explain unfamiliar ideas in terms of more familiar ones. For instance, if a writer tells you that "intussusception" means that one part of the intestine is inverted and received into an adjacent part, you might not have a clear idea of what the writer means; however, if the writer makes a comparison and tells you that intussusception means that the intestine decreases in length *like a telescope* (a simile), you might have an easier time picturing the process.

Draw Contrasts

Just as discovering similarities between pieces of evidence helps you use your evidence effectively, so too, paradoxically, does seeing differences. Identifying differences is necessary for categorizing information, that is, separating various items into groups. Categorizing your evidence also helps you manage the large amount of information you gather in your search for evidence.

Draw Connections

Presenting sensory perception and providing examples and illustrations helps you present your specific information clearly. Drawing comparisons and contrasts helps you show your readers how you have put the related pieces of evidence together into separate groups and started to create meaning. All of those techniques lead up to drawing connections, which is how you create almost all of your meaning.

When you draw connections, you do more than note similarities or differences. Information can also be connected as cause and effect, part of a process, or through other logical relationships. Seeing these relationships gives you new ways of understanding the evidence—ways that are uniquely yours. Because you draw connections in your mind rather than see them as physical characteristics of an object, drawing connections is a form of mental ownership, as well as the primary way of creating original meaning.

EXERCISE 3–3

For this exercise, you will need to work with a classmate. Take several minutes to observe your partner's appearance—clothes, hairstyle, etc. Once you have gathered your facts about your partner's appearance, write a brief description of that person, using sensory details, comparisons, contrasts, connections, examples, and illustrations.

CREATING AND PRESENTING MEANING: PROFESSIONAL WRITING

The following passage shows the great American writer Mark Twain using the techniques of creating meaning and presenting details. Twain gathers facts about the Mississippi River, draws conclusions from those facts to create meaning, selects only those facts that are necessary to clearly present his perspective (the process of selection, however, is not visible in the passage), balances his use of general and specific statements, and uses sensory perception, comparisons, contrasts, examples, and illustrations to present his ideas.

The River as Book and as Picture   Comparison

Mark Twain

The face of the water, in time, became a wonderful book—a book that

was a dead language to the uneducated passenger but which told its

mind to me without reserve, delivering its most cherished secrets as

Comparison   clearly as if it uttered them with a voice. And it was not a book to be

---

Continued

read once and thrown aside, for it had a new story to tell every day. Throughout the long twelve hundred miles there was never a page that was void of interest, never one that you could leave unread without loss. Never one that you would want to skip, thinking you could find higher enjoyment in some other thing. There never was so wonderful a book written by man, never one whose interest was so absorbing, so unflagging, so sparklingly renewed with every reperusal. The   **Contrast**
passenger who could not read it was charmed with a peculiar sort of faint dimple on its surface (on the rare occasions when he did not overlook it altogether) but to the pilot that was an *italicized* passage; indeed it was more than that, it was a legend of the largest capitals with
Connection (signs)   a string of shouting exclamation-points at the end of it, for it meant that a wreck or a rock was buried there that could tear the life out of the strongest vessel that ever floated. It is the faintest and simplest expression the water ever makes, and the most hideous to a pilot's eye. In truth, the passenger who could not read this book saw nothing but all manner of pretty pictures in it, painted by the sun and shaded by the   **Contrast**
clouds, whereas to the trained eye these were not pictures at all, but the grimmest and most dead-earnest of reading matter.

Comparison   Now when I mastered the language of this water, and had come to know every trifling feature that bordered the great river as familiarly as I knew the letters of the alphabet, I had made a valuable acquisition. But I had lost something, too. I had lost something which could never   **Contrast**
be restored to me while I lived. All the grace, the beauty, the
Illustration begins   poetry, had gone out of the majestic river! I still kept in mind a certain wonderful sunset which I witnessed when steamboating was new to me. A broad expanse of the river was turned to blood; in the middle distance the red hue brightened into gold, through which a   **Sensory perception (sight)**
solitary log came floating, black and conspicuous; in one place a long, slanting mark lay sparkling upon the water; in another the surface was
Comparison   broken by boiling, tumbling rings, that were as many-tinted as an

Continued

opal; where the ruddy flush was faintest, <u>was a smooth spot that</u>   Sensory perception (sight)
<u>was covered with graceful circles and radiating lines, ever so delicately</u>
<u>traced; the shore on our left was densely wooded, and the somber</u>
<u>shadow that fell from this forest was broken in one place by a long,</u>
<u>ruffled trail</u> that shone like silver; and high above the forest wall a clean-
stemmed dead tree waved a single leafy bough that glowed like a flame
in the unobstructed splendor that was flowing from the sun. There were
graceful curves, reflected images, woody heights, soft distances; and over
the whole scene, afar and near, the dissolving lights drifted steadily,
enriching its every passing moment with new marvels of coloring.

Comparison   <u>I stood like one bewitched.</u> I drank it in, in a speechless rapture.
The world was new to me, and I had never seen anything like this at
home. <u>But as I have said, a day came when I began to cease from</u>   Contrast
<u>noting the glories and the charms which the moon and the sun and the</u>
<u>twilight wrought upon the river's face; another day came when I ceased</u>
<u>altogether to note them.</u> Then, if that sunset scene had been repeated, I
should have looked at it without rapture, and should have commented
Extended illustration of   upon it, inwardly, after this fashion: <u>"This sun means that we are</u>
contrast begins   <u>going to have wind tomorrow; that floating log means that the river</u>
<u>is rising, small thanks to it; that slanting mark on the water refers to a bluff</u>
<u>reef which is going to kill somebody's steamboat one of these nights, if it</u>
<u>keeps on stretching out like that; those tumbling 'boils' show a dissolving</u>
<u>bar and a changing channel there; the lines and circles in the slick water</u>
<u>over yonder are a warning that that troublesome place is shoaling up</u>
<u>dangerously; that silver streak in the shadow of the forest is the 'break'</u>
<u>from a new snag, and he has located himself in the very best place he</u>
<u>could have found to fish for steamboats; that tall dead tree, with a single</u>
<u>living branch, is not going to last long, and then how is a body ever</u>
<u>going to get through this blind place at night without the friendly old</u>
<u>landmark?"</u>

Continued

No, the romance and beauty were all gone from the river. <u>All the value any feature of it had for me now was the amount of usefulness it could furnish toward compassing the safe piloting of a steamboat.</u> <u>Since those days, I have pitied doctors from my heart.</u> What does the lovely flush in a beauty's cheek mean to a doctor but a "break" that ripples above some deadly disease? Are not all visible charms sown with what are to him the signs and symbols of hidden decay? Does he ever see her beauty at all, or doesn't he simply view her professionally and comment upon her unwholesome condition all to himself? And doesn't he sometimes wonder whether he has gained most or lost most by learning his trade?

Connection (definition)

Comparison

READING QUESTIONS

1. *The annotations above are not exhaustive. What other sensory perceptions, comparisons, contrasts, examples, and/or illustrations can you find in Twain's essay?*
2. *The essay as a whole is organized as a contrast. What particular ideas are being contrasted? How does the contrast help to clearly present Twain's ideas?*
3. *What facts, or evidence, does Twain present in the essay? What meaning does he draw from those facts?*
4. *What influences affect Twain's interpretation of his evidence? How do those influences change the meaning he creates from the facts?*

CREATING AND PRESENTING MEANING: STUDENT WRITING

In the following essay, Rachel Beam, a former student of one of the authors of this book, describes a sculpture called *Woman with Dog*. By employing the techniques for presenting concrete information, Rachel allows the readers to see the sculpture as fully as she sees it herself, and, from those details, she derives her own perspective on the significance of the sculpture.

The Mysterious Journey
Rachel Beam

Together they stand, a woman and a dog. The woman is nude, standing erect and looking off into the distance to the right as you look at her from the front. Her right arm is stretched up, her forearm resting on the top of her head. She looks as though she may be holding her hair back or shading her eyes to get a clear view of something in the distance. Both her left arm and hand look relaxed, her hand remaining open. Her hands are not proportionate to the rest of her body. They look too big for her body, giving her a clumsy appearance. The lack of fingernails on both hands makes her fingers appear mutilated.

She has the body of an old woman. The uneven clay makes her body look old and haggard. She displays no muscle tone, but the lumpiness of cellulite. At her midsection, though she has not much of a waist, her stomach is fairly flat. Her hips widen naturally into her legs, which look wooden, running straight down to her feet. Thus, she has no defined knees, and her ankles are missing completely. Her feet, like her hands, seem too large for her body, making her look awkward. Her toes look like they were an after-thought of the artist. They do not flow smoothly into the foot; rather, they look like they were cut into the sculpture at a later date. Unlike the fingers, each toe has a nail, giving the toes a detailed appearance lacking in the fingers.

In general, her features are not terribly feminine. Her head is attached to her body by a short, thick neck. Her bland, oval face displays no emotion. Her forehead is high and her eyebrows are missing. Similarly, no ears are visible. Her nose is shaped like a plump Christmas tree. Her lips are her most feminine feature, being full and slightly parted to reveal three teeth, which themselves are crooked and spaced apart from each other. Her eyes are simply two round holes cut out of the clay.

Continued

If you walk around to the back of the sculpture, you will see that the head is not finished. The neck comes up to a stump behind her face. Her head looks like a mask that has been placed on top of the sculpture. As you look at her from behind, you can actually lean in and look through her eyes, as if through a telescope. If you look at her from the front, her eyes act as windows into a nonexistent mind. But from the back, you see what she sees. Her hair is attached only at the front of her face. Four wide slabs of clay form her hair flowing horizontally back from her face, like four miniature blankets blowing in a strong wind. Her gaze matches the direction of the wind.

Her companion, the dog, stands about five inches tall between the woman's legs. It leans against her left leg with its back legs crouching slightly. The dog's paws are large with lines etched in to suggest toenails. The tail, short and stumpy, suggests no movement. The dog's front legs are stretched out somewhat, appearing muscular. Its neck stretches upward, giving the head and the eyes the same focal point in the distance as the woman has. Its ears are large and floppy, being lifted upwards and back as if acted upon by the same force as the woman's hair. The snout is large, and the mouth is closed, revealing the dog's silence. The dog's eyes, like the woman's, are hollow, but the head is complete or closed on all sides. However, if you squat and look at the underside of the dog's belly, you can see that it is open, just like the back of the woman's head.

Many of the features of the dog are well-defined, but it reveals no identifying characteristics of any particular breed. Instead of specialized breeding, it appears to be a dog of many backgrounds.

The woman and her companion stand alone, gazing into the distance at what we ourselves cannot see. And yet they gaze with no orbs for seeing, standing riveted to the small mound, which may afford them a higher view. The woman's hair lifted from her neck and flowing back from her face, as well as the dog's heavy ears being lifted, suggests a strong force coming from the direction into which they gaze. Their transfixion

Continued

suggests immobility, yet the gaze contradicts with a quest. And if it is a quest, the dog's position under the protective stance of the woman would suggest a foreboding in the quest, yet it does not cower.

They appear not to be able to return, to remain, nor to go forward. Perhaps the dog seems to be relying on the woman to lead the way, yet what kind of decision can she make when she has no ears to hear, no eyes to see, no mind to think?

READING QUESTIONS

1. *What sensory details does the writer include in this essay? To which sense does each detail refer?*

2. *What comparisons does the writer make in the essay? What is being compared to what? How do the comparisons help you see the writer's ideas?*

3. *What contrasts does the writer draw? How do the contrasts help her or you categorize the details? How do the contrasts help you understand her meaning?*

4. *What other connections does the writer draw? What is the nature of each connection?*

5. *What examples or illustrations does the writer present? How do they clarify her understanding of the figure?*

6. *What influences (knowledge, attitudes, methods of collecting evidence) might have affected the writer's understanding of the details? What effects of those influences do you detect in the essay?*

WRITING ASSIGNMENT: CREATING AND PRESENTING MEANING

Using the techniques explained in this chapter, write an essay based on your examination of the painting reproduced on the next page, Edvard Munch's "The Scream." You can easily access a color version of this painting on the Web. Point your browser at your favorite search engine and use "Edvard Munch" as your search term.

1. Take time to examine the picture carefully in order to gather details about it. As you examine what is in the picture, also think about what is *not* in the picture.

2. Review your evidence—the details you observed—in order to create your meaning. Take into account your knowledge of the painting, any preconceived attitudes you may have about the painting, *all* of the evidence you have gathered, and what methods you used to gather the evidence. All of these factors can affect the meaning you create from Munch's painting.

3. When you write your essay, remember to keep a good balance between general ideas and specific, concrete statements.

4. As you write, also keep the techniques for presenting details in mind: use sensory detail, comparisons, contrasts, connections, examples, and illustrations.

PART TWO

Using Sources

All of your papers in this course are research-based. Therefore, Part Two introduces you to techniques for finding and working with your resources. In Chapter 4, you will learn how to locate and build a bibliography systematically and how to annotate each source so that you know what its contents are and what its relative value to your project is. In Chapter 5, you will learn about making decisions on when to quote, paraphrase, or summarize a source. Furthermore, you will learn how to integrate sources with your own text, instead of just dropping them in. Skill in blending your source material creates a mature style, showing your ownership of your topic.

Chapter 4   Building a Bibliography

Chapter 5   Using Sources in Your Writing

CHAPTER 4

Building a Bibliography

CALVIN AND HOBBES

Ah, if only research were as easy as Calvin thinks it is: a phone call, a couple of questions, and then you're done. But it's not that easy. Research is a lengthy process that is rarely completed in a single sitting. In fact, you will very likely continue to research your project as you work your way through the rest of this book. You will visit the library several times. You will surf the Internet several times. Depending on your plan for primary research, you may conduct several interviews, or create, distribute, collect, and analyze a survey. Wherever you are and whatever research you are doing, keep one rule in mind: *you must thoroughly investigate every possible source you can find.*

Research consists of four steps:

1. Locating sources
2. Previewing sources
3. Gathering information
4. Using sources

This chapter discusses the first two steps, locating and previewing sources. The third and fourth steps, gathering information and using sources, are the topics of the next chapter.

When you locate sources, you search in the library and on the Internet for every source that seems to address your topic. As you locate sources that discuss your researched writing topic, you will record them in a working bibliography. When you preview sources, you examine the sources in your working bibliography individually to see how useful they might be. When you add this information to your list of sources, you are creating an annotated bibliography.

DEFINITION: BIBLIOGRAPHY

> **Bibliography:** A written record of resources on a given topic, organized according to one of several sets of conventions.

The term *bibliography* comes from two Greek words: *biblio*, meaning book, and *graphia*, meaning writing. The term has several definitions, but the one that is important in the context of research is *a list of sources on a particular topic*.

Keeping such a list from the very beginning of your research process is important for several reasons. One of those reasons is that you always know what sources you have looked at so you don't spend time looking at a source more than once. Another reason is that the information you record in a bibliography helps you easily find a source again if necessary. A third reason is that you will be using the information in a bibliography throughout the research process. Recording the necessary information at the beginning of the research process means you don't have to run around a library trying to find necessary information ten minutes before an assignment is due.

Bibliographies record the answers to four basic questions about a source:

1. *Who wrote the source?* The answer to this question is usually the name of an author or several authors. Sometimes, however, the answer includes editors, translators, and other kinds of contributors.
2. *What is the source?* The answer to this question is the title of the source.
3. *Where was the source published?* For books, the answer to this question is the name of the publisher and the city where the publisher is located. For articles, the answer is the title of the magazine, journal, or newspaper and the page numbers of the article. For online sources, the answer is the name of a Web site or service provider and the URL, or address, of the source.
4. *When was the source published?* Like the last question, this question also has three answers depending on the kind of source. For books, the answer is the year the book was published (the year of copyright). For articles, the answer is the date, volume number, and issue number of the particular issue of the magazine, journal, or newspaper that contains the article. For online sources, the answer is the date the article or Web page was authored, as well as the date that you accessed the source.

These answers are very generalized responses to the four basic bibliography questions. Different types of sources require slightly different kinds of information. For instance, the bibliographic entry for a magazine that is numbered nonconsecutively (in other words, each issue starts with page 1) requires only a date as the answer to the question "when was the source published?" A journal that is numbered consecutively (that is, each issue in a given year starts its page numbers where the last issue left off) requires a date, a volume number, and an issue number.

In addition, the order in which you put the answers to these four questions can differ greatly. Different professions and academic disciplines have different bibliographic systems.

Bibliographic Systems
ACS American Chemical Society
AMS American Mathematical Society
APA American Psychological Association
CBE Council of Biology Editors
CM Chicago Manual
MLA Modern Language Association

This textbook teaches two bibliographic systems: the MLA style and the APA style. For further information on other bibliographic styles, you should refer to the official guide for that particular style. The Web site for Duke University's libraries (http://www.lib.duke .edu/reference/style_manuals.html#biosty) lists the style guides for several bibliographic systems, including the ones used for biology, engineering, and health sciences.

You will see examples of MLA-style and APA-style bibliographies throughout this textbook. All of Tobi Raney's work uses MLA style, whereas Julie McDowell's papers use APA style. In addition, you will find a detailed treatment of citation and bibliography in Chapter 10 (MLA) and Chapter 11 (APA).

Your bibliography will include several different kinds of sources: books, periodicals, reference works, and online sources. Each of these sources has its own strengths and weaknesses. The best research strategy is to use a combination of these sources, so that the strengths of one cancel out the weaknesses of another.

Kinds of Sources

During the finding sources step of your research process, you should look at all four kinds of sources: reference works, books, periodicals, and online sources. Here are some characteristics of the different kinds of sources to keep in mind.

Reference works

The reference collection in your library has a wide range of sources that may prove useful to you, such as various kinds of dictionaries, specialized indexes, guides, atlases, and almanacs. The most common reference work that researchers turn to, however, is the encyclopedia. Some instructors tell students not to use encyclopedias now that they are in college because they consider encyclopedias the fast-food version of research. But encyclopedias and other reference works are useful avenues for quick information about an unfamiliar subject. They are also a good starting point for a preliminary survey of sources as you develop your research topic. The important phrase here is "starting point": encyclopedias and other reference works can get you into a topic, but they are usually too superficial to support an entire research project. In addition, an encyclopedia's point of view may be skewed on controversial issues, which will distort your perspective on a topic.

Encyclopedias have another major weakness: unless you have access to electronically updated encyclopedias, the information may be dated. It takes years to gather and process all of the evidence that goes into creating an encyclopedia, and some information changes rapidly. So remember: reference works such as encyclopedias are useful points of entry to your topic, but current information and varied points of view must be sought in works that are recent and that thoroughly investigate a topic.

Books

Like reference works, books not only take time to write but also to publish. Thus, although the writer of a book may be able to analyze information and synthesize it from a unique perspective, the information in the book is typically dated by at least a year and sometimes more.

In addition, when considering book sources, think about the credibility of the author and publisher. Publishing houses employ editors whose job is to ensure that books are accurate and credible, but just because a publisher has a good reputation does not mean that you can automatically trust what it publishes. Erich von Däniken's work illustrates this point very well. Since its first publication in 1969 by Putnam, a respected publisher, von Däniken's *Chariots of the Gods* has had more than forty-four printings and sold more than four million copies. Since Putnam, von Däniken has worked with other reputable publishers, including Bantam Books and Berkeley Books. In *Chariots of the Gods*, von Däniken proposes that intelligent civilizations on Earth were established not by a natural, evolutionary process, but by extraterrestrial visitors. One major flaw in this argument is that if intelligence on Earth was brought about by visitors from another planet, then how did intelligence begin on that planet? The question can be asked backwards ad infinitum, as several easy-to-find articles on the Internet demonstrate. Yet, despite von Däniken's faulty reasoning, his book was regularly published because publishers are sometimes more concerned with making money than with publishing reliable sources.

Even if both the publisher and the author are reliable, information in books may unintentionally mislead simply because facts are misinterpreted, and assumptions based on those facts are therefore flawed. Consider, for example, the five-ring Olympic symbol originally designed in 1914 by Pierre de Coubertin, founder of the International Olympic Council. Coubertin had planned that the circles would represent the first five Olympic games, but World War I intervened. After the war, when the games were reactivated in 1920, the rings were used to represent five continents (North and South America being treated as one).

In the next decade, film director Leni Riefenstahl had the rings carved into a rock wall at Delphi, Greece, as a prop for her 1936 Olympic documentary, *Triumph of the Will*. Many years later, two American authors, Lynn and Gray Poole, observed the carving and mistook it for an ancient symbol dating from classical Greek ages. Other writers who found the description in the Pooles' book borrowed it, thereby establishing a movie prop as an ancient artifact. Even as late as 1980, the Official Olympics Guide included a statement that "The interlocking circles found on the altar at Delphi are considered to be 3000 years old." You can avoid such mistakes by reading your sources critically and by looking at many sources of different types.

Periodicals

Periodicals are magazines, newspapers, journals, newsletters, and similar publications that appear at regular intervals, such as daily, weekly, monthly, yearly, and so forth. Articles and news stories in periodicals have an advantage over books and reference works—immediacy. Reporters can collect information from the principals involved while their memories are still fresh, so news stories in particular impart a feeling of being at the scene. Today, however, television reporting has largely supplanted that function of print sources because television broadcasts live and because the visual impact of some television reporting is indelible. No words are needed to communicate the tragedy of the space shuttle *Challenger* exploding into shards, taking the lives of six astronauts and a New Hampshire schoolteacher. But unless you videotape the program, it is virtually impossible to recover the television report and to use it in a paper; consequently, researchers must depend on print sources.

Material from newspapers, consumer magazines (those available at newsstands or magazine counters), and professional journals, like the material in books, has had at least some filtering through an editorial board. Like the editors who control the publication of books, however, newspaper and magazine editors can make mistakes. Remember that you have to read all of your sources with a critical eye, whether the sources are reliable or not.

Occasionally, a writer makes up a news story and passes it off as fact. One national "media-ized" event involved not just the writer, but also her publisher and editor and the group awarding her the Pulitzer Prize. In 1981 Janet Cooke wrote a series of articles for *The Washington Post* about an eight-year-old boy caught up in the inner-city life of drugs. It was a convincing, heart-wrenching account of a youthful heroin addict, titled "Jimmy's World." After she was awarded the Pulitzer Prize, others attempted to corroborate the "facts" of her story but found nothing. The result? Her award was taken away, she lost her job, and she lost her career (it turned out that she had also fabricated part of her résumé).

Remember to check your sources by looking at several different perspectives on your issue. This is your paper, and if your evidence doesn't check out, you will be the one in the hot seat.

Online sources

The Internet has quickly become a powerful research tool. Like an encyclopedia, it is easily accessible, has enormous amounts of information, and can provide a good starting point for research. But do not fall into the trap of relying solely on the Internet for your sources. Remember that you are trying to develop a broad and balanced combination of sources for your research project.

Moreover, the Internet poses some significant dangers for the unwary researcher. Just as anyone can get information off the Web, pretty much anyone can put information onto the Web, and not all of that information is accurate or reliable. Journals and publishing houses have editors who exert some amount of control over the information they publish, but there is no such control over the Web.

In addition, the amount of information provided on the Internet can be overwhelming. For instance, if you type "Shakespeare" into an Internet search engine, you will find that you still have a long way to go. Yahoo! will return 7 categories and 501 sites; Alta Vista will give you 633,580 sites; and Infoseek lists 455,692 of the "most relevant" sites. Limiting your topic helps reduce the number of sites that search engines will return, but you can still spend a lot of time on the Internet, only to discover that the information you just spent two weeks reading doesn't really fit your topic.

Online sources fall into two groups: The first group includes electronic versions of articles or news reports that also exist in print form. This kind of source can be found on the Web sites of various well-known publications, such as *The New York Times, Atlantic Monthly,* and many other major newspapers and magazines. You can also access electronic versions of print articles from professional and academic journals through services such as EBSCOHost and ProQuest (often available only through a library). In these cases, the online source should be considered the same as the print source.

The other group of electronic sources available on the Internet includes "pure" electronic sources, that is, Web pages, chat rooms, e-mail, Usenet groups, and so forth that exist solely in an electronic format. These sources have a special challenge when it comes to validation. There is absolutely no control over who can post information on the Internet. Therefore, many of the sources you find when researching on the Internet are not credible.

Another limitation of the material on the Internet is currency. A good rule of thumb states that the most recent information is often the most reliable, especially in terms of scientific information; however, looking only at recent material reduces your perspective—remember that you are trying to develop as broad a perspective as you can, and researching an idea over time is one way to broaden your perspective. Suppose, for example, you are looking at the current controversy over the harmful effects of tobacco use and depend only on Internet sources. You may well get the impression that people became concerned about the harm caused by cigarettes only in the late twentieth century. But as early as March 1954, *Playboy* magazine published an article questioning the use of tobacco and highlighting the fact that, ironically, the cigarette manufacturers themselves first raised questions about the dangers of tobacco use. In fact, to get a full perspective on the tobacco issue, you could go all the way back to 1604, when King James I of England wrote *A Counterblast to Tobacco,* probably the earliest anti-tobacco document in English.

As with encyclopedias, then, consider the Internet a good place to start but only one of several sources of evidence for your project.

TECHNIQUES: LEARNING YOUR LIBRARY

In sports, teams scout their opponents before they form a game plan. In the military, reconnaissance gives an army information about the enemy and the battlefield before they form a battle plan. Advance knowledge often leads to easier and greater success. You, too, should gather advance knowledge before forming a research plan by learning about your library.

If you learn how your library is arranged, what resources are available, and how your library can help you get sources that it does not own, then your research process will proceed more easily and quickly. You won't have to interrupt your research to find out, for instance, where last year's issues of *Newsweek* are kept or where to find the library's collection of government documents.

TABLE 4–1

Dewey Decimal System	Library of Congress System
000-099: Generalities	A: General Works
100-199: Philosophy and Psychology	B: Philosophy, Psychology, Religion
200-299: Religion	C: Auxiliary Sciences of History
300-399: Social Sciences	D: History: General and Old World
400-499: Language	E: History: America
500-599: Natural Sciences and Mathematics	F: History: America
600-699: Technology and Applied Science	G: Geography, Anthropology, Recreation
700-799: The Arts	H: Social Sciences
800-899: Literature and Rhetoric	J: Political Science
900-999: Geography and History	K: Law
	L: Education
	M: Music and Books on Music
	N: Fine Arts
	P: Language and Literature
	Q: Science
	R: Medicine
	S: Agriculture
	T: Technology
	U: Military Science
	V: Naval Science
	Z: Library Science

Generally, a library's collection of sources is divided into five types: stacks, reference, periodicals, online sources, and catalogues.

The Stacks

Stacks are where your library keeps the circulating books (books that you can take out of the library). The stacks (a librarian's word for bookshelves) are usually catalogued (or organized) according to one of two systems. One system is the Dewey decimal system, which uses numbers to organize books by topic. The other system is the Library of Congress system, which uses letters to arrange books by topic. You need to find out which system your library uses because the two systems put the same topics in a slightly different order. Refer to Table 4–1 to compare the two cataloguing systems.

The Reference Collection

Your library will also have a collection of noncirculating books (books that you cannot check out but must use while in the library). This collection consists of reference works: dictionaries, encyclopedias, bibliographies, guides, and so forth. These books are usually not kept in the stacks but are collected in the reference room of the library. The reference collection is also arranged according to either the Dewey decimal or the Library of Congress system.

Periodicals

Your library will have a collection of magazines and journals in its periodicals section. Periodicals are usually divided into recent issues (the issues of the current year) and back issues. In order to help periodicals last longer, libraries bind back issues together in books and store them in a different location from the recent issues. Some libraries allow you to check out back issues, but many do not. You should plan to use periodicals in the library.

Libraries keep a list of the periodicals in their collection, which is sometimes called the *union list*. The union list is kept in the periodicals section or online. Knowing your library's holdings (which issues of a periodical the library has in its collection) will save time you might otherwise waste looking for a source not in the collection. The union list or the online list of periodicals gives the library's holdings for each periodical in the collection.

Online Sources

Libraries now offer access to online databases and catalogues that greatly speed up your research process. First, there is an online catalogue of the library's holdings, which will be discussed further in the next section. Another kind of online source is a subscription database, such as EBSCO-Host, ProQuest, the MLA Bibliography, or PsychInfo. These services provide information ranging from bibliographic entries to article abstracts to the full text of articles. These databases allow libraries to provide access to many periodicals at a lower cost. But some of these subscription services are limited by time: the online MLA Bibliography, for instance, only includes records back to 1963. The MLA Bibliography as a whole, however, goes back to 1921. To find the earlier records, you would have to use the hard copy of the MLA Bibliography, which is usually kept in or near the reference section.

Catalogues

Every library has a catalogue, or a list of its holdings. For many years, libraries used card catalogues, huge pieces of furniture with dozens of drawers filled with thousands of three-by-five-inch cards. These cards are organized by title in one section, the author's name in another section, and by topic in a third section. Naturally, if your library has a large collection, it would have a huge card catalogue. To save space and money, many libraries have switched to online catalogues. Online catalogues not only take up much less space, but they are also much easier to search. From one location, you can search by title, author, topic, call number, or several other options. Your library may have an online catalogue, a card catalogue, or a combination of both; your research process will proceed more quickly if you know what the situation is before you start researching.

Learning the Library

Your library may have several other collections as well, including videotapes, sound recordings, rare books, and government documents. Before you start researching, visit your library to find out what special collections it has, where they are located, what circulation restrictions there might be, and how you can obtain sources your library does not have.

Locating the different collections is fairly easy. Your library will likely have a map of the building posted at several locations throughout the building. Especially likely places to find the map are by staircases and elevators. You might also find a copy of the map that you can take with you.

If you need more specific information than maps provide, all you need to do is ask a librarian. Like the scouts who work for a baseball team, librarians can give you detailed and expert information on what is in the library and how the library works. Usually, libraries offer tours that give you most of the advance information you need to begin your research. If you can't take a tour or you still have questions after the tour is over, ask your librarians. They'll know the answer.

EXERCISE 4–1

Visit your library and find the answers to these questions.

1. Where are the periodicals located?
2. Does the library use the Dewey decimal system or the Library of Congress system?
3. What is the name of the reference librarian?
4. Does the library provide online access? If so, where?
5. Where is the *Reader's Guide to Periodical Literature* located?
6. Where are the back issues of *Discover* kept? Can you check them out of the library?
7. Where are the photocopy machines located?
8. What kind of catalogue does your library use? Where is it located?
9. How long can you check books out for?
10. What are the library's hours?

TECHNIQUES: BUILDING BIBLIOGRAPHIES

Now that you have visited the library and know where to find general reference works, books, articles, and online sources, it's time to begin locating sources for your researched writing project. Again, remember to look for every possible source that has anything to do with your topic. Locating more sources now will save you time in the long run. You will likely have to locate sources several times during your research process no matter what, but the more you do now, the less you will have to do later.

As you locate each source, record the source in your working bibliography. Your instructor will tell you whether to use MLA or APA style. Following is a brief introduction to these two styles of bibliography to get you started on your research.

MLA Style

The MLA (Modern Language Association of America) style of bibliography is used in the humanities, especially in the study of literature and languages.

MLA style answers the four basic bibliography questions in this order: author, title, publisher, and publication date. (Occasionally, publisher and publication date are switched around or mixed together. You'll learn more about variations in Chapter 10.) MLA style puts the answers in this order because the scholars in the humanities are most concerned with who wrote the source and the source's content. The first line of all entries is flush with the left-hand margin, and the second and following lines are indented (called a *hanging indent*).

At this point in your research, you probably need to be familiar with only the basic MLA bibliography entries: book, magazine article, newspaper article, journal article, online article, and Web page. If you run into other kinds of sources not covered here, look in Chapter 10, where you will find a larger selection of MLA bibliography entries. If you look there and still don't find what you need, then consult *The MLA Handbook for Writers of Research Papers*, fifth edition, the MLA's Web site (*http://www.mla.org/*), or ask your instructor.

MLA Bibliography Entries: The Book

To write an MLA bibliography entry for a book:

1. Write the author's name (last name first, first name last), followed by a period.
2. Write the title of the book, underlined or in italics, followed by a period.
3. Write the location of the publisher. The location is usually a city's name followed by the two-letter abbreviation for the state. If the city is recognizable (such as New York), then you do not need to include the state abbreviation. The location is followed by a colon.
4. Write the name of the publisher, followed by a comma.
5. Write the year the book was published, followed by a period.

For instance, the MLA bibliography entry for *Blood Memory: An Autobiography*, a book written by Martha Graham that was published in 1991 by Doubleday, which is located in New York, would look like this:

> Graham, Martha. *Blood Memory: An Autobiography*. New York: Doubleday, 1991.

MLA Bibliography Entries: The Magazine Article

The word *magazine* refers to periodicals typically available at a newsstand or bookstore such as *Time, Newsweek, Sports Illustrated, PCWorld*, or *Vogue*. These periodicals are usually published once a week, once every two weeks, or once a month. In addition, their pages are numbered nonconsecutively—each issue begins with page 1.

To write an MLA bibliography entry for a magazine article:

1. Write the name of the article's author (last name first, first name last), followed by a period.
2. Write the title of the article in quotation marks with a period inside the closing quotation mark.

3. Write the title of the magazine, underlined or in italics.
4. Write the date of the magazine's issue, followed by a colon.
5. Write the page numbers of the article, followed by a period. If the article starts in one part of the magazine but finishes in another part, then put the page numbers of the first part followed by a "+" (plus sign) to indicate that there are other parts to the article.

For example, the bibliography entry for "Beating the System," an article written by Mat Edelson that starts on page 46 and ends on page 50 of the April 2000 issue of *Sport*, would look like this:

Edelson, Mat. "Beating the System." *Sport* April 2000: 46–50.

MLA Bibliography Entries: The Newspaper Article

The MLA bibliography entry for a newspaper article is basically the same as the entry for a magazine article. For instance:

Skolnick, Andrew A. "A Professor at WU Warns That a Popular Diabetes Drug Could Cause Liver Problems." *St. Louis Post-Dispatch* 19 March 2000: A6–7.

MLA Bibliography Entries: The Journal Article

The term *journal* refers to professional and academic journals such as PMLA (Publications of the Modern Language Association), *The New England Journal of Medicine, American Anthropologist, Foreign Language Studies, American Scholar,* and *Education Digest.* These periodicals are usually published every other month, four times a year, twice a year, or annually. Often, these journals are numbered consecutively, which means that the first issue of the year begins with page 1, but later issues start their page numbers where the previous issue ended. Thus, the second issue of one of these periodicals could begin with page 200. If the journal in which your article appears is numbered in this way, then you need to include the journal's volume number as part of your answer to the question "when was the source published."

If your source is an article in a scholarly journal that is numbered non-consecutively, then you will need to include the volume number and the issue number of the journal, presented as though it were a decimal number. For instance, "27.3" would indicate issue number 3 of volume number 27. Volume and issue numbers are usually provided on the cover or first page of the journal.

To write an MLA bibliography entry for a journal article:

1. Write the name of the article's author (last name first, first name last), followed by a period.
2. Write the title of the article in quotation marks with a period at the end.
3. Write the title of the journal, underlined or in italics.
4. Write the volume or the volume and issue number.
5. Write the date of the journal in parentheses, followed by a colon.
6. Write the page numbers of the article, followed by a period.

For example, the MLA bibliography entry for "Genesis, Holy Saturday, and the Sistine Ceiling," an article by Lynette M. F. Bosch that starts on page 643 and ends on page 652 of volume 30, the volume for 1999, of *The Sixteenth Century Journal* (a consecutively numbered journal), would look like this:

> Bosch, Lynette M.F. "Genesis, Holy Saturday, and the Sistine Ceiling."
>   *The Sixteenth Century Journal* 30 (1999): 643–52.

MLA Bibliography Entries: The Online Article

Before computers were available in libraries, researchers looking for magazine or journal articles not in the library had to wait while they were obtained through interlibrary loan, travel to distant libraries, or do without the source. Now, researchers can download articles from the Internet with a click of the mouse.

Online articles come in two forms: First, an article can be downloaded from the periodical's Web site. Many magazines and journals (*Time, Sports Illustrated,* and *Entertainment Weekly*, just to name a few) exist both as Web sites and as hard-copy publications. Online articles can also be downloaded at your library through a subscription service such as EBSCOHost or Pro-Quest. Note, however, that neither form is identical with the article that was originally published in the magazine or journal, so the bibliographic entry answers the four bibliography questions differently.

The first difference is that you must indicate that you downloaded this source either by including the word "online" or by naming the subscription service you used. The second difference is that online articles often do not have page numbers. You indicate this in your bibliography entry with the abbreviation "n. pag."

To write an MLA bibliography entry for an online article:

1. Write the name of the article's author (last name first, first name last), followed by a period.
2. Write the title of the article in quotation marks with a period at the end.
3. Write the title of the magazine or journal, underlined or in italics.
4. Write the date of the issue in which the article appears, followed by a colon.
5. Write page numbers or paragraph numbers if they are given for the source, followed by a period; otherwise, put "n. pag." followed by a period.
6. If the source is an online version of a print article, then put the word "Online" followed by a period; if you downloaded the article through a subscription service, then put the name of the service, followed by a period.
7. Write the date you looked at or downloaded the article, followed by a period.

Here's an example of an article from an online magazine:

Ratnesar, Romesh, and Joel Stein. "Everyone's A Star.Com." *Time* 27
    March 2000: 1–4. Online. 28 March 2000.

And here's an article downloaded through ProQuest, a service your library can subscribe to:

> Horn, John. "Triumph of the Willis." *Premiere* January 2000: n. pag. ProQuest. 24 March 2000.

MLA Bibliography Entries: The Web Page

Web pages are becoming a larger part of research as the Internet grows in size and resources become more reliable. The answers to the four basic bibliography questions for a Web page resemble the answers for magazine or journal articles. There are two additional pieces of information that need to be included, however. As part of the answer to the question "where is the source published," you must include the URL (uniform resource locator) of the Web page. In addition, because Web pages and Web sites are updated and revised regularly, you need to include the date when you looked at the source as part of the answer to the question "when was the source published."

In addition, you often have to look a little harder to find the information you need to create the bibliography entry for the Web page. If information such as the author's name, title, or date of publication is not clearly displayed, then here are some places to look:

- *"Last updated" information:* Toward the bottom of the Web page, or the Web site's home page, there is usually a sentence called "last updated" information. In small type is a sentence that starts "Last updated," gives a date, and tells you by whom the page was updated. The date in this sentence is the date of publication; the person or persons who updated the page are the author's name or names.
- *The title bar:* If the title of the Web page or Web site is not clearly displayed, look in the title bar of your Web browser. The title bar is the blue or striped bar toward the top of the browser window. The Web page or Web site title will usually appear in the middle of the title bar.

The illustration on the next page shows these two locations on one of the authors' home page.

To write an MLA bibliography entry for a Web page:

1. Write the author's name (last name first, first name last), followed by a period.
2. Write the title of the Web page in quotation marks with a period inside the closing quotation mark. If the page is a personal home page, it might not have a title, so use the words *Home Page.*
3. If the Web page is part of a larger Web site, then write the name of the Web site, underlined or in italics, followed by a period.
4. If the Web page or Web site is sponsored by an organization, then write the name of the sponsoring organization, followed by a period.
5. Write the date the page was last updated, followed by a period.
6. Write the date you accessed the page.
7. Write the URL of the Web page in corner brackets, followed by a period.

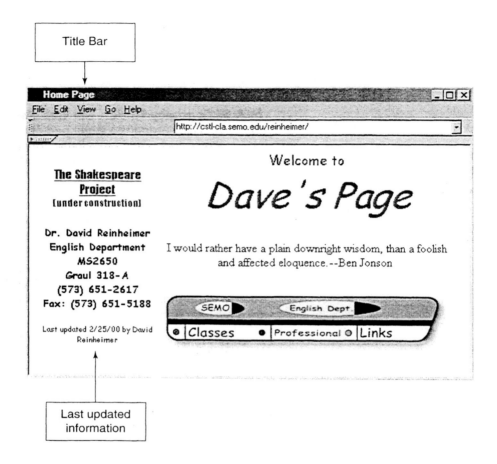

For instance, here's the entry for the Web page in the illustration:

> Reinheimer, David. Home Page. 25 February 2000. 24 March 2000.
> <http://cstl-cla.semo.edu/reinheimer>.

These examples are very basic and general examples to get you started on your research. If your source doesn't fit any of the above patterns, refer to Chapter 10 or the *MLA Handbook*.

APA Style

The APA (American Psychological Association) style of bibliography is used largely in the social sciences, such as psychology, education, and other disciplines. APA-style bibliography answers the four bibliography questions in a different order than does the MLA style. In APA style, the author's name still comes first, the publication date comes second, followed by the title, and finally the publisher. APA style presents the answers in this order because scholars in the social sciences need to know who the author is to see if the source is reliable and when the source was published to see if it is current.

There are also format differences between MLA style and APA style. In APA style, you capitalize only the first letter of book and article titles. Journal titles are capitalized as in MLA style. Book and journal titles are underlined or italicized, as in MLA style, but article titles are not enclosed in quotation marks. These and other format differences between MLA and APA style are shown in the following examples of APA bibliography entries for a book, magazine article, newspaper article, journal article, online article, and Web page.

APA Bibliography Entries: The Book
To write an APA bibliography entry for a book:

1. Write the name of the author (last name first, followed by the author's first initial), followed by a period.
2. Put the year of publication in parentheses, followed by a period.
3. Write the title of the book, underlined or in italics. Capitalize only the first letter of the title, the first letter of any subtitle, and proper nouns.
4. Write the location of the publisher, followed by a colon.
5. Write the publisher's name, dropping words and abbreviations such as Publishers, Inc., or Co.

For example, here's the APA bibliography entry for Martha Graham's *Blood Memory:*

Graham, M. (1991). *Blood memory: An autobiography.* New York: Doubleday.

APA Bibliography Entries: The Magazine Article
The APA bibliography entry for magazine articles also differs from MLA style in the presentation of page numbers. APA style includes all the page numbers, even if an article starts in one part of a magazine and finishes in another part.

To write an APA bibliography entry for a magazine article:

1. Write the author's name (last name followed by first initial), followed by a period.
2. Write the date of the journal in parentheses, followed by a period. Write the year first, followed by a comma, then put the month and day.
3. Write the title of the article, followed by a period. Follow the capitalization rules for book titles. Do not enclose the title in quotation marks.
4. Write the title of the magazine or journal, underlined or in italics, followed by a comma. The comma should also be underlined or in italics. In journal titles, capitalize the first word, nouns, adjectives, and all other words that are longer than five letters.
5. Write the page numbers, followed by a period.

For instance, here is the APA bibliography entry for Mat Edelson's article "Beating the System":

Edelson, M. (2000, April). Beating the system. *Sport,* 46–50.

APA Bibliography Entries: The Newspaper Article

The APA bibliography entry for newspaper articles resembles the APA entry for magazine articles. There is one important difference, however. For newspaper articles (and only newspaper articles) use the abbreviations "p." and "pp." before the page number or page numbers of the article, respectively.
 For example:

Skolnick, A. (2000, March 19). A professor at WU warns that
 a popular diabetes drug could cause liver problems. *St. Louis
 Post-Dispatch,* pp. A6–A7.

APA Bibliography Entries: The Journal Article

APA bibliography entries for journal articles, whether appearing in consecutively numbered journals or nonconsecutively numbered journals, contain the same information as the MLA bibliography entries. The order in the APA entry is different, naturally. In addition, in the APA bibliography entry, the volume number is underlined or in italics, and the issue number is enclosed in parentheses.
 To write an APA bibliography entry for a journal article:

1. Write the author's name (last name first, then first initial), followed by a period.
2. Write the date of the journal issue in parentheses, followed by a period. Write only the year.
3. Write the title of the article, followed by a period. Capitalize only the first letter, and do not enclose the title in quotation marks.
4. Write the title of the journal, underlined or in italics, followed by a comma. The comma should also be underlined or in italics. Follow the capitalization rules for magazine titles.
5. Write the volume number of the journal, underlined or in italics.
6. Write the issue number, if necessary, in parentheses, followed by a comma. Do not underline the volume number or put it in italics.
7. Write the page numbers of the article, followed by a period.

For an example, here is Lynnette Bosch's article from *The Sixteenth Century Journal*:

Bosch, L. M. F. (1999). Genesis, holy scripture, and the Sistine ceiling.
 The Sixteenth Century Journal, 30, 643–52.

APA Bibliography Entries: The Online Article

APA bibliography entries for online articles are different in several ways from MLA style. In APA style, the word *online* is hyphenated: "on-line." Also, the entry includes a brief description of the source in square brackets. A third difference is that the date-accessed information is preceded by the word "Retrieved" in APA style. Finally, in APA style, the URL of the source is not enclosed by corner brackets, and no punctuation follows the URL unless it is part of the URL itself.

To write an APA bibliography entry for an online article, provide as much of the following information as is appropriate:

1. Write the author's name (last name first, then first initials), followed by a period.
2. Write the date of the online article in parentheses, followed by a period.
3. Write the title of the online article, followed by a period. Follow the capitalization rules for magazine article titles.
4. Write the title of the *print* journal or periodical, followed by a comma. Both the title and the comma should be underlined or in italics.
5. Write the date of the *print* journal or periodical (month, day, then year), followed by a period.
6. Write the title of the *electronic* journal or periodical, followed by a period. Both title and period should be underlined or in italics.
7. Write a brief description of the online source in square brackets, followed by a period.
8. Write the retrieval information, followed by a colon. The retrieval information should follow this syntax: "Retrieved [give the date], from [give the source, such as World Wide Web or EBSCOHost]."
9. Write the URL. Do not follow the URL with any punctuation that is not part of the URL.

For instance, here are the APA-style entries for the same two articles that were used as examples in the last section:

> Ratnesar, R., and Stein, J. (2000, March 27). Everyone's a star.com. *Time,* 1–4. [On-line magazine]. Retrieved March 28, 2000, from the World Wide Web: http://www.time.com/everyone/magazine/main.html

> Horn, J. Triumph of the Willis. (2000, January). *Premiere*. Retrieved March 24, 2000, from ProQuest.

APA Bibliography Entries: The Web Page

In APA style, bibliography entries for Web pages are largely the same as entries for online articles. For example:

> Reinheimer, D. (2000, February 25). Dave's page. [Personal Home Page]. Retrieved March 24, 2000, from the World Wide Web: http://cstl-cla.semo.edu/reinheimer

If your source does not match any of these basic patterns, refer to Chapter 11, which provides a larger selection of APA-style bibliographic entries. If you are still unsure of how to create the correct bibliography entry, refer to the APA Publications Manual or ask your instructor.

Familiarize yourself with the basics of bibliography before you begin your research so that you know what information to record when you find sources. Before you start finding sources, you should also familiarize yourself with your library.

EXERCISE 4–2

Write MLA-style and APA-style bibliography entries for the following sources.

1. A book entitled *The Wordsworth Book of Days*, written by Gerald Masters, and published in 1995 by Wordsworth Editions, Ltd., in Ware, England.
2. An article written by Leigh Montville entitled "The Superstar," which appears on pages 44 and 45 of the May 17, 1999 issue of *Sports Illustrated*.
3. A newspaper article entitled "A Second Look at the Writers on Kent Library," written by Sam Blackwell, and published in the March 4, 2000 edition of the *Southeast Missourian*, on page 3A.
4. An article written by Jill Smolowe entitled "Paul McCartney Finds Love Again," downloaded from *People.com*. The article has no page numbers, was posted on the Web site on March 24, 2000, and was accessed on March 26, 2000. The URL of the article is *http://people.aol.com/people/ weekly/features/index.html*.
5. An article written by Tricia Vita entitled "Rescuing Mr. Lincoln." The article originally appeared in the March 2000 issue of *Yankee*. It was downloaded from EBSCO-Host on March 26, 2000, and the downloaded version has no page numbers.
6. The home page of the International E-mail Chess Group, last updated on March 20, 2000 by Vania Mascioni. The URL is http://www.iecg.org/ index.htm, and it was accessed on March 22, 2000.

TECHNIQUES: BUILDING A WORKING BIBLIOGRAPHY

Armed with the knowledge of where sources are located in your library and the strengths and weaknesses of various kinds of sources, you are ready to begin locating sources. At this point in the process, you are not reading your sources. You are simply compiling a list of sources that are likely to be useful. This list is called a *working bibliography*.

A working bibliography is useful in two ways: First, a working bibliography helps you keep track of what sources you have found and what sources you still need to find. Second, a working bibliography compiles the bibliographic entries you will use as you create works cited or references lists in the writing assignments for later chapters in this book. In fact, if you keep your working bibliography on a computer disk or hard drive, then later bibliographies can be compiled easily by cutting and pasting entries from your working bibliography to the files your writing assignments are in.

To build a working bibliography, you should look for sources in the library and sources on the Internet.

Locating Sources in the Library

To find sources in the library, begin with the library's catalogue. Whether your library still uses a card catalogue or has an online catalogue, you will most likely begin your search by looking for sources related to your topic. To search by your topic, you need to employ *keywords* or *subject headings*—important words that catalogues use to identify different topics.

The crucial part of searching by keywords or subject headings is to find the right balance between general and specific terms. The best strategy here is the same as the best strategy for researching generally: use a combination of different keyword searches. For example, Tobi Raney came up with keywords for her researched writing project on women's athletics and self-esteem in two ways. The first way was to brainstorm a list of possible keywords. Tobi's list included the following:

- Women
- Athletics
- Women's athletics
- Title IX
- Basketball
- Soccer
- Gymnastics
- Psychology

The other way to find keywords is to look in the *Library of Congress Subject Headings (LCSH)*. The LCSH is usually kept near the library's catalogues or in the reference collection. Looking in there, Tobi found the following subject headings:

- Exercise for Women
- Physical Education for Women
- Women—Psychology
- Self-esteem in Women
- Sports for Women
- Women athletes

When Tobi used these subject headings to search for sources in the library's online catalogue, she got the following results. For her brainstormed list of keywords, Tobi found:

- Women (5,970 records)
- Athletics (494 records)
- Women's athletics (no keyword matches)
- Title IX (18 records)
- Basketball (353 records)
- Soccer (174 records)
- Gymnastics (200 records)
- Psychology (9,449 records)

Using the Library of Congress subject headings, she found:

- Exercise for Women (188 records)
- Physical Education for Women (79 records)
- Women—Psychology (175 records)
- Self-esteem in Women (10 records)
- Sports for Women (191 records)
- Women athletes (168 records)

Neither of these keyword lists is complete, and the results are only how many records were found but nothing about each record; however, you can see how using the proper keywords can help you search effectively. When Tobi looked under the keyword "psychology," she got 9,449 records; when she limited that search to "women—psychology," she got only 175 records. That's still an awful lot of sources to look at, even on a computer screen. So, when Tobi limited the keyword search even further, to "self-esteem in women," she got only ten records, a very manageable number.

Also note that when Tobi searched for the keyword "women's athletics," she received no matches; however, when the keyword was phrased as "sports for women" and "women athletes," she got more than one hundred records each time. Remember the first law of computing: "Garbage in, garbage out." If you don't phrase your keywords in a way the computer understands, then it will tell you that there are no sources on your topic—even when there actually are.

EXERCISE 4–3

You are researching the topic of global warming.

1. Brainstorm a list of possible keywords to use for a search in your library's online catalogue.
2. Go to the library and look at the Library of Congress Subject Headings. Get a list of subject headings you can use to search your library's online catalogue.
3. Mark the keywords or subject headings you think are properly limited and will give you a manageable number of sources.
4. Search your library's online catalogue, recording the number of records each keyword or subject heading returns.
5. Write a brief summary of your searches. How many sources did you find? Did you correctly predict which searches would return a manageable number of sources?

EXERCISE 4–4

1. Brainstorm a list of possible keywords you can use to search for sources on the topic of your researched writing project.
2. Go to the library and look in the *LCSH*. Compile a list of subject headings you can use to find sources for your topic.

Hard-Copy Searches

Whether or not your library has an online catalogue or access to online databases, you may still have to search through hard-copy resources. Your library's online catalogue may not include all of the library's holdings, so you may have to look through the card catalogue. Your library might not have access to the online database that lists sources on your topic. Some important search tools, such as the *Reader's Guide to Periodicals,* are not available online. Finally, online databases do not always cover the entire range of time that hard-copy bibliographies, such as the *MLA Bibliography,* cover. Thus, you need to be familiar with searching hard-copy sources as well.

Searching the card catalogue allows you to add books to your working bibliography. Card catalogues collect several pieces of important information on a three-by-five-inch card:

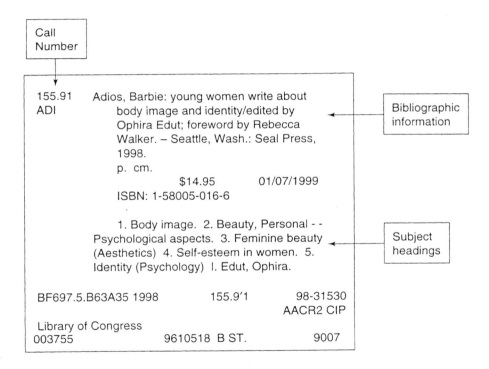

At the top of the entry is the bibliographic information you need for the source. Examine the title of the source because it is the first clue to whether this source will be useful for your research topic. If the title indicates that the source applies to your topic, then copy the bibliographic information into your working bibliography.

In the upper left-hand corner, the card lists the call number of the source. This number allows you to find the source in the stacks. You should include this call number at the end of your working bibliography entry for the source.

At the bottom of the card is a list of the subject headings that apply to the source. This information is important for two reasons: First, the subject headings give you a more specific idea of the topics of the source, so you have a better idea about whether the source will be useful for your researched writing topic. Second, the subject headings can give you more topics to search for as you find sources. Compare the list of subject headings on the card to your own list of subject headings. If the card has a topic listed that sounds like a promising avenue of research, then add it to your list.

Through the card catalogue, you will find book sources for your research topic, and you will also be able to locate periodicals by their titles. To find specific articles, you will have to turn to hard-copy bibliographies. There are two kinds of hard-copy bibliographies: general bibliographies and specialized bibliographies. General bibliographies list articles of general interest on many topics. This kind of bibliography includes *The Reader's Guide to Periodical Literature* and *The New York Times Index*. Specialized bibliographies list articles on a single topic or field. Examples of this kind of bibliography include the *MLA Bibliography* (articles on language and literature) and *The Brandon/Hill Selected List of Nursing Books and Journals* (sources on medicine and nursing).

Many of the specialized bibliographies are available online, as is *The New York Times Index*. *The Reader's Guide to Periodical Literature,* however, is not available online, so you will have to search the hard-copy version. *The Reader's Guide* consists of many volumes, each of which lists several thousand articles from hundreds of periodicals, organized by author's name and by the subject of the article. Each volume contains one year's worth of articles. In order to get all of the possible sources you can, you will need to search through each volume of *The Reader's Guide* in the appropriate time frame for your topic. Note that the most recent issues of *The Reader's Guide* may be in paperback issues rather than hardbound.

Because *The Reader's Guide* contains so many articles, it uses many abbreviations to save space (in 1988, it started using the full titles of all periodicals, although it still uses many other abbreviations); however, *The Reader's Guide* gives a table of the abbreviations and the corresponding full titles of all of the periodicals at the beginning of each volume.

Here is a sample entry from *The Reader's Guide*:

> The amazing new brain surgery for Parkinson's disease. E, Keister. il
> *50 Plus* 27: 24-6+ O '87.

This entry gives the article title first, followed by the author's name. The "il" means that the article is illustrated. It appears in a magazine called *50 Plus,* volume 27. The article begins on page 24, continues through page 26, and then continues on pages later in the issue. The issue is dated October 1987.

Once you have located articles in *The Reader's Guide* or another hard-copy bibliography, copy the bibliographic information in your working bibliography. Then, you have to locate the periodical itself. To do this, return to your library's catalogue, whether the card catalogue or a hard-copy catalogue. Find the location of the periodical and copy that information in your working bibliography. Finally, check your library's holdings to ensure that your library has the issue you need.

EXERCISE 4–5

You are researching the "Star Wars" defense policy of the 1980s for a course in American History. Using "star wars" as a keyword search, you get the following titles. Which of these sources will be useful for your project?

1. Journeying: children responding to literature
2. Star Wars <visual>
3. The wisdom of the dream: Carl Gustav Jung <visual>
4. America invulnerable: the quest for absolute security 1812 to Star Wars
5. Star Wars: the economic fallout
6. Empty promise: the growing case against star wars
7. The Star Wars debate
8. The Fallacy of Star Wars

Online Searches

Online searches follow the same principles as hard-copy searches. You create a list of subject headings or topic keywords, locate sources, check the titles and topics to see if the source talks about your topic, and finally enter the bibliographic information and location of your source into your working bibliography.

To search online, however, you must be able to navigate the interface of the online catalogue. Interface refers to the way a program asks you to interact with it. Your library's own online catalogue will usually have one kind of interface, whereas online databases (which are often accessed through the World Wide Web) will have a different interface. A third interface you will use is searching the Internet through Web-based search engines such as Yahoo! or Lycos.

Although individual libraries' online catalogues often look similar, each individual catalogue often differs in details, such as abbreviations and action keys (the buttons on the computer you press to make the database complete an action). Your library should have a guide to the online database that gives you the specific information you need to search the catalogue. If the guide doesn't answer your questions, then the online catalogue should have an online help file. If you're still unsure of how to search the online catalogue, then ask the reference librarian for help.

When Julie was building her bibliography for her researched writing project on aspartame, she went to the online catalogue. Julie saw this screen on the computer terminal:

```
                                                            SADIE
                                                      Introduction
------------------------------------------------------------------------
     Welcome to SADIE, Southeast Missouri State University's Online Catalog!

              To search for:        Type a command and press <ENTER>
                     Author         a=bronte c
                      Title         t=catcher in the
   Subject, Library of Congress     s=painting
                    Keyword         k=heat moon and highways
     Dewey Decimal Call Number      c=317
   Superintendent of Documents (SuDoc)  cs=prex2.8

        You may begin a new search on any screen.
        Press <ENTER> for more information on searching the online catalog.
        For Library news, type news and press <ENTER>.
        To learn how to search certain collections within the Library
        type set cat and press <ENTER>.
-------------------------------------------------------- - Page 1 of 2  -------------
                Enter search command              <F8>  FORward page
                NEWs
                CR for Course Reserve

NEXT COMMAND: █
```

To begin your search, you enter a *query*. A query consists of three parts. The first part is the *limiter*, an abbreviation that indicates what piece of information you are searching by, such as title, author, or keyword (see the list of limiters on the screen pictured in the previous illustration). These limiters may vary from library to library. The second part is the *search term*—the specific title, author's name, or topic you are looking for. The final part of the query is a *Boolean operator*, which is actually optional. Boolean operators are common words that cause specific logical actions. These actions allow you to focus or expand your search by using more than one search term in the same query. The two most commonly used Boolean operators are "and" and "not." Here's how they work:

Regular search
- Example: k=Abraham Lincoln
- Returns: sources with keywords "Abraham," "Lincoln," and "Abraham Lincoln"

Using "and"
- Example: k=Abraham and Lincoln
- Returns: sources with keyword "Abraham Lincoln"

Using "not"
- Example: k=Abraham not Lincoln
- Returns: sources with keyword "Abraham" except those sources with the keyword "Lincoln"

Your library should have an explanation of Boolean operators available at the reference desk or near the computer terminals that access the online catalogue.

To search the library for sources on aspartame, Julie used the query "k=carcinogen." Here are the results the catalogue came back with:

```
Search Request: K=CARCINOGENS                                    SADIE
Search Results: 20 Entries Found                         Keyword Index
---------------------------------------------------------------------
       DATE  TITLE:                                  AUTHOR:
   1   1996  Cancer free : the comprehensive cancer pre  Winawer, Sidney J
   2   1992  Toxins and targets : effects of natural an
   3   1990  Cancer sourcebook : basic information on c
   4   1990  Indoor air - assessment : methods of analy
   5   1988  Health hazards of nitrite inhalants
   6   1987  Identifying and regulating carcinogens
   7.  1986  Risk management and political culture : a   Jasanoff, Sheila
   8   1984  Mutagenicity, carcinogenicity, and teratog
   9   1980  Degradation of chemical carcinogens : an a  Slein, M. W
  10   1980  Safe handling of chemical carcinogens, mut
  11   1979  Carcinogens and related substances : analy  Bowman, Malcolm C
  12   1977  Cancer testing technology and saccharin     United States
  13   1976  Chemical carcinogens
  14   1975  Occupational monitoring for genetic hazard
-------------------------------------------- CONTINUED on next page  ----
STArt over      Type number to display record         <F8>  FORward page
HELp
OTHer options

NEXT COMMAND:
```

From this list of titles, Julie could make some decisions about which sources apply to her topic. When she wanted more information on a specific title, she typed the record number of the result. For instance, typing the number "12" gave her more information on *Cancer Testing Technology and Saccharine:*

```
Search Request: K=CARCINOGENS                                    SADIE
BOOK - Record 12 of 20 Entries Found                        Brief View
---------------------------------------------------------------------
Author:         United States. Congress. Office of Technology Assessment.

Title:          Cancer testing technology and saccharin.

Published:      Washington : Congress of the United States, Office of
                Technology Assessment : for sale by the Supt. of Docs., U.S.
                Govt. Print. Off., 1977.

Subjects:       Saccharin--Toxicology.
                Carcinogenesis.
                Carcinogens.



---------------------------------------------- + Page 1 of 2 -------------
STArt over      LONg view                             <F8>  FORward page
HELp            INDex                                  <F6>  NEXt record
OTHer options                                         <F5>  PREvious record

NEXT COMMAND:
```

Like the source card in the card catalogue, this screen gives you important information about your source. It shows the bibliographic information you need, the call number to locate the source, and the subject headings of the source. Copy the bibliographic information and the call number into your working bibliography, and check the subject headings against your own list of topic keywords to see if you may have missed any useful topics.

Most online catalogues have a separate database for book sources and for periodicals. The periodical database allows you to find periodicals by title but may or may not allow you to search by article title. To search by article title, you may need to turn to Web-based databases. The interface for Web-based databases operates almost the same way as your library's online catalogue, but it probably looks very different. The most common interface for specialized bibliographies and databases through the Web looks like this:

From this screen, you choose the database you want to search. Clicking on one of the topics in the list on the left-hand side will load a page listing databases specifically focused on that topic. Find the database you want to search and click on the title. Julie, for instance, chose the topic "Medicine and Health Sciences" and then chose to search MEDLINE.

Once you find the database you want to search, you will see this screen:

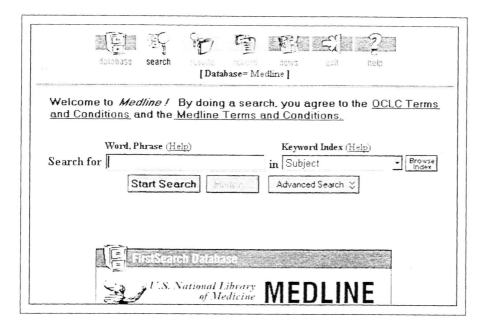

To search the database, type your search term in the textbox, and then find your limiter in the drop-down menu to the right. Then click on "Start Search." Depending on the database you are searching, you may get a list of sources, abstracts of the sources, or even the full text of the source. Use the information the database provides to determine if the source is likely to talk about your topic, to find additional search terms, and to gather bibliographic information. You may have to return to your library's catalogue to find the location information for the periodical if you are not able to download the full text of the article.

EXERCISE 4–6

Using the limiter abbreviations for your library's online catalogue, write queries for the following searches.

1. Search for sources with the keyword divorce.
2. Search for sources written by Harold Bloom.
3. Search for sources written by authors named Smith, but not those written by John Smith.
4. Search for sources on the subject of baseball in Japan.
5. Search for sources written by William Shakespeare, but not sources with the words "complete works" in the title.

Locating Sources on the Internet

Finding Web sites and Web pages to use as sources for your researched writing project works much the same way as using online databases. The first step is to choose an Internet search engine. Then, you use keywords to search the Web by topic. Later, you use the results to see if the source will likely talk about your topic and to gather bibliographic and location information on the source.

Given the millions of pages and sites on the World Wide Web, you use search engine Web sites to locate possible sources. The more commonly known search engines include the following:

- AOL NetFind (aol.com)
- GoTo.com
- Infoseek.com
- Magellan.excite.com
- Snap (home.snap.com)
- AltaVista.com
- Google.com
- NorthernLight.com
- WebCrawler.com
- HotBot.com
- Lycos.com
- Yahoo.com

Again, the best research strategy is to use several search engines, not just one or two.

These sites usually rely on a topic keyword search. You can use Boolean operators to limit or expand your search. Be aware, however, that for some of these sites, the Boolean operators may not be words. For instance, if Julie entered the search term "aspartame and health," she might return results that list Web sites whose description includes the words "aspartame," "health," as well as the word "and." For these sites, the Boolean operator "and" is replaced by "+" (plus sign) and the operator "not" is replaced by "−" (minus sign).

BUILDING A WORKING BIBLIOGRAPHY: STUDENT WRITING

Your working bibliography will grow as you conduct several searches through hard-copy catalogues in your library, online catalogues in your library, and search engine Web sites. List each source that you find during these searches, including full bibliographic information and location information (a call number or URL). You will use this list of possible sources to locate and investigate your sources in the next step of the research process.

Here are Tobi's (MLA) and Julie's (APA) working bibliographies to give you an idea of what a working bibliography looks like.

Working Bibliography
Tobi Raney

Anderson, Judy. "Confidence's Role in Winning." *Long Island Business News* 27 July 1998: 23A. [Periodicals]

Baumeister, Roy F. "Self-esteem." *Encyclopedia of Human Behavior.* 1994 ed. [150.3 En184—Reference]

Branden, Nathaniel. *The Psychology of Self-esteem.* Los Angeles: Nash, 1969. [155.2 B733p]

Cantu, Norma V. "Athletic Experience Vital to Both Sexes." NCAA Title IX Seminar. Baltimore, 20 April 1995.

Coopersmith, S. *The Antecedents of Self-Esteem.* San Francisco: W. H. Freeman, 1967. [155.418 C788a]

Corey, G. "Self-esteem." *Encyclopedia of Psychology.* 1994 ed. [150.3 En191 1994—Reference]

Donovitz, Jean. "Comparison of Personalities of Eight and Ninth Grade Female Athletes and Eighth and Ninth Grade Female Nonathletes." Thes. U of Texas, 1971. [613.7 Or3h 81-174 – 81-175—Microfiche]

Dyer, K.F. *Challenging the Men: Women in Sport.* New York- U of Queensland P, 1982. [796.0194 D988c]

Ebben, William P. "Strength Training for Women: Debunking Myths that Block Opportunity." *The Physician and Sports Medicine* 26.5 (98). <www.hpyssportsmed.com/issues/1998may/ebben.htm>.

Ensley, Gerald. "Sporting Girls Fields and Arenas to Become Athletes." *Tallahassee Democrat Online* <http://www.tdo.com/features/families/stories/0708/>.

Epstein, Bruce, M.D. "Make Your Young Athlete a Winner!" 9 October 1997 <http://www.allkids.org/epstein/articles/athletics.html>.

Faragher, John Mack, et al. *Out of Many.* Upper Saddle River, NJ: Prentice Hall, 1997. [Interlibrary Loan]

Continued

Hanson, Sandra L., and Rebecca Kraus. "Woman, Sports and Science: Do Female Athletes Have an Advantage?" Paper. American Sociological Association Meetings. New York, Aug. 1996.

Harré, Ron, and Roger Lamb. "Self-esteem." *The Encyclopedic Dictionary of Psychology.* 1984 ed. [150.321 En19 1983—Reference]

Horn, T. S. "Coaches' Feedback and Changes in Children's Perceptions of Their Physical Competence." *Journal of Educational Psychology 77* (1985): 174–86. [Periodicals]

Hoyle, Rick H., and Stephen S. Left. "The Role of Parental Involvement in Youth Sport Participation and Performance." *Adolescence* Spring 1997: 234. [Periodicals]

King, Keith A. "Self-concept and Self-esteem: A Clarification of Terms." *The Journal of School Health* Feb. 1997: 69. [Periodicals]

Kunde, Diana. "Women Say Sports Valuable to Future Business Careers" *Dallas Morning News* 15 Oct. 1997: D1. [Periodicals]

Lapchick, Richard. "Participation Helps Keep Kids in School, Provide Life Skills." *USA Today* 4 Apr. 1996: 14C. [Periodicals]

Le Unes, Arnold D., and Jack Nation. Sports Psychology. Chicago: Nelson-Hall, 1996. [Interlibrary Loan]

Mau, Robert E. "Differences of Co-dependency and Self-esteem in College Age Male and Female Athletes and Non-athletes." Thes. Springfield College, 1995. [613.7 Or3h 96-206 – 96-207—Microfiche]

Norder-Pietrzak, Michelle Marie. "Perceived Body Image: Selected Lifestyle Practices and their Relationship to Physical Self-esteem." Thes. U. Of Wisconsin-La Crosse, 1993. [613.7 Or3h 94-192—Microfiche]

Padawer, Ruth. "Sports: a Curb on Teen Pregnancy?" *Berger Record* 16 May 1998. <www.math.lsa.umich.edu/~wolbert/sports.html>.

Continued

Reavill, Gil, and Jean Zimmerman. *Raising Our Athletic Daughters: How Sports Can Restore Self-Esteem and Save Girls' Lives.* New York: Doubleday 1998. [Interlibrary Loan]

Schenkman Kaplan, Leslie. "Self-esteem is Not Our National Wonder Drug." *School Counselor* May 1995: 341–43.

Shields, D. L., and B. J. Bredemeier. *Character Development and Physical Activity.* Champaign, IL: Human Kinetics, 1995. [796.01 Sh61c]

"Sports Lift Self-Esteem in Young Athletes." *American Psychological Associates Monitor* July 1996. 34. [Periodicals]

Spreitzer, Elmer. "Does Participation in Interscholastic Athletics Affect Adult Development?" *Youth and Society* March 1994: 369–71. [Periodicals]

Tyler, Suzanne Jayne. "Differences in Social and Sport Self Perceptions Between Female Varsity Athletes and Class Participants." Thes. Pennsylvania State U, 1973.

Talamini, John T. Sport and Society. An Anthology. Boston: Little, Brown, 1973. [796.08 T141s]

Twin, Stephanie L. *Out of the Bleachers.* New York. Feminist, 1979. [796.0194 Ou8]

Weiss, M. R., and S. C. Duncan. "The Relationship Between Physical Competence and Peer Acceptance in the Context of Children's Sport Participation." *Journal of Sport and Psychology* 14 (1992): 177–91. [Periodicals]

Working Bibliography
Julie McDowell

All about NutraSweet®. (1998). Monsanto Company. http://www.nutrasweet.com/ hml/his_about.html

Appleton, N. (1996). *Lick the sugar habit.* Garden City Park, NY: Avery.

Continued

Aspartame . . . the BAD news! (n.d.). *Aspartame kills.*

    http://www.aspartamekills.com/ symptoms.htm

Aspartame: Pro and con. (1983, September). *Consumers' Research*

    Magazine, 11–15. [Periodicals]

Beridot-Therond, M. E., Arts, I., & De La Guerronniere, V. (1998, August).

    Short-term effect of the flavor of drinks on ingestive behaviors in

    man. *Appetite,* 67–81. [Periodicals]

Bitter reaction to an FDA ban. (1997, March 21). *Time,* 60–61.

    [Periodicals]

Bitter sweetener. (1974, August 26). *Time,* 67. [Periodicals]

Blumenthal, H. J. & Vance, D. A. (1997). Chewing gum headaches.

    Headache: The Journal of Head and Face Pain, 37, 663–664.

    [Periodicals]

Chase, M. (1999, June 7). Amid new confusion, here's the truth about

    aspartame. *Wall Street Journal,* p. B1. [Periodicals]

De Francisco, J.C., & Dess, N.K (1998). Aspartame consumption in rats

    selectively bred for high versus low saccharin intake. *Physiological*

    Behavior, 6, 393–396.

Everything you need to know about aspartame. (1997, November).

    International Food Information Council.

    http://ificinfo.health.org/brochure/aspartame.htm

FDA reaffirms Nutrasweet safety. (1997, January/February). *Foods and*

    Nutrition Digest.

    http://www.oznet.ksu.edu/ext_f&n/_fndigest/1997/janfeb97.htm

FDA statement on aspartame. (1996, November 18). Food and Drug

    Administration. http://vm.cfsan.fda.gov/~lrd/tpaspart.html

Fumento, M. (1997, January). Sweet nothings. *Consumer's Research,* 35.

    [Periodicals]

FYI: What are the differences between the sweeteners saccharin and

    aspartame? (1998, July) *Popular Science,* 80–81. [Periodicals]

Gorman, C. (1999, February 8). A web of deceit. *Time,* 76. [Periodicals]

Continued

Halber, D. (1998). Study reaffirms safety of aspartame. MIT Tech Talk.
    http://web.mit.edu/newsoffice/tt/1998/sep16aspartame:html

Hearing on sweetener. (1979, July–August). *FDA Consumer, 2.*
    [Periodicals]

Harte, J., Holdren, C., Schneider, R., & Shirley, C. (1991). *Toxics a to z.*
    Berkeley: University of California Press. [615.9 T667—Reference]

Holmes, B. (1997, March). Could drinking diet soda give me brain
    cancer? *Health,* 18. [Periodicals]

How sweet it is. (1983, August 29). *Time, 44.* [Periodicals]

Hunter, B. T., & FDA. (1983, September). Aspartame: Pro & con.
    Consumers' Research, 11–14. [Periodicals]

Interview with Dr. Blaylock on aspartame. (1998). Personal Achievement
    Radio, WZHT.
    http://medicinegarden.com/Library/aspartame-interview.html

Lambert, V. (1993, April). Using "smart" drugs and drinks may not be
    smart. U.S. Food and Drug Administration.
    http://www.fda.gov/bbs/topics/CONSUMER/ CON00207.html

Leblang, B. (1992). Sweetness: Trial and error. *American Health
    Magazine* (Vol. 4, Art. 69) Boca Raton: SIRS.

Malaisse, W.J., Vanonderbergen, A., Louchami, K., & Jijaki, H. (1998).
    Effects of artificial sweeteners on insulin release and cationic fluxes
    in rat pancreatic islets. *Cell Signal,* 10, 727–733. [Periodicals]

Notebook. (1997, November/December). *FDA Consumer, 37.*
    [Periodicals]

Olney, J. W., Farber, N. B., Spitznagel, E. & Robins, L. N. (1996)
    Increasing brain tumor rates: Is there a link to aspartame? *Journal
    of Neuropathology and Experimental Neurology, 55,* 1115–1123.
    [Periodicals]

Podolsky, D., Wiener, L., & Chetwynd, J. (1996, December 2). Is
    aspartame sweet but deadly? *U.S. News & World Report, 98.*
    [Periodicals]

Continued

Sapolsky, H. M. (1986). *Consuming fears: The politics of product risks.* New York: Basic. [363.19 C766]

Smith, J. R. (1981, August 28). Aspartame approved despite risks. *Science, 217,* 986–87. [Periodicals]

Spiers, P. A., Saboryian, L., Reiner, A., Wurtman, J. & Schomer, P. L. (1998). Aspartame: neuropsychologic and neurophysiologic evaluation of acute and chronic effects. *American Journal of Clinical Nutrition, 68,* 531–537. [Periodicals]

Stein, P. (1997, September). The sweetness of aspartame. *Journal of Chemical Education, 74,* 1112–1113. [Periodicals]

Sweeteners await a cyclamate decision. (1974, August 10). *Business Week,* 47–48. [Periodicals]

Taylor, E. J. (Ed.). (1988). *Dorland's illustrated medical dictionary* (27th ed). Philadelphia: WB Saunders. [Interlibrary Loan]

Title 21—food and drugs. (1999, rev. April 1) U.S. Government Printing Office. http://frwebgate.access..../ get-cfr.cgi?TITLE=21&PART=172&SECTION=804&TYPE=TEXT.html

Walsh, J., R.D. (1997, March). Aspartame alert. *Parents,* 48. [Periodicals]

WRITING ASSIGNMENT: THE WORKING BIBLIOGRAPHY

For this assignment, you will create a working bibliography for your researched writing project. The bibliographic entries should follow the format (MLA style, APA style, or another style) assigned by your instructor. Basic entries in MLA and APA style are presented earlier in this chapter. A more complete list is presented in Chapter 10 (MLA style) and Chapter 11 (APA style).

1. *Learn about your library.* Tour the library to locate where reference works, books, periodicals, and online resources are kept. Familiarize yourself with lending policies and interlibrary loans procedures for your library. Obtain directions on using online catalogues and databases for your library.
2. *Find sources.* Search the catalogues of your library for possible sources. Use the source's title and subject headings to determine whether a source is likely to apply to your topic.

3. *List sources.* As you find sources, enter them in your working bibliography. For each source, create a full bibliographic entry in the correct style. You should also list the call number or URL you will need to locate the source.

TECHNIQUES: BUILDING AN ANNOTATED BIBLIOGRAPHY

Your working bibliography is the end product of the first step in the research process. The second step of the research process is to investigate your sources. In this step, you locate the source, skim its contents, and write a brief summary of the source. You will then combine the summaries of your sources with your working bibliography to create an annotated bibliography.

The annotated bibliography is an indispensable tool for researched writing projects. It allows you to quickly locate a source that contains specific information for answering questions raised during the researched writing process and developing your ideas.

Previewing Sources

In the first step of the research process—finding sources—you determined which sources in your library and on the Internet probably addressed your researched writing topic. In the second step—previewing sources—you obtain the actual source and see what the source says about your topic. While previewing your sources, you will no doubt find that some sources sounded good but do not in fact address your topic. Simply remove sources that are off-topic from your bibliography.

When you preview your sources, do not read the entire source. That comes later. A close reading of the source belongs to the third step in the process—gathering information—which is discussed in the next chapter. Right now, you need only skim the source to get an idea of what it says about your topic. The process of skimming books and articles varies.

To skim a book, you should perform the following steps:

1. *Read the introduction or preface.* The introduction or the preface gives you important information about the author, the author's profession, and the author's education. Information on the author may also be located in a separate section at the very beginning or end of the book. The introduction also gives you the context for the book: the author's purpose, what other sources say about the topic, and how this source is different. The introduction often includes a brief outline or summary of the book's contents.
2. *Look at the table of contents and the index.* The table of contents shows you the book's organization: what topics it discusses and in what order. Look in the index to find keywords related to your topic, so you know where to look for specific information on your topic.
3. *Read the first paragraph of each chapter.* The first paragraph of each chapter develops the brief summary presented in the introduction. After

reading the first paragraph of each chapter, you will have a clearer idea of the book's contents. You will also have an idea of how the chapters connect to each other.

4. *Read the last chapter or conclusion.* Reading the last chapter or conclusion of the book gives you an idea of how the author ties together all of the information in the book. You can often find the overall claim of the book in the conclusion. In addition, the conclusion often reviews the contents of the book from a new perspective—the perspective created by the book's claim.

When you skim an article or a Web page, you follow the same basic steps as you do when skimming a book. The difference lies in the parts of the source you look at. To skim an article, you should perform the following steps:

1. *Read the byline.* At the beginning or end of each article, there should be a brief statement, usually printed in italics, that gives you some basic information about the author and the author's qualifications.

2. *Read the introduction.* The introduction to an article may range from one to several paragraphs, depending on the length of the article. At the beginning of the article, the author tells you the topic of the article as well as a very brief outline of the contents.

3. *Read the topic sentences of each paragraph.* The topic sentences of each paragraph serve the same function as the first paragraphs of a book's chapters. If your article is divided into sections, then pay special attention to the beginning of each section by reading the first paragraph of each section.

4. *Read the conclusion.* Like the introduction, the conclusion of an article may be a single paragraph, or it may be several paragraphs. The length of the conclusion is based on the length of the article. Reading the conclusion is important because you often find the author's claim at the end of the article.

Take notes as you skim each source. You will use the information you gather as you skim to write the annotations for your annotated bibliography.

Writing Annotations

An *annotation* is a brief commentary on a source. Try to keep your annotations short—about four to six sentences (about fifty to sixty words). If you find a particularly useful book, you may want to write a sentence on every chapter (or key chapters), as shown in the annotation for *Jazz in the Sixties* in the sample bibliography that follows. Include the following information:

- The author's qualifications (profession, experience, and/or education).
- A summary of the source's contents.
- Your general impression of the source. (Is the source clearly written or confusing? Is it a general source or does it deal with a very limited

topic? Is it intended for a special audience? How useful, generally, do you think it will be to you? Why?)

To create an annotated bibliography, you combine the bibliographic entries from your working bibliography with your annotations. The annotation should start on the next line after the bibliographic entry. You should indent the annotations two tabs (one inch) so that it is not confused with the indented lines of the bibliographic entries.

BUILDING AN ANNOTATED BIBLIOGRAPHY: PROFESSIONAL WRITING

Here are some entries from an annotated bibliography for the study of black music.

From *Jazz, Black Music in the United States:*
An Annotated Bibliography of Selected Reference and Research Materials
Samuel A. Floyd, Jr. and Marsha J. Reisser.

189. Berendt, Joachim, E. *The Jazz Book: Ragtime to Fusion and Beyond.* Translated by H. and B. Bredigkeit with Dan Morgenstern. 2nd English ed. Westport, Conn. Lawrence Hill & Co., 1982. xi, 436 pp. musical examples, table. discography. index.

    This book surveys the entire range of jazz from ragtime (classic and New Orleans style) and Louis Armstrong to the AACM and electric jazz, jazz rock, and fusion. In covering the whole scope of the genre, the book necessarily gives superficial and summary treatment to important musicians and significant events. But it is a good introduction to the study of jazz, covering the various styles, the main figures, and the principal elements, instruments, vocalists, and ensembles of the genre. The author's narrative on "A Definition of Jazz" is particularly informative and provocative. The excellent and extensive discography is designed to be used in conjunction with the text.

Continued

190. Blesh, Rudi. *Shining Trumpets: A History of Jazz.* 2nd ed., rev. and enl. New York Alfred A Knopf, 1958. xiv, 410, xviii pp. chart, photographs, musical examples. appendix. index.

> This work purports to "explore the beginnings and trace the progress of jazz, analyze and define its nature, evaluate and compare it with the kinds of music we know" (p. vii). Based on the assumption that "a thorough treatment of jazz as music not only deals with the American Negro but goes all the way back to Africa" (p. viii), the work is divided into two parts. Book One treats "Black Music," "Drums to Africa," folk songs, and the blues; Book Two treats the various jazz styles, starting with "New Orleans and the Beginnings of Jazz" and ending with "Hot Piano." The author's insights, perceptions and conclusions remain fresh today. His treatment of jazz as black music is a relatively early recognition of the validity and propriety of that designation. An interesting feature is the "Chart Showing African Survivals in Negro Jazz and the Development of Negro Jazz."

191. Brunn, H. O. *The Story of the Original Dixieland Jazz Band.* Baton Rouge: Louisiana State University Press, 1960. xx, 268 pp. photographs, tables. appendix. index.

> The thesis of this book, that jazz was created by the ODJB, reveals it as part of the "white origins" literature. The book is a story of a white band in the jazz age; it traces the group's activities from the days before its recording of the first jazz record in 1917 until its final demise around 1940. Interesting, well-written, thorough, and authoritative in tone, it is nevertheless an example of the danger of relying on oral reports and conventional wisdom as evidence for conclusions. It is important that black music scholars be

Continued

familiar with this version of the story and the methodology that produced it.

192. Budds, Michael J. *Jazz in the Sixties: the Expansion of Musical resources and techniques.* Iowa City: University of Iowa Press, 1978. xii, 119 pp. musical examples, appendix. bibliography. index.

The stylistic diversity, new resources, and advanced techniques that came to jazz in the 1960s are briefly discussed in this volume. The work treats the jazz of the 1960s as both a continuation of an evolutionary process that began with New Orleans jazz and as a process involving the disintegration of its structural foundations. After beginning with a "Survey of Jazz Styles before 1960," the study treats 1960s jazz through its musical elements—"Color and Instrumentation," "Texture and Volume," "Melody and Harmony," "Meter and Rhythm," and "Structural Design." The final two chapters treat "Other Influences" and the "Legacy of the Sixties to the Seventies." The "Jazz Styles Before 1960" section is valuable in itself; its brief but comprehensive treatment of the various pre-1960s jazz styles—"New Orleans Dixieland," "Chicago Dixieland," "Swing," "Bop," "Cool," and "Hard Bop"—is a convenient and concise review. The chapter on "Color and Instrumentation" treats the employment of new sound sources and new timbres, including African and previously unused European acoustical instruments, electronic modification, synthesizers, and tape music. The "Texture and Volume" chapter treats textural density; the "Melody and Harmony" chapter includes discussion of modal scales, quartal harmony, and atonal techniques. Regular, irregular, and free rhythm are discussed in the chapter on "Meter and

Continued

Rhythm," and the "Structural Design" chapter focuses on Third Stream structural concepts, "free form," and free group improvisation. The appendix, which lists seventy-five recordings, is a valuable selection of important works of the period.

WRITING ASSIGNMENT: THE ANNOTATED BIBLIOGRAPHY

For this assignment, you will create your own annotated bibliography. You will use this bibliography throughout the researched writing process. It will help you locate sources you need to complete assignments later in the researched writing process.

1. *Locate your sources.* Using the location information in your working bibliography, locate your sources. Some of your sources may not be in your library; in this case, you will need to use interlibrary loan to obtain the source. Ask the librarian how to do that.
2. *Skim your sources.* Take notes on the author and the contents. What is your general impression of the source and why will it be useful to you in your researched writing project?
3. *Write your annotations.* Include information about the source's author, its contents, and your general impression of its usefulness. Try to keep your annotations to about four to six sentences.
4. *Compile the annotated bibliography.* Add your annotations to your working bibliography. Begin the annotation on the next line after the bibliographic entry. Indent the entire annotation two tabs (or one inch).

CHAPTER 5

Using Sources in Your Writing

Chapter 4 explained the first two steps of the research process: finding sources and previewing sources. At this point, you have a completed annotated bibliography for your researched writing project. This chapter discusses the third and fourth steps of the research process: *gathering information* and *using sources in your writing*. Your annotated bibliography is the starting point for these next two steps. You will gather specific information from the sources in your annotated bibliography. Then, you will decide whether to quote, paraphrase, or summarize these sources in your writing, blend the sources into your writing, and correctly cite the sources. First, however, a few words must be said about plagiarism.

DEFINITION: PLAGIARISM

> **Plagiarism:** Using someone else's words or ideas without giving the author or thinker proper credit.

As writers, if we violate the rules of grammar, the penalties are not severe—perhaps a note in the margin from your editor or supervisor or a slightly lower grade from your instructor. If, however, we violate the rules of using sources, the penalties are very severe. In college, you might fail the assignment or the course. In your personal or business life, penalties range from paying thousands of dollars in fines to losing your career.

If you think about what researched writing is all about, you can see how pointless plagiarism is. The whole purpose of researched writing is to use others' words and ideas in order to build on their knowledge. If we didn't use others' work, we would have to reinvent the wheel every time we investigated a topic, so we wouldn't ever progress very far. Others' words and ideas are a big part of your researched writing—all you need to do is give the original authors credit. Tell your reader that the other person's ideas belong to the other person and avoid any possible penalties.

109

Plagiarism can sometimes be embarrassing as well. A former colleague of one of the authors of this book was teaching at the same university she had attended as an undergraduate. As she sat correcting an essay, she kept getting the feeling that she was reading something she had seen before. Eventually, she realized that she was reading an essay that she had written as an undergraduate student. Somehow, the essay had gotten into circulation, and the student had purchased a copy and turned it in as original work. Such situations clearly violate any university's standards of academic honesty, and at some schools the student may be expelled.

Most plagiarism committed in a composition class, however, is not committed on purpose. A student might accidentally handle sources incorrectly. But "accidental" does not mean "excusable." Even accidental plagiarism should be avoided at all costs because it leads to questions about your credibility as a researcher and a writer.

And avoiding plagiarism is a simple matter. First, put quotation marks around all the words, phrases, and sentences that you use unchanged from the original text. Second, give credit to all the sources from which you borrow information.

EXERCISE 5-1

Examine the following situations and determine whether the hypothetical student has committed plagiarism. In two or three sentences, explain why you made your decision.

1. A student writes a paper on recycling for a freshman composition course. After the composition instructor grades and returns the essay, the student turns in the same essay for an assignment in an environmental studies course.
2. A student asks a roommate to read a draft of an essay. The roommate reads the draft and makes specific corrections, such as changing words and rearranging sentences. The student makes those changes and turns the essay in.
3. A student summarizes Geoffrey Elton's *The English* and cites only the author's name and the book's title.
4. A student writes: Somebody once wrote, "All the world's a stage."
5. A student writes: Life is like a movie. All the world's a stage, after all.

TECHNIQUES: USING SOURCES IN YOUR WRITING

Consider the following statements:

- "If you want to keep your children, you have to turn them loose."
- Eighty-seven years back, the Continental Congress hammered out a document which produced our country, based on freedom and the idea that all people have the same rights.
- When he hears that Juliet has died, Romeo rushes off to the local druggist, buys some poison, runs back to Verona, breaks into Juliet's tomb, and kills himself. This kind of rash behavior characterizes the young Italian's approach to life, love, and death; his behavior is also the reason why no fewer than six people die.

Each of these statements is an improper use of a source. The first is a quotation, so we as readers know someone other than the writer said it, but the writer does not tell us who, which the writer should do. The second statement paraphrases the opening of Abraham Lincoln's Gettysburg Address, but without the imagery and ideas of the original; without Lincoln's language, the ideas are not as powerful, so perhaps the writer should have quoted this passage. The third statement summarizes the end of Shakespeare's *Romeo and Juliet* but greatly oversimplifies the action. In this case, the writer should have paid closer attention to all of the information in the original source. Each of these improper uses of the source material creates problems for both the writer and the reader. Improper use of sources damages a writer's credibility; at the same time, improper use of sources confuses the reader.

As you gather sources and incorporate them into your researched writing, you face a series of choices. You must choose which sources to use; you must choose what form each source will take in your writing; and you must choose how to blend the source material with your own writing. Making these choices allows you to claim ownership of your researched writing at the same time that you use others' words and ideas in that writing.

Gathering Information

Gathering information refers to selecting specific passages from the books and articles in your annotated bibliography. There are two basic ways to gather source material: photocopies (including computer printouts) and notecards.

For years, teachers insisted that their students collect their resource information on three-by-five-inch notecards. The student had to go through the tedious process of writing out the notecards, organizing the notecards, and turning the notecards in, at which time the teacher then had to go through the tedious process of checking the notecards for accuracy. Although this method kept the three-by-five-inch card manufacturers in business, technology has given us more efficient ways of gathering source material.

Photocopy machines are one of technology's gifts to the researcher. If you have enough change, you can save yourself the hours of time and effort researchers used to spend transferring words from sources to notecards. You can simply photocopy your sources and highlight material that looks promising. Technology's other blessing is the Internet. You can now download sources directly from the Net and either view them on your monitor or simply print them out.

But before you throw away your stash of notecards, keep the following in mind: Some researchers *prefer* to use them. If you prefer notecards, then work with notecards. Notecards are also useful for recording information from sources that cannot be electronically reproduced. These sources include interviews, oversized materials, and sources so valuable or rare that you would not be allowed to remove them for photocopying.

Regardless of whether you are photocopying your sources or using notecards, whenever you come across a passage you think you can use in your writing, you must make sure you get the exact wording of the original source. On a photocopy, you can simply highlight a passage. If you're using a notecard, you need to be sure to copy down the words exactly. You might not end up quoting the source, but you will need the exact words of the source as a starting point for paraphrasing or summarizing the source.

If you photocopy or print out a source, use a highlighter to mark passages that you think you might want to use in your researched writing. Highlight only what is absolutely necessary. Limit yourself to only those sentences that contain essential information. In the margin by the passage, write the name of the topic or subtopic that you think the passage will be useful for, so you can later put related information together easily. You can also distinguish between topics by using a different-colored highlighter for each topic.

The same principles are true for notecards. Put only what is necessary on the card; limit yourself to one idea or one brief passage. In one of the top corners of the card, write the name of the topic or subtopic to which the information relates. In order to avoid writing out bibliographic information on each notecard, use numbers or letters to key your notecards to your annotated bibliography. When you gather information from a source, put a letter or number in the margin next to the source's entry in your bibliography. Here's an example from Tobi's researched writing project:

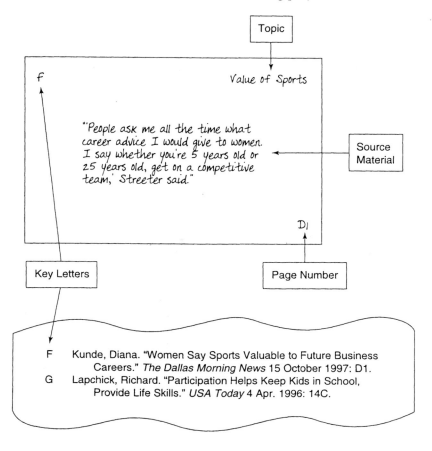

Quoting Your Sources

After you gather information, the next step is to choose how you are going to use your sources. You have three options: (1) you can quote the material; (2) you can paraphrase it; or (3) you can summarize it.

Usually, when an instructor mentions using sources in researched writing, students think about quotations. In a way, quotations are the easiest way to put sources in your writing because all you really have to do is copy down what the original source says. But if that is all you do, then you have surrendered ownership of your writing and handed it over to the author of the source. You need to think carefully about quotations and decide when you, as a writer, want to use them. There are five conditions under which quotation is appropriate.

> **When You Should Quote**
> 1. The source's authority is essential.
> 2. The source's language is exceptional.
> 3. You are discussing the source in detail.
> 4. You want to distance yourself from the source.
> 5. The source is very difficult to paraphrase.

If none of these conditions applies to your source, then do not quote the source. Instead, paraphrase or summarize it.

(1) The source's authority is essential.

Some authors are so expert in their fields that what they say is accepted by readers simply because this particular author said it. The same is true of certain sources. If, for instance, you were defining a difficult word, all you would have to do is quote the definition from the *Oxford English Dictionary,* the most authoritative dictionary of the English language, and your readers would accept the definition because it comes from the *OED.*

(2) The source's language is exceptional.

The source may use language that is so vivid and remarkable that the best choice is to simply let the source speak for itself. If this is true, then quote the source. For example, in a book about his love of fishing, *A Jerk on One End,* author Robert Hughes compares the voracious bluefish to "cuisinarts with fins." Such a vivid image would be hard, if not impossible, to paraphrase.

(3) You are discussing the source in detail.

Sometimes you want to discuss a passage from a source—say, an important paragraph or two—in detail. In this case, it will be easiest for your reader if you reproduce the original text in your writing before you analyze the passage. This way, the reader can easily refer to the original in order to understand your analysis.

(4) You want to distance yourself from the source.

Often, your sources will not agree with what you think, and you will not agree with what your sources say. But you may need to include some of those sources in your writing. Perhaps the position the source takes is extreme, and you want to make sure your readers know that the viewpoint belongs to your source and not to you. This is especially true if the source's language is racist, sexist, or otherwise offensive to you or your reader.

For instance, if you are researching World War II, you might need to turn to Hitler's writings to explain some of the causes of the war. In your paper, you choose to discuss Hitler's views on racial purity, views you would not want your audience to think you agreed with. If you paraphrase or summarize his writing, there is a chance that your reader might take his views to be your views. But, if you quote Hitler directly, your reader will see that the words are not yours, so there will be no chance that the reader will think his views are yours.

(5) The source is very difficult to paraphrase.

You will occasionally use a source that is impossible to paraphrase well. Sometimes the source may depend on technical terms for which there are no synonyms. Other times, the writing style may be too complicated to paraphrase well. An example would be this sentence from a book on computer programming:

> The Math function in JavaScript, when dealing with double-digit precision floating-point numbers, is subject to platform-dependent accuracy bugs when numbers get close to boundary conditions such as +/- Inf, and NaN (Not a Number, a condition found in UNIX systems).

Because this sentence includes so many technical terms for which there are no accurate synonyms, the only possible paraphrase would be so general as to misrepresent the meaning. If you can't paraphrase a passage accurately or well, then you need to quote it. You should, however, put every effort into paraphrasing the material first. In this case, quotation is a last resort.

Once you determine that you should quote your source, you need to remember some basic rules about quotation:

- The quotation must be presented exactly as it is in the original source; you cannot change the grammar, the punctuation, or the spelling.
- If you need to omit material that is not necessary to your purpose, and leaving out the material does not affect the central issue in the quotation, then you can do so, indicating the omission with ellipses (three periods with spaces between them). For example, if your source says, "John Smith, who lives on Elm Street, feels that taxes are too high," you can leave out "who lives on Elm Street" if it's not central to your purpose. The quotation would then read, "John Smith . . . feels that taxes are too high."

Note, however, that this concerns material you leave out of the *middle* of a quotation. It is conventionally understood that you are leaving material out before and after each quotation, so you would not need to use ellipses to indicate omissions in these positions.

- Sometimes you will need to add a word to a quotation. For instance, you may need to supply a noun to make a pronoun understandable to your reader. In these cases, you can add the word by placing it in brackets at the right point in the quotation.

For example, consider again the last example. If the original source read, "He feels that taxes are too high," and you quoted that material in your writing, your reader would not know who "he" is. In this case, you could use brackets to supply the missing information: "He [John Smith] feels that taxes are too high."

- If your quotation includes an error of spelling, grammar, or fact, then indicate the error by placing the word *sic* within brackets immediately after the error. In this way, the reader knows that the original author, and not you, made the error. Here's an example: "John Smith feels that taxs [*sic*] are too high."
- Quote the minimum amount of your source necessary. Quoting unnecessary text looks like you're padding your paper or that you are overdependent on outside sources.

EXERCISE 5-2

For each of the following situations, decide whether the writer should quote the material described.

1. A student is researching mythology and primitive rituals. In Edith Hamilton's *Mythology*, a reference work depended on by scholars for years, the student reads, "The real interest of the myths is that they lead us back to a time when the world was young and people had a connection with the earth, with trees and flowers and hills, unlike anything we ourselves can feel."

2. When reading Richard Selzer's *Mortal Lessons*, a student comes upon this passage: "Do not touch the spleen that lurks below the left leaf of the diaphragm, a manta ray in a coral cave, its bloody tongue protruding. One poke and it might rupture, exploding with sudden hemorrhage."

3. In researching the development of life on Earth for a biology class, a student locates the following passage:

    Our oldest fossils are about 3,600 million years old, and the lush biology of multicellular organisms goes back about 600 million years. With a few calculations, we find that the species living today are only a miniscule percentage of the total number that ever lived, perhaps considerably less than 1 percent. There are arguments about some of the estimates we plug into the calculations, but all agree that most species are extinct.

4. A student is preparing a paper on the use of figurative language in Harlan Ellison's short story "'Repent, Harlequin!' Said the Ticktockman." The student wants to break down all of the figurative language in the following paragraph:

    Jelly beans! Millions and billions of purples and yellows and greens and licorice and grape and raspberry and mint and round and smooth and crunchy outside and soft-mealy inside and sugary and bouncing jouncing tumbling clittering clattering skittering fell on the heads and shoulders and hardhats and carapaces of the Timkin workers, tinkling on the sidewalk and bouncing away and rolling about underfoot and filling the sky on their way down with all the colors of joy and childhood and holidays, coming down in a steady rain, a solid wash, a torrent of color and sweetness out of the sky above, and entering a universe of sanity and metronomic order with quite-mad coocoo newness. Jelly beans!

5. As part of a researched writing project for an astronomy class, a student considers quoting this passage: "Jupiter is so hot that it radiates about 1.5 times as much energy as it receives from the sun."

6. In a researched writing project on vegetarianism, a student is considering using the following passage:

   The May 1992 edition of Countryside *has a story called "The Last Roundup for Beef?" In it, liberal ecopest Jeremy Rifkin argues that without cattle, the world would be well fed, and peaceful.*

7. A student is researching how the idea of family has changed over time and finds this passage: "The joys of parents are secret, and so are their griefs and fears. They cannot utter the one, nor they will not utter the other."

8. A student in an anthropology course is thinking about using this passage in a researched writing assignment:

   For millions of years our ancestors subsisted solely on the proceeds of hunting and gathering, yet within just a few thousand years, between 10,000 and 3,500 years ago, domesticated plants and agricultural economies independently appeared in several different parts of the Old and the New World.

Paraphrasing Your Sources

If none of the five conditions for quoting sources applies, then you must either summarize or paraphrase your source. Whether you choose one method over the other largely depends on how long the passage is. If a passage is a few sentences or shorter, then you can probably paraphrase. If the passage is longer, then you probably need to summarize it. This section of the chapter explains how to paraphrase; the next section discusses how to summarize.

When you paraphrase the source, you reproduce the original source in your own words. The key part of paraphrasing is that you need to reproduce everything the original source says. Thus, paraphrases can often be longer than the original passage, which is why you would paraphrase only short passages—you wouldn't want to reproduce an entire page or chapter of a source.

Consider the following stanza from Robert Frost's "Stopping by Woods on a Snowy Evening":

Whose woods these are I think I know.
His house is in the village though;
He will not see me stopping here
To watch his woods fill up with snow.

A paraphrase of this stanza needs to include all of the ideas in the original. Here is one possible paraphrase:

Frost's speaker believes he is acquainted with the owner of the forest, who lives in the village. Therefore, the owner will not see the speaker pause in the forest during a blizzard.

Here is another example. In a guide to using Microsoft Access, Roger Jennings explains, "When the Office Assistant is on, it displays tips related to activities that you are currently performing and provides a means for you to search for help on specific tasks." A paraphrase of this passage would read:

According to Roger Jennings, the Office Assistant shows hints on jobs you are doing now as well as letting you look for more specific assistance (114).

To paraphrase a source, follow these steps:

1. Highlight the key parts of the sentence(s), such as subject, verb, and modifiers.
2. On a separate sheet of paper, substitute synonyms for these key elements.
3. Change the sentence patterns so that you are processing the concepts in your own thoughts. Otherwise, you are merely substituting synonyms for the original words.
4. Put the original text away and try to draft the information in your own words.
5. Maintain the sense of the passage; do not distort the intent of the original material.
6. Remember to cite the source.

EXERCISE 5-3

Paraphrase the following passages.

1. The number of oxygen atoms in the air is surprising. There will be over 300,000,000,000,000,000,000,000,000 soaring loose in your bedroom as you turn a book's pages, each one vibrating and tumbling in the air. They don't just attack the paper and other substances, but also clang into each other, bumbling into head-on collisions an average of once every seven billionths of a second.
2. The situation of the last days of the dinosaurs is made yet more difficult because the fossil record is rather scrappy. Most dinosaurs lived on land in settings that undergo much more erosion than sedimentation, so that burial and fossilization is a rare occurrence.
3. Aristotle said the sky was the realm of absolute, crystalline perfection. But Galileo showed the Moon's face to be battle-scarred and pocked. He could see with his own eyes that the worlds in the sky were no more perfect than the Earth.
4. Some caterpillars have made themselves unpleasant to eat. They are covered with poisonous hairs or have within their bodies a particularly acrid-tasting substance.

Summarizing Your Sources

If the passage you are working with is longer than a few sentences, then paraphrasing won't work. You will have to summarize it, largely for space purposes. In one sense, summarizing is the same as paraphrasing because you rewrite the original source in your own words. Summarizing is different from paraphrasing, however, because you present only the most important ideas of the passage in a summary, not all of the information in the original.

Consider again the stanza from Frost's poem. A summary of the stanza must mention only the main idea. Here's a possibility:

In this stanza, Frosts' speaker is alone in a forest during a snowstorm.

As with paraphrasing, there is a fairly simple process for summarizing your sources:

1. As you read the original text, identify the main idea that controls the passage, such as the topic sentence in a paragraph or a thesis statement in a longer source. Also identify subtopics if the source is long enough to have them. Finally, identify the meaning the author creates from the evidence.
2. Now paraphrase these key parts using the paraphrasing process you just learned. Then rewrite the paraphrase in your own words so that it expresses your own understanding of what the original source says. Do not interpret or respond to the source. Even though you are using your own words, you are still presenting someone else's ideas.
3. Check your summary for clarity and coherence to be sure you have clearly expressed the relationships between the elements that you have "borrowed" from the original text.
4. Remember to cite the source of the information. Using your own words to restate the original text does not free you from obligation to give credit to the author(s).

Here's another example of summarizing, using a different passage from Robert Jenning's book on Access. The original reads:

If you hide the Office Assistant, it remains hidden until you turn it on again or until you use a wizard or some other feature of Access that automatically invokes the Office Assistant. Access "remembers" the status of the Office Assistant whenever you close Access; if the Office Assistant was hidden at the time you last exited Access, the Office Assistant remains hidden the next time you start Access.

Here's a summary of this passage:

Robert Jennings explains that a hidden Office Assistant stays hidden until you turn it back on, even if you exit the program (115).

EXERCISE 5-4

Summarize the following passages.

1. Many of the swamps around the flood plains of African rivers turn to hard sun-baked mud during the dry season. Yet one fish, the lungfish, manages to live in them and survive from season to season by breathing air. As the pools shrink, the lungfish burrows into the mud at the bottom. There it curls into a ball, wrapping its tail around its head, and secretes mucus to line its hold. As the sun bakes out the last moisture from the mud, the mucus turns to parchment. The bichir and other primitive freshwater fish have a pouch opening from the gut to enable them to breathe air. The lungfish has a pair; and now, out of water, it is totally dependent on them. In burrowing down, the fish made a tube through the mud an inch or so across. Air now passes down this to the mouth of the fish, which is connected to tiny openings in the parchment cocoon. By pumping its throat muscles, the fish draws air down its throat to its pouches. The walls of these are thick with blood vessels, which absorb gaseous oxygen. These organs are simple lungs, and with their aid the lungfish can survive for several months, even years.

2. When a steer is slaughtered, it doesn't all die at once. After the brain waves stop, continued haemorrhaging uses up the oxygen in the animal's system. This destroys the glycogen fuel in its muscles, and that produces lactic acid—the same chemical our . . . chef gets in his legs when through a fate-tempting burst of activity, such as running after a bus, or playing squash at lunchtime with the club's resident killer, he uses up all the oxygen within. When a jogger says his legs feel dead, he's being more accurate than he thinks.

3. One of the less desirable "firsts" of Sumerian civilization was probably in the field of epidemic diseases. Just as there are certain disastrous things a hunter and gatherer can do (e.g., presume on too slight evidence that a cave bear is not at home), one of the worst things a villager can do is mix drinking water with sewage, and this is hard to avoid in a primitive town. Typhoid, cholera, and many other diseases require certain levels of population density to evolve, to maintain a reservoir of infected individuals, and to perpetuate themselves. These levels were probably reached for the first time in Sumer. Once people started digging wells and irrigation canals in areas with many people and animals, disease and epidemics quickly followed.

TECHNIQUES: BLENDING YOUR WRITING AND YOUR SOURCES

You have gathered specific information from your sources, and you have decided whether you will quote, paraphrase, or summarize in each case. Now you are ready to actually put the sources into your writing, a process called *blending*.

Blending source material into your own writing may be the most difficult part of using sources in your writing. A writer can establish any one of several relationships between source material and his or her own writing. At one end is the smoothly blended source material that allows the writer's voice to be heard so that the writer can still claim ownership of the writing. At the other end is the quotation that is not blended at all—there is nothing in the sentence except the quoted material.

Why is an unblended quotation a problem? First, the reader does not know how the quotation connects to your ideas. Second, for the moment when the reader is reading this sentence, you are not speaking at all. You do not own this sentence—the original author does. So, for this sentence (and all other sentences in your writing like it), you cannot claim ownership of your writing. One rule of thumb for blending sources, then, is never to put a quotation in a sentence all by itself. Instead, tell your readers how the quotation fits into your own writing.

There are, in fact, four parts to any blended source material:

1. the introduction (or "blending in")
2. the source material
3. the citation
4. the commentary (or "blending out")

Citing sources will be discussed later in the chapter. First, let's look at the introduction, the source material, and the commentary.

The Introduction

Any time you include source material in your writing, you need to lead into it with your own writing. Exactly what you say when introducing source material depends on your purpose for using it. If you are using the source material for the ideas it contains, then your introduction will probably contain your own ideas about the source's topic. If you are including the source material because the author or the source itself is important, then your introduction will likely state the source. Here's a closer look at these two kinds of introductions.

If you want to concentrate on a source's ideas, you will probably use only part of the original sentence or paragraph. In your introduction, you would want to include your own ideas or a paraphrase or summary of the source material. Here's an example:

The shape and color of the center of the universe make it look like the "bloodied yolk" of a giant egg (Ferris 19).

If, however, you want to focus on the author or source, include the author's name or source's title in the introduction to your source material. When you introduce the author, give the author's name and a brief phrase that gives the reader an idea of who the author is. The identifying phrase can include information such as the author's profession, other accomplishments of the author, or for whom the author works. That is, instead of just "Oprah Winfrey," you might say, "Oprah Winfrey, talk show host and philanthropist." Here's an example:

Timothy Ferris, an astronomer who has popularized the study of his field, uses the language of poetry to educate his readers: "The color of this great egg [the center of our galaxy] is that of a bloodied yolk, the red and orange light of old stars that have been burning steadily for billions of years" (19).

In most cases, you will use this kind of introduction for paraphrases and summaries, so the reader knows for certain that you are presenting source material.

If you are citing the source's title or the author's name, then choose your verb carefully. Verbs like *says, states, continues,* or *goes on to say* give no clue to the nature or importance of the information in the quotation. They convey nothing more than a perfunctory "Here's who said what comes next." Choose concrete verbs that help your reader understand how the source material is being used. Saying that a source "trivializes" a point indicates something very different to your reader than if you had said your source "exaggerates" a point, and both terms are better than "says."

The following table gives you an extensive list of concrete verbs to choose from.

TABLE 5-1

Concrete Verbs for Introducing Source Material

When the source admits an idea, use

acknowledges	admits	concedes	concurs

When the source completes an idea, use

accomplishes	culminates	produces	realizes
achieves	fulfills	proves	resolves
concludes			

When a source intensifies an idea, use

continues	emphasizes	intensifies	specifies
contributes	enlarges	lends	stresses
copies	exaggerates	notes	substantiates
develops	foregrounds	reasserts	supports
echoes	highlights	reinforces	underscores
embellishes	insists	reiterates	verifies

When a source connects ideas, use

analogizes	echoes	recapitulates	recurs
approximates	imitates	reconciles	reflects
compares	mimics	reconsiders	reiterates
conflates	parallels	reconstitutes	repeats
connects	parodies	recounts	reproduces
copies	recalls	recreates	resembles

When a source interprets an idea, use

analyzes	considers	interprets	summarizes
assumes	elevates	misinterprets	sums up
characterizes			

When a source negates an idea, use

challenges	departs from	inverts	subverts
contradicts	discounts	negates	suppresses
contrasts	discredits	nullifies	undercuts
denies	dismisses	questions	undermines

Continued

TABLE 5–1	*continued*

When a source begins an idea, use

adumbrates	commences	invents	prefigures
anticipates	conceives of	opens	proceeds from
begins	confronts	precedes	

When a source changes an idea, use

adapts	reduces	substantiates	trivializes
distorts	revises	translates	

When a source shows a relationship between ideas, use

adopts	detaches	juxtaposes	underlies
applies to	derives from	proceeds from	

When you are focusing the introduction on the author (see #3 in Table 5–2), use

accounts for	contends	establishes	points out
addresses	creates	examines	portrays
advances	defines	explains	presents
announces	demonstrates	explicates	proposes
argues	deploys	identifies	propounds
articulates	describes	informs	recites
asserts	details	introduces	records
chronicles	determines	maintains	refers
cites	devotes	narrates	relates
claims	discusses	notes	remarks
clarifies	dramatizes	observes	takes
comments on	employs	offers	traces
communicates	enumerates	organizes	

When you are focusing the introduction on the text, use

accommodates	depicts	furnishes	occupies
affords	discloses	functions	predominates
alludes to	displays	illuminates	represents
appears	divulges	illustrates	reveals
bears	dominates	implies	serves
betrays	embodies	includes	signifies
compromises	emerges	incorporates	suggests
confirms	epitomizes	indicates	symbolizes
constitutes	exemplifies	insinuates	typifies
conveys	exposes	involves	unfolds
delivers	expresses	marks	yields

Of course, you want to make sure you know what a verb means before you use it in your writing. A dictionary and this list of verbs will help you show your readers how you and your source approach an idea.

The Source Material

Having written an introduction to your source material, you are now ready to decide how you will insert the material itself into your writing. Most paraphrases and summaries do not pose much of a problem because they are already sentences themselves. You will simply put the paraphrase or summary into your writing at the appropriate point. Quotations, however, require specific formatting.

There are four different formats for quotations: one format for when the introduction focuses on the quotation's idea, one for when the introduction focuses on the author or the source and does not use a verb of expression, one for when the introduction focuses on the author or the source and does use a verb of expression, and one for when the quotation is over four lines long. Table 5–2 shows the correct format for each case.

TABLE 5–2

QUOTATION FORMATS

1. Introduction focuses on ideas:

Example: The shape and color of the center of the universe make it look like the "bloodied yolk" of a giant egg (Ferris 19). Not only does this image describe the center of the universe, but it also indicates its creative function.

- The quotation is rarely a complete sentence.
- The quotation must fit the grammar and syntax of your writing.
- The quotation begins with a lowercase letter unless it begins with a proper noun.
- A comma or period after the quotation goes inside the quotation marks; other punctuation usually goes outside.
- If the quotation is immediately followed by a parenthetical citation, then ending punctuation usually goes after the citation.

2. Introduction focuses on author or source and does not use a verb of expression:

Example: Timothy Ferris, an astronomer who has popularized the study of his field, uses the language of poetry to educate his readers: "The color of this great egg [the center of our galaxy] is that of a bloodied yolk, the red and orange light of old stars that have been burning steadily for billions of years" (19). Not only does this image describe the center of the universe, but it also indicates its creative function.

- The introduction (or blending in) is usually a complete sentence, so the quotation is usually preceded by a colon.
- If the quotation is a complete sentence or begins with a proper noun, then start the quotation with a capital letter; otherwise, begin with a lowercase letter.
- End punctuation follows same rules as format #1.

3. Introduction focuses on author and uses a verb of expression:

Direct quotation

Example: Timothy Ferris, an astronomer who has popularized the study of his field, writes, "The color of this great egg is that of a bloodied yolk" (19). Not only does his image describe the center of the galaxy, but it also indicates its creative function.

- A comma follows the verb of expression.
- The first letter of the quotation is *always* capitalized.
- End punctuation follows the same rules as format #1.

Indirect Quotation

Example: Timothy Ferris, an astronomer who has popularized the study of his field, explains that "the color of this great egg is that of a bloodied yolk" (19).

Continued

TABLE 5–2   *continued*

Not only does his image describe the center of the galaxy, but it also indicates its creative function.

- The word "that" follows verb of expression.
- The first letter of the quotation is lowercase, unless the first word is a proper noun.
- End punctuation follows the same rules as format #1.

4. The long quotation:

Example: Timothy Ferris, an astronomer who has popularized the study of his field, describes the center of our galaxy:

> After decades of travel, the interstellar clouds at last fall away. Ahead lies the central region of the galaxy, an elliptical cosmos of stars glowing through the relatively unsullied spaces with fantastic clarity. The color of this great egg is that of a bloodied yolk, the red and orange light of old stars that have been burning steadily for billions of years. Behind us the inner portions of the dusty disk hang like the walls of a canyon; thousands of light-years down one wall we can discern the elbow joint where one spiral arm emerges from the central regions and begins a winding path that will eventually take it out past our sun. (19)

Ferris' vivid, even poetic, language shows how he has been able to bring astronomy to the masses.

- Quotation is indented.
- No quotation marks are used.
- End punctuation goes before parenthetical citation.

EXERCISE 5-5

Proofread the following quotations for correct format. If the format is not correct, then revise the quotation.

1. To describe the appearance of the liver, surgeon Richard Selzer poses a riddle: "What is the size of a pumpernickel, has the shape of Diana's helmet, and crouches like a thundercloud above its bellymates, turgid with nourishment?" (62).
2. David Willis McCullough characterizes the unique nature of Europe's barbarian peoples. "Again and again, the barbarian enemies came from nowhere. They were unexpected. They were people no one had ever heard of. They were perhaps not altogether human." (xviii).
3. According to Jonathan Weiner, "Earth has destroyed all its Genesis rocks. Wind, rain, and weather, drifting continents, restless sea floors, and the great wheel of the revolving seasons have destroyed all the original rock that was here when our planet was born" (157).
4. Jonathan Weiner says "the ocean of air is like the kind of glass paperweight in which a miniature carved Eskimo plods across snow toward his igloo. Turn the paperweight over, right it again, and a blizzard of white powder swirls through the fluid in the glass and settles to the bottom". (101)
5. Contrary to what most people think of the comma, Lewis Thomas argues that "the commas are the most useful and usable of all the stops" (126).

6. Herbert Kohl offers a clear definition of *metonymy:*

   > "Metonymy is a **trope** or figure of speech in which a thing, concept, person, or group is represented by something closely associated to it. Referring to a baseball player as the glove, referring to the presidency as the Oval Office, or referring to a person who bets on horse races as the Horse are examples of metonymy" (34).

7. A poker game and a lawsuit taught the playwright David Mamet that "You can neither bluff nor can you impress someone who isn't paying attention (11)".

The Commentary

In order to fully blend sources into your writing, you need to connect the quotation to your writing at both ends, just as a bridge is connected to both banks of a river. Your introduction takes care of one connection. The other connection is provided by your commentary. The commentary explains how the evidence in the source material connects to the point you are making— your meaning.

Once again, we can use the material from Timothy Ferris.

> Good science writers entertain at the same time that they explain. For example, Timothy Ferris, an astronomer who has popularized the study of his field, uses the language of poetry to educate his readers: "The color of this great egg [the center of our galaxy] is that of a bloodied yolk, the red and orange light of old stars that have been burning steadily for billions of years" (19). Not only does Ferris's writing clearly describe the center of the galaxy, but his vivid language also keeps the reader interested and entertained.

TECHNIQUES: CITING YOUR SOURCES

The last part of using sources is citing them, which is itself a complex process. Part of what makes citation so complex is that there are many different systems for citing sources. Each professional field has its own system described in its own handbook. Here are just a few examples:

> *American Chemical Society Style Guide*
>
> *The AMS Author Handbook* (American Mathematical Society)
>
> *Style Manual for Political Science*
>
> *The CBE Manual for Authors, Editors, and Publishers* (Council of Biology Editors)
>
> *Writing About Music: A Style Sheet*

Most college students use either the MLA or APA style of citation, so, as was true of the last chapter, this chapter also focuses on these two styles.

In the last chapter, you were introduced to basic bibliographic entries for both the MLA and APA styles, and then told to refer to later chapters for a more complete listing of entries. This chapter follows the same pattern: you will learn only basic citation formats for both MLA and APA style. A more complete selection of citation formats is found in Chapter 10 (MLA style) or Chapter 11 (APA style). If, after looking in those two chapters, you still cannot find the citation format you need, then refer to the style guides for these two styles: *The MLA Handbook for Writers of Research Papers* and the *Publication Manual of the American Psychological Association.* Before looking closely at citations, though, a quick word about when you need to cite.

The definition of plagiarism given at the beginning of this chapter insisted that you give credit to all of the ideas and words that you borrow from someone else. Citation is the way that you give that credit. If you are unsure whether you should cite something or not, cite it. It's better to be safe than sorry; however, there is some information that you do not need to cite. It's called "common knowledge," sometimes called material in the "public domain."

Consider this example: Most people could identify George Washington as the first president of our nation, but very few could tell you which number president Bill Clinton is. If you do not know, then you could look it up, but you would not have to document the source you found it in because facts of public record do not require documentation. Nor would you have to document a source that provides the molecular formula for water (H_2O). Most educated people have that knowledge.

Facts, then, that are common knowledge to many people or that are part of the public record do not need citation. Everything else—claims, statistics, ideas, language—needs to be cited so that the originator of the material receives proper credit.

EXERCISE 5-6

Determine if the information that follows is common knowledge or if it is information that should be cited.

1. The capital of Spain is Madrid.
2. Water boils at 212 degrees Fahrenheit.
3. The most effective way to boil water is over an open gas flame.
4. Madrid is Spain's most beautiful city.
5. A college education is necessary for a successful career.

Citing Your Sources (MLA Style)

The MLA style of citation consists of two parts. One part is a list of works cited at the end of your researched writing. To create a Works Cited list,

1. Start a new page.
2. Center the words "Works Cited" at the top of the page.
3. Copy the bibliographic entries from your annotated bibliography.

   • Include only those sources that are quoted, paraphrased, or summarized in your writing.
   • Put the bibliographic entries flush with the left-hand margin.
   • Use a hanging indent.
   • Do not number the sources.
   • Do not include the call number or your annotation.

Unlike the bibliography you built in the last chapter, the Works Cited list includes only those sources you actually quote, paraphrase, or summarize in your essay.

The other part of the citation style is a parenthetical citation that appears in your writing whenever you include an outside source. The parenthetical citation includes the minimum information necessary to direct your reader to the correct source in the Works Cited list.

Parenthetical citations are usually placed at the end of a quotation:

Timothy Ferris, an astronomer who has popularized the study of his field, uses the language of poetry to educate his readers: "The color of this great egg [the center of our galaxy] is that of a bloodied yolk, the red and orange light of old stars that have been burning steadily for billions of years" (19).

If your sentence continues after the quotation, however, then you should place the parenthetical citation at the end of the sentence, so you do not distract your reader:

The shape and color of the center of the universe make it look like the "bloodied yolk" of a giant egg (Ferris 19).

Similarly, if you include several brief quotations, paraphrases, or summaries from a single source in one paragraph, wait until the end of the paragraph to cite the source, so that you do not interrupt the flow of your writing. In this case, do not put any of your own writing between the source material and the citation.

Exactly what information goes into the parenthetical citation depends on two things: (1) what bibliographic information you put in your sentence, and (2) how many sources in the Works Cited list come from the same author. The flowchart on the opposite page outlines the choices you can make.

You will find examples of the most common kinds of parenthetical citations in the following list. If you have a citation that is not covered by these examples, then ask your instructor or refer to any of the MLA sources listed previously. The following examples are keyed to the examples of bibliographic entries in Chapter 10.

1. Citing by Author

   - One author: (Dillard 46).
   - Two authors: (Johanson and Edey 244).
   - Three authors: (Lass, Kiremidjian, and Goldstein 95).
   - More than three authors: (Turnbull, et al. 199).

2. Citing by Title: (*Practical* 244).
3. Citing Multiple Works by One Author: (Selzer, *Mortal* 130).
4. Citing Authors of the Same Last Name

   - (A. Smith 100)
   - (C.R. Smith 125)

5. Citing More than One Source: (Johanson and Edey 44; Hunter 93-5).

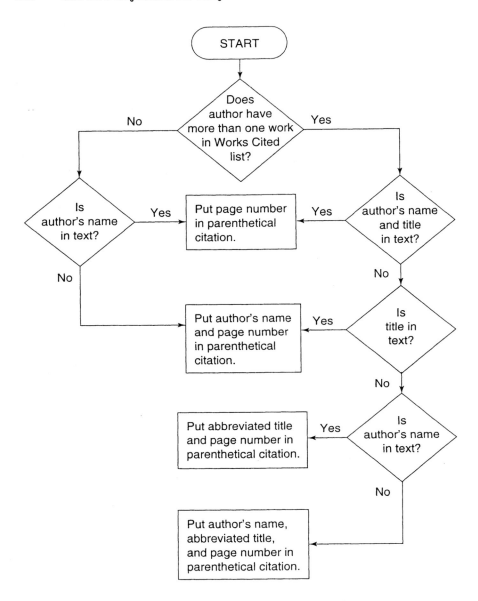

6. Citing a Corporation or Government Office: (Department of Health and Human Services 24-5).

7. Citing Sources with Several Volumes: (Graves 2: 10).

8. Citing Online Sources with No Pages: (Stotsky)

EXERCISE 5–7

Use the following list of works cited to create the parenthetical citations requested.

WORKS CITED

Bloom, Harold. *The Western Canon: The Books and School of the Ages.*
New York: Harcourt Brace, 1994.

Eliot, George. *Middlemarch.* Ed. Gordon S. Haight. Boston: Houghton
Mifflin, 1956.

Eliot, T.S. *The Complete Poems and Plays 1909-1950.* New York:
Harcourt, Brace and World, 1971.

Grene, David, and Richmond Lattimore, eds. *Greek Tragedies.* 3 vols.
Chicago: U of Chicago P, 1960; 1991.

James, Henry. *The American.* Ed. and intro. William Spengeman.
New York: Penguin, 1986.

——. *The Portrait of a Lady.* Ed. Robert D. Bamberg. Norton Critical
Edition. New York: W.W. Norton, 1975.

Parmeter, Sarah-Hope, Ellen Louise Hart, Paul M. Puccio, and Ann Marie
Wagstaff. "Successful Teaching Practices for Sexual Minority
Students in Writing Courses: Four Teachers at Work." *Voices in
English Classrooms: Honoring Diversity and Change.* Ed. Lenora
(Leni) Cook and Helen C. Lodge. Classroom Practices in Teaching
English 28. Urbana, IL: NCTE, 1996. 131-47.

Stross, Randall E. "My New Best Friend, Tiger." *U.S. News & World
Report* 6 March 2000: n. pag. Online. EBSCOHost. 20 March
2000.

---

1. Cite page 174 of T.S. Eliot's *Complete Poems and Plays.*
2. Cite pages 135 through 142 of "Successful Teaching Practices for Sexual Minority Students in Writing Courses."
3. Cite the article "My New Best Friend, Tiger."
4. Cite page 5 of *The American,* assuming you have mentioned the author's name in the text.
5. Cite page 10 of volume 3 of *Greek Tragedies.*

Citing Your Sources (APA Style)

The American Psychological Association cites sources using the same general method, although the format is different. Like MLA style, APA style uses parenthetical citations in the text. The parenthetical citations are keyed to a list of references at the end of your paper. You compile a list of references the same way you compile an MLA-style Works Cited list, with one difference: you center the word "References" as the title.

In general, you insert APA parenthetical citations in the same places you would an MLA citation. One exception occurs when you refer to an author in the introduction to your source material. In this case, cite the year of the source directly after the author's name. Another difference between APA and MLA citation is that APA style does not require you to cite page numbers of summaries or paraphrases. The following flowchart will lead you through creating APA-style parenthetical citations:

1. Citing by Author
   - One author: (Dillard, 1999, p. 46).
   - Two authors: (Johanson and Edey, 1981).
   - Three to five authors: (Lass, Kiremidjian, and Goldstein, 1987).
     - ◇ Identify all of the authors when they are first cited, but in subsequent citations, name only the first author, followed by the phrase et al., as in (Lass et al., 1987).
   - Six or more authors: (Choate et al., 1987).

2. Citing by Date: (2000)

   - When you use the author's name in your text, you only need to cite the date for summaries and paraphrases. Cite the date and page number for quotations in this case.

3. Citing by Title: (*Practical,* 1991).
4. Citing Multiple Works by One Author: (Smith & Weiss, 1997a).

   - If you are using more than one work by an author published in the same year, then alphabetize the works by title in the Reference section and assign them an alphabetical code according to their sequence.

5. Citing Authors of the Same Last Name:

   - (A. Smith, 1984)
   - (C.R. Smith, 1998)

6. Citing Multiple Sources: (Johanson and Edey, 1981; Korbeck, 1996).
7. Citing a Corporation or Government Office: (U.S. Department of Health and Human Services, [USDHHS], 1988).

   - In the first citation, use the full name of the corporation or office and include an abbreviation in brackets. Use the abbreviation in subsequent citations.

8. Personal Communications

   - Personal Interview: (R. Zahner, personal communication, June 27, 1999).
   - Telephone Interview: (D. Brooks, telephone interview, June 28, 1999).
   - Personal Survey: (Classroom Cheating Questionnaire, personal survey, June 25, 1999).
   - Letter: (M. Brooks, letter to the author, 23 June 1999).
     - ◇ Letters, interviews, and e-mail messages are not considered "recoverable sources." In other words, your reader cannot access them. Therefore, cite them in your text only, not in the list of References.

EXERCISE 5–8

Use the following references list to construct the APA citations requested.

References

Bloom, H. (1994). *The western canon: The books and school of the ages.*
New York: Harcourt Brace.

Eliot, G. (1956). *Middlemarch.* (G. S. Haight, Ed.). Boston: Houghton
Mifflin.

Eliot, T.S. (1971) *The complete poems and plays 1909-1950.* New York:
Harcourt, Brace and World.

Grene, D., & Lattimore, R. (Eds.). (1991) *Greek tragedies.* (Vols. 1-3).
Chicago: University of Chicago Press.

James, Henry. (1986) *The American.* (W. Spengeman, Ed. and Intro.).
New York: Penguin.

——. (1975). *The portrait of a lady. Norton Critical Edition.* (R. Bamberg,
Ed.). New York: W.W. Norton.

Parmeter, S., Hart, E., Puccio, P., & Wagstaff, A. (1996). Successful
teaching practices for sexual minority students in writing courses:
Four teachers at work. In L. Cook & H. Clark (Eds.), *Voices in
English classrooms: Honoring diversity and change. Classroom
Practices in Teaching English 28* (pp. 131-47). Urbana, IL: NCTE.

Stross, R. (2000, March 6). My new best friend, Tiger. *U.S. News &
World Report* [On-line magazine]. Retrieved March 20, 2000,
from EBSCOHost.

---

1. Cite page 174 of T.S. Eliot's *Complete poems and plays.*
2. Cite pages 135 through 142 of "Successful teaching practices for sexual minority students in writing courses."
3. Cite the article "My new best friend, Tiger."
4. Cite page 5 of *The American,* assuming you have mentioned the author's name in the text.
5. Cite page 10 of volume 3 of *Greek tragedies.*

The following flowchart will lead you through the process of using sources in your writing:

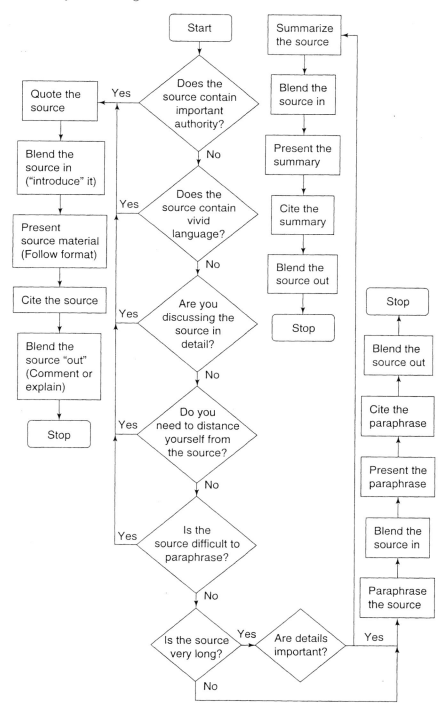

USING SOURCES IN YOUR WRITING: PROFESSIONAL WRITING

In this excerpt from *The Alphabetic Labyrinth*, Johanna Drucker discusses the connections between the written word and the practice of magic, especially prophecy, in ancient Greece and Rome. Drucker uses summary, paraphrase, and quotation in this passage. As you read, try to figure out why she uses her sources as she does.

From *The Alphabetic Labyrinth*

Johanna Drucker

Magic in its many forms was an exceedingly common element of religious practice among both Greeks and Romans. The materials in this section are drawn from sources traced to Greece, Hellenistic Egypt and the far flung reaches of the Roman empire. The written word was believed to have very definite and real power throughout this period—the power to curse, to heal, to empower and to constrain. Whether such oracles[1] as the famous ones at Cumae, Delphi and Dodona made extensive use of writing is difficult to determine. There are no remaining written documents and there is only sporadic mention of the use of writing in the oracles' activities. It is clear that answers to inquiries were sometimes given in writing, and both the visual augury[2] of entrails and the divination by lots[3] were common practice. But oracles depended largely on ecstatic speech trance[4] and there are few, if any, recorded instances of actual oracular pronouncement involving alphabetic letters as symbols (Parke). Later depictions of the Cumaean Sibyl, of the Delphic Pythia, or other less renowned oracles, are frequently depicted with inscribed messages on scrolls in long cryptic lines. But in classical times the use of writing was far more common in the form of amulets[5] and curse tablets and various kinds of imprecations[6] protecting everything from city or field to private property from violation. Customs varied locally, Greeks in their homeland, for instance, were less involved with burial imprecations than were Greeks in

---

Continued

Anatolia and Asia Minor (Strubhe 33-59). These were activities which were known as early as the 5th century BC and extended almost five centuries into the Christian era.

Various kinds of curses and tablets are associated with burial rituals in antiquity. These range from curses applied to newly dead enemies, curses against those who would violate a tomb, and phylacteries[7] designed to aid or protect the dead. For example, curse tablets were commonly buried near the site of a fresh tomb in order to punish a deceased enemy by giving the spirits of the dead greater power over the victim. Funerary imprecations were inscribed on tombs or inserted into them on tablets in order to protect them from material or spiritual violation. Such imprecations were often worded to prescribe the price to be paid in both spiritual and economic terms should such a violation occur: "The man who acts against these prohibitions will be a wrongdoer towards the gods of the underworld, and he will pay a fine of 1,500 denarii to the most sacred [imperial] treasury" (Strubhe 34).

[1] *Oracle:* A person who served as the mouthpiece of a divinity.

[2] *Augury:* Prophecy; here, foretelling the future by the shape, size, and arrangement of animals' internal organs.

[3] *Divination by lots:* Foretelling the future by reading the random arrangement of, usually, marked pieces of wood or bone.

[4] *Ecstatic speech trance:* A trance an oracle falls into when speaking with the "voice" of a divinity.

[5] *Amulets:* An object worn on the body as magical protection against evil.

[6] *Imprecation:* An oath or curse that calls divine vengeance or evil upon another.

[7] *Phylacteries:* Amulets, usually a case containing a holy relic.

In this passage, author Michael Shermer discusses the different kinds of beliefs used by cults. He depends here on quotation. Using what you learned in this chapter, why do you think he chooses to use his sources in this way?

From *Why People Believe Weird Things*
Michael Shermer

The ultimate statement of Rand's moral absolutism heads the title page of Nathaniel Branden's book. Says Rand,

> The precept: "Judge not, that ye be not judged" . . . is an abdication of moral responsibility: it is a moral blank check one gives to others in exchange for a moral blank check one expects for oneself. There is no escape from the fact that men have to make choices; so long as men have to make choices, there is no escape from moral values, so long as moral values are at stake, no moral neutrality is possible. To abstain from condemning a torturer, is to become an accessory to the torture and murder of his victims. The moral principle to adopt . . . is "Judge, and be prepared to be judged."

The absurd lengths to which such thinking can go are demonstrated by Rand's judgments on her followers for even the most trivial things. Rand argued, for example, that musical taste could not be objectively defined, yet, as Barbara Branden observed, "if one of her young friends responded as she did to Rachmaninoff . . . she attached deep significance to their affinity." By contrast, Barbara tells of a friend of Rand's who remarked that he enjoyed the music of Richard Strauss: "When he left at the end of the evening, Ayn said, in a reaction becoming increasingly typical, 'Now I understand why he and I can never be real soul mates.

Continued

The distance in our sense of life is too great.' Often, she did not wait until a friend had left to make such remarks" (1986, p. 268).

In both Barbara and Nathaniel Branden's assessments, we see all the characteristics of a cult. Deceit and sexual exploitation? In this case, exploitation may be too strong, but the act was present nonetheless, and deceit was rampant. In what has become the most scandalous (and now oft-told) story in the brief history of the Objectivist movement, starting in 1953 and lasting until 1958 (and on and off for another decade after), Ayn Rand and Nathaniel Branden, twenty-five years her junior, carried on a love affair and kept it secret from everyone *except* their respective spouses.

WRITING ASSIGNMENT: USING SOURCES IN YOUR WRITING

This exercise will give you practice in quoting, paraphrasing, and summarizing source material.

1. Choose one of the sources from your annotated bibliography to work with.
2. Choose a passage that you would quote, another that you would paraphrase, and a third that you would summarize. Because these three methods of using source material serve different purposes, you probably would not use the same passage for all three.
3. For each passage you have selected:

   - Type out the separate passages you have selected.
   - Present each passage as you would quote it, paraphrase it, or summarize it. Remember to blend the source material properly. Cite the source using MLA style with parenthetical citations and a Works Cited list.
   - Present each passage as you would quote it, paraphrase it, or summarize it. Remember to blend the source material properly. Cite the source using APA style with parenthetical citations and a References list.
   - Include an explanation of why you decided to quote, paraphrase, or summarize a particular passage.

PART THREE

Reading Sources Critically

In Part Three, you begin to work directly with the resources in your working bibliography. Because sources report "facts" so differently, you start by comparing and contrasting the information in your various sources. Thus in Chapter 6 you check the validity of the facts by consulting a variety of sources, instead of relying on a limited number of references. After ascertaining the validity of your information, you are ready to increase your perspective and understanding of the topic by looking at its background, context, or connections with similar issues. In Chapter 7, you are asked to look beyond the specific topic to gain an understanding of influences affecting that topic. Giving perspective will enhance your credibility with your readers.

The activities in Chapters 6 and 7 increase your knowledge and understanding of your topic, helping you to make judgments about a source's value. Judging the value of a source leads you to the goal of Chapter 8, "Critiquing Sources." Because the credentials and objectives of authors are as varied as their audiences, you want to determine which argumentative techniques have been used before you accept the source. Now you are ready to use your resources in your own text, creating meaning from them. In Chapter 9, you lean how to draw inferences from the evidence or facts you have collected. At this point in your writing, you are in full ownership of your topic, making the most original contribution to its study.

Chapter 6   Validating Sources

Chapter 7   Discovering Connections and Context

Chapter 8   Critiquing Sources

Chapter 9   Drawing Inferences

CHAPTER 6

Validating Sources

The "facts" depend on where you stand in the communication line.

When someone reports another person's spoken words, the possibility that the original words will change is almost guaranteed. You can demonstrate this yourself, taking your cue from the cartoon. Either in a group or as a class, take a moment to play the "telephone game." Whisper a sentence to your neighbor; your neighbor then whispers it to the next student in line; when the sentence has made it around the group, compare what the last student says the sentence is to what you started the game with.

There are other reasons beyond simply mishearing words that explain why primary and secondary sources can vary in the information they present. Three of the more common reasons include the following:

- A source misquotes information
- A source purposely misrepresents information
- A source changes its perspective or understanding of information

These three kinds of variation are more common than you might think. Here are just a few examples.

Kenneth Arnold, a civilian pilot, was apparently misquoted with long-range consequences. Arnold was the first individual to use the expression "flying saucer," but he used it to describe the motion of what he saw, not to offer a description of the shape of what he had observed. Arnold reported seeing something during a flight near Mount Ranier on June 24, 1947. Nearly a year later, in an interview with Edward R. Murrow, Arnold complained that his statement was not reported accurately:

> *When I told the press they misquoted me, and in the excitement of it all, one newspaper and another got it so ensnarled up that nobody knew just exactly what they were talking about. . . . These objects more or less fluttered like they were, oh, I'd say boats on very rough water. . . . And when I described how they flew, I said that they flew like they take a saucer and throw it across the water. Most of the newspapers misunderstood and misquoted that, too. They said that I said that they were saucer-like; I said that they flew in a saucer-like fashion.*

One newspaper's misquotation of Arnold's information set off a chain reaction that put the words "flying saucer" into our everyday language—with a different meaning from what Arnold intended.

An example of purposeful misrepresentation can be found as recently as 1990. In December of that year, an article in *Time* reported that rapper Vanilla Ice claimed "he grew up street-tough in Miami, went to the same school as rapper Luther Campbell of 2 Live Crew and won three national motocross championships." The article goes on to report, however, that "Vanilla is actually Robert Van Winkle, the product of a white, middle-class Dallas suburb who never went to high school in Miami or won a single national motocross championship." Misrepresentation may have earned Vanilla Ice millions, but it left the facts rather poverty-stricken.

Over a period of time, some sources may change their perspective on information. This change in perspective will cause the source to understand the information differently, so what the source says at two different points in time may change. Consider the example of Rosa Parks. Soon after her heroic actions in Montgomery, Alabama, Rosa Parks (central figure in the 1956 Montgomery bus strike) stated in a 1956 interview with Sidney Rogers, "I had been pushed as far as I could stand to be pushed. . . . I had decided that I would have to know once and for all what rights I had as a human being and a citizen." But in an interview three decades later, Mrs. Parks explained her refusal to give up her seat "because I was so involved with the attempt to bring about freedom from this kind of thing. . . . I felt just resigned to give what I could to protest against the way I was being treated." Her second statement does not invalidate what she first stated. Rather, the second statement simply reveals that over time Mrs. Parks understood her own complex emotions during the bus strike in a different way.

The last two chapters guided you through the research process, and you should, by this time, have gathered a large amount of information. Some of that information will likely vary from source to source. But, in order to create the best meaning that you can out of your sources, you need to use accurate and reliable information. In this chapter, you will learn the techniques of validating, or corroborating, evidence. You will then apply those techniques to the validation paper. A *validation paper* establishes which pieces of information that you've found are the most accurate and reliable. You will then be armed with the best information you can, ready to create your own meaning and perspective out of your research.

DEFINITION: VALIDATION

Validation: Ensuring that the evidence we are working with is accurate and reliable.

As you can see, the reliability and accuracy of both the primary and secondary resources you use can easily be called into question. The reasons for the lack of reliability are various: an author misunderstands what is said; an author applies metaphorical interpretations; an author hears only partially because of his or her emotional states; an author simply does not remember accurately; or an author is careless and lazy.

After you have determined your topic and purpose, the next step is to begin gathering evidence, but that evidence might not be reliable, accurate, or consistent, as the previous anecdotes have shown. Therefore, you must validate your evidence: consult a wide number and variety of sources to establish accurate and reliable facts. Without such validation, the meaning you create from your evidence may be flawed.

Imagine the following scene: it takes place in a composition classroom much like the one you are in right now, and you may, in fact, have unknowingly played one of the roles. The instructor enters and distributes a handout to the class. "All right, students, here is your assignment," she says. "You are going to write a research paper. The topic will be of your choice, but it should be tightly focused and personally meaningful. And it must be no longer than five pages. A title page and a works cited page are required. Do you have any immediate questions?"

Every hand in the room shoots up with the same burning question. The instructor calls on a student in the front row. "Yes?"

"How many sources do we need?" the student replies. The rest of the hands go down with a classwide sigh of relief—the important question has been asked.

The instructor, looking crestfallen, mutters to herself, "How many years do I have till retirement?" She turns back to the class and announces, *"As many as it takes!"*

No wonder the teacher is frustrated. There is no magic number of sources that adds up to an "A." The problem here is a discrepancy between goals: the teacher is looking for the maximum possible, whereas the students are hoping for the minimum necessary. The teacher's goal is that the students will read as widely as possible for the topic, become well-informed, make judicious choices, and write a paper that responds to the sources in an original way. The students' goal is to conserve effort, time, and energy in getting yet one more of the seemingly endless writing assignments for the semester out of the way.

But, when you accept ownership of your research project, you also accept the responsibility to pursue the project with diligence and enthusiasm and do the best work that you can. Remember that your name goes on this project—make sure that your project is worthy of bearing that name.

If you study a topic using just a few sources, you will get only a rough sketch or outline of the issue. A few sources allow you to stitch a couple notes together to get a connected series of bits of information that appear to hang together. But an informed reader—such as your instructor—will quickly see how sketchy the material is if it does not include all of the relevant detail and important variations from an appropriate number of sources. Consulting many sources provides you with a fuller, richer perspective on the topic you are investigating. One source or two sources or three, even for a brief paper, will hardly help you understand the depth and breadth of your topic. How many sources should you use? *As many as it takes!*

When you examine a wide variety of sources, you run into a problem that all writers have experienced—"the sanctity of the script." This problem occurs when a writer relies unquestioningly on what is in print, accepting it at face value. But, as the opening scenarios show, sources, for various reasons, are not always accurate. In addition, as you go from source to source, you find that different writers—because they have different purposes and different audiences—focus on different parts of the same story. Thus, action will be important to one reporter, but the names of the people involved are the focus of another. From the first reporter, you may discover many details about what happened, but not much information about who did what; from the second reporter, you find out much more about who was involved, but not very much detail about the events.

Another problem you often run into with sources concerns the nature of a "fact" itself. You might think that facts and evidence exist independently, but that is not exactly true. The object under consideration—such as a tree—usually exists independently. But any "facts," descriptions, or details about that object—the tree is tall, the bark is rough, the color of the leaves is beautiful—are products of the human mind. The human mind does not receive information about an object in a direct manner. Rather, received information is modified by what communication specialists call *noise*, which is any type of interference that causes a person to perceive information differently than what it literally is.

There are different kinds of noise. One kind of noise occurs because humans simultaneously perceive objects through more than one sense: as we observe, we also hear, touch, and possibly even taste or smell. Associations are another kind of noise. Associations can come from memory; sensory perceptions; what our parents, teachers, or other acquaintances have told us; or from what we have read. Our minds are not merely computers that store data and then spit it back out exactly as it came in: exact recall is difficult without the information being modified by the pizza we ate last night, or by our emotional state after being dumped by a sweetheart, or by our intense fear of snakes caused by a childhood trauma. Even "direct observation" is a form of short-term memory subject to all the influences that shape the information we "observe." Therefore, as a researcher, you should not only validate the evidence you find in your sources but also consider the noise that might have influenced the author of the source.

When you first begin to work with sources, you will discover many discrepancies among sources. So, you consult more sources. But then you begin to notice that the details of a story or event are not duplicated exactly from source to source. At this point in your research process, you need to validate the accuracy and reliability of your sources in order to determine which sources you will depend on.

EXERCISE 6–1

The *Letters to the Editor* section of many magazines includes letters from readers who "correct" a writer on some point of fact. Look in three recent issues of a single publication for letters to the editor that correct writers. Write a brief paper (one to two pages) that describes the incorrect facts and what you think caused the writer to include the incorrect fact.

TECHNIQUES: VALIDATING YOUR EVIDENCE

The first step in obtaining the most valid evidence is simply to consult a wide variety of sources: primary sources and secondary sources in both print and electronic media. If you consult only one or two sources, then you will have to rely on just those authors for the "factual" data, for the points of view, and for their inferences; however, the chances are not good that the first one or two authors you find will give you all the information you will need. If you consult more sources, you will find more variations in the "facts," more variations in points of view, and wider variances in the inferences drawn from the data or evidence.

Are you beginning to worry that finding accurate and reliable evidence is an impossible task? Don't. Keep in mind that you are not necessarily trying to find one set of evidence upon which everyone agrees. Remember, too, that validating many different pieces of evidence will give you the best evidence from which to derive meaning.

As you read your sources, you will soon see that "facts" are not always "factual" because facts often depend on an individual furnishing the data; therefore, in many walks of life, a single source is not sufficient to establish what is a "fact." Lawyers, judges, and officers of the law know the frailty of facts all too well, so they seek a parade of witnesses, not just a single witness, to corroborate the facts of a case.

Consult a Variety of Sources

Just as you will need to use a considerable number of sources to verify the reliability of the information, you will also need to make sure that relying on one type of source does not skew your information. One way to begin validating your evidence is to look at sources written by authors from different professions and aimed at different audiences. A second way to begin the process of validation is to look at sources from a variety of media: print, video, electronic, and so forth. If you follow these two principles as you do research, you will be able to see the evidence from a variety of perspectives. The more ways you can look at your evidence, the easier the validation process will be.

Recently, one of the authors of this book assigned a paper in which students were to look for a variety of sources on their research topics. One student, whose topic was how AIDS was being reported in the media, found only two sources, an article from *Time* and a series of articles from the professional medical journal *The Lancet*. Because he limited himself to only these two sources, the student did not have enough evidence to fully discuss his topic. Instead, he could write only one paragraph on how these two sources reported the topic of AIDS, so he had to fill the rest of the paper with information not related to his topic at all. Because the student did not consult a *wide* variety of sources, he did not do very well on the assignment.

The best research strategy uses a combination of secondary resources: print, audio and video media (if available), and electronic. The key word here is *combination*. A combination of resources helps you avoid the limitations of any one type of source and gives you the advantages of all. Relying on only one type of source may save you time, but it short-changes you in terms of perspective and fullness of information. Remember the frustrated teacher whose students wanted to know how many sources were required? Teachers are also frustrated by researchers who look at one of every kind of source and figure that all the bases are covered because those researchers are still thinking, "How many sources do I need?" rather than, *"As many as it takes!"*

Keep a Reflective Journal

In addition to reading your sources critically, you also need to record your critical responses. You should do this immediately, too, before you forget what you were thinking. A reflective journal helps you record this information.

When you read your sources, you are not the receptacle in a one-way stream of information. Rather, you should engage the source in a kind of discussion: ask it questions, reply to its statements, restate what it says. This kind of active reading not only leads you directly to the process of validation, but it also starts you on the road to owning your evidence. No longer are you simply accepting what somebody else says. Now you are taking your source for a "test drive" to see if you want to "buy" it.

Try to make the notes in your journal open-ended, leading to further questions, further connections, further points of view, further follow-up responses. Writing as if you were sending a telegram (in abbreviated words and phrases) will not accomplish the intent of the reflective journal. "Reflection" derives from the Latin *reflexio*, literally meaning "to bend back": you want to bend the information around your own ideas and back onto itself. This process involves turning matters over in your own mind and spending time with the issues or information you encounter in your reading.

A reflective journal has four columns. The first, labeled "Source," identifies the source with full bibliographic information—you'll need this information later in the project, and it's better to get it now than to have to find it later. The second column, labeled "Category/Topics," includes quotations, summaries, and paraphrases of your source (with the page number). In the third column, "Interactions/Questions," you record your reactions to the evidence and ask questions about it. In the last column, "Connections/ Answers," you ask follow-up questions, answer the questions you asked in the third column, make connections between sources, and reflect on the source and its evidence.

Table 6–1 is an excerpt from a reflective journal to give you an idea of how to actively engage your sources in a critical dialogue. Mary Stone, the author of this journal, is researching euthanasia and medical technology.

Reflective Journal, Mary Stone

TABLE 6–1

Source	Category/ Topic	Interactions/ Questions	Connections/ Answers
Elina Hemminski, Paivi Santalahti, Pekka Louhiala, "Ethical Conflicts in Regulating the Start Of Life," Jan/Feb 1998 Vol. 11 No. 1 Intensive Care p. 42	Technology has expanded possibilities in regulating life + death with ethical + social issues raised. In elderly patients, question of heroic treatment, lengthening of life + euthanasia are formulated uniformly even though THEY ARE LARGELY UNRESOLVED. P 42	What does this statement mean? Treatment + euthanasia are formulated evenly but are unresolved? Do we apply measures without knowing the end result? Isn't this backwards? Shouldn't we determine the ethical first? p. 42	
Ethical Conflicts p. 44 In the author's note, this article is a reprint from Perspectives in Biology in Medicine The Univ. of Chicago Press. Louhiala is from the Univ. of Helsinki, Finland	(1) They suggest using common principles in different interventions (2) Classify the intervention by the ethical principle on which it is based (3) ACKNOWL-EDGE the ethical principles with which they are in conflict. If the ethical grounds of the different forms of	Seek to organize interventions /or lack of/ into categories with the ethical principles for each. When they are in conflict, acknowledge it and discuss openly. Through a logical approach combined with ethics, open forums might bring new norms + practices	

Continued

TABLE 6-1 *continued*

Source	Category/ Topic	Interactions/ Questions	Connections/ Answers
	regulation were openly discussed, the discussion might lead to better means of formulating societal norms + practices + help people personally confronting the situation p. 44	which could be shared with patients in families having to make decisions. p.44	
American Thoracic Society "Quality of Life Resource" pub. American Lung Association 1999 pp. 1-3	Flanagan has a typical taxonomy which puts 15 areas of life quality under 5 domains. Health Status, Health Perceptions 1. Some ill people, think of themselves as healthy. Other healthy people, consider themselves ill. Functional Status "...individual's ability to perform normal daily activities required to meet basic needs, fulfill usual roles, and maintain health and well-being." P. 2	How is it defined? And...What are the 5? Are they necessary to this paper? How does health affect quality of life? Can we possibly consider people on mechanical ventilators to meet this definition of functional status and quality of life? If not, is it any of our business?	Taxonomy—science or techniques of classification No, focus on the first domain. Maybe if society is bearing the additional cost
American College of Chest Physicians Chest, May 1998; "Ethical Issues Consensus Statement" p. 1	Informed Decision Making + Advance Directives 1st technical ability makes the question: should this be done instead of can this done? 2. Patient + family should have a major role in decision making + understand their health-care rights.	Why does this group of physicians feel strongly enough about the issue to publish their ethical issues statement?	Anesthesiologists also have their own. I think that specific groups that deal daily with issues have a better handle on the ramifications. They don't hide from it + I think that they are under scrutiny from the public.

TABLE 6-1 *continued*			
Source	**Category/ Topic**	**Interactions/ Questions**	**Connections/ Answers**
	3. Patients should understand A. Medical conditions and prognosis B. Options for care C. Plan of care advised by the physician + multidisciplinary team. D. Provide benefits + risks + <u>BURDENS</u> of long-term mechanical ventilation. E. Patients with COPD, CF, ALS + kyphoscoliosis should DISCUSS the <u>potential</u> need for mech. ventil. with an experienced physician (read pulmonologist) <u>PRIOR</u> to initiation of vent. assistance.		
	Informed patient's wishes about advance directives of invasive + noninvasive vent. should be known by staff. Some because of misinformation might not choose it, while others strongly opposed find themselves on it as a result of emergency +critical care.		
	Surveys show many patients with ALS, even with severe physical limitations,		

TABLE 6-1   *continued*

Source	Category/Topic	Interactions/Questions	Connections/Answers
	rate this q. of life as satisfactory + would choose vent. again.		
	ALS patients who can't be weaned from invasive mech. vent. feel quality of life is satisfy. Even in situations appearing inappropriate + burdensome. Many patients who decline mech. vent. will try NIV	What is noninvasive ventilation?	
ICU area Registered Respiratory Therapist Questioned June 25, 1999 Local Hospital	<u>Patient wants expressed</u> 1. CPR? 2. Intubation + Reintubation 3. Limits of care/ aggressiveness of care Discuss + Record Identify Surrogate dec. maker in case they can't. Use of a legal Durable Power of Attorney is encouraged. Patients <u>CANNOT</u> legally be required to identify advance directives or a surrogate decision maker	How long a trial period? Several days usually shows if it will work. Why is NIV better?	Answer Continuous Positive Airway Pressure or Bilevel Positive Airway Pressure CPAP done with a mask blowing into the airway. No need for intubation or tracheostomy BIPAP 2 set pressures (epop which is end positive airway pr. + ipop which is inspired airway pressure. No need for intub or trach
			CPAP
			BIPAP

EXERCISE 6-2

Set up and begin to fill in your own reflective journal. Divide your journal into the four columns described previously. As you read each source, put the full bibliographic citation in the first column. Then, put information from the source in the second column, being sure to include the page number. Use the third and fourth columns to reflect on the source. Remember that you are trying to interact with your source, to engage it in a kind of discussion about its information.

Compare the Evidence in Your Sources

To start validating your evidence, use your reflective journal to discover and explore the following aspects:

- Discrepancies in "factual" data
- Omissions of specific detail
- False or misleading statements
- Opposing views
- Lack of confirming evidence

Discrepancies in the "factual" data

For instance, Tobi Raney, one of the student researchers we introduced in Chapter 2, found that education and psychology specialists use approximately 30 different definitions of the term self-esteem. She needed to validate these definitions to determine which she should use in her researched writing.

Omissions of specific detail

Another student was validating the evidence about Mark McGwire's record-setting baseball season of 1998. She found three articles that suggest that McGwire's relationship with his ex-wife indicates his "wonderful personality"; she also notes that only one of the articles tells the reader that McGwire's ex-wife is named Kathy. What details a writer includes or excludes will help you find the source's focus. The writer who included Kathy's name focuses on her as a more important part of the story than do the other writers.

False or misleading statements

Some sources state that Rosa Parks had no prior involvement in civil rights activities. Had the reporters done their homework, however, they would have discovered that she had attended a civil rights training camp at Monteagle, Tennessee, and that she had a history of civil disobedience with the same bus driver who had her arrested for refusing to give up her seat.

Opposing views

Opposing views are important issues in validation. One of the authors' students discovered that there were different perspectives on the relationship between science and religion: some authorities, such as the Center for Theology and the Natural Sciences, see science and religion in a "continuously emerging" relationship, whereas others see the two "locked in mortal combat." Sometimes, techniques such as confirming evidence can validate one side or the other of such opposition. Other times, the opposition cannot be resolved and will have to be presented as ambivalent evidence.

Lack of confirming evidence

A research rule of thumb states that primary sources are generally more reliable than secondary sources. But, as the Vanilla Ice example at the beginning of the chapter shows, even primary sources can sometimes be unreliable. In these cases, you want to do what lawyers and police officers do: corroborate your evidence. If you find that two or more sources report the same information, you can be more certain that the information is more accurate than information found only in one source.

The student researching Mark McGwire acknowledges this when discussing contradictory views of Roger Maris:

> My problem with the contradictions was that they were based on the memory of one young boy excited about baseball. There was a lack of real evidence to support the views. This caused me to realize another point: the fact that so many people were voicing their opinions in the other direction. One has to decide whether to believe them or one boy's experience.

You may recall from Chapter 3 that creating meaning—or interpreting facts—often results in views that are quite opposite from each other. Thus, when you consult different sources you will often find different interpretations, leaving you with the question of which is "correct." The answer is that perhaps none is; however, validating your evidence puts you in a position to create meaning from the most reliable and accurate information.

EXERCISE 6-3

Examine the information you have included in your reflective journal. Compare the evidence and identify discrepancies, omissions, inaccuracies, opposing views, and unconfirmed evidence. For each occurrence, describe how you plan to validate the evidence in a sentence or two.

TECHNIQUES: WRITING THE VALIDATION PAPER

At this point, you should have completed an inventory of your interests, finished a proposal for your research project, gone to the library, gotten on the Internet, and built a bibliography of possible sources. You should have read the sources in your bibliography and analyzed the evidence you found in a reflective journal.

Now, you are ready to write the validation paper. In the validation paper, you discuss the credibility and reliability of your sources and attempt to validate the information that you find.

You should, of course, employ the usual techniques of effective writing that were reviewed in the first chapter. Here is how to adapt the general principles of good writing to the validation paper assignment.

Limit the Scope of the Topic

You will probably have limited your topic somewhat when you wrote your research proposal. For instance, Tobi Raney limited the topic of her researched writing project from "self-esteem" to "the self-esteem of adolescent and young adult females in popular high school and college sports." But this limited topic is still too broad for the validation paper assignment. So Tobi focused her validation paper on a fundamental piece of information for her project: the definition of self-esteem.

For the validation paper, you should also focus on only a part of your final researched writing project. Look at the information in your sources. Is there an important idea that you need to validate? Is there a particular piece of information that is reported very differently by your sources? Is there a particular point of contention that your sources disagree about? The answers to these questions will help you identify a limited topic for your validation paper.

Limit the Focus of the Topic

Chapter 1 discussed how limiting the focus of your topic leads you directly into your essay's thesis. This discussion mentioned several traps that writers fall into when they create their thesis statements. Here is what these traps might look like in a validation paper:

- **The "garbage can" thesis:** *There are many sources on my topic and they all agree on some points while disagreeing on many others.* This thesis allows the writer to pretty much say whatever he or she wants in the body of the essay, but it doesn't really provide the reader with any useful information. The garbage can thesis can be plugged into virtually any validation paper and work. Make sure your thesis is specifically focused on your topic and expresses the results of your research in concrete terms.
- **The "vehicle reminder" thesis:** *In this paper, I will corroborate the evidence by comparing the sources I have read.* The problem with this thesis is that the writer is simply telling the readers what he or she will do in the essay, rather than showing them the validation essay's main idea. In fact, all the writer has told the reader is that he or she is going to do what the assignment says should be done, which means the writer has told the reader absolutely nothing of value. Make sure that your thesis gives your readers a clear picture of the main idea of your validation paper by showing them your topic and your claim.
- **The "clothesline" thesis:** *When corroborating my evidence, I found that my sources presented different facts, omitted some facts, made inaccurate statements, and presented different interpretations of the evidence.* This thesis is slightly better than the vehicle reminder thesis, although the

clothesline thesis is still telling much more than it is showing. A simple list of the essay's topics gives the reader some indication of what the paper will discuss. But the topics list information the reader already knows, if he or she is familiar with the techniques of validation. A better approach here would be to present a version of that list while focusing on the specific points of validation: "It is difficult to get a clear picture of this issue because the sources contradict each other on who was involved and the order of events and give four different causes for the events themselves."

At this point, you might be thinking, "I know how to recognize ineffective thesis statements, but how can I recognize an effective thesis statement?" In general, an effective thesis presents the final, limited topic and the claim that shows the writer's original approach to the topic. The student essays at the end of this chapter show you some examples; here is Julie McDowell's thesis: "At this time, the issue over the safety of aspartame appears to be far from being settled because no definite evidence supports one side or the other." Julie clearly presents her limited topic—the safety of aspartame—and her original understanding of the topic—that both sides of the controversy lack definite support.

Select Either the Inductive or Deductive Scheme

In a *deductive* paper, you present your thesis first and then your supporting evidence. In other words, the evidence "leads away" from the thesis (deduction comes from the Latin *de* and *ducere*, meaning to lead away from). Conversely, in an *inductive* paper, you present your supporting evidence first and "lead into" your thesis by analyzing and synthesizing the evidence ("induction" comes from the Latin *in* and *ducere*, meaning to "lead into"). Either of these formats will work for a validation paper: you choose the format of your paper, and you make your choice based on your purpose as a writer.

Because validation is essentially a discovery activity, you could structure your paper to reflect your process of uncovering the "facts" of your topic. You would be taking an inductive approach, not presenting your thesis until the end of the paper. Julie McDowell chose to follow this structure. On the other hand, if you have gathered information objectively, and you find that the material you have gathered clearly lends itself to a certain point of view, then you may feel secure enough to present that point of view as the thesis in the introduction. This approach would give your paper a deductive structure. Tobi Raney decided to use this structure.

Don't, however, make this decision while you are still researching—wait until you have gathered and analyzed all of your information. Once you have all of the information at hand, you will be able to choose the most effective format for your essay.

Determine the Most Effective Arrangement

Form follows function: in other words, what goes into your validation paper will determine how your paper should be arranged. In the validation paper, you will be looking at multiple sources to determine their consistencies and inconsistencies, which suggests that *comparison and contrast* would be an effective pattern. But the essay as a whole will probably need to be arranged according to a different principle.

How you arrange the whole essay should be based on how you have focused and limited your topic. For example, Julie McDowell uses an *ascending* arrangement, going from the least important evidence (the chemical composition of aspartame) to the most important (the effects of aspartame on the human body). In their article analyzing U.S. journalists' reporting of the nuclear power plant disaster at Chernobyl, William A. Dorman and Daniel Hirsch approach their analysis *conceptually,* looking at the various ways the event was presented to American readers. You may want to review the section in Chapter 1 on arranging an essay. Choose an arrangement that makes sense for your limited, focused topic and the information in your essay.

Use Formal Citation of Sources

Every time you write with sources, you must cite those sources to avoid plagiarism. Chapter 5 showed you briefly how to cite sources in both MLA and APA style; you may want to review those sections. If you need further information about citation, look in Chapter 10 for MLA style and Chapter 11 for APA style. Your instructor will let you know which style you should use.

EXERCISE 6–4

Below are some thesis statements you might find in a validation paper. Referring to the information presented in this section and in Chapter 1, determine whether the thesis statement is an effective, a garbage can, a vehicle reminder, or a clothesline thesis. If the thesis is not effective, then suggest revisions that you believe would improve its effectiveness.

1. Available evidence on the destruction of the rainforest is in general agreement, although some discrepancies can be found.
2. It is clear that the medical community feels that too much cholesterol is unhealthy, although doctors do not agree on how much is too much.
3. Carbon monoxide pollution can be reduced through greater use of public transportation, development of alternative fuel sources, legal limits on driving, financial assistance to carpoolers, or outlawing personally owned vehicles.
4. Many educators insist that college athletics pose several problems, but coaches, athletes, and athletic directors see only the benefits of athletic programs; clearly, these sources are limited by their bias.
5. In the following essay, I will show the disagreement in my sources about the causes of urban congestion, and then I will show how the sources all suggest different solutions to the problem.

VALIDATING YOUR EVIDENCE: PROFESSIONAL WRITING

The following pair of articles about the Chernobyl nuclear disaster appeared in the August/September 1986 issue of *Bulletin of Atomic Scientists*. The two articles show different approaches to validating evidence.

In the first article, "A Chronology of Soviet Media Coverage," Alexander Amerisov presents reportage from various Soviet news sources (radio, television, newspapers). By simply listing the coverage over 15 days, Amerisov shows why researchers need to look at many sources from a varied time span to get a clear and reliable perspective on an issue.

In the second article, "The U.S. Media's Slant," William A. Dorman and Daniel Hirsch validate the information U.S. journalists reported about the event. Their results show what happens when researchers do not validate their evidence.

A Chronology of Soviet Media Coverage

compiled by Alexander Amerisov

How much did Soviet citizens learn about Chernobyl from the Soviet media, and when? Following is a chronology of key items about the disaster primarily as reported in the government daily *Izvestiya* and the party newspapers *Pravda* and *Pravda Ukrainy*, including as well some radio and television reports from the first few days after the accident. This timetable spans a 15-day period from the first accounts of the accident, more than 48 hours after it took place, to newspaper accounts of General Secretary Gorbachev's May 14 [1986] television appearance in which he proclaimed, "the worst is over." For about the first week, almost all newspaper information about the accident could be found only in the foreign news sections.

April 28. At 8:00 p.m. Moscow time, two days after the explosion, Radio Moscow broadcasts TASS's statement that an accident occurred at the Chernobyl Nuclear Power Station: "Measures are being taken to eliminate consequences of the accident. Aid is being given to those affected. A government commission has been set up." One hour later the broadcast is repeated in English for listeners abroad.

Continued

April 29. The sixth item on the main television evening news program, *Vremya*, says that two people died during the accident, a portion of the reactor building was destroyed, and residents of Pripyat and three nearby towns were evacuated.

April 30. TASS carries a government statement denying Western reports of mass casualties. The statement repeats the earlier assertion that only two people died during the accident, adding that 197 have been hospitalized and levels of radiation are decreasing.

May 1. May Day parades and demonstrations nationwide. Happy people, smiling faces. A government statement reported by *Vremya* says the clean-up continues and radiation levels are dropping rapidly; 18 are injured and in serious condition; there are no foreigners among those affected; and information on the accident has been provided to ambassadors of Great Britain, Finland, the Netherlands, Austria, and France.

May 2. Newspapers provide extensive coverage of the previous day's celebrations. Radio Kiev reports on angler fishing in the Dnieper River.

May 3. Radio Moscow says that the day before a government commission headed by the prime minister visited "population centers where [commission members] met working people temporarily evacuated from the area of the nuclear power station."

May 4. The first film footage of the nuclear power station, shot from a helicopter, is shown on *Vremya*. The commentator says the film disproves Western reports of massive destruction.

May 5. A government report says an embankment is being constructed on the Pripyat River to prevent it from being contaminated. Television reports that vegetables and fruits from the Ukraine are being checked for contamination, and evacuees are being given temporary jobs in nearby collective farms outside an established 30-kilometer zone.

May 6. The first extensive report on the situation appears in *Pravda*. The article says Pripyat is empty. Emergency crews are staffing the three other Chernobyl reactors. It also describes the first few hours after the

Continued

accident: Responding to sirens, two fire commands arrive on scene to find the machine room on fire. The firemen's boots stick to melted asphalt, and they find it difficult to breathe. [Later, it was reported that many of these first fire-fighters died.] The Soviet press makes its first accusations that the West is "enjoying somebody else's misfortunes." [This line will be taken up by the Soviet media to condemn all criticism of government handling of the situation.] The *Pravda* article also claims that immediately after the accident the weather station operator at Chernobyl sent a telegram about it to Ukraine's Weather Central. At the same time, evacuation began in Pripyat. Within four hours, the town was evacuated by teams of all-volunteer drivers. The evacuees were received warmly by people in neighboring villages.

TASS reports that the American Dr. Robert Gale has arrived in Moscow and director general of the International Energy Agency, Hans Blix, is on his way. It says that Western reports are politically motivated. *Pravda Ukrainy* quotes a newly released report by Ralph Nader's Public Citizen organization citing approximately 20,000 accidents at nuclear power stations in the United States.

May 7. TASS reports that many Kiev residents are trying to leave the city and that additional trains and flights have been scheduled. The media drops its insistence that everything is under control. *Sovetskaya Rossiya* quotes the Kiev regional party secretary Gregory Revenko, who describes the situation as "alarming." He emphasizes that "it is too early to say everything is back to normal." *Pravda* reports on a May 6 news conference in the Ministry of Foreign Affairs, where it was announced that radiation levels in the Ukraine and nearby Moldavia and Belorussia have not exceeded international safety levels and that the injured were brought to Moscow on April 27 and are receiving the treatment they need. The time of the explosion is given as 1:23 a.m., April 26. Along with the emphasis on the struggle to fight the fire, *Pravda Ukrainy* portrays the nuclear accident as a natural calamity, and, in *Izvestiya*, TASS says the

Continued

accident was the result of "highly improbable and consequently unforeseeable failures."

May 8. In an interview with *Izvestiya,* academician Yevgeny Velikhov, vice president of the Soviet Academy of Sciences and the chief scientist sent to Chernobyl, says the disaster is "without precedent." Numerous articles describe life and work in the "special zone."

May 9. Day of Victory Over Nazi Germany, a national holiday. *Pravda* publishes a detailed report of Blix's news conference the day before, where he said the situation in Kiev is normal. *Pravda Ukrainy,* for the first time in the Soviet press, gives the public recommendations on how to protect themselves from the effects of radiation.

A large article in *Pravda* by G. Arbatov calls Chernobyl the 152d major nuclear accident worldwide, "albeit a fairly serious one." The article admits for the first time in the Soviet press that "radiation levels rose not only in the USSR but in other countries, although not dangerously enough to affect health." The article also thanks thousands of foreigners for offering to be bone-marrow donors, while rejecting the thesis that the Soviet Union had not "instantly" informed the governments of other countries about the accident. Arbatov reminds readers of the *Challenger* and Bhopal disasters, acid rain, and worldwide delays in reporting accidents; he says Western reporting on Chernobyl will backfire by increasing the popular outcry against nuclear power in the West.

An article in *Izvestiya* says "thousands of street vendors of ice cream, doughnuts, and cool drinks" have gone indoors in Kiev. Fruits and vegetables are being checked twice, although plenty of meat and greens are available. The authors call Chernobyl "an expensive lesson."

A *Pravda* article says some families got separated during evacuation. The article admits: "Maybe in the beginning, the Kievans had not received full information on the things that were taking place. Hence the foundation for various rumors, helped along by foreign radio stations." Better information in the past few days, the article continues, "helps people to better imagine what

Continued

actually happened and therefore more effectively fight the consequences."
Again it is stated that radiation levels in Kiev pose no health hazards.

Pravda Ukrainy runs an interview with the minister of health of the
Ukraine. He says a few days ago he appeared on local television to tell
Kievans how to cope with radioactivity: "The number one enemy is dust."

May 10. Newspapers carry fuller reports of Blix's May 8 press
conference. They say that at the end of the 30-kilometer restricted zone
the radiation level was 10-15 millirem at the time of the accident. By May
8, the level has dropped to 0.15 millirem. *Pravda* publishes a report on
the May 8 Politburo meeting. One-third of the report is devoted to
Chernobyl, but the accident follows other topics, such as capital
investment in Leningrad. TASS reports on the bans by some Western
countries on food and commodity imports from some parts of Eastern
Europe and the Soviet Union.

May 11. *Izvestiya* says 150 people continue working on the other
three reactors to keep them cool: "Only male volunteers are working at
the station." *Pravda Ukrainy* quotes the chief doctor at the station as
saying, "I can say with all certainty that there is absolutely no danger for
those who are fighting the consequences of the accident." Another article
in the same paper says that a government commission is working in
Chernobyl. [This is supposed to indicate that the area is safe. On July 4,
TASS will report that the government official in charge of the cleanup,
Boris Shcherbina, was replaced. It is rumored that he was hospitalized
with massive doses of radiation.]

May 12. An *Izvestiya* article reports that transport is being checked
on all roads leading to Kiev. It also reports on evacuees: more than 9,200
people have been evacuated so far. Two thousand people, mostly mothers
with children, have been given free passes to sanatoriums. The evacuees
are divided by occupation and placed in houses with people of similar
backgrounds. The article says many are not psychologically prepared to
live in a new place for a long time.

Continued

In Kiev City Hall, experts announce the levels of radiation and the amount of drinking water [was drinking water rationed?] every morning at 9:00 a.m. One expert predicts normal radiation levels by May 19. The *Izvestiya* article observes that what is normal has been redefined. Instead of 0.5 rem per year, the standard for those who live near factories where radioactive chemicals are produced, Kiev was measured by a standard of 10 rem per year applicable in a crisis situation. To get this dosage, residents must experience the current level of 0.35 or 0.4 millirem per hour for five years [under the old norms the exposure would only have to continue for two months].

The same article also quotes Velikhov, who said on May 10: "The possibility of catastrophe which was written about so much in the Western press can now be excluded. Indeed, until today, theoretically the possibility of catastrophe existed—a large quantity of fuel and reactor graphite was in a red-hot state. It is no longer so."

Pravda says two Communist Party officials were dismissed from their jobs, and a third was reprimanded, for callous attitudes toward their evacuees.

May 13. *Pravda* says the "battle continues." It says that 10 days after the accident, the situation still could possibly have worsened. *Pravda* reports it is receiving tens of thousands of telegrams from individuals offering to volunteer their aid. Factories supplying equipment for the cleanup are working day and night. Employees at the Ukrainian Chmelnitsky Nuclear Power Station decided to turn over all of the 144 apartments prepared for them to newly arrived evacuees.

May 14. *Izvestiya* explains a cancelled soccer game in Kiev with the need to prepare for the world championship games in Mexico. Gorbachev makes a televised address on *Vremya*.

May 15. All papers carry Gorbachev's speech, insisting there was no cover-up: "The moment we received reliable data we gave it to the Soviet people and sent it abroad."

READING QUESTIONS

1. *Alexander Amerisov, the author of this article, is the editor of the* Soviet-American Review. *The article itself appeared in the August/September 1986 issue of the* Bulletin of the Atomic Scientists. *Do you feel that this article is a credible and reliable source? Why or why not?*

2. *Apply the list of evidentiary characteristics in the section "Compare the Evidence in Your Sources" to this article. What discrepancies among facts show up in different sources at different times? What omissions or false statements are present? What contradictory statements can you find? Is any evidence corroborated? How and by whom? What different interpretations of the evidence are offered?*

3. *Examine the credibility of the sources in this article—Izvestiya, Pravda, and Pravda Ukrainy. Are these sources reliable? Why or why not? How does their reliability, or lack thereof, affect your attitude toward their evidence?*

The U.S. Media's Slant

William A. Dorman and Daniel Hirsch

In international news, first impressions usually are lasting ones. The impressions about the Chernobyl tragedy, given currency by the news media and most likely to linger for many Americans, are that a similar nuclear disaster could not happen in the United States and that the affair was further evidence that the Kremlin cannot be trusted to carry out a nuclear arms agreement. Yet a sampling of early crisis coverage poses the troubling possibility that these impressions were the product of a Cold War journalistic rush to judgment rather than the result of sound news practice in a situation that demanded more than the usual prudence.

Of course, the Soviets' failure to promptly warn neighboring countries invited suspicion. And clearly the media's job was severely complicated by a news vacuum created by the Soviet Union's grudging release of only meager information after the initial announcement, although it is still not clear how much the Soviets knew early on or when they knew it. An official at a Nuclear Regulatory Commission (NRC) briefing on May 8 concluded: "It is most likely that the Soviets do not yet know with certainty

Continued

the actual sequence of events. This is similar to our knowledge of the sequence of events at TMI-2 within the first week or so after the accident."

Still, at least for those concerned about a better understanding of both the Soviet Union and nuclear matters, the Kremlin's behavior cannot justify the news media's rush to fill the information void with rumor and an uncritical presentation of the views of the Reagan Administration and the nuclear power industry.

The most disturbing aspect of U.S. press coverage was the willingness to give currency to speculation about casualties and thereby to charge, implicitly or explicitly, that the Soviets were trying to cover up the true death toll. An egregious example of such irresponsibility was a *New York Post* front page, whose headlines screamed, "MASS GRAVE—15,000 Reported Buried in Nuke Disposal Site," a report that relied on nothing more than a Ukrainian weekly in New Jersey.[1]

Perhaps an even more serious lapse, given its prestige and number of clients throughout the United States, was United Press International's handling of the death toll. Its report of 2,000 deaths received wide play, and the wire service did not retract its story until almost a month later. The report was based wholly on the word of a single unidentified source in Kiev whose story could not be confirmed.

Several major news organizations—including the *New York Times*, the *Washington Post*, the Associated Press, and the three television networks—exercised varying degrees of caution in using the figure of 2,000 supposed deaths but used it nevertheless. It is doubtful that caveats about lack of confirmation counted for much in the superheated atmosphere. The Soviet announcement that two had been killed in the initial accident was all but dismissed by the news media.

U.S. government sources dominated the news. For instance, prominent play was given to Kenneth Adelman, director of the Arms Control and Disarmament Agency, who called the official Soviet statement regarding casualties "frankly preposterous," and Secretary of State

Continued

George Shultz, who said he would "bet $10" that the deaths were "far in excess" of the figures given by the Soviets. The press can be expected to report what prominent members of the Administration have to say, but journalists did not challenge these and other assertions about Chernobyl, nor were these officials pressed for hard evidence despite their obvious bias. Coverage gave little sign of a journalistic hunt for contrary views.

Ironically, the initial Soviet statements turned out to be largely correct on a number of significant concerns—for example, the number of casualties, the number of reactors on fire, and whether the fire had been contained—while those of the Reagan Administration, which were taken by journalists at face value, proved not to be. Yet elements of the national press were all too quick to echo the Administration's position that the whole affair demonstrated that negotiating arms control with the Soviets was senseless because they could not be trusted to tell the truth on nuclear matters. The *New York Times* intoned in a May 1 editorial: "Gorbachev cannot win confidence in his pledges to reduce nuclear weapons if he forfeits his neighbors' trust over the peaceful uses of nuclear energy." U.S. journalists frequently erased the distinctions between verifying nuclear weapons treaties, with all of the technical safeguards that such schemes have to provide, and the slow release of information by the Soviets about a totally unexpected explosion at a civilian nuclear plant—a situation for which no treaty obligations currently exist.

The U.S. nuclear industry seems to have made a major effort to use the press to distance itself from the Soviet accident, apparently in order to preserve deregulation gains achieved under the Reagan Administration. The *New York Times*, belatedly but to its credit, pointed out some three weeks after the accident: "Nuclear proponents and industry officials have tried to minimize Chernobyl's relevance to American power plant operation by contending that American units have better features." The article quoted a mailing from the Atomic Industrial Forum to reporters as flatly stating that Chernobyl had no containment structure, and cited

Continued

industry-sponsored advertisements claiming that many Soviet reactors—including those at Chernobyl—lack the steel and reinforced-concrete containment structures common to U.S. reactors.[2]

Similar views were advanced by spokespersons for the Electric Power Research Institute—Chernobyl "was not encased in a reinforced-concrete containment building, as is required of reactors in the United States" and therefore "there was nothing to stop" radioactivity escaping the plant—and the Edison Electric Institute: "We have not and will not have a Chernobyl-type plant accident here."[3]

At least during the early period of the crisis, there is evidence that the industry's efforts were successful. For instance, the theme pushed by the industry that allegedly backward Soviet technology was the sole explanation for the accident at Chernobyl was caught in the April 30 editorial judgment of the *New York Times*: "The accident may reveal more about the Soviet Union than the hazards of nuclear power. . . . Behind the Chernobyl setback may lie deeper faults of a weak technology and industrial base." While the editorial did carefully conclude with the observation that Americans are as vulnerable as Soviets to "technological disasters and human error," its overall tone and that of other mainstream coverage was markedly less humble.

The impression conveyed by the news media during the early stages of the accident was that Americans had little to fear from a Chernobyl-like disaster. Virtually absent in news columns as well as editorials was the perspective that the real lesson to be learned from Chernobyl was the fallibility of complex technology, not Soviet backwardness.

In particular, editorial writers seemed quick to accept the industry's contentions about the total lack of containment at Chernobyl. As early as April 30, the *Los Angeles Times* told readers: "Minimum safety standards . . . clearly have not been met in the Soviet Union, where most nuclear reactors—apparently including the ill-fated plant at Chernobyl—do not have containment structures of the sort that are almost universal outside

Continued

Russia." A May 2 editorial in the *San Jose Mercury News* echoed these views with the conclusion that "the U.S.S.R. simply has not built safe reactors." According to the *Mercury,* the Soviets "have been exposed as reckless with the atom."

The possibility that the plant had some form of containment should have been immediately obvious to reporters and editors. Both the *New York Times* and the *Los Angeles Times* reported the first day that, although older plants were often built without containment structures, the Soviets began adding them for newer nuclear plants in 1980, in the wake of the Three Mile Island accident.[4] Both papers furthermore reported that the four units at Chernobyl had been completed between 1977 and 1983. Unsure of which unit was involved or its construction date, the *New York Times* was careful to state that "it is not known" at which of the Chernobyl reactors the accident had occurred nor whether it had containment.

Such caution, however, appeared to evaporate the following day, even though by this time the Times was able to report that the accident had occurred at the newest of the four reactors at the facility, which went into operation in 1983, and therefore—at least based on what was reported the day before—presumably had some form of containment.[5] Rather than pursuing this line of inquiry, the media opted to repeat the no-containment theme advanced by U.S. nuclear power advocates. Nor was it pointed out that, even if Chernobyl had no containment, the failure or bypass of such structures remains one of the most troubling potential aspects of severe accidents in U.S. reactors.

American minds had probably long since been made up on the question of containment by the time the *New York Times* reported on May 19, three weeks after the first story on the accident, that the reactor which exploded had a large containment structure of heavy steel and concrete, and "that at least some of this containment structure was designed to withstand pressures similar to those in many American reactors." The

Continued

Times also reported that the stricken reactor "had more safety features and was closer to American designs than Western experts had assumed," and in fact "incorporated enough of the advanced safety features used in American reactors to raise questions . . . about the effectiveness of plant designs in the United States."

Why this information took so long to surface in the national press is puzzling. Much of the material in the *Times* story, for instance, was revealed at the May 8 NRC briefing in a room packed with reporters, 11 days before the *Times* or other major news organizations finally ran its story. And two days before that briefing, NRC Commissioner James Asselstine had testified at a House hearing that Chernobyl indeed did have containment and that it was built to withstand greater pressure than some U.S. containments. Yet his disclosure received only passing mention in paragraphs 12 and 13 in a *Wall Street Journal* article and barely surfaced elsewhere.[6]

In short, mainstream journalists first ignored the strong possibility apparent from day one of the crisis that Chernobyl might have containment, and then for whatever reasons continued to ignore the possibility even after NRC officials brought it to their attention. While uncertainty remains about the nature of containment at Chernobyl, it is clear that flat claims of "no containment" were overreaching.

Throughout the early days of the Chernobyl story, U.S. journalism seemed determined to make the disaster into a morality tale about U.S. and Soviet cultures. Over and over, the accident was linked to the nature of Soviet society, the absence of debate, and state control of the press. Editorialists and commentators adopted a self-congratulatory tone, implying that the virtues of U.S. democracy—in particular of a free press—made such a tragedy practically impossible in the United States. Journalists should have been alert to the possibility that they were being manipulated by those with a vested interest in portraying the Soviets in the worst possible light.

Continued

A number of news organizations eventually took a critical view of Chernobyl coverage, but the usual explanation for the media's questionable behavior during the crisis let journalists off the hook with little more than a mild reproach. According to *Newsweek:* "For all the frenzy, the press was just obeying a natural law: journalism abhors a vacuum."[7] Thus, Soviet secrecy was blamed for defective U.S. coverage of the Chernobyl accident.[8] While journalism does indeed abhor vacuums, such an explanation avoids the question of how vacuums are to be filled, which is not a matter of nature but rather of choice. These choices may have had as much to do with a reflexive instinct to believe the worst of the Soviets as with a journalistic rush to fill the void.

1. The *Post's* actions are recounted in "Did the Media Hype Chernobyl?" *Newsweek* (May 26, 1986), p. 31.

2. Stuart Diamond, "Chernobyl Design Found to Include New Safety Plans," *New York Times*, May 19, 1986.

3. Michael Benson, "Soviet Reactor to Contain Leak, Expert Says," *San Jose Mercury News*, April 29, 1986; Diamond, op. cit.

4. Lee Dye and Larry B. Stammer, "Moscow Rated Damaged Plant Among Safest," *Los Angeles Times*, April 29, 1986, p. 1; Theodore Shabad, "Development of Nuclear Power a Consistently High Soviet Priority," *New York Times*, April 29, 1986, p. A10.

5. Serge Schmemann, "Soviet, Reporting Atom Plant 'Disaster,' Seeks Help Abroad to Fight Reactor Fire," *New York Times*, April 30, 1986, p. 1.

6. John J. Fialka and Robert E. Taylor, "Soviets Say Confusion at Chernobyl Led to 36-Hour Delay in Evacuating People," *Wall Street Journal*, May 7, 1986. The Chernobyl containment features and their design pressures were described in briefing materials prepared for the NRC

Continued

commissioners by their staff in preparation for the congressional hearing. See Question and Answer C.4 in briefing paper dated May 5, 1986.

   7. "Did the Media Hype Chernobyl?"

   8. See, for example, Thomas B. Rosenstiels, "Soviet Society Blamed for Exaggerated American Reports on Chernobyl Disaster," *Los Angeles Times*, May 10, 1986, p. 21.

READING QUESTIONS

1. *The* Bulletin of the Atomic Scientists *gives the following information about the authors: "William A. Dorman is a professor of journalism at California State University, Sacramento, and a research affiliate of the Adlai E. Stevenson Program on Nuclear Policy at the University of California, Santa Cruz. Daniel Hirsch is director of the Program on Nuclear Policy at the University of California, Santa Cruz, and serves on a Nuclear Regulatory Commission advisory panel examining problems associated with the potential for containment failures in U.S. reactors during severe accidents." Based on this information, do you feel that this article is a credible source? Are the authors qualified experts in the field? Is the publication a credible journal?*

2. *Make a list of the sources the authors use in this essay. How many of the sources are primary sources and how many are secondary sources? Does their use of primary or secondary sources affect their credibility? For instance, many of the articles the authors discuss are editorials; how does this type of source affect their discussion of the "U.S. media"?*

3. *What information do the authors claim was mistakenly published by members of the U.S. media? What mistakes did the media make? Why did they make these mistakes?*

4. *Put yourself in the position of the U.S. media. What might you have done differently to avoid making the mistakes the authors discuss in this essay?*

EXERCISE 6–5

Use the Internet to research the chain of events in a recent news story of national importance (e.g., the Monica Lewinsky scandal, the Microsoft anti-trust hearings, the conflict in Kosovo, etc.). Use newspaper accounts as well as other Web pages. Many major newspapers can be easily located by going to a search engine such as Yahoo! and looking under "News and Media: Newspapers" or a similar heading. Construct a timeline like the one in Alexander Amerisov's article. Look for answers to these questions: When was information released? Did the information come from a credible source? Was conflicting information released? If so, when and by whom? What might account for the way information was released to the public?

VALIDATING YOUR EVIDENCE: STUDENT WRITING

Here are the validation papers from our student researchers. As you read these papers, you can see two important ideas. First, you can see how both Tobi and Julie limited the topics of their validation paper to a single, important idea within their researched writing topic. Second, you can see how the writers concentrate on what the sources say and how the sources present information, rather than arguing a point about their topic. The sources, rather than a point of contention, are the focus of the validation paper.

Defining Self-Esteem

Tobi Raney

It has become one of the most commonly used words in classrooms and workplaces, not to mention the countless references made to it by psychologists and counselors. It has been blamed for every negative epidemic from racism to teen pregnancy and credited for successes and accomplishments (Huebner B 10; King 69; Lapchick 14C). It even has its own National Council (Schenkman Kaplan 341). However, does anyone know what this popular term really means? It is referred to as self-esteem, but the implications of the word are as varied as the people who use it. The only way to limit the interpretation of self-esteem is to look at all the explanations of it and its many counterparts and to research the antecedents of self-esteem. The means by which a person achieves self-esteem are even more important than the vocabulary itself. The concept of self-esteem begins to take a more recognizable shape after discussing the development of the concept; however, even after outlining all of these aspects, the complex principle of self-esteem will probably never have a concrete definition.

The National Council of Self-esteem surveyed hundreds in the field of education and came up with 27 distinctly different explanations of self-esteem (Schenkman Kaplan 341). Psychologists, too, present different meanings for this word that has become more and more important to

---

Continued

modern society. The *Encyclopedic Dictionary of Psychology* calls self-esteem the "evaluation an individual makes of, and applies to himself" (Harré and Lamb 561). The *Encyclopedia of Human Behavior* echoes that explanation, but words it as "the evaluative dimension of self-knowledge, referring to how a person appraises himself or herself (Baumeister 83). Like these two similar versions, most definitions state that self-esteem is an evaluative term that results from self-appraisal, conscious or not (Coopersmith in King 69; Branden 103; Gergen and Coopersmith in Mau 83; Martens in Le Unes and Nation 181). Still others see it as the difference between the ideal self and the actual self (Brooks and Lawrence in King 69; Calhoun and Acocella in Le Unes and Nation 181).

Many authors agree that self-esteem has two interrelated aspects, personal efficacy and personal worth (Branden 104; Anderson 23; Corey 369). Others add the requirement that the individual must feel successful in order to complete his self-perception (Mau 83; Calhoun and Acocella in Le Unes and Nation 181; Schenkman Kaplan 342; Hoyle and Left 234). There are those who believe self-esteem is a multidimensional system. Several resources referred to Morris Rosenberg, a psychologist in the late 1970s (Norder-Pietrzak 11; Mau 84; Spreitzer 369). Rosenberg's Scale consists of 12 items used to measure self-esteem. He defined self-esteem as all the little things that relate and interact within one's total existence. Individuals place value on various aspects of their lives according to the priorities they set for themselves (Norder-Pietrzak 11). These "little things" can be placed in four major categories: emotional, social, physical, and mental (Mau 84; Norder-Pietrzak 12; Corey 370). Individuals assess themselves in these areas and gain self-esteem when they feel a sense of self-respect, self-confidence, and competence (Schenkman Kaplan 341; Corey 369; Mau 83).

Attempts to explain a confusing term involve more terminology, equally complex. One author found this explanation in one of his sources: definitions focused only on how people think and feel about themselves

Continued

cause misunderstanding between self-concept, self-centeredness, selfishness, conceit, and self-esteem. However, to sort through all the ideas regarding self-esteem, a basic concept of these related terms is necessary. Even the notion of "self" is debatable. The idea was introduced by American psychologist William James in 1890. He concluded that the self consisted of many different forms: social, spiritual, and material. On the other hand, all of these forms added together equaled one's self. Self-esteem is a combination of how one perceives himself and how he senses others see him (Tyler 7).

There is still a sea of terms that accompany "self" and contribute to misunderstandings of the term self-esteem. Self-concept is probably the term most similar to self-esteem. But, it too, has many interpretations. It has been called a "mental self-portrait" (Le Unes and Nation 181) and "the perception one has of oneself in terms of personal attributes and the various roles which are played or fulfilled by the individual" (King 69). This sounds similar to several of the definitions for self-esteem. The difference, though, is explained in an example found in *Self-Concept and Self-Esteem: A Clarification of Terms*. Individuals describing themselves as tall may feel happy or unhappy about being tall. Self-concept refers to the perception of tallness, whereas self-esteem refers to the feelings (happy or unhappy) about that perception (King 69).

Exploring similar components of self-esteem helps narrow the definition to "feelings" or "satisfaction with oneself," according to the evaluation of personal priorities. Delving into the origins of this self-esteem will further clarify what it is and how we can achieve it. While virtually all sources state that self-esteem is formed as a child (Corey 369; Harré and Lamb 561; Schenkman Kaplan 343; Mau 85), many disagree on whether it can be changed later in life or if we are stuck with our childhood perception of self.

Perhaps the most famous illustration of the antecedents of self-esteem is provided by Abraham Maslow. Maslow's hierarchy of needs explains

Continued

what one must have before healthy self-esteem can be developed. At the base of his pyramid are survival needs, followed closely by safety needs for security, stability, dependency, and protection. Then there is the essential need for love and affection (Corey 369; Le Unes and Nation 183). If this basic need is met, our esteem needs are tended to next. In her book, *Our Inner Conflicts,* Karen Horney contends that if children do not receive enough parental love, acceptance, and approval they develop a neurotic need for attention and affection. Their self-esteem needs are unfilled because their safety needs have not been met (Corey 369).

Is low self-esteem reversible? Are individuals locked into the self-esteem their parents allowed them to shape at an early age? A few think so. One source stated that studies show it is very difficult to change one's level of esteem after middle childhood (Harré and Lamb 561). Another source leaned more towards genetics, stating that some people will never be successful and others will be no matter what they experience in life (Kunde D1). Others argue that "a multifaceted self-esteem structure exists from an early age, and gradually becomes more complex with age" (Mau 85). Indeed, many sources agree that as an individual becomes older, more aspects of their life interact with and help define their self-esteem (Norder-Pietrzak 11; Corey 370). Approval of peers seems to weigh very heavily in adolescents' and even adults' self-evaluation (Donovitz 26; Mau 86; Schenkman Kaplan 341). In order to strike a healthy esteem balance, areas that an individual excels in must be advocated and value on areas of weakness must be reduced. However, if peers place strong merit on an area of someone's personal weakness, it is up to the individual to balance the feelings resulting (Mau 87).

After wading through definition after definition and trying to hack a path through the forest of terms and antecedents of self-esteem, we can reach a few conclusions. While all of the sources worded it differently, self-esteem is broadly defined as the way we feel about our personal qualities, as we have weighed them. Most references insist that self-esteem

Continued

is present at childhood and may not change drastically from its original state, but that it has the capability to adapt to each new life-situation. Basic needs must be met before an individual can shape his or her self-esteem. However, once these needs are met, self-esteem becomes a central component of our personalities, our behaviors, and our relationship with the world.

WORKS CITED

Anderson, Judy. "Confidence's Role in Winning." *Long Island Business News* 27 July 1998: 23A.

Baumeister, Roy F. "Self-esteem." *Encyclopedia of Human Behavior.* 1994 ed.

Branden, Nathaniel. *The Psychology of Self-esteem.* Los Angeles: Nash, 1969.

Corey, G. "Self-esteem." *Encyclopedia of Psychology.* 1994 ed.

Donovitz, Jean. "Comparison of Personalities of Eighth and Ninth Grade Female Athletes and Eighth and Ninth Grade Female Non-athletes." Thes. U. Of Texas, 1971.

Harré, Ron and Roger Lamb. "Self-esteem." *The Encyclopedic Dictionary of Psychology.* 1984 ed.

Hoyle, Rick H. and Stephen S. Left. "The Role of Parental Involvement in Youth Sport Participation and Performance." *Adolescence* Spring 1997: 234.

King, Keith A. "Self-concept and Self-esteem: A Clarification of Terms." *The Journal of School Health* Feb 1997: 69.

Kunde, Diana. "Women Say Sports Valuable to Future Business Careers." *Dallas Morning News* 15 Oct. 1997: D1.

Lapchick, Richard. "Participation Helps Keep Kids in School, Provide Life Skills." *USA Today* Apr 1996: 14C.

Continued

Le Unes, Arnold D. And Jack Nation. *Sport Psychology.* Chicago: Nelson-Hall, 1996.

Mau, Robert E. "Differences of Co-dependency and Self-esteem in College Age Male and Female Athletes and Non-athletes." Thes. Springfield College, 1995.

Norder-Pietrzak, Michelle Marie. "Perceived Body Image: Selected Lifestyle Practices and their Relationship to Physical Self-esteem." Thes. U. Of Wisconsin-La Crosse, 1993.

Schenkman Kaplan, Leslie. "Self-esteem is Not Our National Wonder Drug." *School Counselor* May 1995: 341-343.

Spreitzer, Elmer. "Does Participation in Interscholastic Athletics Affect Adult Development?" *Youth and Society*; March 1994: 369.

Tyler, Suzanne Jayne. "Differences in Social and Sport Self Perceptions Between Female Varsity Athletes and Class Participants." Thes. Pennsylvania State U, 1973.

READING QUESTIONS

1. *Tobi's paper follows a deductive structure. What kind of arrangement (for example, comparison and contrast) does the essay follow?*
2. *What two interrelated aspects do most authors agree self-esteem has?*
3. *What contribution does Abraham Maslow make to the definition of self-esteem?*
4. *Examine the list of works cited for this paper. Do you think Tobi has looked at a sufficient variety of sources, both in kind and in date? Why or why not?*

Too Much of a Sweet Thing?

Julie McDowell

While drinking a can of Diet Coke, I glance over the ingredient list. There, among all the other chemical names, I see a word that jumps out at me. Perhaps it is because of the asterisk next to it, or because I cannot figure out how it is pronounced. The name: aspartame, pronounced ah-spar`tam

Continued

(Taylor, 1988). So what is it that makes this ingredient any different from the others on the can? How about the many controversies it has been the subject of since its approval eighteen years ago? Every few years the topic of aspartame's safety seems to resurface and cause new allegations and consumer worry. The past five to ten years have shown numerous articles devoted to the topic. Now, the Internet has become a major battleground with many pro- and anti-aspartame Web sites, as well as a widely received e-mail earlier this year (Chase, 1999; Gorman, 1999). Whom should we believe?

Aspartame has a fairly simple composition, with its main components being aspartic acid, phenylalanine, and methanol (Appleton, 1996; "All," 1999; "Everything," 1999). Chemically, it is known as "the methyl ester of the dipeptide aspartyl-phenylalanine" (Stein, 1997, p. 1112); "N-L-a-aspartyl-L-phenylalanine" (Taylor, 1988, p. 155; Harte, Holdren, Schneider, & Shirley, 1991, p. 225); or "1-methyl N-1-a-aspartyl-1-phenylalanine" ("Title," 1999, n. pag.; Harte et al., 1991, p. 225). More simply aspartic acid and phenylalanine are non-essential and essential amino acids, respectively ("All," 1999; Leblang, 1990). According to NutraSweet corporation's Web site "All About NutraSweet," the manufacturing process, during which ingredients are combined by fermentation, is "a lot like making bakers' yeast" (1999, n. pag.).

All of this chemical jargon results in a low-calorie sweetener that is used by many dieters and diabetics. Although the calorie content of aspartame and table sugar is about the same (4 calories per gram), much less aspartame is needed to achieve the sweetness of a particular amount of sugar ("All," 1999; "FYI," 1998). Most sources consulted, including the FDA, state that aspartame is 200 times sweeter than sucrose (table sugar). However, a few were more precise, saying that it is 180 times sweeter ("FYI," 1998; Leblang, 1990).

Although the sources have only minute discrepancies pertaining to the chemical composition of aspartame, opinions vary widely about the effect

Continued

of the sweetener on the body once ingested. The Food and Drug Administration, along with the NutraSweet corporation and others, maintain that aspartame is simply broken down into its main components—aspartic acid, phenylalanine, and methanol—and then absorbed by the body like foods that are consumed everyday ("Everything," 1999; "All," 1999). Methanol especially has been the topic of much discussion. Some sources speak of methanol "toxicity" or poison. The Web site <http://www.aspartamekills.com> states methanol is further reduced to formaldehyde and formic acid, and accumulates in the body rather than being used ("Aspartame," 1999). Other sources counter that methanol is found in higher amounts in fruits and vegetables than it is in aspartame. For example, a *Time* article by Christine Gorman states that a glass of tomato juice contains about four times as much methanol as a soda sweetened with NutraSweet (1999).

In addition to methanol "toxicity" the anti-aspartame Web site claims that when heated above 86 degrees Fahrenheit, the methanol by-product becomes even more toxic ("Aspartame," 1999). However, the FDA approved in 1996 the use of aspartame in heated foods because a loss in sweetness due to chemical instability was the only consequence past this temperature ("Everything," 1999; Harte et al., 1991).

Though not common knowledge, there is an established acceptable daily intake, or ADI, for aspartame. This level is 50 milligrams per kilogram of body weight per day (Stein, 1997; "Everything," 1999). Paul J. Stein, writing in the *Journal of Chemical Education*, states that "surveys indicate that the 90th percentile of consumption is between 2 and 10 mg/kg/day" (1997, p. 1112). The International Food Information Council adds to this information by comparing the level to the consumption of one pound of sugar every day ("Everything," 1999).

Aspartame has also been accused of causing numerous side effects and ailments, from memory loss to death ("Aspartame," 1999). However, the most common of the 7000-plus consumer complaints that the FDA has

Continued

received in relation to aspartame is headaches (Chase, 1999). This theory or claim may have been discredited somewhat by a study led by Susan Schiffman, a Duke University researcher, in which aspartame caused fewer headaches than did a placebo. Ms. Schiffman pointed to a greater probability that the cause of these headaches stems from the caffeine contained in many beverages (Chase, 1999; Gorman, 1999). Nevertheless, much media attention is given to the claim that aspartame has contributed to an increased number of malignant brain tumors.

Leading the way of this allegation is Dr. John Olney, a staff member at the Washington University School of Medicine in Saint Louis, Missouri. A major player in the debate over the original approval of aspartame, Dr. Olney published the results of a study he conducted, in a 1996 issue of the *Journal of Neuropathology and Experimental Neurology* (Podolsky, Wiener, & Chetwynd, 1996). The study was highly regarded, and thus was mentioned in other periodicals (Walsh, 1997; Fumento, 1997). Although the study claimed that aspartame was linked to an increased number of cases of brain cancer in 1985, many publications were quick to cite other statistics that cast doubt on the findings.

Health showed that the greatest increase in brain cancer rates occurred between 1984 and 1985. In the following years, the rate stabilized. The later trend has occurred despite the doubling in the use of aspartame (Holmes, 1997). In addition, *Parents* and an FDA Talk Paper have cited a slight decrease between 1991 and 1993 (Walsh, 1997; "FDA," 1996). Perhaps most damaging to Dr. Olney's study are public statements he made in 1987. At that time he said that the effects of NutraSweet in cancer statistics would not emerge for 20 years (Fumento, 1997). Since aspartame did not gain FDA approval until 1981 and was not widely used until 1983, Michael Fumento contends that the sweetener has nothing to do with the trends in cancer rates (1997). Taking these statements into account, we should begin to see the effects in 2001 or 2003.

Continued

Other studies conducted over the last several years lend more confidence to the safety of using products containing aspartame. The *FDA Consumer* cited findings of a study published in the July 16, 1997 issue of the *Journal of the National Cancer Institute*. In this study, conducted at five United States medical research centers, no link was established between aspartame consumption and the occurrence of brain cancer in children. Neither could researchers establish a connection to brain tumors in children whose mothers drank aspartame-containing products while carrying the child in the womb ("Notebook," 1997). A similar story was found in *The Wall Street Journal* (Chase, 1999).

Still, there is the warning "Phenylketonurics: Contains Phenylalanine," found on all products containing aspartame (Stein, 1997, p. 1112). Phenylketonuria (PKU) is a genetic disorder and is the only known disorder that is affected by the use of aspartame, according to Christine Gorman in *Time* (76). Victor Lambert, whose article "Using 'Smart' Drugs and Drinks May Not Be Smart" appears on the U.S. Food and Drug Administration's Web site, concurs with this information and adds that "diet products made with aspartame (NutraSweet) contain phenylalanine at low, safe levels for people who don't have PKU and must bear labels warning people with PKU of the presence of this amino acid" (1993, n. pag.).

At this time, the issue over the safety of aspartame appears to be far from being settled because no definite evidence supports one side or the other. However, most sources are not concerned about the toxic effect of aspartame in the body. Those that are concerned are not found often in mainstream media sources, but are abundant on the Internet. Perhaps, until further studies are conducted and supported, consumers of aspartame-containing products should continue using the product but in moderation.

Continued

References

All about NutraSweet. (1998). NutraSweet. Retrieved June 25, 1999,
from the World Wide Web:
http://www.nutrasweet.com/html/his_about.html

Appleton, N. (1996) *Lick the sugar habit.* Garden City Park, NY: Avery.

Aspartame...the BAD news! *Aspartame kills.* (n.d.) Retrieved June 23,
1999, from the World Wide Web:
http://www.aspartamekills.com/symptoms.htm

Chase, M. (1999, June 7). Amid new confusion, here's the truth about
aspartame. *Wall Street Journal,* p. B1.

Everything you need to know about aspartame. (1997, November)
International Food Information Council.
Retrieved June 25, 1999, from the World Wide Web:
http://ificinfo.health.org/brochure/aspartame.htm

FDA Statement on Aspartame. (1996, November 18) Food and Drug
Administration. Retrieved June 23, 1999, from the World Wide
Web: http://vm.cfsan.fda.gov/~lrd/tpaspart.html

Fumento, M. (1997, January). Sweet nothings. *Consumer's Research,* 35.

FYI: What are the differences between the sweeteners saccharin and
aspartame? (1998, July) *Popular Science,* 80-81.

Gorman, C. (1999, February 8). A web of deceit. *Time, 76.*

Harte, J., Holdren, C., Schneider, R., & Shirley, C. (1991). *Toxics a to z.*
Berkeley: U of California Press.

Holmes, B. (1997, March). Could drinking diet soda give me brain
cancer? *Health,* 18.

Lambert, V. (1993, April). Using "smart" drugs and drinks may not be
smart. U.S. Food and Drug Administration.
Retrieved June 29, 1999, from the World Wide Web:
http://www.fda.gov/bbs/topics/CONSUMER/CON00207.html

Continued

Leblang, B. (1992). Sweetness: Trial and error. *American Health Magazine* (Vol. 4, Art. 69) Boca Raton: SIRS.

Notebook. (1997, November/December). *FDA Consumer, 37.*

Podolsky, D., Wiener, L., & Chetwynd, J. (1996, December 2). Is aspartame sweet but deadly? *U.S. News & World Report,* 98.

Stein, P. (1997, September). The sweetness of aspartame. *Journal of Chemical Education,* 74, 1112-1113.

Taylor, E. (Ed.). (1988) *Dorland's Illustrated Medical Dictionary* (27th ed.). Philadelphia: WB Saunders.

Title 21—food and drugs. (1999, rev. April 1) U.S. Government Printing Office. Retrieved June 23, 1999, from the World Wide Web: http://frwebgate.access..../get-cfr.cgi?TITLE=21&PART=172 &SECTION=804&TYPE=TEXT.html

Walsh, J. (1997, March). Aspartame alert. *Parents* 48.

READING QUESTIONS

1. *What do the sources Julie looks at generally agree about? What do they disagree about?*
2. *What are some of the effects of aspartame, according to Julie's sources?*
3. *Who is Dr. Olney and what does he contribute to the aspartame controversy?*
4. *What pattern does Julie discern regarding print and Internet sources? Does this pattern imply anything about the credibility of the claims made about aspartame?*

WRITING ASSIGNMENT: THE VALIDATION PAPER

This assignment is the third step toward your researched writing project. This assignment will help you look at as many resources as needed to get "the whole story," to determine what information is reliable, and to discard the misinformation. It will also help you learn about the nature of factual information and the different perspectives on that information.

Your purpose in this paper is to determine where the sources are reliable and where they distort the story or events by leaving out information, presenting distorted or erroneous information, or repeating misinformation. You are trying to find out as much of the full story on your topic as you can; however, in the validation paper, telling that story must remain a secondary purpose to assessing the reliability of the sources. You will be comparing and contrasting items of information and the news sources themselves.

1. Research your selected topic. Continue trying to restrict the scope of your topic in time and space. In fact, for this assignment, you may even want to put more restrictions on your topic than you will put on the topic for your final researched writing project.
2. As you research, be sure to consult a variety of sources, including books, magazine and newspaper articles, newspaper columns, and Internet sources, as well as primary sources such as interviews. You should work with no fewer than 15 sources for this assignment.
3. As you read through your sources, record the results of your critical reading in a reflective journal. Your reflective journal should include comparisons of the evidence in your sources: discrepancies, omissions, misleading statements, opposing views, and any lack of confirmation.
4. As you write the validation paper, remember the principles of good writing described earlier in the book. You may also want to review the Techniques section of this chapter to see how those general principles apply to this particular assignment.

CHAPTER 7

Discovering Connections and Context

Daddy Data
Number of single fathers in America with custody of their children in 1970: 393,000. Today: 1.9 million.

In the previous chapter, you learned the importance of validating the facts in your sources. Yet by themselves, facts do not mean very much. If you are given only the one statistic on how many single fathers had custody of their children in 1970, your reaction might be a resounding "So?" But put that number next to another statistic—the number of fathers with custody today—and the numbers begin to mean something.

For example, when you consider the current number of single fathers with custody along with the number in 1970, you make a *connection*—you notice an increase. Now you are in a position to discover the context for your connection by asking what caused the increase. Asking questions leads you to dig for other numbers and make other connections. You might compare the number of single fathers to the number of divorces in 1970 and today. If the numbers remain the same, you might look elsewhere; if the percentages are markedly different, then you can move beyond making connections between statistics and look at the *context*—in this case, the reasons for that increase. You might look at the changes in how judges determine which parent is the more responsible caregiver, or you might look at how fathers and their lawyers today are more aggressive in pursuing "fathers' rights."

The work of discovering connections and context begins in your reflective journal. This chapter takes a closer look at the different ways facts can be connected and put into a context, and how you can apply those methods to your own research. By finding connections and discovering context, you become more than a recipient of information—you become a maker of meaning. And by making meaning, you are claiming ownership of your own research.

DEFINITION: CONNECTION AND CONTEXT

> **Connection:** The links among two or more pieces of evidence, usually parallel or sequential.
> **Context:** The background information that explains and clarifies the connections among evidence.

Connections and contexts are closely related ideas; context is, in some ways, a kind of connection, and connections help create context. But, as similar as these two ideas might be, they are different, and keeping the difference in mind will help to simplify your tasks for this chapter.

"Connection" and "context" can be distinguished by their etymology. They both share the same Latin prefix, *con-*, meaning "together" or "with," but the roots of the two words are very different. The *-nect-* in *connection* comes from the Latin *nectare,* which means "to bind." Thus, *connection* indicates being bound together or linked. But the root *-text* in *context* means "to weave," which suggests a broader, more substantial link between pieces of evidence. If strands are woven together, they are closer and more difficult to separate than if they are merely tied to each other.

The distinction between *connection* and *context* has far-reaching implications for you as you look at the facts and evidence of the subject you are researching. Making connections between two facts is fairly easy, but such connections are not very useful to a researcher until they are put into context. For instance, you might notice the fact that the number of single fathers with child custody has nearly tripled over the last three decades, but by itself, the fact does not help us understand the issue of child custody very well. To understand what part the two statistics play in the issue of custody requires you to look for the cause of the connection, to weave the connection into a tapestry of context.

In a sense, finding connections and discovering context go hand in hand: making a connection should lead you to look for context to determine if the connection applies to the subject you are researching. Perhaps the number of single fathers with custody has increased because courts are granting fathers custody more often. Perhaps the number has grown simply because the overall number of divorced parents has grown, or perhaps it has grown because the statistical methods used to measure which parents have custody have changed. Discovering a context for the connection by looking at court decisions, census figures, and the methods used to create the statistics will show whether the connection is useful. If your topic is father's rights, but the larger number of single fathers with custody was caused by a change in how single fathers are counted by statisticians, then the connection will not be very helpful; however, if the statistical change is caused by a different approach to custody by the courts, then the connection is likely to be extremely helpful. Discovering the context of your connections gives you the information you need to determine a connection's usefulness.

TECHNIQUES: MAKING CONNECTIONS

The work you will do in this chapter builds directly on what you did in the last chapter. The validation paper required you to find and validate facts about your research topic. Now you will connect those facts and put them into context—in other words, you will start to create meaning from your evidence. In this chapter, you will start on the road to full ownership of your topic by finding your unique perspective on your research topic.

Discovering Connections
1. Gather Facts
2. Review Your Knowledge
3. Look for Parallel Connections
4. Look for Sequential Connections

Before discussing how to make connections, however, a quick reminder: Making connections and discovering context will often lead you to ask more questions—which usually means doing more research. Don't think that you are finished with research because you have finished your validation paper. Actually, you will probably continue to do research, validate facts, make connections, and discover context until your final researched writing project is due.

Keeping that in mind, here's how to go about making connections.

Having written the validation paper, you've already completed the first step in making connections—gathering facts. The second step is to review your knowledge. Ask yourself, "What do I know about my topic?" The answer to this question will include both your own knowledge as well as the facts you found in your sources.

A good way to review your knowledge of your topic is to use the prewriting activities we discussed in Chapter 1. Brainstorming can be particularly effective for getting your knowledge down on a piece of paper—and you might even surprise yourself with how much you know. Other prewriting methods—such as clustering and mapping—can help you review your knowledge and start making connections at the same time. You can use clustering and mapping as either your primary way of reviewing knowledge, or as a follow-up to some brainstorming.

Regardless of how you use prewriting methods such as clustering and mapping, you have started on the last step of making connections—actually making the connections themselves. Connections generally follow one of two patterns: they will be either *parallel connections* or *sequential connections*. In parallel patterns of connection, pieces of information can be placed next to one another and compared or contrasted. In sequential patterns of connection, one piece of information leads to another, often (but not always) by time or cause.

A closer look at the first pattern of connections shows that finding parallel connections involves putting facts next to each other and seeing how they are the same and how they are different. You will usually find one or more of these common patterns:

- **Comparisons:** Similarities among facts
- **Contrasts:** Differences among facts
- **Categories:** Groups of facts with common characteristics

Another way to look at parallel connections is to think of them in terms of a picture. As part of a picture, parallel connections would look like this:

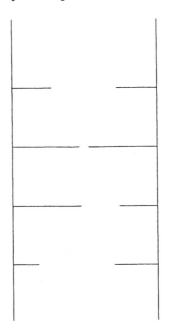

In this picture, the lengths of the lines show how closely the facts are connected and how important the connection is.

Now that you know what parallel connections are, take a look at them in action. In the following example, the historian Timothy Garton Ash examines the war in Kosovo and compares and contrasts it with World War II and the war in Vietnam. The results of the comparisons and contrasts he makes are his parallel connections.

The New Adolf Hitler?

Timothy Garton Ash

In the war over Kosovo, one weapon is being used by both sides: Adolf Hitler. Yugoslav President Slobodan Milosevic accuses the West of acting like Hitler and appeals to his people's proud memories of the Partisan war against Nazi forces. And isn't the German Luftwaffe engaged in the NATO bombing? Meanwhile, in justifying that bombing, U.S. President

---

Continued

Bill Clinton says, "What if someone had listened to Winston Churchill and stood up to Adolf Hitler earlier? How many people's lives might have been saved? And how many American lives might have been saved?

So Clinton, we understand, is Churchill. But hold on. Who has been the American President for the past six years while this Milosevic-Hitler has been rampaging through the former Yugoslavia? And whose Administration has been seeking peace in our time by negotiating with him? So perhaps, after all, Clinton is not Churchill but the British Prime Minister whose policy of appeasement Churchill fiercely criticized in the 1930s: Neville Chamberlain.

Tricky things, historical analogies. They tend to cut several ways. But they also help clarify thought, if only by showing up the differences between then and now. Let's try five for size:

1) Kosovo as Kosovo, the Milosevic version. Once again the Serbs are engaged in a heroic defense of Kosovo, as they were against the Turks in the great battle of 1389. Today Serbian propaganda appeals constantly to this mythology of martial sacrifice. There's only one problem: the Serbs lost the battle of Kosovo in 1389.

2) 1999 as 1914. Clinton used this one too, recalling that World War I started in this part of Europe. Here the differences are revealing. In 1914 the great powers of Europe lined up on opposing sides. Today they are united—except for Russia, but it won't go to war for Serbia.

3) Milosevic as Hitler. Well, not exactly. Milosevic is the most dangerous European leader of the 1990s. He is a menace, a thug, a postcommunist villain who has cynically manipulated nationalism. He has blood on his hands. But his state does not have either the power or the ideological will to conquer Europe. While Germany under Hitler grew ever bigger, Yugoslavia under Milosevic has shrunk. The element of truth in this analogy is President Clinton's point about appeasement: the longer you put off standing up to aggressive dictators, the higher the price. If we had called Hitler's bluff when he remilitarized the Rhineland in 1936,

Continued

50 milion lives might have been spared. If we had stood up to Milosevic when his forces besieged the Croatian town of Vukovar in the fall of 1991, perhaps a quarter of a million men, women and children might still be alive. But we—West Europeans and Americans—didn't, and so we now face the prospect of . . .

4) Kosovo as Vietnam. Yes, but whose Vietnam? The Vietnamese people in this analogy are actually the overwhelming Albanian population of Kosovo, and the analogue to the Viet Cong is the Kosovo Liberation Army. Kosovo is the Serbs' Vietnam, not ours. If NATO really does eventually destroy Milosevic's army from the air, as General Wesley Clark has threatened (although he hasn't explained how this can be done without inflicting extensive civilian casualties), then the K.L.A. will soon be riding into Pristina as if into Saigon. Then the remaining Serbs living in Kosovo will probably flee. Milosevic knows this. He knows such a loss is the one thing that might finally turn the fury of people in Serbia proper against him. That's why he is unlikely to give up swiftly, which leaves us with . . .

5) Slobo as Saddam. Yes, alas, the closer to the present, the more plausible the analogy. Air power alone will probably not depose the Serbian dictator any more than it did the Iraqi one. The bombing has not yet achieved even its first proclaimed objective of stopping Serbian atrocities in Kosovo.

So, analogies past, we reach the unique dilemma of the present. One may feel a bit like the proverbial pedestrian at the crossroads who is asked the way by a motorist and says, "I wouldn't start from here." The story of wrong turnings goes right up to Rambouillet. Yet here is where you always have to start. Having recently studied the situation in Kosovo and Serbia at first hand, I reached a drastic conclusion. I hope against hope that the bombing will stop the murderous rampage and bring the Serbian side back to the negotiating table. But if, as I expect, it does not, then there is only one way for NATO not to be seen on its 50th anniversary as either impotent or complicit in a savage ethnic war. This is

Continued

to assemble a large international force that will physically occupy Kosovo, make it an international protectorate and stop Serbs from killing or expelling innocent Albanians—and, as important, vice versa.

This would be a nightmarish task, of course, and a very grave international precedent. However, at this stage of Europe's worst crisis in the whole decade, all we may be left with is a choice of nightmares.

If we were to put the comparisons and contrasts Timothy Ash makes in this article into the graphic model of parallel connections, it would look like this:

Kosovo in 1389	Kosovo in 1999
Start of World War I (1914)	War in Kosovo (1999)
Adolf Hitler	Slobodan Milosevic
War in Vietnam	War in Kosovo
Saddam Hussein	Slobodan Milosevic

READING QUESTIONS

1. *The first connection made is between Kosovo and World War II. What specific connections are made? Are the connections comparisons, contrasts, or categories?*
2. *The author presents five different connections between Kosovo and historical events, as shown above. What kind of connection is each one? How does the author evaluate each connection?*
3. *What effect do these connections have on you, the reader? Do you understand more or less about the war in Kosovo? Why do you think the connections are successful or unsuccessful?*

EXERCISE 7-1

Draw as many connections as you can between the following items (using prewriting techniques may help you). Then divide your connections by type: comparisons, contrasts, and categories. Finally, diagram your connections to show the relative closeness and importance of the connections.

1. Thanksgiving
2. Martin Luther King, Jr. Day
3. Arbor Day
4. Thursday
5. Christmas

6. Monday
7. Independence Day
8. Mother's Day
9. Your birthday
10. The day after tomorrow

If you take a closer look at the other pattern for connecting, *sequential connections,* you will find that you are putting facts in the order that they happened when you make sequential connections. As with parallel connections, there are three common patterns for sequential connections:

- **Chronology:** Connecting facts in the order they happened in time
- **Cause and Effect:** Showing how one fact produced another
- **Problem and Solution:** Showing how one fact solves the problem raised by another

These patterns are not the only ones you find in sequential connections, just the most common ones. Any time you connect facts by saying "this one comes before that one," you are making a sequential connection regardless of why the facts go in that order.

Use a model like this to help you make sequential connections:

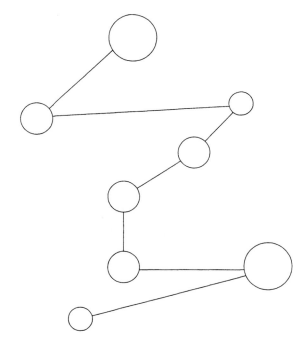

Some of the circles in the picture are bigger than others because the facts that would go in the bigger circles are more important to the chain of events. Likewise, the closer circles have a more direct connection to each other than the circles that are farther apart. If your sequential connections follow the cause-and-effect pattern, then you would put major causes in larger circles and minor causes in smaller circles. Likewise, if one idea is an immediate cause of another, then you would connect the ideas with a shorter line. The more remote a cause one idea is, the longer the line that connects it to its effect.

In the following example of sequential connections, the author connects several habits—chewing, biting, and sucking—as a chain of events.

Nervous Habits Often Reflect a Developmental Need (Abstract)

Barbara F. Meltz

Now a mother of three and a pediatrician who, perhaps not so coincidentally, researches children's nervous habits, she understands how much her biting must have bugged her parents. She also understands why they were never able to get her to stop. It turns out that nail or cuticle biting is one of the hardest habits for children to break; 20 percent of those who do it, like [Susan] Swedo, will still be picking or biting as adults.

Luckily, most of the habits our children engage in do go away on their own. While they last, though, any one of them—from hair twirling to lip picking, thumb sucking to shirt sucking, finger tapping to knuckle cracking—can make you crazy. And therein lies the rub. Just because a habit bothers you doesn't mean it bothers your child. Indeed, most children pick, bite, or suck without even realizing it. Not only that, but most of the time, the habit serves an important purpose and a developmental need, usually for comfort.

It's easy to see that the baby who sucks his thumb is trying to comfort himself. It's also easy to connect it to the primitive suckling reflex. It's harder to make the connection with a 9-year-old who one day starts to suck on his shirt sleeve but [Laura Gutermuth] Foster says it's the same need. In fact, she says many kids migrate from one form of oral gratification to another, typically pacifier to thumb to pencil chewing to shirt sucking.

If we diagram this article to show the sequential connections, it would look like this:

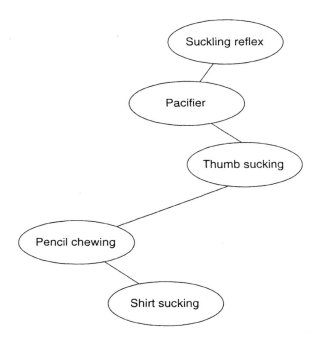

READING QUESTIONS

1. *List the connections the author makes concerning nervous habits.*
2. *What pattern of sequential connections does this example follow? (It may follow more than one.)*
3. *Does the author provide any explanation of cause for the chain of habits? Is any solution suggested?*
4. *Can you extend the chain of habits beyond what the author lists?*

EXERCISE 7–2

Below are the first and last steps in several processes. Fill in the sequential connections that lead from one to the other. Then, diagram the connections, using the size and position of the circles to show the relative closeness and importance of your connections.

1. Buying groceries/Doing dishes
2. Going on a first date/Getting married
3. Getting up in the morning/Attending your first class
4. Applying to college/Graduating from college
5. Getting an essay assignment/Turning your essay in

At this point, you have gathered and validated the facts about your research topic. You have reviewed what you know about your topic, recalling both your personal knowledge and the information you discovered through research. You have found connections among your facts—some parallel (such as comparison and contrast) and some sequential (connected by order in time). Now, it is time to move on to the next step in creating unique meaning from your sources: discovering context.

TECHNIQUES: DISCOVERING CONTEXT

Discovering context is important in every field of study and in every profession: police investigators depend on context, as do stock market analysts, historians, sociologists, literary scholars, and doctors—the list is endless. In short, nearly everybody seeking to understand nearly anything depends on context. Indeed, an Internet search can show how many different kinds of people are interested in the context, or surrounding environment, of many different kinds of information. As of December 31, 1999, Infoseek returned 730,483 Web pages that had "context" in their title. AltaVista returned 1,002,165 sites for the same search. The first 10 sites on AltaVista's list included sites on art, music, education, and computer software.

In your research project, you will be discovering the context of your facts in order to explain and support the connections that exist among them. You are looking for the background information that surrounds the fact: What was going on in history when this fact "happened"? What did people of that time know and not know? How did the culture view the world and the universe? What did people like to eat? There are just as many questions as there are facts to be found because each fact has a context.

To answer such questions, you are probably going to have to do some more research. During this visit to the library or the Internet, however, you need to broaden your search some and look in areas that might not seem to be directly related to your topic. Think for a moment about "muscle cars": In the 1960s, American car makers introduced several models of small (for the time) cars with large, powerful engines, such as the Pontiac GTO. To discover the context of this fact, you would need to research several topics that have nothing to do with cars, such as, perhaps, the increase in the number of teenagers with disposable income, a growing permissiveness in moral behavior, and the surfer culture of Southern California.

The Rosa Parks story offers another example. To discover the context, or background information, for her refusal to give up her seat on the bus, you might research the 1954 Supreme Court decision on *Brown vs. Board of Education of Topeka, Kansas* (the initial step to desegregate schools). You also might want to read about the experience of African-American World War II veterans who returned to a segregated country after fighting to free other peoples in other nations. The information you find will help you understand and explain why Rosa Parks did what she did. It will also help you develop and support connections you might make between Rosa Parks and other facts.

A diagram of context would look very different from the models for connections. Whereas connections link several facts together into one pattern, context looks to surround a fact with background information. A picture of discovering context might look like this:

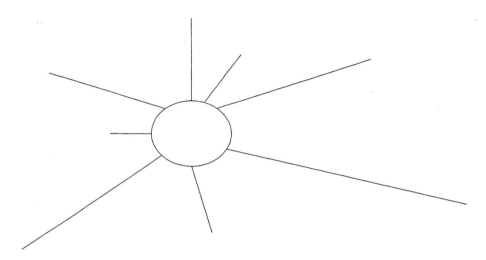

Whatever fact you are putting into context would go in the circle in the middle. The background information you discover would go at the ends of the lines. The shorter lines would lead to more important information that is closer to the central fact, and the longer lines would lead to information that is farther away from the fact and less important to the context.

The following example shows context in action and how the model works. Ronald L. Ecker looks to the Bible and other elements of Hebrew culture and society to discover a context for Adam and Eve's sexual relations.

Adam and Eve, *And Adam Knew Eve: A Dictionary of Sex in the Bible*

Ronald L. Ecker

When God creates the first man (Hebrew *adam*) and woman (named Hawwah ["Eve"], similar to Hebrew *hayyah*, "life"), he commands them, "Be fruitful and multiply." It should follow, then, that Adam and Eve engage in sex early on. The book of Genesis, however, is silent on this question. The couple remains childless while in the Garden of Eden, and until their loss of innocence Adam and Eve are not even aware of their nakedness. Some interpreters take this to mean that Adam and Eve before

---

Continued

the Fall are not aware of their sexuality. But that makes nonsense of the divine command to procreate. It also suggests that sex is somehow to be associated with the Fall and is thus tainted with sin and shame. Such a view reflects a later ascetic Christian, not a biblical Hebrew, attitude toward human sexuality. (See "Lovemaking" and "Virginity.")

One can speculate, based on Gen. 1:27, that Adam and Eve were originally one androgynous being—"God created man in his own image, . . . male and female created he them"—meant to reproduce in some asexual way. But again this associates sex with the couple's Fall (their original state being androgyny or asexuality), an un-Hebrew notion that also conflicts with Genesis 2, according to which man and woman were not created simultaneously.

Perhaps Genesis makes no mention of Adam and Eve making love in the Garden of Eden because it is taken for granted. James Barr, in *The Garden of Eden and the Hope of Immortality,* points out that there was no reason, given the acceptance of sexuality as normal in ancient Hebrew culture, for the couple to abstain. In the noncanonical book of Jubilees (3:6), Adam and Eve have sexual relations as soon as God introduces them. It is literally love at first sight. According to rabbinic tradition, Eve is not even Adam's first wife. His first wife is Lilith, who leaves him because during sexual intercourse Adam wouldn't let her be on top. (For more on this failed relationship, see "Gender: Male and Female Created He Them.")

Sex, in any case, has nothing to do with Adam and Eve's Fall from grace in Genesis. Their sin is one of disobedience, specifically eating fruit from the "tree of the knowledge of good and evil," that is, reaching for godlike knowledge ("ye shall be as gods," the serpent tells Eve, "knowing good and evil" [Gen. 3:5]) (see Gaster). Eve, tempted by the serpent to partake of the fruit, gets blamed by Adam, ("she gave me of the tree," Adam tells God, "and I did eat," as if Eve had a choice but poor Adam didn't). (The woman is given all the blame also by the early Christian church; see "Paul.") God punishes them both, with the punishment of Eve

Continued

being pain in childbirth ("in sorrow thou shalt bring forth children") and unequal status ("thy desire," God tells her, "will be to thy husband, and he shall rule over thee"; see "Gender").

The first sex act described in the Bible comes after the departure from Eden: "And Adam knew Eve his wife" ("to know," Hebrew *yada*, being a euphemism for sexual intercourse) "and she conceived, and bare Cain." As Barr notes, intercourse is here described for the first time because it is the first time that a child is produced. Adam and Eve then have a second son, Abel, and when Adam is one hundred and thirty years old he knows Eve again, fathering Seth.

How many times Adam knows Eve after that, or how many more wives Adam knows, is unknown, but he begets "sons and daughters" for eight hundred more years. (Gen 1:26-5:5).

READING QUESTIONS

1. *Ecker draws both parallel connections and sequential connections in this piece. What connections can you find?*
2. *What information does Ecker use to help create a context for his connections?*
3. *Ecker repeatedly suggests you "see" other entries in his encyclopedia. Why do you think he does this? How might these additional entries help to create context?*

Ecker provides us with background information on the question of Adam and Eve's intimate relations by looking at surrounding information. In the diagram showing context, Adam and Eve go in the middle, and the background information is placed at the ends of the lines:

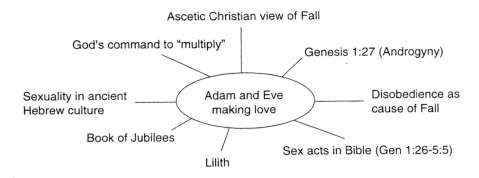

EXERCISE 7-3

This section of the chapter mentioned the context for the popularity of muscle cars in the 1960s. America's taste in automobiles has changed many times since then: until the mid-1970s, large sedans were the car of choice; in the 1980s, the most popular models were fuel-efficient compact cars; and in the 1990s, the vogue was SUVs and minivans. Do some research and write a one- to two-page paper explaining the context behind America's taste for a certain kind of vehicle.

Taking Connections Out of Context

Chapter 3 listed the dangers of creating meaning, one of which was not paying attention to all of the evidence. Paying attention to all of your evidence is especially important when making connections and discovering context. In fact, it is so important that there's a common phrase about it: Statements or actions are said to be "taken out of context." You've probably heard politicians or other people in the news complaining that they were misrepresented by the media. They claim that, on purpose or by accident, the media didn't provide all of the background information.

Another frequent example comes from Hollywood. A movie critic might write, "This movie is one of the best examples of wasted time, money, and talent I've ever had to sit through." But the ad for the movie leaves out the context, and says, "John Jones, critic for the *Los Angeles Times,* says, "one of the best...ever."

The following article tells how a New Zealand company apparently ignored part of the context in a story about Microsoft.

"Quote taken out of context" says Microsoft

Aardvark News

In response to the feature story in this week's *Aardvark Weekly,* Microsoft have replied that the quote used by NBR *(National Business Review)* in its advertising and attributed to them was taken "out of context."

It seems that the phrase "New Zealand's most frequently visited Web site" was used only in reference to a very small sector of the market, namely those business or financial sites based on Microsoft server technology.

In this context it's very likely that the claims hold water, but it's also rather naughty of NBR to use the quote in this manner without any clear indication that it was so specific.

Just another case of excessive exuberance on the part of the advertising department?

As this example shows, one piece of evidence can completely change meaning depending on the context. If the context is ignored, it sounds like the Web site is enormously successful, and that Microsoft is a popular and powerful company for all of the people who surf the Web. If the context is acknowledged, then suddenly the Web site's popularity is limited to only a small group of people. There are probably many Web surfers who have never heard of the site, and Microsoft, in this example, no longer seems quite as important.

You also need to be careful when making connections. You cannot simply make whatever connections you want to make. You have to have a good reason for making a connection, including some background information to support it. Here's an advertisement for a book that makes some questionable connections between events that occurred years apart and in different countries.

The true story behind the Jonestown massacre,

including connections to the Kennedy and King assassinations,

Heavenly Deceptor

Heavenly Deceptor is a true story involving sex, torture, profit, cunning deception and mass murder.

The author, Nathan Landau, explores new links between the Kennedy, King and Jonestown murders which are revealed through an examination of historical files hidden from the public for fourteen years.

In a thoroughly documented and exhausting research work, the author raises and answers the following questions:

- Who was second in command at Jonestown and why was her identity never revealed before, although she is still at large?
- What really happened to the millions of dollars hidden in the Swiss banks?
- Suicide or murder—Who really killed Jim Jones and why?
- What was the connection between Jonestown, the mayor of San Francisco and Harvey Milk—and why were they killed nine days after the massacre?
- What was the secret escape plan of the top leadership of Jonestown?
- What is the hidden connection between Jim Jones, Lee Harvey Oswald and James Earl Ray?

This advertisement does not provide any context for these unusual connections, which makes them unsupportable, if not absurd. Providing some background information to link these connections would make them appear less random and thus more probable.

Read the following two articles on two female artists, Vinnie Ream and Maya Yin Lin, who lived a century apart. Both created works that have deeply affected millions of Americans who have viewed them. Yet the works provoked a storm of controversy that nearly prevented their realization. After you read the articles, make a list of the parallel connections between the artists themselves and their experiences in bringing their work to completion. You will want to consult other periodical and newspaper articles about these two artists, especially Maya Lin and her design for the Vietnam Memorial, to supplement these articles. In addition to the connections between the artists, you may want to look at the connections made in the *Time* article to other monuments that faced storms of controversy before they were brought to completion.

From *Teenage Lincoln Sculptor*
Ethel Yari

Congress's 1866 decision to award a $10,000 commission to 18-year-old Vinnie Ream for a marble statue memorializing the nation's recently assassinated president, Abraham Lincoln, vaulted the young sculptor into the center of a storm of controversy. The art world and the press were incensed. Not only was Vinnie a neophyte sculptor, she was just a teenager and a female! Eighteen other sculptors—all more experienced than she and all but one (Harriet Hosmer) a man—had competed for the appointment and been passed over.

The issue of Vinnie's selection was passionately debated by senators and members of the House of Representatives. Those from western states supported her appointment, while easterners—who considered themselves the cultural elite—vigorously opposed giving such a significant commission to an unknown, inexperienced girl.

But when the full-length statue of America's sixteenth president, which still graces the rotunda of the U.S. Capitol in Washington, D.C., was unveiled in

Continued

1871, Senator Matthew H. Carpenter of Wisconsin spoke for many when he declared, according to a press account, that while no judge of the statue's artistic merit, he was "able to say . . . that it is Abraham Lincoln all over."

The story of how the petite Vinnie Ream—barely five feet tall, she weighed less than ninety pounds—came to win such a coveted award began in 1862 with a chance meeting between Vinnie and Missouri congressman James S. Rollins in the U.S. Capitol. She had been introduced to Rollins three years before, when she was 12 and a star pupil at the academy division of Christian College in Columbia, Missouri. The congressman, a trustee at the college, remembered the artistically gifted youngster, whose portrait of Martha Washington had been chosen to hang in the school's administration building.

As they spoke in Washington, Rollins offered to take Vinnie to visit the studio of an acquaintance, the nationally known sculptor, Clark Mills, which was located in a wing of the Capitol. When Vinnie arrived at the studio, Mills was working on a clay model. "As soon as I watched the sculptor handle the clay," she wrote later, "I felt at once that I, too, could model. . . ." Mills gave Vinnie a bucket of clay, from which "in a few hours I produced a medallion of an Indian chief's head. . . ."

Mills was so impressed with her carving that he immediately invited Vinnie to be his student-helper. The visit sparked her desire to be a sculptor, but although she was eager to accept Mills's offer, her mother disapproved of the entire notion. She expected her daughter to marry and become a homemaker, not pursue a professional career, especially in such an unladylike field as sculpting.

But Vinnie was determined. She persisted in her appeals until her parents agreed to a compromise. If, when she reached her sixteenth birthday, she still wanted to be a sculptor, they would permit her to work part-time in Mills's studio. . . .

On her sixteenth birthday, Vinnie began her part-time apprenticeship with Mills, who received frequent visits from House and Senate members

Continued

curious to see the sculptor at work in his Capitol studio. While there, they were attracted to his pretty, young assistant with her chestnut curls. Vinnie's effervescent personality and the energy with which she carved and modeled clay intrigued the visitors, leading several to agree to pose for her.

Determined to master the art of sculpting, Vinnie strove to recreate the natural facial expressions and moods of her models. One of her first subjects was Congressman Thaddeus Stevens of Pennsylvania, then considered to be the most powerful man in the House of Representatives. Vinnie's finished bust of Stevens realistically captured his beetle-browed, pugnacious expression, a look he used to intimidate opponents. Pleased with her work, Stevens became one of Vinnie's staunchest friends and supporters. Before long, Vinnie had enough commissions to allow her to leave her clerical job and devote all her energy and enthusiasm to sculpting.

Often, while walking the streets near the Capitol, Vinnie observed President Lincoln striding along in his stovepipe hat, head down and deep in thought. Struck by his sad expression and gaunt features, she yearned to model a bust of the president, but attempts to recreate his features from memory proved unsatisfactory. When she mentioned her desire to sculpt Lincoln to Congressman Rollins, he agreed to appeal to the president on her behalf.

At first, Lincoln, who hated to pose for anyone, considering it a waste of time, refused. "Why would anyone want to make a bust of a homely man like me?" he said. But when told that Vinnie was poor and came from humble beginnings similar to his own, he jokingly replied in the vernacular, "Well that's nothing agin her. Tell her she can come."

In later years, Vinnie recalled that Lincoln, whose favorite son, Willie, had recently died, "seemed to find a sort of companionship in being with me, although we talked but little. . . . I made him think of Willie and he often said so and as often wept." She was struck by the image of "his great form slouched down into a chair at his desk, his head bowed upon

Continued

his chest, deeply thoughtful. I think he was with his generals on the battlefield appraising the horrible sacrifices brought upon his people and the nation." He was, as had often been said, "a man of unfathomable sorrow," and she tried to capture this emotion in her work, which was nearly completed when he was assassinated in April 1865.

Gradually, the nation's shock at Lincoln's murder gave way to a desire to memorialize the martyred president, and a competition was announced for a full-length marble statue of his likeness. Vinnie's mother, by now proud of her daughter's sculpting efforts, encouraged her to apply, as did her congressional friends. Convinced that she should make an effort to win the commission, Vinnie appealed to Mary Todd Lincoln for an endorsement, but the president's widow declined.

Vinnie was undeterred by this rebuff. During five months of sittings, she had become aware of the president's pain, and she was determined to portray all the emotion that she had observed in President Lincoln in a life-size statue. But she knew that to win the competition, she would have to overcome several obstacles, especially criticisms aimed at her limited sculpting experience, her age, and her gender.

Fired by ambition, Vinnie appealed to the senators and congressmen whose portraits she had modeled and to other supporters familiar with her work. Together they came up with a plan that saw Representative Thaddeus Stevens propose House Resolution 197, which would bypass the selection committee's review of the models submitted and award the commission directly to the teenage sculptor. Stevens waited until the day before Congress adjourned, hoping to push the measure through in the last-minute rush of business.

The strategy worked. The House quickly passed the bill and sent it on to the Senate for approval. Seeking to aid her own cause, Vinnie had gathered additional support throughout the capital. She had loaned some of her plaster busts and medallions of well-known Washington faces to jewelry stores, where they were placed on display in show windows.

Continued

More significantly, Vinnie had obtained recommendations from many of the most notable figures in Washington politics. Four months before the Senate committee reached its decision on the commission, a formidable group of prominent men signed and submitted a petition vouching for Vinnie Ream's competence. Making no mention of the pending decision on the Lincoln statue, the petition, addressed "To Whom it May Concern," merely expressed confidence in "an accomplished young lady [of] rare genius in the beautiful art of sculpture. . . ."

Probably because she did not meet the standards of the proper Victorian female to which they subscribed, a number of Vinnie's critics were women. One of the most outspoken was Mrs. Jane Grey Swisshelm, a newspaper columnist, who accused Vinnie of using her "feminine wiles" to win the commission. Ream, she wrote, "has a pretty face, bright black eyes, long dark curls and plenty of them . . . has been studying her art for a few months, never made a statue, has some plaster busts on exhibition, including her own, minus clothing to the waist. . . . [She] sits in the galleries [of Congress] in a conspicuous position and in her most bewitching dress, . . . and nods and smiles as a member rises and delivers his opinions on the merit of the case. . . ." To soften the impact of Swisshelm's article, the editor of the *Times* printed it under the title, "A Homely Woman's Opinion of a Pretty One."

It was clear that Vinnie's physical attractiveness and youthful exuberance were both a help and a hindrance to her career as a sculptor. Male admirers were drawn to her by the very qualities that her female critics found objectionable. The *St. Louis Evening News,* an early critic that reversed its negative stance on Vinnie, observed that "Miss Ream has a pleasing face, which may be a serious drawback for an artist but which is no fault of hers."

In the meantime, a long, drawn-out debate about eastern and western notions of what makes great art raged in the Senate. Reflecting the opinions of the educated art world, Massachusetts senator Charles Sumner

Continued

declared his belief that art should glorify the ideal in human culture, raising it above everyday life. And Sumner questioned Vinnie's ability to create such great art. The Senate was being asked, he declared, "to commission an unknown artist, of possible merit, but who has given no assurance that she can produce a work worthy of so large a sum . . . She cannot do it."

Irritated by Sumner's remarks, Oregon's Senator James Willis Nesmith, a northwestern pioneer and Indian fighter, disagreed, arguing that the statue should be an "exact imitation of nature," a replica of President Lincoln as he was in real life. Practical and self-educated, Nesmith ridiculed the notion that anyone needed to be well read in order to judge the quality of a work of art.

Only Senator Jacob Howard of Vermont rose to defend Sumner's position. He complained that Vinnie's model was without meaning or spirit. Stated Howard: "I will go further too, and say [that] in view of her sex, I shall expect a complete failure in the execution of this work."

As the senators debated on the night of July 27, the hands of the clock moved past midnight into the next day. Many of those present had had enough and were anxious to return to their home states. Called to vote on HR 197, they passed the bill 23 to 9, making Vinnie Ream the youngest person and the first woman to receive a government sculpting commission.

Congress provided Vinnie with a rent-free studio in the basement of the Capitol, where she became a popular tourist attraction. Wearing a plaster- and clay-spattered smock and work shoes and perched on a ladder, often with a white, pet dove on her shoulder, the tiny wisp of a girl started work on the full-length Lincoln statue.

Having no previous experience at carving a full-size figure, Vinnie wanted to be certain that her model would portray Lincoln exactly as he looked. To recreate the great man as realistically as possible, Vinnie worked meticulously on the unclothed model and then, according to the Washington *Evening Journal,* "submitted it to the critical examination of

Continued

the most eminent surgeons of the city, including the doctor who was in attendance at the death of Mr. Lincoln, and one of the best sculptors of New York City who came to Washington purposely to examine it, all of whom pronounced it a piece of faultless work."

In 1868, while she was still working on the incomplete model, Vinnie, through no fault of her own, almost was evicted from her studio. A group of Republicans bent on impeaching President Johnson learned that Senator Ross, the Reams's boarder and an opponent of the impeachment effort, had invited undecided colleagues to meet in her studio for tea. The Republicans went to the Ream home and warned Vinnie that they would force her out of the studio if she did not persuade Ross to change his vote. Vinnie refused to be intimidated or to attempt to influence Ross's vote in any way.

Ordered to vacate the Capitol studio, Vinnie moved her clay busts, medallions, plants, and two pet doves to her home. Only the soft, wet clay model of Lincoln remained in the studio, since any attempt to move the 6'11" statue would have resulted in serious damage.

The attempt to impeach Johnson failed, and Senator Ross's vote was the deciding factor. Disgruntled anti-Johnson forces struck at those who had thwarted their impeachment efforts. Congressman Benjamin Butler of New Orleans demanded that Vinnie be "cleared out" of the Capitol, adding, "if the statue be spoilt . . . I shall be very glad of it." Vinnie turned to her friend, Thaddeus Stevens, who, despite being very ill and the leader of the pro-impeachment faction, once again came to her rescue; she was allowed to remain in the studio.

After completing the plaster model the following year, Vinnie presented it to Interior Secretary Orville H. Browning, who approved it without reservation. Only then did she receive half of the $10,000 award. The balance would be paid when the marble statue was finished and accepted. On viewing the model, Vinnie's critics, including Swisshelm, ceased their attacks. . . .

Continued

On January 25, 1871, Vinnie's statue of Abraham Lincoln was unveiled during ceremonies at the Capitol in Washington. When the silk covering of the statue was removed, there was, the *Washington Star* reported, a "momentary hush," followed by rounds of warm applause. Then, according to the paper, "everybody turned to where the little sculptor-girl stood, a little to the rear with glad tears in her eyes, and congratulations were poured in upon her from all quarters. . . ." In her diary, Vinnie described the night as "the supreme moment of my life . . . I had known and loved the man! . . . my country had loved him . . . with shouts they . . . received his image in the marble."

Praise poured in from press and critics alike. The statue was "the most real likeness of Lincoln that I ever saw," said one reporter. "Boldly and powerfully executed," highlighted by "the unfathomable melancholy of the eyes," said another. Vinnie was at last accepted as a sculptor. . . .

To the end of her life, Vinnie was humble and appreciative of her success . . . Although she had created more than a hundred monuments, portrait busts, and reliefs in her lifetime, Vinnie Ream, the teenage girl with curls, is best remembered for her masterpiece, the white marble statue of Abraham Lincoln in the rotunda of the U.S. Capitol.

Storm over a Vietnam Memorial
Wolf Von Eckhardt

Though Vietnam veterans never got big parades, by next year they should at least be able to dedicate a memorial to their fallen comrades. But as with so much else touched by that tragic war, the memorial's eloquently understated design is stirring controversy.

Designated for a site on two acres of gently rolling park land on Washington's Mall, the monument will consist of two black granite walls that meet in a V and recede into the ground. One critic, Vietnam Veteran

Continued

Tom Carhart, calls it "a black gash of shame." The *National Review* labels it "Orwellian glop."

The winning design, picked from among 1,421 entries last May in a national competition, was submitted by a Chinese American, Maya Yin Lin, 22. "I've studied funerary architecture, the relation of architecture to death," says Lin. She has pointed the 200-ft.-long walls of her memorial west to the Lincoln Memorial and east to the Washington Monument. On those walls will be listed the names of the 57,709 Americans who died or were declared missing in Vietnam. The names will appear in chronological, not alphabetical, order (another source of criticism). The roll begins on the right wall, with the name of the first American killed in Vietnam, in 1961. It continues on the left and ends with the year 1975. Thus the first and last to die meet in the center and, as Lin puts it, "the war is 'complete,' coming full circle."

A lively, articulate woman who was born in Athens, Ohio, Lin graduated only last May from Yale, where she majored in architecture (and beat out one of her mentors in the Vietnam competition). It was her concept, rather than her hazy pastel rendering of it, that won over the eight-man jury (four architects, three sculptors and one critic).

The first sour note to mar the initial symphony of praise came from Pulitzer prize-winning Architecture Critic Paul Gapp of the Chicago *Tribune*. "The so-called memorial," he wrote, is "bizarre" because it is "neither a building nor a sculpture." But of course it is precisely those unclassifiable qualities that make Lin's design so eminently right. It fits. At this time in the history of our architecture, and at this place in the monumental heart of Washington, additional buildings or sculptures would intrude. In retrospect, it is hard to conceive of anything but a horizontal landscape design that could meet the criteria that the memorial be "neither too commanding nor too deferential."

This is confirmed by a look at some 50 of the other entries that will go on display next week at the American Institute of Architects

Continued

headquarters in Washington. They illustrate our time's bewildering embrace of almost anything: from architectural stunts to sculptural theatrics, from the pompous to the ludicrous, from the innovative to the reactionary.

The rejected entries include such kitsch as a house-high steel helmet and a number of handsomely styled columns, pylons, tablets and structures that belong at a world's fair or amusement park. Other designs accommodate the thousands of names on various layouts of slabs, blocks and other geometric stones and look depressingly like constructivist graveyards.

The sculpture is mainly of the socialist realism school. Not that realism is unacceptable; we are rediscovering its value. The trouble is that no sculptor since Augustus Saint-Gaudens has been able to come up with a convincing metaphor that can be realistically rendered. The gods of Greek mythology have fled.

None of the runners-up, however sincerely conceived, deserves a place near the Lincoln Memorial. While there is nothing sacred about the Mall, the majesty of this green carpet demands dignified simplicity, if not nobility, of any newcomer. Lin's design meets that demand.

That simplicity disturbs those who want a more assertive memorial. The *National Review*, calling for a sculpture, sees the black granite, sunken walls and unalphabetical roster as a conspiracy to dishonor the dead. Carhart, a Purple Heart winner who lost out in the design competition (he proposed a statue of an officer offering a dead soldier heavenward) says the jury should have consisted of war veterans, as if a beauty contest should be judged only by beauties.

However heated the criticism has been of the Vietnam veterans' dark chevron, it has been tepid compared with the storms that have raged over other public monuments. The Franklin D. Roosevelt memorial, approved in 1960 and still unbuilt, was smothered in epithets like "instant Stonehenge" and "bookends out of a deep freeze." Not until next spring, incredibly,

Continued

will Washington get its first monument to General Pershing and the American Expeditionary Forces of World War I. Those bothered by abstract design might consider that grand obelisk, the Washington Monument. We have come to love it. Some day the Vietnam memorial, too, may win the hearts and minds of the American people.

DISCOVERING CONNECTIONS AND CONTEXTS: PROFESSIONAL WRITING

Connectivity prompted two mathematicians, Steven Strogatz and Duncan Watts, to study and write a formal paper on the phenomenon popularly known as "six degrees of separation," the idea that any two people in the world are separated by no more than six acquaintances. One whimsical manifestation of the phenomenon is played out by identifying how close you are to persons of fame or infamy. For example, one of the authors has only two degrees of separation from two persons who waged war against each other on a grand scale: Dwight Eisenhower and Adolph Hitler. Phil, a college acquaintance, was introduced to Eisenhower as the youngest businessman (he was 18 and a service station owner) in Salina, Kansas, Eisenhower's hometown. Ted, a former colleague who was born in Nazi Germany, was held up by his mother to be patted on the head when Hitler passed by on parade. Consider also the connectivity of the student writers brought together by inclusion in this text.

The following article by Polly Shulman makes it very clear, however, that the concept of "six degrees of separation" can be anything but an amusing "trivial pursuit." Ideas too are interrelated. As you conduct your research, you can be on the alert (especially as you record your findings, questions, and observations in your reflective journals) for material that connects.

From Muhammad Ali to Grandma Rose

Polly Shulman

When Duncan Watts was pursuing his Ph.D., his adviser was Steven Strogatz, who has written scientific papers with Rennie Mirollo, who was a teaching assistant for Steve Maurer, whose mother used to live down the hall from my Grandma Rose in a high-rise in Hackensack, New Jersey. Small world, huh?

Continued

Such coincidences crop up a lot. They feel so familiar that there's even a popular legend to explain them. According to cocktail-party lore, every pair of people on the planet—a randomly chosen Inuit and a Parisian, a Solomon Islander and a dude from Nebraska—are connected by a chain of at most 6 acquaintances. I personally, to drop only a few names, am 2 steps from Prince Charles and Stephen Hawking, 3 steps from Marilyn Monroe and King Carl XVI Gustaf of Sweden, 4 steps from King Juan Carlos of Spain, and close friends with the brother of a childhood buddy of the crown prince of Holland. The *Discover* art department has grislier connections: The picture editor is 3 steps from John Hinckley, Ted Bundy, and Adolf Hitler. The assistant picture editor is 2 steps from Charles Manson and Bugsy Siegel. The associate art director is 2 steps from Gary Gilmore and 3 from Jeffrey Dahmer (through 1 of his victims). The associate production editor knows a friend of the grandson of the man who assassinated Rasputin. And chances are you too have similar connections.

Without coincidences like these, literature as we know it, from *Oedipus Rex* to *Great Expectations*, could hardly exist. Two recent examples have lent their names to, or maybe borrowed their names from, the phenomenon: *Six Degrees of Separation*, a play and film by John Guare (who's pals with my best friends' father), and *Small World*, a farce about academics who all seem to know each other's colleagues, by the British novelist David Lodge (no connection that I know of).

Strogatz and Watts have also written about the phenomenon, but their paper is a work of math, not fiction. The "small worlds" they study are networks that consist of lots of little cliques, but in which a few members of each clique have connections to other, more distant parts of the network. These longer connections make it easy to find short paths through the network from any one point to any other. "The small-world effect is not just a curiosity about social networks," says Strogatz, an applied mathematician at Cornell. "It occurs in many different kinds of

Continued

networks throughout nature and technology. We give examples of that in our paper, and we also try to give a mathematical way of understanding why it might be so common."

The small-world effect could have a lot to do with how diseases like AIDS spread, for example: the idea that everyone is at most 6 degrees apart takes on a sinister significance when we look for shared sexual partners instead of shared acquaintances. It could also explain how rumors spread, says Watts, who is now a post-doctoral fellow at the Santa Fe Institute. It could explain how a blackout could propagate across an entire power grid, how year 2000 bugs could bring down vast computer systems, and perhaps even why neurons in the brain are connected the way they are.

The popular conception of the small-world phenomenon may have arisen from a 1967 experiment by Harvard sociologist Stanley Milgram, who asked people in Kansas and Nebraska to get letters to strangers living in Boston by sending the letters to friends who they thought might have a chance of knowing the Boston targets, or of knowing people who did. Milgram found that half the letters took 5 intermediaries or fewer to reach their targets. "That was the experiment that I think led to the idea of 6 degrees of separation," says Strogatz. But for 30 years, until he and Watts turned their attention to the problem, it remained mostly social-science territory. . . .

Watts and Strogatz started by looking at the kinds of networks mathematicians already know quite a bit about: highly structured networks—such as the graph-paper lattice of atoms that make up a crystal of salt—and completely random networks. "Cubic lattices are great to study," says Watts, "because any part of the lattice looks the same as any other part. It's relatively easy to do analysis on things like that." It's also easy to do analysis on networks that are completely random "because even though you can't figure things out exactly for random networks, you can do things approximately or statistically. . . ."

Continued

Networks that are neither completely random nor as regular as graph paper are much harder to understand mathematically. And very many real-world networks, perhaps even most, seem to fall in the middle. So Watts and Strogatz built model networks that fell in the middle, too. They began with a beautifully structured network called a ring graph. Although it's not quite as symmetrical as a lattice, it would still warm a control freak's heart.

"Think of a lot of people standing in a circle holding hands," says Watts. "Say there are a million people and you know 100 of them. You know 50 people on your left and 50 people on your right, and they are the only ones you can communicate with. What if you want to get a message to person number 500,000 on the other side of the circle—how do you do that? Well, you just shout the message to your farthest friend, number 50 on your left side, and say, 'Pass it on.' The best they can do is shout to their fiftieth friend to the left, and so on. So you have to go from 0 to 500,000 in steps of 50 That's 10,000 steps. From you to the farthest person in the world, in this particular world, is 10,000." The distance between you and number 250,000, a quarter of the way around the circle, will be 5,000. Between you and number 125,000, an eighth of the way, it will be 2,500; between you and number 300,000, a bit more than a quarter of the way around the circle, it will be 6,000. On average, there are 5,000 steps between pairs of people in this world. And 5,000 degrees of separation, as Watts points out, is an awful lot.

Now imagine the same million people standing in the same circle. Each still has 100 friends. But instead of knowing only the 50 people to the left and the 50 to the right, everyone chooses friends at random from the million people available. "Because you can pick from a million, and there are only a few people standing near you, chances are you will almost always pick someone who is not physically close to you," says Watts. Now when he and Strogatz calculate the average degree of

Continued

separation between two people, it comes out to about 4, which is easy to believe—start multiplying 100 by itself and in 3 steps you've hit a million. ("Why do we say 4 on average and not 3?" asks Watts. "Because by the third step, it's quite likely that people will be picking friends who have already been selected, so some people will have been reached twice and others not at all. If you go out another degree, to 4, you probably really have reached just about everyone.")

The other thing you'll notice about this random network, says Watts, is that almost none of your friends know one another. The first, orderly circle, in contrast, is what mathematicians call highly clustered. It's full of cliques. "The guy next to you knows almost everyone you do," says Watts. "You have an almost complete overlap of friendship. And even your farthest friend knows half of your friends. Each person is not adding much to the pool of acquaintances, whereas in the random world it's very clear that each new person is opening new doors."

But what happens between the orderly world and the random one? To find out, Watts and Strogatz started with an orderly model and carefully messed it up, making worlds that were progressively random. "On the computer you build the first world, the ring, and then you just start picking up connections between people at random and moving them, as if they were made of bungee cords," says Watts. So instead of knowing the 50 people to your right and the 50 to your left, you might know the 50 to your right and 49 of the 50 to your left. But number 17 to your left is a stranger; instead you're close friends with number 307,411.

These new connections quickly bring the world closer together. In a big world, says Watts, "if you make one of these random connections, the chances are that you will connect to somebody who is many, many degrees of separation away from you. When you do that, a lot happens. Before that connection was made, you were maybe 1,000 degrees of separation apart; now you're 1 degree apart. So that's a big difference for the 2 of you. But it's not just the 2 of you involved, it's also your

Continued

friends. All your 100 friends are now 2 degrees of separation away from that person, and they are only 3 degrees of separation away from all of that person's friends. So suddenly, whereas they were all more than 1,000 degrees of separation apart, now they're only 3 degrees. And your friends of friends and their friends of friends are only 5 degrees of separation apart. So huge chunks of the world are being brought closer together by virtue of a single connection."

It takes only a tiny number of rewirings—less than 1 percent of the total connections—to bring the average degree of separation down from 5,000 to just over 4, close to the average degree of separation of a random world. With a few random encounters, the big, wide world becomes virtually as small as a random world. . . .

But how common are small worlds in nature? Strogatz and Watts began looking around for networks in which every connection was known, allowing them to determine the shortest possible path between any 2 points. Such networks were hard to find, but they turned up 3: the neural network of *Caenorhabditis elegans,* a nematode worm; the power grid of the western United States, a map of power stations connected to one another by high-voltage transmission lines; and the Hollywood graph, a database of everyone who has ever acted in a feature film. "That includes silent movies, movies made in India—everything," says Strogatz, "so that's an enormous graph, with currently about 300,000 actors in it—although it gets bigger every day. You say that 2 actors are connected if they've ever been in a movie together." People use this very database—available on the Web at *http://www.cs.virginia.edu/~bct7m/baco.*html—to play a game called Six Degrees of Kevin Bacon, tracing connections between the *Footloose* thespian and other Hollywood luminaries. Charlie Chaplin, for example, is only 3 steps from Kevin Bacon—he was in *The Countess from Hong Kong* with Marlon Brando; Brando was in *Apocalypse Now* with Laurence Fishburne; and Fishburne was in *Quicksilver* with Kevin Bacon.

Continued

Although Watts and Strogatz chose those three examples because they were the only networks they could find in which all the connections were known—"It's not like this was some crafty choice," says Strogatz—all turned out to be small worlds. Bingo, all three times. So the researchers suspect that the natural world is teeming with small worlds. But, of course, they don't know for sure. "Is this as widespread a phenomenon as we guess it is?" asks Strogatz. "I would look forward in the future to work by, say, neurologists mapping out brain networks or other nervous systems. The people who study ecology could study food webs—which organisms are eating each other. In economics it would be interesting to trace out networks of markets and consumers and buyers and sellers. I'm sure there are people who are thinking about networks theory in economics and finance—it could be at the level of whole nations interacting, or even just individual people."

READING QUESTIONS

1. *When they began to study the small-world effect, Strogatz and Watts looked at completely random networks and highly structured networks. Why did they start with these two kinds of networks? Why are these networks not like most networks in the real world?*

2. *Looking for real-world examples, Strogatz and Watts came up with the neural network of a certain kind of nematode worm, the power grid of the western United States, and the Hollywood graph. Polly Shulman, the author, suggests many other uses for the small-world theory, including the spread of AIDS and the effect of the Y2K bug. What other uses do you see for the small-world effect?*

EXERCISE 7–5

In this article, Polly Shulman describes an experiment by Stanley Milgram in 1967: "He asked people in Kansas and Nebraska to get letters to strangers living in Boston by sending the letters to friends they thought might have a chance of knowing the Boston strangers, or of knowing people who did." Using e-mail and the Web, run a version of Milgram's experiment. Using a function like the "People Search" on Yahoo!, locate a random stranger in a city at least 1,000 miles from your location. Then, send an e-mail to someone you know who you think might know the stranger or who might know someone who knows the stranger. In your e-mail, you should explain what you are doing and why you are doing it; you should also ask that the stranger you are trying to get in touch with send you an e-mail when he or she is contacted. See how many people it takes to get an e-mail to your targeted person.

EXERCISE 7-6

Shulman also mentions a Web site at the University of Virginia that can be used to play "Six Degrees of Kevin Bacon." The same people have constructed a site that allows you to find the connections between any two stars. Point your browser at *http://www.cs.virginia.edu/oracle/star_links.html,* and play the game. See if you can find two stars that are linked by more than six degrees of separation.

The study of history is very much concerned with drawing connections and discovering context. In the following article, Richard Stengel draws connections among several minor figures in history and places those connections in the context of major twentieth-century events.

Dubious Influences

Richard Stengel

We all know about Carlyle's Great Man theory of history, but what about the Creepy Guy Behind the Curtain theory of history or the Meddlesome Housemaid Who Spikes the Punch theory or the Wife Who Whispers in the Great Man's Ear theory?

History is written by the victors, but what of those who called in sick that day? Or those who opted not to play? What of the individual who performed one small act that set in motion a great, grand tumult of actions that changed history?

Consider Gavrilo Princip.

He is the 19-year-old Serbian student who assassinated Archduke Francis Ferdinand in Sarajevo in 1914, which ignited the conflagration of World War I, which yielded the Treaty of Versailles, which deeply embittered an Austrian corporal named Adolf Hitler, who in response booted up the great horror of World War II, which yielded the Treaty at Yalta, which divided Eastern Europe in such a way that another Serb named Slobodan Milosevic felt the need to ethnically cleanse Kosovo.

Continued

Gavrilo Princip, Trigger of the Century.

History belongs not only to the victors but also to the morally ambiguous. We tend to cite those individuals who divide most conveniently into black and white, good and evil, like characters in an old western. Those who are shades of gray, who are moral relativists, are relegated to a place outside the canon. This group includes those who may have the right idea but whose biography is dodgy, to say the least.

Heidegger was a towering philosopher but an odious man with Nazi sympathies. Whittaker Chambers was mostly right about communism and Alger Hiss, but he was a nasty piece of work and no one likes a snitch. Even Joe McCarthy may have been on to something, but he was a crude and cruel man who ruined people's lives for 48-point type. You might call this the When Bad People Spoil Good Things school of history.

Of course, there are those whose intentions were malign but not all that influential, whose perniciousness petered out. Father Coughlin's anti-Semitic rants on the wireless never really amounted to much. Preacher Billy Sunday swore that when Prohibition finally came, "Hell would be rent forever." Fat chance of that happening any time soon. George Wallace's cry of "Segregation now, segregation tomorrow, segregation forever!" lasted only a decade before it was relegated to the dustbin of ugly 19th century prejudices. Call this the When Bad People Don't Do All That Much Damage theory of history.

There are also those who started a movement or hitched their wagon to an idea that never quite panned out. Or the idea succeeded, but it's one that makes us uncomfortable. Chiang Kai-shek was a contender for a billion people's loyalty but played his cards wrong. Marcus Garvey preached racial separatism and opposed interracial marriage; his ideas seem rather quaint now. Whether Hugh Hefner was a pioneer of the sexual revolution or just piggybacked on it is impossible to know, but in the age of AIDS and poverty caused by out-of-wedlock births, his hedonism-without-tears philosophy makes him look like Austin Powers with

Continued

better teeth. Timothy Leary preached the liberating power of psychedelic drugs, but aside from *Lucy in the Sky with Diamonds,* the legacy of LSD seems to be a lot of boring baby-boomer anecdotes and some black light posters in the attic. But who knows: Is Leary's time past, or is it yet to come? The great caveat of historians is "It's too soon to tell."

Then there are those folks who altered history but in ways that make us a bit squeamish. They launched notions that we're not proud of and that may have engendered consequences we regret. Edward Bernays, the father of public relations (what we now blithely call spin), figured out how to get people to buy things they did not really want and feel things they did not really believe in. His legacy may be political campaigns without content, women who thought Virginia Slims were liberating, and an epidemic of credit-card debt.

History looks backward, not forward, so there are those for whom the jury is still out. Legions of computer whizzes in Silicon Valley are certain that they're remaking history as we speak. Maybe they are. Patrick Steptoe, the British doctor who created the first test-tube baby in 1978, has certainly changed the history of thousands of families. And who is to say that one of those test-tube babies will not change history? What new Gavrilo Princip is yet to be born?

It's too soon to tell.

READING QUESTIONS

1. *Stengel starts his article with a reference to Carlyle's "Great Man theory of history." What is this theory? (You might have to go to the library to find the answer to this one or look it up on the Internet.)*
2. *What are the alternate "theories" of history that Stengel proposes? How are these theories different from Carlyle's?*
3. *What facts does Stengel connect in this article? Are these connections parallel or sequential?*

EXERCISE 7-7

Draw a diagram of the connections in Stengel's article using the appropriate model.

DISCOVERING CONNECTIONS AND CONTEXTS: STUDENT WRITING

The connections and contexts papers from our student writers show two of the many directions that this assignment can take. Note that the writers are focusing on only a part of their topic as they look at connections and context for their facts. Tobi Raney's project looks at self-esteem, but for this assignment, she focused on the development of the female athlete and its connections to the advent of bicycling, the two world wars, and the civil rights and peace movements of the 1960s.

Julie McDowell shows another way to go after this assignment. She narrows her focus from the effects of aspartame to look at the parallel connections between the development and testing of cyclamates, saccharin, and aspartame.

From Corsets to Converse

Tobi Raney

"You've come a long way baby," read the words of a modern cigarette ad for women. Indeed, black and white pictures of corseted ladies demurely sipping tea look ridiculous next to bright pictures of women riding motorcycles, working in the office, and striding confidently down large streets. It is hard to believe that teaching, nursing, and homemaking were once the only careers available to young women when today they aspire to become executives, doctors, and police officers. Looking at another scope of life, it's also unbelievable that, once, women were not allowed to physically exert themselves. Today televisions broadcast the feats of women boxers, WNBA stars, and female Olympians. These radical changes of women in society raise many questions, particularly in the athletic realm. How did civilization change from defining the perfect female as a quiet, gentle species to allowing rough, sometimes violent competition between women? Clearly, when we investigate this change in the sporting realm, we cannot ignore the context of the society in which these changes took place. It is only when we understand the world's view of women and how that view has changed that we can begin to investigate the evolution of women's sports.

Continued

Up until, and even throughout, much of the 1900's, a woman's future plans consisted of growing up, marrying and bearing children. Her career options were extremely limited. If she did work, it was for ridiculously low pay. The "perfect" woman was genteel, modest, shy, fragile, conventional, and above all else, subordinate to men. Almost every aspect of her life was dictated by society's standards of women. Her dress was to be modest and, consequentially, restricting; layers upon layers of thick, tight undergarments topped by long, full skirts (Talamini 278). Women had few rights other than those afforded them by their husbands. No women's trade unions existed for the working middle class females. Few labor-saving devices eased the burden of housework. Women could not vote. They dared not break convention and propose a new idea or thought. Until 1848, there was very little public recognition of women's rights, and only a brave few dared to argue for such privileges (Dyer 121).

However, in 1848 the first Women's Rights Convention in America began to address the limitations facing women. At this meeting, it was decided that, although fighting for women's suffrage was too radical, efforts would be made to guarantee women the right to own property, have custody of children in cases of divorce, obtain a higher education, and participate fully in religious activities. It took many years before their goals were reached, but slowly the Women's Movement began to reshape society's "ideal woman" (Faragher et al. 371).

At this same time, the very beginnings of women's athleticism were slowly emerging. Until the 19th century, the only forms of recreation available to women were horse riding and dancing (Dyer 120). At the turn of the century, it became acceptable for women to participate in croquet, lawn tennis, archery, and some golf. These "sports," though, were hardly such. Due to the ridiculously modest dress, women could hardly bend over to hit a tennis ball. The few existing women's sports were played standing straight up. Furthermore, competition was considered unladylike. The sport was played merely "for playing's sake."

Continued

Women were discouraged, even forbidden, to take the game seriously. Such an offense would make a woman appear masculine and not at all attractive.

It was not until the growth of secondary and then later tertiary education that women's sport truly began. The popular new sport of bicycling helped set athletics into action (121). The incompatibility of current dress and bicycling spurred a rise in ladies' hemlines. Soon, lawn tennis dresses revealed the female ankle (Talamini 278). With a bit more freedom of movement, women began to realize they could enjoy and benefit from sports. In 1903, studies were published that linked health to physical activity in women. Soon after, the American Physical Education Association appointed a women's athletics committee (Twin xxiv; Dyer 121). Slowly, women were allowed, even encouraged, to engage in light physical activity. The "ideal girl" shifted from an inactive, delicate creature to an active, graceful girl who was skillful in one sport, but did not make her athletic ability her chief hobby.

World War I brought on another big change in the role of the American woman. With their men off to war, women were forced to take on heavy industrial jobs. Women proved to be more capable than anyone had thought. Similarly, in the sports world, women temporarily filled men's role in athletic entertainment by drawing crowds to their softball games (Twin xxvii). In this era, women truly began to realize the scope of their own worth. At the end of the war, women finally attained the right to vote. However, feminism is said to have died with the victory of women's suffrage (xxxii). While the right to vote allowed her freedom, it did not change the role of the woman in the public eye (Talamini 280).

Athletic feminism followed shortly behind the women's movement, but it too lay dormant after a while. Its first wave ended in 1936, and not much was changed in the world of women's rights until the 1970's. However, historical events continued to reshape the woman's role in society. The Great Depression of the 1930's required women to assist in

Continued

providing income for their family. World War II, much like the First World War, obliged women to take on new capacities. Rosie the Riveter, a strong, confident woman of the work force, became the poster girl of the World War II era. A few women went even farther and joined the armed forces. By the end of the war, the role of the woman had expanded. She was still primarily a homemaker, but her emancipation in the 1920's, additional income during the Depression, and robustness during the Second World War brought her a responsibility almost equal to that of men (281).

As women slowly grew in autonomy, education, and economic productivity, the woman's movement emerged once more. The percentage of women in the work force doubled from 1920 to 1975 (Twin xxxvi). This drastic change instigated a feminist revolution in the late 1960's (Faragher et al. 950). The new women's movement revived sports as a feminist issue. It was not long before Title IX ensured equal representation of women's and men's athletics in federally funded institutions (Twin xxxvi). This directive abolished sex discrimination that had been present in sports since the first Olympic games in ancient Greece. It is not hard to understand this radical change when we, again, observe the context that it took place in. The roots of the modern feminist movement lay in the civil rights and peace movements of the 1960's. These movements emphasized equality and fought for their objectives through legal means. Sex discrimination could not reasonably be found constitutional. Therefore, all it took was someone willing to appeal for gender equality in the area of sports, and the Supreme Court was obligated by the Constitution to grant it.

The main obstacles then lay in society's view of women. They were quite liberated from corsets and petticoats, but the average female was still not able to compete athletically and fulfill America's standards of femininity. The changes that would eventually allow women to be both athletes and "ladies" came gradually. Scholastic intramural programs

Continued

expanded in the 1940's. Society adjusted to women's participation in various sports. Not all sports became socially acceptable at once, though. Female tennis athletes were quickly approved of, but competitive female swimmers were long disgraced. Then, as they grew in number, swimmers did not seem so radical anymore. The new scandal existed in the daring female track athletes. However, women's track events were gradually added to the Olympics, particularly in the mid 60's and early 70's. Slowly, more and more women began to participate in basketball, track, weightlifting, and other "masculine" sports. Slowly, they gained admission, and eventually acceptance. As demand increased for such activities, new teams and clubs formed. As their opportunities increased, the number of women in sports grew. As female athletes grew in abundance, they were no longer a shocking minority, but a brave assemblage. Little by little the female athlete gained respect and recognition.

It seems phenomenal that the female athlete, once nonexistent, has become the strong, assertive, conditioned woman we see on the court and in the field today. This impact is a huge one in the eyes of society. Yet even more powerful is the change that has occurred in women's perception of themselves. It is evident that women, as a whole, have become more self-confident as their rights progress. How much have sports had to do with this progression? When the Olympics first started, women were punished by death for even watching certain events (Dyer 120). Now we don't think twice about attending the many events where women sweat, grunt and lay their hearts and bodies on the line. This drastic change took many years and came about only because the role of the woman changed in society. It is only in this context that we can understand the growth and changes in women's sports.

Continued

Works Cited

Dyer, K.F. *Challenging the Men: Women in Sport.* New York: U of Queensland P, 1982.

Talamini, John T. *Sport and Society: An Anthology.* Boston: Little, Brown, 1973.

Twin, Stephanie L. *Out of the Bleachers.* New York: The Feminist Press, 1979.

Faragher, John Mack, et al. *Out of Many.* New Jersey: Prentice Hall, 1997.

Passing the Sugar Bowl
Julie McDowell

Sugar, how sweet it is. These tiny crystals are today found in numerous items from cereal, ice cream, and cookies, to Coca-Cola, lemonade, and iced tea. Popular, too, are another class of sweeteners—artificial. Also known as sugar substitutes, artificial sweeteners have given humans a low-calorie option to their favorite foods. Especially alluring to diabetics and dieters, their satisfying taste may come at a price.

The artificial sweetener, aspartame, has been a common staple in American "diet" foods and beverages since the early 1980s. Although much controversy has surrounded it since it was first submitted for FDA approval, aspartame is not the first artificial sweetener to face such problems. In fact, two other sweeteners, cyclamates and saccharin, were subjects of investigation after published studies linked them to cancer in laboratory rats.

In 1937, Michael Sveda, a University of Illinois doctorate student, "accidentally" discovered cyclamates while conducting experiments on sulfamic acids and its salts. The sweet taste he noticed on a cigarette that

Continued

had touched the mixture was later identified as sodium cyclohexyl-sulfamate (cyclamate).

In 1950 Abbott Laboratories began production of a cyclamate mixture, Sucaryl, which was used as a tabletop sweetener. Thirty times sweeter than sugar, it was marketed in the forms of cyclamic acid, sodium cyclamate, and calcium cyclamate. Noted for its versatility (solid and liquid forms, heat stability, etc.), cyclamate was initially sold as an aide to those with medical complications such as diabetes. However, as dieting gained popularity in the 1950s, manufacturers began to aim Sucaryl at those who wanted to lose weight (Sapolsky, 1986).

Despite the popularity of cyclamates in America, the sweetener was found to be a carcinogen. Japanese studies found that when ingested, the sweetener is partly broken down into cyclohexylamine, a toxic substance that can cause a danger to the unborn and newborn whose mothers consumed cyclamates. Cyclamate's not-so-sweet end came in October 1969 when Dr. Jacqueline Verrett, a biochemist employed by the FDA, announced on national television the birth defects that she had observed in chickens given cyclamate while in the egg ("Bitter Sweetener," 1974). Another FDA study also published that month linked a calcium-cyclamate and saccharin mixture to causing bladder cancer in rats. These events led to almost-immediate removal of most cyclamates from foods and beverages and its eventual ban on August 27, 1970 ("Bitter Sweetener").

With the ban on cyclamates, Americans had only saccharin to use for an artificial sweetener. This substance, the oldest known sugar-free sweetener, was also an accidental discovery. Johns Hopkins University chemist, Constantin Fahlberg, found in 1879 that a toluene/petroleum compound resulted in a substance 300 to 400 times sweeter than sugar ("Saccharin," 1999). Charles Remsen, also of Johns Hopkins, is additionally given credit for the discovery (Sapolsky, 1986).

At the turn of the century, saccharin made its mainstream appearance, primarily as a preservative and antiseptic. Over eighty years

Continued

ago, however, it began to be recognized for its sweetness, and thus began saccharin's use in foods and beverages. Other items containing the sweetener include toothpastes, cosmetics such as lipstick, as well as prescription and non-prescription drugs. In contrast to cyclamate, saccharin produces a bitter aftertaste and loses its stability when exposed to heat.

Following the ban on cyclamates, investigations began to look into possible carcinogenic effects from saccharin. The Wisconsin Alumni Research Foundation found a link to bladder cancer in male rats in a 1972 study (Sapolsky, 1986). The study that led the FDA to seriously consider a ban on saccharin, though, was a three-year Canadian government observation of two generations of rats.

In the study one hundred rats were fed high doses of saccharin and were compared to one hundred control rats. Of the first generation, three of the rats being given the saccharin developed tumors of the bladder, while fourteen of the second generation—whose mothers were fed saccharin while pregnant—died ("Fight," 1977).

The FDA's announcement on March 9, 1977, of an intended ban on saccharin led to much public outrage. Those who were pro-saccharin argued that one would have to drink 800 servings of twelve-ounce, saccharin-sweetened drinks every day for a lifetime in order to achieve the equivalent amount that test rats received. Even the American Cancer Society spoke out in defense of saccharin. The ACS's president, R. Lee Clark, commented that "banning saccharin may cause great harm to many citizens while protecting a theoretical few" ("Cancer," 1977, p. 276). This statement was in reference to the fact that many diabetics relied on the sweetener to control their blood sugar.

Despite the plan of the FDA, Congress enacted a moratorium that restricted the use of saccharin until further research could be conducted. In addition, manufacturers were required to place a warning label on all products containing saccharin. The saccharin moratorium ended on May

Continued

23, 1979, and today the sweetener is still used under FDA restrictions ("Saccharin," 1999). Because of the restrictions, only twelve milligrams per fluid ounce can be used in beverages; thirty milligrams per serving in processed foods; and twenty milligrams as a table sweetener for every teaspoon of sugar (Harte, Holdren, Schneider, & Shirley, 1991).

In the cases of both cyclamates and saccharin, a clause that came to be known as the Delaney amendment was cited. Included in Section 409 of the 1958 Food Drug and Cosmetic Act, the amendment called for a "zero cancer risk" (Holland, 1997). This clause meant that any study linking a substance to causing cancer would have to be banned. More precise science measurements, however, increased the complexity of the amendment because trivial amounts of substances that could produce minute risks were being found and would, nevertheless, have to be removed.

Due to the ban on cyclamates and the controversy over saccharin, aspartame was looked to as a new alternative in the artificial sweetener craze. The FDA originally approved aspartame, a 1965 discovery by G.D. Searle scientist James M. Schlatter, in 1974. Questions from Dr. John Olney and James Turner, a Washington, D.C. lawyer, about a link between aspartame and brain cancer resulted in an ensuing investigation into the effects of aspartame on the body. In 1979, a precedent three-person board of inquiry was assembled to evaluate the conclusions of these studies and to decide whether or not to allow the sale of aspartame ("Hearing," 1979). Although the board recommended that approval be withheld until more concrete evidence could be found, two of the three board members eventually reversed their opinions (Sapolsky, 1986).

As a result, FDA Commissioner Arthur Hayes, Jr. announced the approval of aspartame in July of 1981. At that time, it was approved only for use as a tabletop sweetener and for use in mixes such as Kool-Aid. These products were required to carry a warning label informing consumers of the presence of phenylalanine, an amino acid that cannot

Continued

be tolerated by people with the genetic disorder phenylketonuria. By 1983, the FDA had also granted permission to use aspartame in beverages.

Though the most costly of the three sweeteners, aspartame (approximately 200 times sweeter than sugar) quickly became more used for foods than saccharin (Harte et al., 1991). Today, question and debate pertaining to whether aspartame causes ailments and diseases—from brain cancer to memory loss—still looms. However, it does not appear to have stopped many consumers. NutraSweet, the brand name of aspartame, is found in over 6,000 products ("All," 1998).

Despite the potential risks of artificial sweeteners, Americans have been reluctant to trade in their sugar substitutes for sugar's calories. An example of this attachment came when the saccharin ban was announced in 1977: "At many stores, weight conscious buyers stripped the shelves bare of their favorite low-calorie products" ("Bitter Reaction," 1977, p. 60). With the evolution of accepted sweeteners, one can only wonder if an even safer alternative will someday replace aspartame in the same way that it replaced saccharin, and saccharin replaced cyclamate.

REFERENCES

All about NutraSweet. (1998). NutraSweet Co.: Author. Retrieved June 25, 1999, from the World Wide Web: http://www.nutrasweet.com/ html/his_about.html.

Bitter reaction to an FDA ban. (1977, March 21). *Time,* 60-61.

Bitter sweetener. (1974, August 26). *Time,* 67.

Cancer Society takes pro-saccharin stand. (1977, April 15). *Science,* 276.

Fight over proposed saccharin ban will not be settled for months. (1977, April 15). *Science,* 276-8.

Continued

Harte, J., Holdren, C., Schneider, S., & Shirley, C. (1991). *Toxics a to z.* Berkeley: University of California Press.

Hearing on sweetener. (1979, July-August). *FDA Consumer, 2.*

Holland, E. (1997, Summer/Autumn). The Delaney era ends. *Frontiers.* Retrieved July 12, 1999, from the World Wide Web: http://www.acs.ohiostate.edu/units/cancer/sa97front/Delaney.html.

Saccharin. (1999). *World Book* [CD-ROM]. Chicago, IL: IBM.

Sapolsky, H. (1986). *Consuming fears: the politics of product risks.* New York: Basic Books.

WRITING ASSIGNMENT: DISCOVERING CONNECTIONS AND CONTEXT

In the last writing assignment, you discovered that many sources need to be consulted to ensure that you get the right facts and get the facts right. In this writing assignment, you will be drawing connections among pieces of your validated evidence and looking for context to help you make sense of those connections.

1. You have already gathered your facts in the validation paper. Now, review your knowledge. Using prewriting or another method, recall what you know about your research topic—this information will include personal knowledge as well as facts from your research.
2. Focus your topic for this essay. You will not be able to address your whole researched writing topic in this essay. Like Tobi and Julie, you will need to focus your essay on a single part or aspect of your topic.
3. Discover connections between the facts you have recalled. Remember that connections can be either parallel (for instance, comparison and contrast) or sequential (for example, chronological).
4. Look for the context of your connections (remember that this step may require further research). What information surrounds the connection? Examine historical events, knowledge, culture, and ways of thinking that might help to explain the connections that you see.
5. Determine the significance of the contextual or connective material—this significance will be the central focus of your essay.
6. As you write your essay, remember to balance general statements (meaning) with concrete, specific statements (facts and evidence).
7. Remember to document your sources according to the format assigned by your instructor.

CHAPTER 8

Critiquing Sources

Selling *It*

Sentimental (and short) journey

For its U.R. the Star videos, Sentimental Journeys Inc. uses a customer's photo as the face of the star of one of several cartoons, thus "personalizing" the video by turning a child (or adult, or pet) into Hercules or Circus Star, for instance. The brochure promises "a 13 to 15 minute adventure. Similar to a Saturday morning cartoon without the commercial interruptions." When a reader complained about a video she had bought, we ordered our own, "Amazing Kid," and submitted the photo of a 4-year-old we know. As our reader had found, our kid's adventure (above, left) was abbreviated: It lasted all of 8½ minutes, at a cost of almost $3 per minute. True, no commercials interrupted the cartoon. Instead, one big commercial—how the videos are made and how to order more (above, right)—came at the end. It lasted three minutes—time for Amazing Kid to have saved at least one more planet from destruction.

Four score and seven gimmicks ago . . .

"This fountain pen," says the spring catalog from Fahrney's Pens Inc., "contains the 'genetic essence' of America's greatest president. Using the most advanced technology, a replication of Lincoln's DNA has been crystallized and embedded in the amethyst stone on the crown of each limited edition pen." What in heaven's name could this mean? asked a reader. We asked Fahrney's. "Someone indirectly connected to the company had a patent on being able to recreate DNA from hair," a customer-service representative told us. "Some of Lincoln's hair was saved and passed on in the family." That hair was used to make a copy of Lincoln's DNA, which was stuck atop the pen's cap. The price per pen: $1,650. So, we asked the representative, could someone clone the sixteenth president from your pen? "No, no, no," she replied.

Before you check, double-check

The form below went to a reader who had ordered a Texaco credit card. If he had checked "yes" (to indicate he'd received his card), signed the form, and followed instructions to "return this form immediately!" he would have signed up for OneCall Protector, to guard his credit cards against fraud. And that service, says the form's flip side, costs $15 per year. How necessary was it, really, to return the form? Not at all, the small print reveals.

Amazing—and true!

This antenna's boasts—it needs no cable box, pulls in all local VHF and UHF channels, requires no satellite fees, and works via "RF technology" —are a tad undermined by the ad's final point. Perhaps the catalog company, Bright Life, thought twice about this revelation: In a later catalog, the last point was missing. For the record, our television expert notes that the antenna has nothing to do with satellites and, at best, would work as rabbit ears do. As for RF (radio frequency) technology, he says, "Every single antenna in the world works that way. That's like saying we all live by breathing."

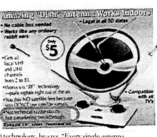

Please Return This Form Immediately!

The following Texaco Credit Card(s) was mailed to you recently:

Please confirm that the card(s) arrived safely.

It's our pleasure to pay you less

In a recent letter, L.L. Bean thanked customers for providing "valuable information to improve" its Outdoor Advantage Program, which gives discounts to those who use an L.L. Bean Visa card. "Today," the letter added, "it is my pleasure to introduce you to the new Outdoor Advantage Program." The letter listed two modest benefits (free mono- gramming and a small drop in the card's annual rate) and two features from the old program (free delivery and no annual fee). The last "improvement"? For every dollar charged at L.L. Bean, cardholders earn 3 percent in coupon dollars; for every dollar charged elsewhere, 0.5 percent. That's nice, but under the old program, they earned 5 percent and 1 percent.

Are you familiar with *Consumer Reports* magazine? It's the publication of an independent agency that evaluates products of all sorts—from cars to dishwashing liquid to frozen pizza and mattresses. *Consumer Reports* often runs a feature on shockingly misleading and false advertising. The preceding illustration is from a recent issue. Some of these ads are pretty humorous, but they're written to be taken seriously—to sell a product.

Obviously, not everyone is taken in by these ads, but a significant enough number of people are. How does this happen? One possibility is that many people simply do not slow down and read carefully. If they did, they'd spot when an advertisement claimed the obvious (the antenna offer), or promoted greater expense as an improvement (the L.L. Bean credit card offer), or made a false claim (the fountain pen offer). Could P.T. Barnum have been right when he said there's a sucker born every minute?

Even when people have nothing to sell, they may still have an agenda to promote. A columnist surveying teen attitudes for *Parade Magazine* asked this question: "Who are more judgmental: boys or girls?" Leslie Taylor, 15, of Haven, Kansas, responded, "Why would you ask us to stereotype either of the sexes? By doing this, you are just asking *us* to be judgmental and stereotypical." Rather than accepting the either-or choices offered to her, Ms. Taylor responded to the way the question itself was asked. A high-five for her—she's a critical thinker.

In Chapter 6, your task was to validate the facts of your topic, and in Chapter 7, you examined how those facts fit into a larger perspective. Now you are ready to critique your sources. Just because something happens to be in print or on the Web doesn't mean it's a reliable and accurate source. In the Information Age, we can access enormous amounts of data by simply logging on to the Internet. That access also multiplies the number of traps awaiting the unwary, uncritical reader. This is not to suggest that we have to be overly suspicious of every article or book we encounter, yet we can still make judgments about even the most well-intended views.

You want to validate your sources' ideas—the claims, conclusions, and deductions the sources use to present their facts—just as you validated the facts themselves. How you validate *ideas* is different from validating *facts*, however. In this chapter, you will learn how to critique your sources: how to read your sources critically and how to organize your thoughts into a coherent evaluation. You will also look at logical fallacies and how we determine an author's credibility because both affect the validity of a source's ideas. Your assignment for this chapter will be to write a critique of an article you have found while researching your project.

DEFINITION: CRITIQUE

| Critique: To decide rightly. |

The word *critique* calls to mind the word *criticize*. And *criticize* has some negative connotations. Normally, we think of criticism as pointing out only what is wrong. Therefore, criticism is unpleasant, especially when it's directed at us. But a closer look at the words *critique* and *criticize* shows that the negative connotations are misleading. Both words are derived from the Greek *kritikos,* which means "able to discern or to judge." *Judge* is derived from the Latin *jus,* which means right or correct, and from *dicere,* which means to decide. So, to critique is to "decide rightly"—to evaluate or judge something.

"To decide rightly" also means that we claim ownership of our judgments. Furthermore, proper criticism requires responsibility. To critique something, we must understand it, know its elements, analyze how those elements are put together, and, finally, evaluate it—judge its worth.

When you critique your sources, you determine their value, truth, quality, and merit. If you discover that a writer is biased in his or her presentation of the material or using "loaded" language to manipulate the reader, you can then choose to use the source with cautionary notation or reject it and move on to another source.

The key word here is *choose.* We critique our sources in order to decide what information suits our purposes. If we do not critique our sources, then we end up using material merely because it somehow relates to our topic. When we do this, we give up control of our researched writing: the writing is no longer our own, but rather a collection of other people's voices.

Critiquing is important in many areas of life beyond academic researched writing. Musicians, photographers, cooks, and travelers critique all the time. In fact, anyone who has to evaluate information and the way information is presented is critiquing. You can use what you learn in this chapter to evaluate a movie, a restaurant, a book, or an offer from a car salesperson. In many (if not all) areas of our lives, critiquing makes it easier for us to make the right choices by deciding rightly.

EXERCISE 8–1

Select two or three advertisements from a recent issue of a popular magazine, and critique the claims that the advertisers make. Are the advertisers being clear and straightforward? Or are the advertisers trying to fool unsuspecting readers? What is your evidence for these claims? Write a one- to two-page summary of your findings.

EXERCISE 8–2

One way to find out about how to critique something is to look at the different kinds of critiques. Using the Internet search engine of your choice, enter "critique" as a search term, and write a one- to two-page summary of the Web pages you find.

TECHNIQUES: CRITIQUING SOURCES

When we encounter information from an outside source, we have certain expectations—the information should be true, logical, clear, coherent, honest, free of bias and prejudice, complete or whole, and reliable. These are the characteristics we use to judge the information. If what we are critiquing fails in any one of these criteria, then we may complain to the editor of a magazine, not buy a book, not return to a restaurant, or tell our friends that such-and-such was a bad movie and they shouldn't waste their money.

Simply reading a source straight through is an uncritical approach that will gain us little beyond understanding what the source says. This is a necessary first step—understanding the content—but it is not sufficient. We also need to look at how the source presents information. After we establish this kind of control, we can begin to make the "right decisions" about the source.

Reading Critically: Encountering the Source

QUESTIONS FOR READING CRITICALLY
1. Is the text presented deductively or inductively?
2. How is the text partitioned?
3. What are the sources of information?
4. How accurate is the information?
5. What is the author's attitude?
6. What is the significance of the piece?

Critical reading involves more than simply discovering the author's ideas: we must actively engage the information, much as you do in a reflective journal. If you don't, you are merely a passive recipient, not a reader or a researcher. As we read a source, we want to answer several questions:

Asking these questions about every source you read is not as overwhelming as it may sound. You probably ask most of these questions already; you just aren't conscious of the process. You will see how familiar these questions are as we take a closer look at each in turn.

(1) Is the text presented deductively or inductively?

In deductive writing, we, as readers, expect to see the thesis at the end of the introduction. Typically, deductive writing attempts to persuade or inform its readers; thus, the readers need to know "up front" what the writer intends to accomplish in the piece, what the writer's purpose is, and what the value of that purpose is for us.

In inductive writing, we expect to learn the thesis at the end of the paper. When the thesis is not presented at the end of the introduction (the opening of the piece), we can expect that the author's purpose is exploratory or analytical and we will be led to the implications of the material near the end of the writing. This approach reflects the "scientific method" of examining the evidence—looking at specifics to determine a conclusion.

Thus, when an author chooses a deductive or inductive organization, he or she establishes a set of expectations for you as the reader, expectations based on the writer's likely purpose. As you read, pay attention to whether or not these expectations are fulfilled.

(2) How is the source partitioned?

Recognizing the source's organization helps you find the thesis. The thesis tells you the specific topic the author is concentrating on and the claim made for that topic. The next step is to locate the topic sentences of the body paragraphs because they partition, or divide into sections, the source's topic.

Typically, you can find the topic sentences at the beginning of the paragraphs, which makes the individual paragraphs themselves deductive in structure. But sometimes an author will structure paragraphs inductively, and place the topic sentence at the end of the paragraph. Occasionally, an author will not directly present the topic sentence, but imply it in the discussion itself.

On a separate sheet of paper, find and list the topic sentences to understand the scope of the topic, the claims made for it, the topic's subtopics, and the organizational patterns that develop the thesis. As you look over your list of topic sentences, ask yourself if the author has included all of the sections that you need to understand the source's topic and claim, and if the author has presented those sections in an order that makes sense to you.

(3) What are the sources of information?

Next, look at the source's own sources to evaluate the support for the topic sentences you just listed. Does the source provide enough evidence to verify the author's claims or conclusions? Merely citing one example, for instance, does not provide adequate support or proof for an author's claim or conclusion. Does the source provide different kinds of evidence as support for the author's claims? A source should provide both primary sources (material originated by the author) and secondary sources as evidence. As in your own researched writing, the author should take ownership of his or her work, so the balance should be tilted toward primary information. Primary and secondary information should be evaluated by slightly different criteria.

When examining primary information, you will need to find out how the author generated it: Did the author conduct original field or laboratory research or conduct surveys? If the author did original research, you want to check if other experts in the field of research have accepted it. If you were researching alternative energy sources, for instance, you might run into the work of Stanley Pons and Martin Fleischmann of the University of Utah. In 1989, these two scientists claimed to have discovered cold fusion—that is, a nuclear reaction that can occur on a tabletop and create a usable power source. Cold fusion, however, is not at all accepted by the scientific community, largely because no one can re-create Pons and Fleischmann's laboratory results.

For surveys, you want to be sure that the number of people surveyed was large enough to be representative of the group being studied or the views being examined. If two people tell you that they plan to vote for the Republican candidate for President, you cannot use those opinions to represent the opinions of a town, state, or country. To get an accurate prediction of a large group's opinions or attitudes, you would need to ask several dozen or even a few hundred people how they would vote. Statisticians and pollsters have mathematical formulas by which they can determine the correct size of a "sample." What you need to look for is that the sample is fairly large (at least 50 to 100 would be a safe number) and that it was randomly selected. If both of these criteria apply to the survey, then the results are likely accurate.

A source can use secondary information as either facts or opinion. If the source is using secondary information as fact, then you want to check the original source of the facts and pay close attention to how your source uses the facts. If your source is using secondary information as opinion, then you want to critique the source of the opinion in the same way you are critiquing your source—ask yourself if the source of the opinion is reliable and accurate.

Then, you need to ask yourself whether your source is presenting original ideas or simply re-presenting others' ideas. If the source is creating original meaning from others' opinions, then the source is likely to be effective in your project. If the source is only presenting the ideas of other authors without creating anything original, then you would be better off using the original source of the opinion.

(4) How accurate is the information?

This question is similar to the last one, except that here we want to separate the facts and the opinions of the source we are critiquing, rather than the source's sources. "Facts" themselves, as we have discussed in earlier chapters, have a way of being elusive. Opinions, or claims, may fool us by the way they are presented, especially if they appeal to our own mindsets or biases. Politicians, among others, know the value of appealing to their listeners' prejudices.

Any claims that a writer makes must be thoroughly grounded in evidence that is accurate and to the point. You can determine whether the evidence is appropriate by validating the source's facts, a process you learned in Chapter 6.

(5) What is the author's attitude?

The author reveals his or her attitude toward the subject through the tone of the writing. If the author is interested primarily in sharing knowledge, then the tone will be neutral. Sometimes, however, writers use tone to emphasize the point they are making. In 1729, for instance, Jonathan Swift wrote an essay entitled "A Modest Proposal" about the starvation and poverty in Ireland. He suggested that Irish infants be sold and served as food, much as cattle were. Obviously, he wasn't serious—and he showed he wasn't serious by using an ironic tone. By making this outrageous proposal, he was in fact criticizing the English policies that created the starvation in Ireland.

The tone of some writers exhibits their prejudices. Rush Limbaugh, for instance, clearly shows his own bias in the terms he uses, such as *femi-nazi, ecopest, wackos,* and *enviro-wackos:* the tone of these words shows that he looks down on these people. If a writer stereotypes people, objects (Sports cars are death traps), animals (Pit bulls are savage killers), or even ideas (Liberalism is unpatriotic), then take a very close look at the writer's conclusions. Is the writer basing conclusions on sufficient evidence or is the writer simply presenting biased attitudes? If the former is true, then the source is likely usable; if the latter is the case, however, then you would be better off looking for a different source to use in your research project.

(6) What is the significance of the piece?

In the old TV show "Dragnet" (which can still be seen in syndication), Sergeant Joe Friday demanded "just the facts." It worked for a TV detective, but just-the-facts doesn't work very well for writers. If writing presented nothing beyond the facts, then we would have little more than a collection of dictionary or encyclopedia entries. Writing becomes more significant only when it uses facts to create unique perspectives or meaning. The more significant a source, the more useful it will be in your research project.

When critiquing a source, you must consider the significance of the meaning the writer creates. Ask yourself: Is the source merely an encyclopedia-like list of facts? Does the author's meaning apply only to the objects or topics he or she is discussing in the source? Is the meaning limited by time or space? Does the meaning apply to other situations or objects in addition to those the author discusses?

EXERCISE 8–3

Using the "Questions for Reading Critically," analyze one of the readings from the last chapter, and summarize your analysis in a one- to two-page paper. Choose from "The New Adolf Hitler?," "Adam and Eve," the excerpt from "Teenage Lincoln Sculptor," and the excerpt from "From Muhammad Ali to Grandma Rose."

TECHNIQUES: DETECTING FALLACIES

When a writer attempts to get you to agree with or understand a position, he or she can use three basic strategies. The most common strategy is to appeal to your reason: the author presents an objective, rational explanation of his or her perspective. In trying to sell you a car, for instance, a salesperson could explain that this particular model gives you the greatest number of features for the least amount of money and will cost the least to operate and maintain, and then the salesperson supports those assertions with specific and concrete evidence.

Another common strategy is to appeal to your emotions: here, the writer tries to manipulate your feelings in an attempt to win you over. You have resisted the salesperson's logical argument, so she tries a new tactic. You need to buy this car because it's a beautiful piece of machinery, because it will make you appear desirable to members of the opposite sex, and because you've worked hard and you deserve this car. No longer trying to convince you to think with reasonable assertions and concrete evidence, the salesperson is trying to get you to feel that you should buy this car.

The third strategy is to appeal to your character: the writer calls upon your morals or values as a way to create agreement. You have resisted all of the salesperson's attempts to sell you a car, so now she tries something new. You should buy this car because you're an American, and it's an American-built car, she says. This car works hard and doesn't quit, she says, just like you at your job. In her final attempt to sell the car, the salesperson has appealed to your values of patriotism and your work ethic.

In creating arguments, writers often make mistakes, or "fallacies." Sometimes these mistakes are made by accident, and while we may feel sympathy for the writer, as readers we must still question the writer's competence and expertise. Sometimes these mistakes are made on purpose—if so, we must question the writer's credibility. Fallacies generally find their way into writing in two ways: One way is through mistakes in thinking when the writer creates an argument, called *logical fallacies*. The other way is through mistakes in presenting the argument to the reader, or *rhetorical fallacies*.

TABLE 8–1

LOGICAL FALLACIES Mistakes made when creating meaning	RHETORICAL FALLACIES Mistakes made when presenting meaning
Begging the question Circular argument False analogy False dilemma Hasty generalization Hypothesis contrary to fact *Non sequitur* *Post hoc, ergo propter hoc* Slippery slope	*Ad hominem* *Ad ignorantium* *Ad misericordiam* *Ad populum* Appeal to tradition Bandwagon Card stacking Equivocation False authority Loaded language Red herring Straw man

Table 8–1 lists the most common fallacies. The list separates the fallacies that occur when we think, and the fallacies that occur when we write. The names alone, however, aren't very helpful, especially because several of the fallacies are usually known by their Latin names. We discuss each fallacy separately in the following sections.

Begging the Question
Assuming the truth of the statement that is being argued.

Example: *This new and improved dishwasher will make your life better.* In this example, the arguer is begging the question of whether the dishwasher is improved. If it is improved, then the dishwasher may very well make life better, but the arguer needs to prove that it is improved. Instead, this arguer simply claims that the dishwasher will make life better, which assumes that the improvements have been demonstrated by evidence.

Circular Argument
Proving an assertion by restating the assertion itself.

Example: *The story is so true to life that the reader knows it is realistic.* The writer here says that the story contains reality and is realistic, which are both the same idea.

False Analogy

Employing an analogy in which the two elements being compared cannot match.

Example: *Students should be allowed to vote on tuition increases because the university is a democracy.* An analogy compares two elements from different contexts. In this case, the comparison is that student is to voter as university (from an education context) is to democracy (from a political context). A university is not a democracy, so the analogy is false.

False Dilemma

Making an either-or, black-and-white, all or nothing assertion that does not allow for possible middle ground.

Example: *If you don't give me a higher grade, I'll be unemployed and homeless for the rest of my life.* The two options presented here are complete failure or complete success. A person can be successful in life even without receiving straight A's.

Hasty Generalization

Drawing a conclusion based on an insufficient number of examples.

Example: *This writer doesn't write very well—he wrote "Web cite" instead of "Web site."* Here, the writer makes a general conclusion about a writer's skill based on a single spelling error. One such mistake, however, is not enough evidence to justify the overall evaluation.

Hypothesis Contrary to Fact

Making an assertion that simply cannot be proven.

Example: *If I had not gone to college, I never would have met the love of my life.* No matter what support you provide here, you cannot prove that this statement is true.

Non sequitur ("It does not follow")

Following one statement with another, unrelated statement.

Example: *If you respected your students, you would curve your grades.* There is no relation between respect for students and curving grades. Thus, it is said that the second idea does not follow on the first idea.

Post hoc, ergo propter hoc ("After this, therefore because of this")

Presenting a temporal relationship as a causal relationship.

Example: *It rained because I washed my car.* Ever notice how it always seems to rain right after you spend hours washing your car? Although it may seem otherwise, there is no causal relationship between the two events. The only relationship is one of time—the rain happens after you wash the car.

Slippery Slope

Claiming that if a course of action is taken (or not taken), then an irreversible set of consequences will inevitably follow.

Example: *If the university cancels English 101 this semester, then my degree will mean nothing.* Despite the writer's argument, canceling one course will not render an entire college education pointless.

Ad hominem ("To the person")

Attacking a person instead of the person's ideas.

Example: *How can my opponent, who grew up in a big house and went to a fancy college, understand the problems of the unemployed and homeless?* Here, the writer cites her opponent's "character"—his upbringing and education—as evidence for his ignorance. This element of the opponent's character is irrelevant to the claim, however. The writer's opponent might, in fact, not understand the problems of the unemployed and homeless, but his upbringing and education do not support the claim.

Ad ignorantium ("To ignorance")

Assuming the truth of a claim because it cannot be proved false.

Example: *Obviously there's life on other planets; we just don't have the technology to contact these beings.* Because we don't have the technology to communicate with aliens, the claim cannot be proved or disproved. There might be life on other planets, but this writer would need to provide evidence that directly supports the claim.

Ad misericordiam ("To pity")

Appealing to the audience's sympathy rather than focusing on the issue.

Example: *Would you mind if I got in line ahead of you? I'm late for an appointment.* The arguer here calls on the audience's pity for her hectic life. What the arguer is ignoring is that she should have started out earlier if she planned to stop at the bank or grocery store before her appointment.

Ad populum ("To the people")

Appealing to the audience's biases or prejudices rather than addressing the issue.

Example: *This is the best car because it's built in America.* This argument appeals to the audience's patriotic bias for products built in this country. It avoids, however, the real issue: an evaluation of the quality of the car itself. Note that this statement also begs the question of the quality of American cars—claims can involve more than one fallacy at once.

Appeal to Tradition

Citing the way things have been as evidence.

Example: *This is the best way to make bread because that's the way my mom made it, and her mother before her, and her mother before her.* Although there may be a long-standing tradition of breadmaking in this family, that fact alone does not prove that the traditional way of making bread is the best way.

Bandwagon

Citing popularity as evidence.

Example: *But, Mom, you have to let me get my tongue pierced—all of my friends have done it.* In this case, although we might not all have been asking for a piercing, we have all attempted to appeal to a parent's sympathy as a way to get what we want. This kind of emotional appeal is faulty, however, because we imply that what is popular is therefore appropriate.

Card Stacking

Ignoring evidence that would weaken the argument.

Example: *This is a wonderful town to live in. It has twelve parks, over a hundred churches, a university, a business school, two hospitals, and a newspaper that supports old-fashioned American values.* Although the town may well include these features, this argument ignores important evidence that might change our perspective, such as unemployment, a high tax rate, and an inept town government.

Equivocation

Using a word or phrase with one apparent meaning but another hidden meaning.

Example: *I didn't steal the car; I just borrowed it without asking.* The writer here wants the audience to understand a difference between the two activities, based on an apparent difference in language. The underlying meaning of the words revealed by the context of the statement, however, shows that the difference is small or nonexistent.

False Authority

Calling on the authority of a person who is not an expert in the field.

Example: *Jim Palmer and Dan Marino are spokespeople for money-lending institutions.* Using sports figures and other celebrities as spokespeople is the most common use of false authority. The advertisers are appealing to our values of hero-worship and respect in one field to demonstrate expertise in an unrelated field. Being a baseball or football great does not qualify someone as a financial expert.

Loaded Language

Using the connotations of words rather than their denotative meaning.

Example: *The cult of "how does this class get me a job" works against the point of a liberal arts education.* The writer allows the negative emotions sparked by the word "cult" to make the argument, rather than offering evidence to support an objective claim.

Red Herring

Providing irrelevant information in an attempt to distract the readers from the real issue.

Example: *I know I should have done my homework, but I saw the greatest movie ever made.* The assertion that the movie the arguer saw is the best ever is presented as a distraction from the real issue of why the homework was not completed.

Straw Man

Distracting the reader by creating an easily refuted issue where no issue exists.

　　Example: *By supporting a bill that lets parents choose what kind of school to send their children to, all the senator is doing is trying to make money for his friends.* Here, the writer tries to distract the reader with an unsubstantiated accusation of corruption, so that the reader does not pay attention to the senator's actual position on the bill.

EXERCISE 8–4

The essay below identifies and explains several logical fallacies, but there are others. Identify and explain the additional fallacies.

Animals Have No Rights: Go Ahead and Lick That Frog
Rush H. Limbaugh III

Rights versus Protection

I'm a very controversial figure to the animal-rights movement. They no doubt view me with some measure of hostility because I am constantly challenging their fundamental premise that animals are superior to human beings. They may deny holding that belief, but the truth is inescapable when you examine the policies they advocate and their invariable preference for the well-being of animals, and their disregard for humans and their livelihoods. It especially bothers them when I state my belief that animals have no fundamental rights. In fact, this statement has bothered more than just animal-rights wackos. Many fellow animal-loving members of my audience misunderstand my point on this as well. But before you jump to the conclusion that I am callous, insensitive, and a heartless animal hater, hear me out. Before beginning the discussion of rights, let me make it perfectly clear that my belief that animals don't have rights is not equivalent to saying that human beings have no moral obligation to protect animals when they can. I am not saying that at all. But this is more, my friends, than a semantic distinction. The animal-rights movement knew what it was doing when it

> **Loaded Language:**
> Persons concerned about the well-being of animals are not as a class mentally unbalanced.

Continued

deliberately adopted the label "animal rights." The concept of "rights" is
very powerful in the American political lexicon. It carries with it no small
amount of clout. If the movement can succeed in drilling into the American
psyche the concept that animals have rights, then there will be far less
outrage at the antibusiness policies the animal-rights people foist onto the
public. If animals have rights, which is after all what we humans have,
then what legal or moral basis do we have to protect ourselves in this war
for dominance of the planet? Let me try to explain the concept of "rights"
and why animals have none.

Rights are either God-given or evolve out of the democratic process.
Most rights are based on the ability of people to agree on a social
contract, the ability to make and keep agreements. Animals cannot
possibly reach such an agreement with other creatures. They cannot
respect anyone else's rights. Therefore they cannot be said to have rights.

Thomas Jefferson, in drafting the Declaration of Independence, did
not begin by saying, "We hold these truths to be self-evident: that all
animals are created equal; that they are endowed by their creator
with certain unalienable rights; that among these are life, liberty
and the pursuit of happiness."

Straw Man: Animals are irrelevant to the issue that Jefferson was addressing.

Webster's defines a "right" as "something to which
one has a just claim. The power or privilege to which one is justly
entitled. A power, privilege, or condition of existence to which one has a
natural claim of enjoyment or possession. A power or privilege vested in a
person by the law to demand action or forbearance at the hands of
another. A legally enforceable claim against another that the other will do
or will not do a given act. A capacity or privilege the enjoyment of which
is secured to a person by law. A claim recognized and delimited by law
for the purpose of securing it."

False Authority: No specific text is cited.

Notice the words *one*, *person*, a claim against *another*. All of these 5
words denote human beings, not animals or any other creatures. Inherent
in the concept of "rights" is the ability to assert a claim to those rights.

Continued

Loaded Language

Implicit in all of these dictionary definitions is that in order to have rights one must know that he has a just claim to them; one must be able to assert them. Only a moron would argue that an animal has the capacity to assert a claim to any rights. An animal cannot avail himself of legal protection through our judicial system or otherwise. Only if humans intervene on its behalf will it have any protection at all.

In my opinion, at the root of the assertion that animals have rights is the belief that animals and men are equal in creation, that man evolved from apes, and that creation is an allegorical myth contained in that wonderful piece of literature known as the Bible. There is no escaping the connection between secular humanism and animal-rights activism.

Non Sequitur: Secular humanism is not relevant to the issue.

The Bible teaches that God created man in His own image and that He placed him on this earth in a position superior to all other creatures, and gave him dominion over animals and nature. God did not create other animals in His own image.

Even if you reject the Bible as the Word of God—even if you believe in evolution and disbelieve in creation—you must still admit that man is the only earthly creature capable of rational thought.

Mortimer Adler, associate editor of the Great Books of the Western World—part of the classics, for those of you in Rio Linda—explains that in the great tradition of Western thought, from Plato right down to the nineteenth century, it was almost universally held that man and man alone is a rational animal. He says that only since the time of Darwin has the opposite view gained any acceptance; and it's mostly among scientists and the educated classes. This relatively new view holds that the difference between man and other mammals is one of degree, not kind. All animals have intelligence, man just has more of it. Adler then goes on to articulate his belief that the traditional view (that man is essentially different from other animals) is undeniable. In support of his belief he cites man's unique ability to make things. Sure, he concedes, bees make hives,

Continued

birds make nests, and beavers make dams, but those productions are purely instinctive. Man's creations involve reason and free will. "In making houses, bridges, or any other of their artifacts, men invent and select. They are truly artists, as animals are not."

Adler also points out that men build machines which are themselves productive. Animals solve problems when they are confronted with a biological urgency of finding a way of getting what they need. But no animals sit down and ponder things and think through problems as man does. Human thinking, he notes, is discursive and involves language. Animals make sounds and communicate; but they do not communicate thought. No animal ever utters a sentence which asserts something to be true or false. Sorry to offend you porpoise and dolphin worshipers out there.

Finally, Adler posits that man is the only animal with a historical development. Men transmit ideas and institutions, a whole tradition of culture, from one generation to another, and it is this which accounts for the history of the human race. In that regard I should like to pose the question to animal rights purveyors: Who is it that writes books about the history and development of animals? Maybe there is dolphin literature in the depths of the ocean, but I'm not going to enroll in the Kennedy Scuba School to find out. . . .

Human beings are the primary species on this planet. Animals and everything else are subspecies whose position on the planet is subordinate to that of humans. Humans have a responsibility toward lower species and must treat them humanely. *Humanely,* now that's an interesting term. Doesn't that mean as a human would like to be treated? Why not treat them animally? Because that would mean killing them. Can't you see? That's my point exactly. Animals often treat each other with no respect, and they have no redress, absent human intervention on their behalf. . . .

False Analogy: Human history is replete with examples of humans killing each other.

The easiest way for the left to exploit animals politically is to try to play upon this notion that the difference between animals and man is only

Continued

one of degree. They seem to go even farther by forwarding the notion that the only difference between us and other mammals is that we have the capacity to subjugate other species. An entire myth has evolved that animals have special abilities and deserve to become a new protected class in society. If you don't believe me, here are some examples I've collected showing just how far the movement to accord animals rights that equal, or even exceed, those of humans, has gone. All of these items are completely true.

The *New York Times* science section recently carried a piece on what it seemed to be saying was the most intelligent being roaming the planet today, our good friend, the dolphin. Many people are convinced that human beings would be infinitely better off if they were only smart enough to understand the dolphin. You see, man is the dunce of the planet, according to animal-rights enviro-wackos. The dolphin is a noble, pure creature.

This twaddle has even crept into science reporting. The *New York Times* reported, "As much as puppies, or pandas or even children, dolphins are universally beloved. They seem to cavort and frolic at the least provocation, their mouths fixed in what looks like a state of perpetual merriment, and their behavior and enormous brains suggest an intelligence approaching that of human beings or even, some might argue, surpassing it."

Non Sequitur: A dolphin's inability to create constructions has nothing to do with its intelligence in its own environment.

I was offended by that. Could somebody please show me one hospital built by a dolphin? Could somebody show me one highway built by a dolphin? Could someone show me one automobile invented by a dolphin?

But vengeance was mine. The *Times* article went on to say that researchers off the coast of Australia have come across male dolphins that engage in very chauvinistic behavior toward female dolphins. This activity is called "herding." "The males will chase after her, bite her, slap her, hit her with their fins, slam into her

Equivocation: Earlier, the author argued the difference between "humanely" and "animally," but now applies the alleged behavior of one human to that of dolphins.

Continued

with their bodies." In other words, Mike Tyson behavioral rules dominate the male dolphin population.

Despite the dolphin's poor dating manners, it's clear that people had better be careful in how they approach this noble creature. Consider Allen Cooper, a hapless fellow from Sunderland, England, who last year was accused of "indecent behavior with a dolphin." Animal-rights activists on a pleasure boat testified that they had seen Cooper fondling a dolphin's penis. Cooper was totally humiliated by the resulting publicity, but a court finally cleared him of indecent-assault charges after expert witnesses testified that dolphins often extend their penises to swimmers as a "finger of friendship."

Apparently not all animals are created equal, according to some animal-rights activists. Some animals that have been happily owned by humans turn out to be politically incorrect and presumably have to be curbed. Take the poor cow. The May 1992 edition of *Countryside* magazine has a story called "The Last Roundup for Beef?" In it, liberal ecopest Jeremy Rifkin argues that without cattle, the world would be green, well fed, and peaceful. He claims that 1.28 billion cattle are now taking up 24 percent of the world's land mass, a ridiculous figure that few in the media will ever challenge.

Rifkin is bent out of shape because he says the cattle consume enough grain to feed hundreds of millions of people. The reason the cattle are eating the grain is so they can be fattened and slaughtered, after which they will feed people, who need a high-protein diet. The combined weight of the cattle exceeds that of the world's human population. I presume Rifkin somehow supports curbing the cow population to limit the damage they are inflicting on mankind.

You may recall that Martin Sheen, the actor, once declared Malibu, California, a sanctuary for the homeless when he was honorary mayor. Well, the Malibu City Council recently went him one better by passing a resolution declaring that Malibu was a "human/dolphin shared

Continued

environment," and urging "warmer relationships between humans and animals." Francis Jeffrey, the cofounder of the Great Whales Foundation, hailed the resolution: "This is a new concept, to say that dolphins are citizens of the community." Mary Frampton, the head of the local Save Our Coast group, told the council that "the dolphins thank you." I wonder how Frampton knows when any dolphins are thanking anyone. Why can't the little talking geniuses communicate this message themselves? After all, Frampton may be lying about what the dolphins told her. We need to hear it from the dolphin's mouth—that is, if we are smart enough to understand what they are trying to tell us. This whole episode just proves what happens when rich people in trendy coastal communities have too much free time on their hands.

Many ski boots are lined with dog fur, and the New York City ASPCA wants to outlaw such boots. Once again, animal-rights activists are lunging for the law rather than examining the facts. Technica US, a ski boot maker in New Hampshire, says all of its boots are made using dog skin from China, where dogs have been raised for food for thousands of years. At least they aren't using cat hair to line their boots. Then Technica's products would be called "Puss in Boots.". . .

Have you heard of frog licking? Now I know you all lead busy lives, so you probably missed it when it showed up in the papers. But I was amazed when I read that frog licking has become a major preoccupation in Colorado. How could this possibly get started? It had to be this way. An environmentalist is out in the woods communing with nature. Probably some overgrown Boy Scout in little green shorts, a backpack filled with

Ad Hominem: Attacks on environmentalists and Boy Scouts.

wheat nut mix. He's wearing his Walkman, skipping along some nature trail listening to Madonna music, probably the *Don't Bungle the Jungle* album.

So he's communing with the Nature Goddess and maybe even humming. Ommmmmm-Ommmmmm-Ommmmmmm. He looks at a tree and maybe he says, "Hi, Greg." Maybe he hugs the tree. "Oh, I am at

Continued

one with this tree." Then he spies a frog and suddenly stops. "Oh, look at that frog. Maybe I should pick it up and lick it." And gets high as a result. You see, the Colorado spotted toad secretes a hallucinogenic substance that can get you high if you lick it near the back of its head. Well, I'm sorry, but most people I know wouldn't lick a frog even if it did give them a buzz. Can you imagine doing that? Well, somebody did it. Somebody had to—otherwise we wouldn't know of this enlightened and marvelous way of turning on. But the amazing thing is that the first person who did it had to tell someone else he did it, who then passed it on for posterity's sake.

Tell me, who would do that kind of thing? I don't know, but they couldn't be considered normal. There may even be a conflict here between environmentalism and animal-rights types. Isn't it a violation of the frog's rights if he is licked?

Frogs aren't the only creatures we have to worry about, of course. You know, the sea turtle is an endangered species too. How so, you ask? Well, evil shrimpers happen to nab a couple of sea turtles now and then while murdering zillions of shrimp. Anyway, a guy in Florida was hauled into court for stealing some sea turtle eggs. The judge found him guilty and fined him $106,000. He said, "Wait a minute, these are not sea turtles, these are sea turtle eggs, and there's no law saying I can't steal them." "Sir," the judge replied, "they're going to be sea turtles. Guilty." The guy was stuck with a $106,000 fine. All this makes me wonder about our priorities. When does a sea turtle's life begin? At conception or when it's laid?

By the way, did you ever wonder why people always worry about sea turtles but ignore the lives of the shrimp? Flipper, the dolphin, is high on everybody's protection list. We kill maybe two dolphins for every 1 million tuna, and yet nobody is expressing any concern for the tuna. They're just a bunch of useless creatures. But dolphins are another matter. They're smart and they're cute. They even have a smile on their face!

Continued

And they try to talk to us. Too bad we're not intelligent enough to understand them.

Conclusion

The point is that animals do not have rights but are accorded protection by human beings. When we establish laws against cruelty to animals, some mistake the laws to be the same as rights. They are not, however.

I received a letter on this subject from a listener, Chris Huson, of Champaign, Illinois. He agreed with the premise that animals have no rights but are instead accorded protection by humans. He then illustrated the difference by observing that the "right to privacy" is not a right, but rather a protection granted by the government. The "right to privacy" does not allow you to take drugs in your car or home with impunity. The privacy is protected but does not therefore allow you to break the law.

He further stated in his letter that the basic right to life of an animal — which is the source of energy for many animal-rights wackos — must be inferred from the anticruelty laws humans have written, not from any divine source. Our laws do not prevent us from killing animals for food or sport, so the right to life of an animal is nonexistent.

He is right and I don't think it can be stated much better. Yet, we are confronted daily by people who wish to obstruct human progress and individual economic choices by virtue of elevating the importance of animal existence to that of human existence. The only way this can happen is for the force of law to be used to devalue human life.

Well, it is time some of us began to speak up for the sanctity of *human* life and the glories of humankind, which was created in God's image. If the wackos prefer to live in caves, let's provide them with free transportation there. As for the rest of us and our posterity, let's do what we can to treat ourselves with the respect and dignity that God intended.

Non Sequitur: Where opponents of the presented point of view choose to live is irrelevant to the issue.

CRITIQUING SOURCES: PROFESSIONAL WRITING

We have already mentioned Erich von Däniken's *Chariots of the Gods,* a book that argues that intelligence was established on the earth by aliens. The following essay is one of the many critiques of von Däniken's book available on the Internet. In this critique, the author takes a close look at the book's argument.

Ancient Astronauts and Erich von Däniken's Chariots of the Gods
Robert Todd Carroll

The term 'ancient astronauts' designates the speculative notion that aliens are responsible for the most ancient civilizations on earth. The most notorious proponent of this idea is Erich von Däniken, author of several popular books on the subject. His *Chariots of the Gods? Unsolved Mysteries of the Past,* for example, is a sweeping attack on the memories and abilities of ancient peoples. Von Däniken claims that the myths, arts, social organizations, etc., of ancient cultures were introduced by astronauts from another world. He questions not just the capacity for memory, but the capacity for culture and civilization itself, in ancient peoples. Prehistoric humans did not develop their own arts and technologies, but rather were taught art and science by visitors from outer space.

   Where is the proof for von Däniken's claims? Some of it was fraudulent. For example, he produced photographs of pottery that he claimed had been found in an archaeological dig. The pottery depicts flying saucers and was said to have been dated from Biblical times. However, investigators from *Nova* (the fine public-television science program) found the potter who had made the allegedly ancient pots. They confronted von Däniken with evidence of his fraud. His reply was that his deception was justified because some people would only believe if they saw proof!

Continued

However, most of von Däniken's evidence is in the form of specious and fallacious arguments. His data consists mainly of archaeological sites and ancient myths. He begins with the ancient astronaut assumption and then forces all data to fit the idea. For example, in Nazca, Peru, he explains giant animal drawings in the desert as an ancient alien airport. The fact that the lines of the drawing would be useless as a runway for any real aircraft because of their narrowness is conveniently ignored by von Däniken. The likelihood that these drawings related to the natives' science or mythology is not considered. He also frequently reverts to false dilemma reasoning of the following type: "*Either* this data is to be explained by assuming these primitive idiots did this themselves *or* we must accept the more plausible notion that they got help from extremely advanced peoples who must have come from other planets where such technologies as anti-gravity devices had been invented."

There have been many critics of von Däniken's notions, but Ronald Story stands out as the most thorough. Most critics of von Däniken's theory point out that prehistoric peoples were not the helpless, incompetent, forgetful savages he makes them out to be. (They must have at least been intelligent enough to understand the language and teachings of their celestial instructors—no small feat!) It is true that we still do not know how the ancients accomplished some of their more astounding physical and technological feats. We still wonder how the ancient Egyptians raised giant obelisks in the desert and how stone age men and women moved huge cut stones and placed them in position in dolmens and passage graves. We are amazed by the giant carved heads on Easter Island and wonder why they were done, who did them, and why they abandoned the place. We may someday have the answers to our questions, but they are most likely to come from scientific investigation not pseudoscientific speculation. For example, observing contemporary stone age peoples in Papua New Guinea, where huge stones are still found on top of tombs,

Continued

has taught us how the ancients may have accomplished the same thing with little more than ropes of organic material, wooden levers and shovels, a little ingenuity and a good deal of human strength.

We have no reason to believe our ancient ancestors' memories were so much worse than our own that they could not remember these alien visitations well enough to preserve an accurate account of them. There is little evidence to support the notion that ancient myths and religious stories are the distorted and imperfect recollection of ancient astronauts recorded by ancient priests. The evidence to the contrary—that prehistoric or 'primitive' peoples were (and are) quite intelligent and resourceful—is overwhelming.

Of course, it is possible that visitors from outer space did land on earth a few thousand years ago and communicate with our ancestors. But it seems more likely that prehistoric peoples themselves were responsible for their own art, technology and culture. Why concoct such an explanation as von Däniken's? To do so may increase the mystery and romance of one's theory, but it also makes it less reasonable, especially when one's theory seems inconsistent with what we already know about the world. The ancient astronaut hypothesis is unnecessary. Occam's razor should be applied and the hypothesis rejected.

READING QUESTIONS

1. *What is the topic of Carroll's critique? How does the author limit that topic?*

2. *In the second paragraph, the author reports that von Däniken said that "his deception was justified because some people would only believe if they saw proof." What kind of logical fallacy does von Däniken commit here?*

3. *In the third paragraph, the author discusses giant drawings in Nazca, Peru. Von Däniken's analysis of those lines contains a logical fallacy in addition to the false dilemma the author notes. What is that logical fallacy?*

4. *Critique the author's argument: What are the major points of the argument? Are these claims arranged clearly and logically? Does the author provide enough support for his claims? What is the author's attitude? Is it appropriate to the argument?*

The second sample of professional critiquing does not follow the traditional essay format. Nonetheless, the authors provide a detailed critique of the evidence, argument, and author of a *Time* article that deals with online pornography.

A Detailed Critique of the Time *Article:*

"On a Screen Near You: Cyberporn" (DeWitt, 7/3/95)

Donna L. Hoffman and Thomas P. Novak

Time magazine published an exclusive story reported on the cover on Marty Rimm's published, yet not peer-reviewed, undergraduate research project concerning descriptions of images on adult BBSs [Bulletin Board Systems] in the United States. Given the vast array of conceptual, logical, and methodological flaws in the Rimm study, (documented in Hoffman & Novak's "A Detailed Analysis of the Conceptual, Logical, and Methodological Flaws in the Article 'Marketing Pornography on the Information Superhighway'"), at least some of which *Time* magazine was aware of prior to publication, *Time* magazine behaved irresponsibly in accepting statements made by Rimm in his manuscript at face value. At the least, *Time* magazine should have sought the detailed opinions of objective experts as to the validity of the study. *Time* further compounded this error by making other erroneous statements about the nature of pornography in "cyberspace," and in some cases, even misinterpreted Rimm's results. Below we detail the numerous errors in the *Time* magazine article.

p. 38, 3rd graf [The word "graf" is short for "paragraph."]: The Rimm study is not "an exhaustive study of online porn—what's available, who is downloading it, what turns them on…" The Rimm study is instead an unsophisticated analysis of descriptions of pornographic images on selected adult BBSs in the United States. The study findings cannot be generalized beyond this narrow domain.

Continued

p. 38, 4th graf: *Time* says the study "tells us about what's happening on the computer networks, [and] also what it tells us about ourselves." The statement is misleading, because the study tells us only what happens on selected private adult BBSs in the United States and can only generalize to those networks and those individuals using those networks.

p. 38, 4th graf: *Time* quotes Rimm as saying, "We now know what the consumers of computer pornography really look at in the privacy of their own homes,"... "And we're finding a fundamental shift in the kinds of images they demand." However, the study does not reveal what consumers look at in their own homes (or anywhere else). The study did not examine consumer behavior, but aggregate download counts of descriptive listings of images available on adult BBSs. Although download patterns would be expected to correlate with viewing, we do not know the extent to which individuals actually *looked* at the images (or, indeed, whether they looked at *all*). Additionally, the study provides absolutely no evidence for the statement that there is a "fundamental shift" in demand for certain types of images.

p. 38, 5th graf: *Time* says, "There's an awful lot of porn online." But in fact, Rimm's own figures suggest that the amount of pornography on Usenet and the World Wide Web represents an extremely small percentage of the total information available on the Internet. *Time* further neglects to clarify this by noting that the vast bulk of Rimm's study concerns files that reside exclusively on adult BBSs, which is a very minor portion of "online," and does not include the Internet.

Time then supports this by saying that "917,410 sexually explicit pictures, descriptions, short stories and film clips" were "surveyed." However, the 917,410 files do not represent porn online, as all of these 917,410 images came from "adult" BBSs. None of these 917,410 files came from Usenet or the Internet. Rimm states that of the 917,410 "descriptive listings," 450,620 with complete download information came from 68 different "adult" BBSs, 75,000 with partial download information came from 6 different "adult" BBSs, and 391,790 with no download information came from 27 different "adult" BBSs.

Further, of the 917,410 files, all text and audio files were deleted from analysis, only a very small number of images were actually examined, and the actual number of *descriptions* of images retained for the content analysis on which the study's conclusions are based was 292,114.

In comparison with the 917,410 pornographic files located on the adult BBSs, how many pornographic images did Rimm locate on the Usenet? Rimm states: "Between April and July of 1994, the research team downloaded all available images (3254)…the team encountered technical difficulties with 13% of these images, which were incorrectly uploaded by the poster. This left a total of 2830 images for analysis." Thus, while 917,410 pornographic files were found on adult BBSs, only 2830 pornographic images were found on the Usenet! In addition, out of 11,576 World Web Sites in December 1994, Rimm found only nine Web sites, which is only eight one-hundredths of one percent, contained R or X-rated Adult Visual Material. *Time*'s statement that "there is an awful lot of porn online" is thus blatantly misleading and irresponsible.

p. 38, 5th graf: *Time* says that 83.5% of images in Usenet binaries groups are pornographic; however, this number is simply incorrect. What Rimm actually wrote (p. 1867) was "Among the pornographic newsgroups, 4206 image posts were counted, or 83.5% of the total posts." This is based upon 17 alt.binaries groups that Rimm considered "pornographic" and 15 alt.binaries groups that Rimm considered "non-pornographic." However, Rimm does not provide a listing of the names of these groups, so there is no objective evidence of whether these groups are, in fact, "pornographic." Also, no information is provided on the degree to which these 32 groups comprise the complete universe of Usenet imagery. Further, as the methodology for counting the number of images is not specified, it is likely that even given Rimm's definitions

Continued

and selection of 32 groups, the percentage is inflated due to the inclusion of non-pornographic text comments and multi-part images in the counts.

To make matters worse, Rimm overgeneralizes his results in his summary (p. 1914): "83.5% of all images posted on the Usenet are pornographic." This is a particularly misleading interpretation.

p. 38, 40, 6th graf: *Time* says that "[t]rading in sexually explicit imagery, according to the report, is now 'one of the largest (if not the largest) recreational applications of users of computer networks.'" But there is no evidence for this statement as Rimm's study does not examine "trading behavior" on Usenet news groups, only aggregate *postings*.

p. 40, first full graf: *Time* says that the "great majority (71%) of the sexual newsgroups surveyed originate from adult" BBSs, "whose operators are trying to lure customers" to those boards. This percentage is unsubstantiated as Rimm provides *absolutely no support* for it. Further, no evidence is presented that operators are engaged in luring customers to the adult BBSs via Usenet newsgroups.

p. 40, third full graf: *Time* says that "there is some evidence that...the 1.1%...women [on BBSs] are paid to hang out on the 'chat' rooms and bulletin boards to make the patrons feel more comfortable." But in fact, Rimm provides no evidence for this supposition (nor any credible evidence that there are 1.1% women and 98.9% men).

p. 40, fourth full graf: *Time* says that demand in the adult BBS market is driven by images that "can't be found in the average magazine rack." Yet, Rimm did not study the existence, availability or extent of "analog" pornography, so no such conclusion is warranted, nor possible. Further, Rimm's study, due to methodological flaws, does not demonstrate the demand for such images (over and above other types of images) on adult BBSs.

p. 40, first column, last graf: *Time* says that this material appears on a "public network accessible to men, women and children" globally,

Continued

yet as stated above, there's no evidence that material from private, restricted-access adult BBSs ever makes its way to public networks like the Internet. In this case, Rimm casually discusses the method, but not the data the method is supposed to have generated.

p. 40, second column, first full graf: *Time* reports that "only about 3% of all messages on the Usenet newsgroups [represent pornographic images], while the Usenet itself represents 11.5% of the traffic on the Internet." But *Time* neglects to take the interpretation to its logical conclusion, which is that less than 1/2 of 1% (3% of 11%) of the messages on the Internet are associated with newsgroups that contain pornographic imagery. Further, of this half percent, an unknown but even smaller percentage of messages in newsgroups that are "associated with pornographic imagery" actually contain pornographic material. Much of the material that is in these newsgroups is simply text files containing comments by Usenet readers.

p. 40, second column, 3rd full graf: *Time* speculates that pornography is "different" on computer networks, and although the Rimm study suggests this, as well, absolutely no evidence is presented to support this hypothesis.

p. 42, third column, second full graf: *Time* wonders "[h]ow the Carnegie Mellon report will affect…the cyberporn debate" and notes that "[c]onservatives…will find plenty" of "ammunition." Yet *Time* fails to note that the "Carnegie Mellon report" is in fact a sole-authored study by an undergraduate student in Electrical Engineering that was not subjected to the usual rigors of peer-review and revision that are common for this type of research.

p. 42, third column, fourth full graf: *Time* notes that "1 million or 2 million people who download pictures from the Internet represent a self-selected group with an interest in erotica." Yet, this 1 to 2 million number is completely fictitious and unsubstantiated because it is not known *and it is not possible to know* how many people download pictures from the

Continued

Internet. *Time* provides no reference for this figure, and the figure itself is not mentioned in the Rimm report.

p. 42, third column, last graf: *Time* suggests that Rimm's study will be a "gold mine for psychologists, social scientists, computer marketers and anybody with an interest in human sexual behavior." Yet *Time* fails to note that it is highly unlikely (at least without a cover story by *Time*) that an unsophisticated, poorly executed, weakly documented study conducted by an undergraduate in electrical engineering that was not published in a rigorously peer-reviewed scholarly behavioral science journal would ever be perceived as a "gold mine" by experts in these areas.

Curiously, Rimm has been surprisingly uninterested in making the study available to such experts. The study was embargoed for at least six months prior to publication in the *Georgetown Law Journal*. Scholarly researchers who requested a copy of the manuscript from Rimm were refused access to the manuscript prior to publication.

p. 43, top graf: *Time* says that the "more sophisticated operators were able to adjust their inventory and their descriptions to match consumer demand," yet the Rimm study provides very little evidence that this is actually occurring except in isolated incidents.

READING QUESTIONS

1. *This article actually presents two critiques: one of the* Time *article and one of Marty Rimm's report. Summarize the main points of each critique.*
2. *Each paragraph of the* Time *article is critiqued based on a specific rhetorical or logical fallacy. Identify the fallacies used to critique each paragraph.*
3. *Using the "Questions for Reading Critically," critique this critique. How credible are the authors? How reliable is the article as a source?*

CRITIQUING SOURCES: STUDENT WRITING

Here you will see the results of our student researchers when they critiqued sources from their research projects. Also included are the sources that are being critiqued so you can better analyze the students' responses.

Leslie Schenkman Kaplan:

Her Problem Unsolved

Tobi Raney

Over the past decade, with a new awareness of the individual, self-esteem has become a much-discussed topic. Increasingly, however, it has shifted to being a much-debated question. As people begin to blame a wide variety of social problems on poor self-esteem, questions arise as to how responsible a person's self-view is for their behavior. Leslie Schenkman Kaplan brings a new perspective to the self-esteem debate as a middle school administrator. She has seen firsthand many contrasting levels of self-esteem in one of the most vulnerable age groups. She has also witnessed the way school counselors both diagnose and prescribe self-esteem as a solution for many discipline problems. In her article, "Self-esteem is Not Our National Wonder Drug," Kaplan asserts that self-esteem is overrated, oversold, and overemphasized. In her own words, self-esteem has become a "psychological wonder drug, a social vaccine that many people believe can inoculate individuals against teen pregnancy, school failure, drug and alcohol abuse, crime, and welfare dependency." She argues the contrary. Self-esteem alone is not responsible for and can not solve all of these problems. Her article provides valid points concerning the way society regards self-esteem. Kaplan also provides some nice solutions in the educational setting for her perceived problem. On the other hand, she leaves several important questions unanswered. The focus of her article seems to encourage alteration in the way school counselors treat self-esteem. However, when establishing the self-esteem problem, she mentions very little about the school setting. Instead she provides information that shows the problem is found throughout society. The article, while providing a strong start in her debate for reform, does not always connect to its main focus, how school counselors can properly represent self-esteem.

Continued

Kaplan introduces the paper by summarizing what she contends is the basic problem. She sees people valuing self-esteem over actual ability and argues that this is harmful to human progress. If people are incompetent, but still feel good about themselves, what is going to motivate them to change? Kaplan maintains that nothing will, that the only way troubled persons can achieve true self-esteem is to prove to themselves, through their own actions that they are worthwhile. Then she adds that this self-esteem will lead to further accomplishments, which will in turn contribute to higher self-esteem, It is a circular process, reminiscent of "the chicken and the egg."

The heading of Kaplan's first main section, *Self-esteem Oversold in the Media,* indicates where she feels self-esteem has been granted unnecessary importance. She cites, within this section, several examples where self-esteem is over-used to cure or prevent a wide variety of problems. Then she jumps into a definition of self-esteem. This outlining section begins with a few documented definitions and opinions about the issue. Then Kaplan defines self-esteem in her opinion and establishes an interpretation that will be used throughout her argument. She sees self-esteem as a "function of mastery." In her opinion, self-esteem cannot be truly achieved without competence. It is only through various accomplishments that we gain a sense of self-worth. Kaplan disagrees with the "I exist; therefore I am wonderful" ideal that she sees many authorities trying to sell. She also contends that self-esteem can not be given to an individual, that it must come from within.

As soon as she has defined a problem and instituted a working definition of self-esteem, Kaplan begins to suggest a solution. Her recommendations apply to school counselors. She states that a counselor's job is to "help children learn how to increase their competence, responsibility, self-respect, resourcefulness, tolerance, and confidence." She then encourages that, by helping young people in this way, counselors will have instilled in them the qualities that it takes to build

Continued

a healthy self-esteem. The way to do this, Kaplan insists, goes beyond just empathizing and talking to students about their problems. It is to employ them in real-life problem solving situations, to teach them useful skills and provide them with opportunities to practice those skills. Kaplan furnishes examples of abilities these students need to be developing: how to ask teachers for help, how to effectively resolve conflicts, how to deal with feelings of pain and guilt, etc. Follow up on the academic progress of these children is also encouraged. Kaplan believes that this process will "rejoin 'lovable' with 'capable.'"

A second part to Kaplan's proposed solution is the involvement of parents. Counselors need to listen to the concern of both parents in their community and those beyond their school. Particularly, though, parents need to feel a sense of involvement when their child is seeking guidance from a school official. Kaplan understands the concerns of parents who hear their child's school talk about self-esteem as an alternative to education, rather than as a supplement of learning. Her solution, to guarantee confidence in a student's counseling experience, is to keep communication open with parents. They will be more inclined to let their child leave class to get help if they know that the intent of the counselor is to help their child become a more confident and competent individual. School officials should also be very open to suggestions, concerns, and criticisms regarding their style of guidance. In this way, a trust can be formed between the parent, the child, and the counselor.

Kaplan uses her last few paragraphs to recap her main ideas; that self-esteem is not a cure-all, but a function of mastery. She restates that it has been overemphasized by the media and the professional world. Then she sums up her proposal to counselors: represent self-esteem correctly and involve parents in a program that is geared towards arming children with problem-solving strategies.

Leslie Schenkman Kaplan has begun a very convincing argument. A large flaw in her article, though, exists when she begins to establish the

Continued

problem that she will later attempt to resolve. While her solution sounds very intelligent and workable, it does not necessarily match up with the declared problem. The heading for this section is *Self-esteem Over-sold in the Media*. If the following three paragraphs covered the media, they would fit the title. If they concerned the educational setting, they would tie nicely with the solution. Unfortunately they do not completely fall into either category. Kaplan opens by stating that, "the popular media has celebrated a self-aggrandizing version of self-esteem, contributing to its public loss of credibility." We never fully discover how the media has done this. She cites examples of self-esteem taken too far in the workplace, on talk shows, and in schools. While all these scenarios together show that there is a problem with the way society views self-esteem, none of them tie to her supposed main subject. She has only one strong reference that indicates the harm over-emphasizing self-esteem has caused in schools. It is an international study that found that United States school children rank greatly above Japanese, Taiwanese, and Chinese students in their self-confidence of their math abilities. Ironically, though, these same American students' actual math performance is far inferior to Asian students. This is a very powerful bit of information, and Kaplan includes it appropriately. What she fails to provide is back-up evidence. No supplemental information in her article supports the opinion that self-esteem is failing students. If she could make a connection between her other examples, some of which occur in the media, and the problem in education, she would have a persuasive establishment of a distinct problem.

Next, Kaplan attempts to define a term very central to her article—self-esteem. She begins with a small establishment of her own authority. She says "after reading dozens of definitions . . . I believe that experts do agree that self-esteem is a function of mastery." This bit of information, that she has read up on the subject, does not satisfy the expertise required to cage such a broad term. Were she to give us a documented

Continued

source that convinced her of the definition she employs, we may be satisfied with her authority on the subject. To her disadvantage, she does not. In fact, the following four paragraphs blatantly state that the interpretation she relies on is only her opinion. She begins sentences with "In my opinion," "I think," "I believe," "I do not think," and "it seems to me." The definition and explanation she provides sound intelligent, and probably are, but this lack of authority causes critical readers to doubt their validity.

A small, but important, fallacy also exists in this section that attempts to define self-esteem. Kaplan says that "success is both the source of self-esteem as well as the outcome of self-esteem." Then she says that it is wrong to believe that increasing a person's self-esteem alone will increase their achievement. However, this is a contradictory argument. If self-esteem is the source of success, then why *wouldn't* raising a person's self-esteem increase their level of accomplishment? It would, if we use Kaplan's explanation of the process of gaining self-esteem. These two statements can not be both true without further clarification, which Kaplan fails to provide.

Despite the fact that she has not clearly proven the problem, Kaplan is close to success in supplying an answer to the misrepresentation of self-esteem in schools. She encourages counselors to outfit students with the ability to solve real problems, which will, in turn, provide them with a sense of pride. This self-satisfaction will better enable them to solve problems the next time on their own. Kaplan assures that it is a circular process, just like her explanation of the connection between self-esteem and success. A major question that she leaves unanswered regards children who will not understand the material. How much worse will they feel, when they have been assured by their mentors that this will help them achieve their goals, and it does not? A particular concern for disabled students arises when a counselor's focus shifts from self-esteem to accomplishments. With so much emphasis in the world already placed

Continued

on being the smartest, the strongest, the fastest, the opposite should be stressed to children who are physically or mentally incapable to be so.

Kaplan also includes advice for counselors on how to involve parents and alleviate fears that their children are sacrificing their education to receive guidance. This section of her article, while logical, addresses something that counselors have known for years. Her advice is basic— communicate very honestly with parents, listen to their concerns, and take their criticism into consideration. These recommendations are valuable, but not original. They fail to address a more important issue how to deal with parents who will not involve themselves in their child's counseling experience.

Kaplan explains that it takes more than just self-esteem to propel a person towards success. She points out situations that support her position that self-esteem is blamed for too many problems. Then she attempts to solve this problem by arming school counselors with techniques to properly raise their students' self-esteem and achievement levels. It is due to a lack of connection between these points that Kaplan's article fails to cohere. Until she shows her readers that *students'* self-esteem is the real problem, her solution will do very little to save the inner selves of the multitudes she sees being led astray.

Self-esteem Is Not Our National Wonder Drug
Leslie Schenkman Kaplan

School counselors are self-esteem advocates. They believe that people with a strong positive sense of their own worth and competence are better able to make positive and life-enhancing decisions both in school and out.

Continued

Increasingly, however, the self-esteem concept has become politicized, targeted by ultra-Fundamentalists as undermining parental authority, promoting sinful selves rather than God, (Marzano, 1993), and keeping students from necessary academic learning (Simonds, 1993). McCullough (1993) wrote in the *American Counseling Association's Guidepost* (now *Counseling Today*) that guidance and counseling self-esteem materials and programs are being challenged nationally by communities that find them suspect, and school counselors are losing their jobs.

In addition, the media has oversold self-esteem as a national cure-all. A component of many other things, self-esteem has become a catchall term used to make sense of wildly different addictions, dependencies, and self-defeating behaviors. Naively, people would like to believe that one solution exists to so many problems and that having positive thoughts about oneself can bring out the individual's innate goodness and responsible behavior. No wonder that Sarler (1992) wrote that the United States has received international criticism for our preoccupation with self-esteem as a national reluctance to grow up.

How can self-esteem, an idea at the very center of our profession, become the center of a conservative firestorm and international ridicule? To a large extent, counselors, educators, and the popular press have been promoting self-esteem as the newest psychological wonder drug, a social vaccine that many people believe can inoculate individuals against teen pregnancy, school failure, drug and alcohol abuse, crime, and welfare dependency. Yet no conclusive research evidence shows a direct relationship between self-esteem and any of these variables. In addition, self-esteem is often expressed as self-aggrandizement rather than as developing self-competence. Given the preceding information, I think that Americans, and even counselors, are over-selling and misunderstanding self-esteem. I suggest that counselors who understand how the popular press and our own profession are widely misrepresenting and

Continued

inadvertently discrediting self-esteem and who understand what self-esteem is, will be better able to respond to community challenges to counseling programs.

Self-esteem Oversold in the Media

The popular media has celebrated a self-aggrandizing version of self-esteem, contributing to its public loss of credibility. Newsweek (Adler et al., 1992) reported that churches have discovered that the term low self-esteem had fewer negative connotations than did the term sin. When Pee Wee Herman was arrested a few years ago, one Jesuit scholar partially excused him with the observation that "masturbation isn't the problem; its lack of self-esteem" (Adler et al., 1992, p. 48).

Sherman (1993) reported that people outside society's mainstream appear on national talk shows to discuss their experiences with rape, incest, child abuse, trans-sexuality, sex addiction, or bulimia. They bare their souls before millions on TV to increase their self-esteem and to feel validated rather than victimized. In another mistaken twist on self-esteem, businesses now believe that improved employees' self-esteem, called "empowering," can be a more effective motivator than costly, old-fashioned raises.

Psychologist Harold Stevenson (1992) found in his international studies that school children in the United States rank far ahead of students in Japan, Taiwan, and China in self-confidence about their math abilities. Unfortunately, these same American children perform far below Asian students in their actual math performance. The National Council of Self-Esteem polled hundreds of educators and found 27 distinctly different definitions for self-esteem. With so many different definitions, I suspect that research studies on self-esteem would be strongly criticized for their lack of construct validity, because no two investigators define, or use instruments that define, self-esteem the same way.

Continued

What Is Self-esteem?

Experts do not agree on one meaning for self-esteem. After reading dozens of definitions, however, I believe that experts do agree that self-esteem is a function of mastery. Self-esteem includes a combination of self-respect, self-confidence, and competence. Self-esteem comes from competence and accomplishment, which lead to more accomplishment. Self-esteem is the belief that what we do, think, feel, and believe matters, and that we can have an effect on our own lives, on others' lives, and on our environment.

In my opinion, self-esteem is learned and dynamic. Self-esteem does not form wholly during a child's first 5 years and then remain stable. Although nurturing individuality, trust, and competence during a child's early years is very important, self-esteem is malleable and affected by life's later stressful and successful experiences. McCarty (1991), a leading self-esteem educator, has said it takes 3 to 5 years for self-esteem to change.

Furthermore, I think that self-esteem grows through an interactive cycle. The cycle includes initial anxiety at solving a difficult problem, struggle and perseverance through the challenge of the problem, accepting mistakes and disappointments, working hard, and gradually demonstrating mastery. When one is able to do today what one was not able to do yesterday, the individual develops an "I can do it!" attitude toward the next learning challenge. The self-confidence and meaningful achievement interact in a reciprocal way. As with the chicken and the egg, we are not sure which came first, but the interaction is critical. Over time, the individual with good self-esteem takes responsibility for her or his own learning, choices, and outcomes.

I believe that a proper definition of self-esteem includes our views and feelings about our own value as competent, responsible, successful individuals in the world. I do not think that self-esteem means that we like ourselves just because we're us. In my opinion, self-esteem is not unconditional. Self-esteem

Continued

does not mean that we exist and therefore we are wonderful. Self-esteem cannot be given to a person, no matter how much positive attention is received from parents and teachers. To a large extent, it must be earned by individual effort, persistence, mastery, and meaningful achievement.

Finally, it seems to me that the relationship between self-esteem and achievement is interactive and reciprocal, with each influencing the other. Success is both the source of self-esteem as well as the outcome of self-esteem. It is simplistic and wrong to believe that solely by increasing an individual's self-esteem, one can increase their achievement.

What Counselors Can Do

A counselor's work is to help children learn how to increase their competence, responsibility, self-respect, resourcefulness, tolerance, and confidence. Helping young people learn how to make good decisions and supporting their efforts to solve real personal problems and to build actual personal competence in educational, personal, and social areas increases their self-esteem.

Counselors can address this issue with interventions that affect real-world behaviors in school. Empathizing and talking with students are only means; ends include engaging students in real-world problem solving. Individual and small group counseling can help students learn, for example, how to ask teachers for help, how to express anger toward classmates with conflict-resolving words instead of with fists, or how to feel understandably sad at a parents' divorce without unjust and overwhelming self-blame for the loss.

In addition, counselors can survey students, teachers, and parents as well as gather concrete data from attendance, grades, and discipline referrals to see how well their counseling interventions are helping young people become better learners. Effective counseling does make a difference in important ways, and counselors can amass data with their own students to show it. Furthermore, counselors can rejoin "loveable"

Continued

with "capable" when they talk about self-esteem. Self-esteem is not a wonder drug, cure-all, fad, or subversive belief system. It is part of what parents want for their children: respect, hard work, and achievement.

Working with Concerned Parents

Counselors need to remember that their core beliefs about human worth and dignity and an individual's responsibility to make wise decisions may be culturally different from those of many sincere and concerned parents. Counselors need to read widely about parent challenges to counseling philosophy and programs in other communities and to listen carefully to parent concerns in their own locales. This will help them learn how these others see and interpret the world and how these views have an impact on school counseling beliefs and practices.

Most parents worry about their children's safety in the neighborhood and in school. They read the bad press about schools failing to educate children, and they worry that their own children will not have the knowledge or the thinking, communicating, and problem-solving skills needed to be successful in future education and careers. Many parents do not fully understand what counselors do to help support parents' efforts to raise responsible and competent children. Other parents do not want to be shut out of important issues that affect their children. They worry that counselors will learn family secrets and will not let parents help solve children's problems. These concerned parents are easy prey for ultra-Fundamentalists playing on their natural fears.

All parents want their children to learn and to be successful in school. They want their children to master and to achieve. Many will hear counselors talk about self-esteem as an alternative to, rather than as an enhancer of, student learning. If counselors want parents to permit students to leave the classroom to participate in counseling experiences, counselors would do well to link counseling activities clearly with important classroom and social learning results.

Continued

Counselors can work successfully with most parents through regular, open communication about what counselors do to help students become confident, competent, and achieving individuals. By conducting annual and ongoing orientation programs, forming and using guidance advisory committees that include parent membership, creating opportunities for parents to review and discuss counseling materials and resources used with students, hosting parent discussion and support groups, making opportunities for informed parental consent for student participation in certain counseling activities, and seeking frequent ways to involve parents in their students' problem solving, concerned parents can learn to see school counselors as their allies.

Furthermore, counselors need to listen genuinely and carefully to parents' concerns. Especially when the two adults do not agree, counselors must refrain from defensiveness and denial. Instead, counselors should listen for valid criticisms of their practices and programs. It is useful to employ open and structured discussions so that all arguments can be met with counterarguments, and evidence with counterevidence. Becoming informed about parents' concerns helps counselors develop strategies to address these fears and charges. Effective listening and responding also builds trust. Communicating can also help counselors and parents find areas in which both agree.

Conclusion

Self-esteem is not a wonder drug or a cure-all for our nation's social ills. The concept has been so misunderstood and misused in the media and on street corners as to make a valuable construct almost meaningless. What is worse, public and professional misunderstanding of self-esteem has actually made counselors look to some as if they are agents who undermine parental authority and oppose children's educational need for cognitive knowledge.

Continued

Counselors need to remember to link capable with lovable. Self-esteem is not just a function of self-appreciation but also a function of mastery. The more a young person learns to do well, the more competent a young person becomes, the more self-worth he or she develops. Competence increases self-esteem, which increases competence.

In addition, informed and supportive parents are school counselors' best allies and partners. Counselors strengthen their programs by representing self-esteem correctly and by involving parents in the program development and problem-solving processes.

References

Adler, J., Wingert, P., Wright, L., Houston, P., Manly, H., & Cohen, A. D. (1992, February 17). Hey, I'm terrific! *Newsweek,* pp. 46–51.

Marzano, R. J. (1993). When two world views collide. *Educational Leadership, 51*(4), 6–11.

McCady, H. (1991, November). Stress and energy in the learning process. A new approach to classroom management. Paper presented at the meeting of the Virginia Counselors Association, Norfolk, Virginia.

McCullough, L. (1993). Guidance programs, outcome based education face tough challenges. *Guidepost, 36*(6), 1, 12–13.

Sarler, C. (1992, February 17). Stiffen your lips, Yanks. *Newsweek,* p. 52.

Sherman, B. (1993, March 9). Talk show confessional. Society's misfits gain self-esteem by going on TV. *The Daily Press,* Newport News, Virginia, pp. C1, C2.

Simonds, R. L. (1993). A plea for children. *Educational Leadership, 51*(4), 12–15.

Stevenson, H. W. (1992). Learning from Asian schools. *Scientific American, 267*(6), 70–76.

"Pro and Con": Equal Representation
Julie McDowell

Introduction

Beginning in July 1983, the sweetener aspartame gained FDA approval for use in carbonated beverages. The following September, *Consumers' Research Magazine* published an article entitled, "Aspartame: Pro and Con," a balanced piece which describes the characteristics, history, studies, and conclusions from studies that led to aspartame's original approval, as well as its acceptance in colas. Divided into five sections—written in part by Beatrice Trum Hunter, the food editor of the magazine, and followed with FDA extracts pertaining to the approval—the material examines several specific views with little prejudice.

Summary

Ms. Hunter commences by highlighting aspartame's milestones, from its discovery, to its critics, to its green light from the FDA. She also details the physical appearance and composition of the substance, categorized as neither an "artificial sweetener (saccharin is) nor as a traditional carbohydrate sweetener (such as table sugar)." Hunter goes into further detail by explaining the controversial component, phenylalanine, known to cause great damage to those suffering from the genetic disorder phenylketonuria.

Next, the FDA provides information (particularly reviews of the stability of aspartame at varying temperatures and storage lengths) that was included in its decision in the beverage debate. Additionally, reasoning—based on two criteria—was given for the FDA Commissioner's finding that aspartame most likely did not play a large part in contributing to brain tumors and lesions, retardation, etc.

Analysis

Except for a couple of statements in the first part of the article, there are very few fallacies which could lessen the piece's credibility. These flaws,

Continued

which come in Hunter's contribution, are minor, however. For example, she begs the question when suggesting that, "because of the recognized actions of such compounds in the brain, the effects of reported subtoxic surges should be of utmost concern." Hunter could also have provided more evidence, such as studies, statistics, or expert testimony, that "the issue of possible brain tumors [from aspartame] created the greatest controversy."

Despite these splinters, Ms. Hunter presents a very specific account of aspartame and the events surrounding its controversy. She also clarifies scientific terms and provides background information, such as Dr. John Olney's reservations to the safety of aspartame in humans.

Though supported with more scientific data, the FDA's portion of the article is somewhat difficult for those unfamiliar with scientific jargon to comprehend. Such passages as "sensitive chromatographic and analytical techniques were used," and "sustained elevations of plasma-phenylalanine . . . can lead to mental retardation in those infants who are homozygous for the gene coding for the deficient form of the enzyme phenylalanine hydroxylase," can be confusing for the average reader of a consumer publication. Still, FDA actions are backed up with the detailed results of studies pertaining to the agency's claims which, in turn, produce a very credible account of events.

Evaluation

By presenting (as the title foreshadows) the "Pro and Con" of aspartame, as well as the FDA's position on the topic, Hunter and *Consumers' Research* have established a neutral viewpoint. Rather than attempting to persuade the reader for or against, they inform the consumer of what aspartame is, in addition to the studies and findings that have made the sweetener one of controversy. Though a bit too technical at times, the article succeeds in giving a very fact-based report that lets the reader come to his or her own conclusion.

Aspartame: Pro and Con

Beatrice Trum Hunter and the FDA

The artificial sweetener aspartame has recently been approved by the Food and Drug Administration for use in carbonated soft drinks. The following discussion addresses both sides of the aspartame question; the first section is written by CR food editor Beatrice Trum Hunter, the second excerpted from recent FDA material on the subject.—Ed.

Many consumers are interested in food products that contain "natural" ingredients, have fewer calories and less sugar than their traditional counterparts. Some food processors are responding to this interest by making use of the approved sweetening agent, aspartame. By regulatory definition, aspartame is "a nutritive substance with sweetening and flavor enhancing properties." It is not classified as an artificial sweetener (saccharin is) nor as a traditional carbohydrate sweetener (such as table sugar.)

Aspartame is a white crystalline low-calorie sweetener synthesized from two amino acids normally found in the human body. One, aspartic, is flat tasting; the other, phenylalanine, is bitter. Yet, in combination, the two amino acids form a sweet-tasting compound, with about 200 times the sweetening power of table sugar. This discovery was made accidentally in Searle, a pharmaceutical laboratory, in 1965, by a scientist who was scrutinizing various substances for their possible usefulness as drugs. For nearly a decade the substance was researched.

In 1974, aspartame gained FDA approval for all uses except with cooked foods and bottled soft drinks, for heating causes aspartame to degrade to diketopiperazine (DKP). Although this breakdown product was judged to be harmless, FDA requested further data. The agency viewed DKP as a technical problem, not a safety issue.

At an earlier date, Dr. John W. Olney, of the Washington University School of Medicine, and colleagues had studied both aspartate and

Continued

glutamate, the salts of aspartic and glutamic acids, as well as their structural analogs. They had reported that these two amino acids, similar in molecular structure, are neurotoxic and capable of inducing brain lesions in experimental animals. Test results had demonstrated that monosodium glutamate induced brain lesions in infant mice and rats, and in a newborn monkey. Aspartate, fed to young mice, induced a similar type of brain damage.

A month after FDA had approved aspartame, Olney charged that FDA "has presented a seriously misleading case for the safety of aspartame." Olney was concerned that children were especially at risk, due to their high intake of sweetened foods (which might contain aspartame) plus their high intake of processed foods (which frequently contain monosodium glutamate). Olney reported that FDA's margin of safety for aspartame fell far short of the traditional safety margin for adults, and was mathematically *off-base a hundredfold for children.*

Phenylalanine

Apart from the potential problem of the aspartate fraction in aspartame, the other amino acid, phenylalanine, posed another problem. This amino acid must be avoided by people who suffer from phenylketonuria (PKU), an inborn metabolic error. Untreated, this health problem can lead to irreversible mental retardation. One in 10,000 children is born with PKU. Damage can be avoided by early diagnosis and rigid adherence to a phenylalanine-free diet. Olney insisted on the importance of an appropriate warning label on any aspartame-sweetened products. FDA agreed. An obligatory statement gives warning: PHENYLKETONURICS: CONTAINS PHENYLALANINE.

Olney and other critics made three charges. 1) FDA had acted hastily in granting aspartame approval. 2) FDA's decision was based on industry research; FDA's own studies were limited to taste tests, not safety. 3) Consumers were not invited to participate in FDA's review of submitted

Continued

data. Olney and others petitioned FDA to 1) withdraw approval of the sweetener, 2) conduct more detailed studies, 3) allow public access to the data, and 4) hold public hearings.

As a result of these objections, a half-year after FDA granted approval to aspartame, the agency stayed approval and prohibited further marketing until all safety issues could be examined and resolved. FDA appointed a board of inquiry and a trial judge.

Unforeseen events, however, made it necessary to postpone the hearings. DKP, the breakdown product formerly considered harmless, now was suspected to be capable of combining with nitrite in the human stomach to form nitrosamines, a group of powerful cancer-inducing compounds. Also, DKP appeared to cause liver cancer in rats, and at medium to high doses, produced uterine polyps in female rats.

Several unresolved safety questions remained. What were the long-range DKP effects? Was DKP hazardous because of its potential to form nitrosamines? What was the significance of certain pathological findings, such as brain tumors, and liver and kidney changes noted during a lifetime study in some animals? What was the significance of adverse findings in the study with newborn rats? What was the meaning of an increased incidence of hyperplasia (an increase in size of a tissue or organ due to abnormal increase in the number of cells) in aspartame-fed mice? Or tumors observed in urinary bladders in DKP-fed mice, and in a 26-week study, using urinary bladder implant?

The manufacturer submitted additional data to clarify these issues. The FDA chose an outside advisory panel to review the data. By 1979, the panel had worked its way through only 12 of some 100 submitted studies. The research techniques and records were validated. Again, FDA decided to review the safety data. This time, the agency convened a scientific board of inquiry, which held marathon sessions. There were charges and countercharges. The issue of possible brain tumors generated the greatest controversy. The board reported that it had "no choice but to

Continued

conclude that the data reported . . . do not rule out an oncogenic [tumor-causing] effect of aspartame," and that the findings "appear to suggest the possibility that aspartame, at least, when administered in the huge quantities employed in these studies, may contribute to the development of brain tumors."

Disapproval

FDA organized a new scientific board of inquiry which held hearings in early 1980. By late 1980, the board gave *a qualified disapproval* to aspartame, with a recommendation that no approval be granted until further long-term animal tests could be conducted, in order to rule out the possibility that aspartame might cause brain lesions or tumors.

Despite this recommendation, and catching both the business world and food processors by surprise, FDA announced in July 1981 that approval for aspartame use would be granted for cold cereals, drink mixes, sugarless gums, instant coffees and teas, gelatins, puddings and fillings, and dairy products and toppings. Aspartame would also be approved for retail sale in tablet form and as a free-flowing sugar for home use.

Approval had not been granted for certain uses. Approval had not been sought for use in carbonated soft drinks or in bakery products, since aspartame loses sweetness with heating or in long storage of products.

Earlier this year, FDA was petitioned to permit the extension of aspartame use in carbonated beverages. A food scientist urged the agency to deny this petition, charging that existing data do not establish "reasonable certainty" that this proposed use would *not* be harmful. On July 1, 1983, however, FDA approval was granted.

The question of DKP degradation in carbonated beverages, and the release of free amino-acids should be addressed. High amounts of these amino acids may cause brain damage. Both phenylalanine and aspartic acid are substances that are well recognized as being capable of

Continued

increasing neurotransmitter activity in the central nervous system. This activity may occur at far lower levels and shorter periods of time than those commonly used in toxicologic tests.

There is a narrowed margin of safety between the physiological effects of amino acids in the typical American diet, with its high level of protein food (containing amino acids) and the pharmacological (drug-like) neuroexcitatory levels. The latter, over a period of time, might result in the production of brain lesions. The FDA expressed apprehension about the possibility of brain lesions being produced *by a single surge* into the bloodstream of glutamic acid and aspartic acid above some toxic threshold. Because of the recognized actions of such compounds in the brain, the effects of repeated subtoxic surges should be of utmost concern.

The following discussion is excerpted from FDA's final rule concerning the safe use of aspartame in carbonated beverages.

Studies on aspartame's stability in carbonated beverages and syrup concentrates were provided by Searle in the current petition to demonstrate the safety and functionality of the sweetener in carbonated beverages during typical storage periods (up to 52 weeks), and over a range of temperatures 5° to 55° C (11° to 131° F).

These stability data were submitted under section 109(b)(2)(C) of [The Federal Food, Drug and Cosmetic Act] which requires that a food additive petition contain a bearing on the physical or technical effect the additive is intended to produce. Sensitive chromatographic analytical techniques were used to identify and quantify aspartame and its decomposition products in the aged carbonated beverage preparations. Taste panel tests also verified that taste characteristics were retained for typical shelf-life periods.

For example, levels of aspartame remaining in carbonated beverages stored for 8 weeks at 20° C (68° F) were shown to be between 84 and 89 percent of the original amount. The lost aspartame is degraded to

Continued

diketopiporazine (DKP) and its component amino acids, aspartic acid, phenylalanine, plus aspartyl-1-phenylalanine (the deesterified dipeptide), and methanol. The DKP formed was 3 to 4 percent of the added aspartame. Approximately one-third of the decomposition products were in the form of DKP, a result which was shown to be relatively considered for four flavors of carbonated beverages as well as for the syrup concentrates. At average aspartame use levels, 67 milligrams (mg) per 100 milliliters (mL) of carbonated beverage, the level of DKP formed was demonstrated to be approximately 2 mg/100 mL under these conditions. Storage at 5° C (41° F) for 52 weeks results in residual aspartame levels similar to the above. After 8 weeks at 5° C, aspartame levels were 90 percent of the amounts added.

Storage tests at 30° C (86° F) for 8 weeks resulted in 62 percent of the added aspartame remaining in a cola-type beverage, with 12 percent of the residue in the form of DKP. At temperatures above 30° C the stability drops off markedly.

The petition shows that storage at 40° C (104° F) and 55° C (131° F) results in less than one-half of the added aspartame remaining after 9 weeks and 3 to 4 weeks, respectively. The agency believes, however, that storage at these times and temperatures can be avoided by attention to handling and distribution. More important, although this lack of stability might result in a marginally acceptable product, it would not lead to an unsafe product.

Any concern over possible toxic effects from DKP has been eliminated as a result of long-term animal studies conducted using DKP itself as the test compound.

Effects
The Commissioner's decision approving the food additive petition for aspartame found that there was not reasonable expectation that aspartame ingestion could influence either of two distinct types of brain

Continued

damage. Specifically, the Commissioner found that there was a reasonable certainty that aspartame; (1) Does not cause brain tumors in rats and (2) does not pose a risk of contributing to mental retardation, brain lesions, or undesirable effects on neuroendocrine regulatory systems in humans.

1. Aspartame's Potential for Causing Brain Tumors. Interpretation of the results of the chronic rat feeding studies designed to determine aspartame's potential for causing brain tumors was one of the major scientific issues before the Board, and consequently one of the most comprehensively deliberated issues relative to aspartame's safety.

The administrative record shows that the regulatory approval of aspartame is supported by a complete series of toxicological tests in animals. These studies have been thoroughly reviewed by FDA scientists. Based on that review and for the reasons stated in the Commissioner's decision, the agency reaffirms the conclusion that there is a reasonable certainty that aspartame does not cause brain tumors in rats.

2. Aspartame's Potential for Causing Mental Retardation, Brain Lesions, and Other Effects. High blood levels of aspartic and glutamic acids have been associated with focal brain lesions in animals after parenteral (nondietary) administration of large doses of aspartate or glutamate.

Searle's petition for carbonated beverage use of aspartame specifically addressed the issue of the potential glutamate and aspartate toxicity through the submission of new clinical safety studies. In these studies, the effects on amino acid blood levels resulting from the acute administration of high doses of aspartame were observed on different human subpopulations: normal adults, adolescents and children, diabetics, lactating mothers, infants, and obese and glutamate-sensitive individuals.

These studies demonstrated that, when ingested aspartame doses are several [times] the highest projected daily intake levels, only one-tenth, i.e., 10 micromoles/dL, of the conservatively derived toxic threshold value

Continued

noted above is attained in humans. This margin of safety is considerable and adds additional support to the Commissioner's conclusion that the proposed use of aspartame, either alone or in combination with glutamate, will not cause focal brain lesions under conditions of use that include use of aspartame to sweeten carbonated beverages.

Sustained elevations of plasma-phenylalanine, resulting from the genetic disorder known as phenylketonuria (PKU), can lead to mental retardation in those infants who are homozygous for the gene coding for the deficient form of the enzyme, phenylalanine hydroxylase.

The agency believes that [comments] regarding potential phenylalanine induced changes in neurotransmitter function appear to be unwarranted extrapolations. Even though elevated plasma amino acid ratios may produce similar elevations of the amino acid in the brain as claimed, recent detailed studies in the rat by Fernstrom, et. al., the best evidence submitted to FDA thus far, do not support the view that neurotransmitter activity is altered.

In one study, serum and brain levels of amino acids were measured in rats given up to 200 mg/kg of aspartame by gavage. The results of this work indicate that the elevations in phenylalanine plasma ratios and brain levels are not sufficient to influence either the levels or the rate of turnover of catecholamine or indoleamine neurotransmitters in the brain of the rat.

Conclusion

FDA, having evaluated the data in the petition and other relevant material, concludes that the proposed food additive use is safe and that the regulations should be amended as set forth below.

The administrative record shows that the regulatory approval is supported by more than 100 studies on the safety of aspartame and its decomposition products. These studies include an extensive program of clinical testing in various human subpopulations, as well as a complete series of toxicological tests in animals. All of these studies have been

Continued

thoroughly reviewed by FDA scientists and the agency finds no basis upon which to alter the Commissioner's conclusions regarding the potential of aspartame to cause toxic effects, including brain tumors.

Further, the agency does not agree with the comments asserting that aspartame consumption beyond currently regulated uses will lower the margin of safety based on a toxic threshold of 100 micromoles/dL of combined aspartame and glutamate in blood, or that abnormal neurotransmitter activity might occur. Rather, the agency concludes that: (1) Ingestion of aspartame at high but conceivable amounts does not result in toxic plasma levels of amino acids; (2) these aspartame constituents are food-like and well-characterized with respect to metabolic fate and demonstrate no evidence of metabolic overload, and (3) clinically, no subpopulations, except homozygous PKU individuals needing to control phenylalanine intake, have been identified that can suffer ill effects from long-term or excessive aspartame ingestion.

WRITING ASSIGNMENT: CRITIQUING SOURCES

The writing assignment for this chapter is to select an article pertaining to your researched writing project and critique it using the techniques from this chapter and the format outlined as follows.

Critique Format:

1. Create an original title

   - A title should grab the reader's attention and identify your unique slant on the work, so merely using the title of the work you are critiquing will not do (using the same title, by the way, is one form of plagiarism). So crank up your creative juices and cue your reader into your critique.

2. Introduce the work

   - The critique has to be deductive in structure. The reader needs to know the title of the work, the author, the subject or issue of the work, and the author's claim about that issue immediately. You also need to present your thesis at the beginning of the essay. In drafting your thesis, remember that you do not have to address every word in the source. Instead, limit the scope of your topic according to your own project proposal (after all, for this assignment, the point of the critique is to determine the source's value to you for your research project).

3. Summarize the work

- You need to identify the author's main point, from the start of the work to its conclusion. Be careful here: a good summary presents the ideas in the source as a whole, rather than as a disconnected string of topic sentences. One way to avoid a "stringy" summary is to avoid such expressions as "The author says/states/continues/goes on to say." This style of writing is wordy and does not show what the author was trying to do. Instead, focus on accurately presenting the ideas rather than presenting the author. How long should the summary be? For this assignment, perhaps one or two paragraphs. Be sure that your summary is not longer than your analysis.

4. Analyze the components

- In this section you should identify which parts of the text succeed or fail and how or why they succeed or fail. In doing so, you must be fair to the author: If you misrepresent the text, your critique is either invalid or suffering from card stacking. To avoid misrepresentation, read critically: Many of the elements that you are concerned with in the reading phase are addressed in this section of the assignment. Elements that may be addressed here include (but are not limited to) the following:
- the design or organization of the text
- the author's assumptions
- sufficiency of supporting details or evidence
- reliability of the information
- the author's originality
- logic or logical fallacies
- the credibility of the author
- the author's perception of the reader

5. Evaluation

- Judge the effectiveness of the text. You are not simply discussing whether you liked the article or not based on your personal preferences. Instead, you are evaluating the article according to certain criteria that are applied to sources by all critical readers. In order to present an effective evaluation, you need to identify the specific criteria that govern your decision, a judgment based on those criteria, and evidence to support the judgment.

CHAPTER 9

Drawing Inferences

What Beetle Bailey does in this cartoon should seem very familiar to you. He sees a fact (the number of men outside the mall) and he creates meaning from that fact (that there are a lot of women shopping). This process of creating meaning from evidence is exactly what Chapter 3 discussed. This chapter takes a much closer look at the process. Just as importantly, this chapter examines how to present your inferences in written form, creating clear and effective arguments.

First, use the Beetle Bailey cartoon to review Chapter 3. Be sure to pay attention to the influences on creating meaning. If you look closely at Beetle Bailey's inference, what influences can you detect? He seems to be influenced by his own biases (especially the roles of men and women when it comes to shopping) and by his methods of collecting facts (his inference is based on very limited evidence). The information in Chapter 3 will help you prepare to look closely at the process of drawing inferences.

DEFINITION: INFERENCE

Inference: A probable conclusion drawn from a fact.

Everyone draws inferences every day. It's a Tuesday morning, for instance. As you are leaving for school or for work, you notice that the ground is wet. "Aha," you say to yourself, "it must have rained."

You just drew an inference.

A closer look at the parts of this definition starts with the word *fact* because without facts, there can be no inferences. Chapter 6 talked about the difficulty of ascertaining "facts." In that context, facts were second-hand evidence—information obtained from someone else. In this part of the chapter, however, "fact" has a different definition: a fact is a piece of information that can be verified by one of the five senses. In the previous example, the wetness of the ground is the fact because you can verify it through feeling (the tactile sense).

The second part of the definition is the word *conclusion*. A conclusion is an idea created by you that is based on evidence. In this case, an inference is a conclusion based on factual evidence. You created the idea of rain based on the fact of wetness.

The third part of the definition is the word *probable*. An inference is never certain—it is at best *likely* to be true. Although it is probable that the wet ground was caused by rain, it is also possible that an underground leak from a water main caused it.

Inferences are perhaps most commonly found in detective stories. One of the most famous literary detectives is Sherlock Holmes, a British detective who lived in London during the late 1800s. Holmes's assistant, Dr. Watson, could never understand Holmes's inferences, so Sherlock always gives him—and thus the reader—a clear explanation of his reasoning process. Read the following passage and look for the inferences Holmes makes and the facts he bases them on.

In this story, a man's body is found on a London street. He has no identification, but he is holding a dead goose. Holmes is attempting to determine the corpse's identity by examining the man's hat.

From *The Adventure of the Blue Carbuncle*

Sir Arthur Conan Doyle

"Then, pray tell me what it is that you can infer from this hat?" [asked Watson].

He [Holmes] picked it up and gazed at it in the peculiar introspective fashion which was characteristic of him. "It is perhaps less suggestive than it might have been," he remarked, "and yet there are a few inferences which are very distinct, and a few others which represent at least a strong balance of probability. That the man was highly intellectual is of course obvious on the face of it, and also that he was fairly well-to-do within the last three years, although he has now fallen upon evil days. He had foresight, but has less now than formerly, pointing to a moral

---

Continued

retrogression, which, when taken with the decline of his fortunes, seems to indicate some evil influence, probably drink, at work upon him. This may account also for the obvious fact that his wife has ceased to love him."

"My dear Holmes!"

"He has, however, retained some degree of self-respect," he continued, disregarding my remonstrance. "He is a man who leads a sedentary life, goes out little, is out of training entirely, is middle-aged, has grizzled hair which he has had cut within the last few days, and which he anoints with lime-cream. These are the more patent facts which are to be deduced from his hat. Also, by-the-way, that it is extremely improbable that he has gas laid on in his house."

"You are certainly joking, Holmes."

"Not in the least. Is it possible that even now, when I give you these results, you are unable to see how they are attained?"

"I have no doubt that I am very stupid; but I must confess that I am unable to follow you. For example, how did you deduce that this man was intellectual?"

For answer Holmes clapped the hat upon his head. It came right over the forehead and settled upon the bridge of his nose. "It is a question of cubic capacity," said he; "a man with so large a brain must have something in it."

"The decline of his fortunes, then?"

"This hat is three years old. These flat brims curled at the edge came in then. It is a hat of the very best quality. Look at the band of ribbed silk and the excellent lining. If this man could afford to buy so expensive a hat three years ago, and has had no hat since, then he has assuredly gone down in the world."

"Well, that is clear enough, certainly. But how about the foresight and the moral retrogression?"

Sherlock Holmes laughed. "Here is the foresight," said he, putting his finger upon the little disk and loop of the hat-securer. "They are never sold

Continued

upon hats. If this man ordered one, it is a sign of a certain amount of foresight, since he went out of his way to take this precaution against the wind. But since we see that he has broken the elastic, and has not troubled to replace it, it is obvious that he has less foresight now than formerly, which is a distinct proof of a weakening nature. On the other hand, he has endeavored to conceal some of these stains upon the felt by daubing them with ink, which is a sign that he has not entirely lost his self-respect."

"Your reasoning is certainly plausible."

"The further points, that he is middle-aged, that his hair is grizzled, that it has been recently cut, and that he uses lime-cream, are all to be gathered from a close examination of the lower part of the lining. The lens discloses a large number of hair-ends, clean cut by the scissors of the barber. They all appear to be adhesive, and there is a distinct odor of lime-cream. This dust, you will observe, is not the gritty, gray dust of the street, but the fluffy brown dust of the house, showing that it has been hung up in-doors most of the time; while the marks of moisture upon the inside are proof positive that the wearer perspired very freely, and could, therefore, hardly be in the best of training."

"But his wife—you said that she had ceased to love him."

"This hat has not been brushed for weeks. When I see you, my dear Watson, with a week's accumulation of dust upon your hat, and when your wife allows you to go out in such a state, I shall fear that you also have been unfortunate enough to lose your wife's affection."

"But he might be a bachelor."

"Nay, he was bringing home the goose as a peace-offering to his wife. Remember the card upon the bird's leg."

"You have an answer to everything. But how on earth do you deduce that the gas is not laid on in his house [he does not have gaslight in his house, so he must still use candles for light]?"

Continued

> "One tallow stain, or even two, might come by chance; but when I see no less than five, I think that there can be little doubt that the individual must be brought into frequent contact with burning tallow — walks upstairs at night probably with his hat in one hand and a guttering candle in the other. Anyhow, he never got tallow stains from a gas-jet. Are you satisfied?"

EXERCISE 9-1

This exercise will break down the inferences in this passage. Take a sheet of paper and divide it into five columns. Label the first column "Fact" and the third column "Inference." Now, fill in the columns with the dozen or so inferences Holmes makes in this passage. The first one he makes is that the man is highly intellectual — put that in the "Inference" column. Holmes bases that inference on the fact that the man's hat is very large — put that evidence in the "Fact" column. Continue filling in the chart with the other inferences Holmes makes about the dead man. Hang onto this chart — you'll fill in the other three columns later in this chapter.

TECHNIQUES: DRAWING INFERENCES

The Steps to an Inference
1. Compare evidence to your "mental model."
2. Compare evidence to familiar information.
3. Look for connections between evidence.

Now that you have had some practice recognizing inferences, the next step is to work on drawing your own inferences. Inferencing is an inductive process—you start with some evidence and create meaning from it. If the process is broken down, it usually involves the following steps:

Here is what is involved in each of these steps:

- *Compare evidence to your "mental model."* Everyone looks at the world through a *mental model,* or a certain intellectual framework. That framework is defined by culture, education, and many other influences. This model shapes how people understand information. In Holmes's mental model, for instance, the size of a person's skull determines how smart the person is. That idea is most likely not part of your mental model, so you would probably not draw the same inference Holmes did.

- *Compare evidence to familiar information.* Your mental model is filled in with familiar information that you gather as you go through life. You tend to process evidence through familiar channels first. The information that rain causes widespread wetness is familiar to you—so that is the first inference you might draw when you see that the ground is wet.

• *Look for connections between pieces of evidence.* Sometimes, information neither fits your mental model nor is familiar to you. When this happens, turn to the techniques you learned in Chapter 7 for discovering connections between pieces of evidence. Look for cause-and-effect connections, chronological connections, problem-and-solution connections, comparisons, contrasts, and categories. Holmes is able to connect several pieces of evidence to infer much about the man's hairstyle and his recent visit to the barber, for instance. When looking for connections, also look for places where information seems to be missing. Further, be sure to look at all of the possible connections—inferences are often found in unexpected places.

Another very common place to find inferences is in riddles. Riddles provide us with some evidence, but we must infer the answer. Put the process of drawing inferences into action and try to infer the answers to these three riddles (the answers appear at the end of this chapter).

"The Motley Fool," a financial advice column that appears regularly in the newspaper, often includes riddles. Here's a recent one:

> *I was born in Boston in 1986, aiming to provide small-business owners the same low prices on certain supplies that only large corporations enjoyed then. Within 12 years, I was raking in more than $5 billion per year. I'm a superstore pioneer and have nearly 1,000 stores in the United States, Canada and Europe, offering more than 6,000 items in most. I also sell online and by catalog. The U.S. market for the products I sell is estimated at $225 billion, growing 7 percent to 10 percent per year. My name is a pun. Who am I?*

Here is a riddle from J.R.R. Tolkien's *The Hobbit*:

> *A box without hinges, key, or lid,*
> *Yet golden treasure inside is hid.*

And one final riddle, again from *The Hobbit*:

> *Thirty white horses on a red hill,*
> *First they champ,*
> *Then they stamp,*
> *Then they stand still.*

EXERCISE 9–2

Answering riddles is one way to draw inferences. Another way to learn about inferencing is to write riddles. Choose an object, and write a riddle for a classmate to answer. Your riddle can contain only facts that are verifiable by your classmate's senses. Take a look at the previous riddles for examples. Share and exchange riddles with your classmates.

TECHNIQUES: PRESENTING INFERENCES AS ARGUMENT

An inference is a building block of thinking. It is a way to create ideas. It is also an inductive process, leading from evidence to a conclusion. But when you present inferences to a reader, you often need to present your conclusion first, and then your evidence. In other words, you often (but not always) present the material deductively.

When you put inferences into written form, you are creating arguments; however, an argument often needs more than a piece of evidence and a conclusion to be clear and effective. Most arguments are put together according to one of two models: the *syllogism* and the *Toulmin model*. The following sections describe how a syllogism is constructed, and then how the Toulmin model works.

The Syllogism

The Greek philosopher Aristotle first explained the syllogism about 2,500 years ago. A syllogism is an argument made up of three statements—a major premise, a minor premise, and a conclusion. The most familiar kind of syllogism is probably the "categorical" syllogism, which draws a conclusion regarding groups or classes of objects. Here's an example:

- All humans walk on two legs. (The major premise; it states a generalization about a group of objects—humans.)
- Joe walks on two legs. (The minor premise; it describes a particular case.)
- Therefore, Joe is a human. (The conclusion.)

Syllogisms are straightforward ways of constructing an argument. In fact, it is easy to rewrite Holmes's first inference as a syllogism:

Major Premise: All highly intellectual people wear big hats.

Minor Premise: This man wears a big hat.

Conclusion: Therefore, this man is highly intellectual.

There are some problems with syllogisms, however. On the one hand, complete syllogisms rarely appear in writing or in speech. Instead, writers and speakers tend to rely on what is called an *enthymeme*. In an enthymeme, the writer or speaker states only one premise, implies the other premise, and then states the conclusion. Holmes tells Watson that the dead man is probably highly intellectual because he has a big hat. Which premise is implied in this enthymeme?

Another problem is that syllogisms can be used to reach clearly incorrect conclusions. Consider this example.

Major Premise: Generals in the army do many things.

Minor Premise: Napoleon was a general in an army.

Conclusion: Therefore, Napoleon did many things.

Major Premise: Octopi do many things and have eight arms.

Minor Premise: Napoleon did many things.

Conclusion: Therefore, Napoleon had eight arms.

Logical? Yes. Syllogistic? Certainly. True? Hardly. Because of these problems, writers often turn to another model of argumentation, called the Toulmin Model.

EXERCISE 9-3

For each of the following syllogisms, supply the missing statement.

1. The sun always shines during the daytime.
   The sun is shining right now.
   Therefore, _____.
2. People who are over 7 feet tall do not fit in this car.
   _____.
   Therefore, Sally is over 7 feet tall.
3. _____.
   Melissa takes aerobics every day.
   Therefore, Melissa is in good shape.
4. Golden retrievers are good family dogs.
   _____.
   Therefore, Fred is a good family dog.
5. _____.
   Harry does his homework every night.
   Therefore, Harry gets good grades.

EXERCISE 9-4

Indicate whether the major premise or minor premise is implied in the following enthymemes.

1. The sun is shining, so it's daytime.
2. George is a liberal—he lives in California.
3. This book must be boring like all really thick books are boring.
4. Jenny runs her own business, so she must be wealthy.
5. Math classes are hard to pass, so it will be hard to pass Mr. Smith's class.

EXERCISE 9-5

Determine whether the following syllogisms are true. If not, briefly explain why not.

1. Love is blind.
   Stevie Wonder is blind.
   Therefore, Stevie Wonder is Love.
2. People in jail are guilty.
   George is in jail.

> Therefore, George is guilty.
>
> 3. All teachers have a college education.
>   Mary is a teacher.
>   Therefore, Mary has a college education.

EXERCISE 9-6

In the chart of Holmes's inferences, the third column that you labeled "Inference" contains Holmes's conclusions, and the first column that you labeled "Fact" contains the minor premise. Label the fourth column "Major Premise" and fill in the chart with a statement about groups of objects or people that connects the fact and the inference.

EXERCISE 9-7

Follow these sentence patterns to write out each inference as a syllogism and as an enthymeme:

> Syllogism: [Minor Premise] *so* [Conclusion] *because* [Major Premise].
>
> Enthymeme: [Major or Minor Premise] *so* [Conclusion].

Which pattern presents Holmes's inferences more clearly and more effectively? (Note: One pattern might not be the best choice for each inference.)

The Toulmin Model

The Toulmin model is named after Stephen Toulmin, who developed the model in the early 1900s. At its heart, the Toulmin model is essentially a syllogism, although the order and the names of the parts are different. Here is Holmes's inference about the size of the hat using Toulmin's model:

> *Data:* The hat is big.
>
> *Claim:* (Therefore) the man is highly intellectual.
>
> *Warrant:* (Since) men who wear big hats are intellectual.

Here, the *data* has replaced the minor premise, the *claim* has replaced the conclusion, and the *warrant* has replaced the major premise. In Aristotle's syllogism, the major premise states a generalization about a group of objects. That generalization explains how and why you can draw the conclusion you do about the object in the minor premise. In the Toulmin model, the warrant serves the same function as the major premise: it is the idea or general principle that explains how and why you get from the data to the claim.

Whereas the syllogism stops at three statements, the Toulmin model can have up to six parts. This is the advantage of the Toulmin model—it is more flexible than the syllogism. Each Toulmin model must have some data, a claim, and a warrant. But it can also include any or all of the following three parts as well.

The fourth, and really important, part of the Toulmin model is the *qualifier*. The qualifier is a word such as "probably" or "usually" that indicates the possibility that the claim is incorrect. The syllogism does not have a similar part, which is why the Toulmin model is more helpful for creating written argument.

The fifth part of the Toulmin model is the *rebuttal*. This takes the qualifier a step further. For a rebuttal, you must put yourself in the shoes of someone who disagrees with your position. You must ask yourself, "What objection can be raised to rebut my claim?" By presenting a rebuttal, you show your readers that you have looked at the issue objectively, which makes you more credible as an author. If the rebuttal is strong enough, then you may have to spend time in your essay answering the rebuttal—your answer will simultaneously strengthen your position and weaken that of the rebutter.

Take another look at Holmes's inference regarding the man's intelligence. What objections could be raised? Perhaps the hat didn't fit the man very well. Perhaps it wasn't his hat at all—he may have borrowed it from a friend. And of course, the obvious one—perhaps the size of his head has absolutely nothing to do with how intellectual the man is. The first two of these rebuttals are not very effective, and thus could be mentioned very briefly, if at all. The third, however, would challenge Holmes's inference, and he would have to come up with a response to this last rebuttal.

The final part of the Toulmin model is called *backing*. Backing is like adding warrants. Again, Holmes's hat size inference clarifies this definition. The actual inference is not that the man is highly intellectual because his hat is big. The actual inference is the man's hat is big, and therefore his head is big. Holmes needs additional inferences (ones he does not mention) to reach the conclusion that the man is highly intellectual: the man's head is big, and therefore his brain is big; his brain is big, and therefore he is highly intellectual. The two extra steps in that chain of reasoning would be the backing to Holmes's inference.

Let's put all of the parts of the Toulmin model together:

Data: The man's hat is big

Claim: (so) he is highly intellectual

Qualifier: probably

Warrant: (since) people with big heads are highly intellectual

Backing: (because) people with big heads have big brains

Rebuttal: (unless) head size has nothing to do with how intellectual a person is.

The additional information you come up with when you construct a Toulmin model makes it easier to present your inferences clearly and effectively.

EXERCISE 9–8

For each of the following arguments, identify the claim, the data, and the warrant.

1. This movie made $10 million its first weekend, so it must be a good movie because good movies make lots of money.
2. Joe is a human because he walks on two legs and all humans walk on two legs.
3. Interest rates are a good indicator of economic strength: right now, rates are very low, so the economy must be strong.
4. Dieticians know what healthy eating is, and my dietician says breakfast is the most important meal of the day, so I try to eat breakfast every morning.
5. Writing classes are important because classes should give students skills they can use on the job, and writing is an on-the-job skill.

EXERCISE 9–9

For each of the previous arguments, add a qualifier and, if necessary, backing.

EXERCISE 9–10

For each of the arguments in Exercise 9–8, brainstorm to foresee as many rebuttals as possible. Indicate whether the rebuttal is significant enough to deserve a response and, if so, how you would respond to it.

EXERCISE 9–11

The warrant of an argument is often left unstated. What are the implied warrants in each of the following arguments?

1. The New York Yankees are the greatest sports franchise in history because they have won the most championships.
2. Reducing the speed limit was a good idea because there are fewer fatalities from car accidents now.
3. A vegetarian diet is healthier because it is lower in fat.
4. TV shows are better nowadays because they are more like real life.
5. Soccer is a good sport because almost anyone can play.

EXERCISE 9–12

Take out the chart of Holmes's inferences you started earlier in the chapter. Label the second column "Qualifier" and the fifth column "Rebuttal." Fill in the chart with the appropriate information.

EXERCISE 9–13

Toulmin arguments can be written as a single sentence, although you wouldn't always write them that way when presenting inferences in a paper. Here is the sentence pattern:

[Data] *so* [Qualifier] [Claim] *since* [Warrant] *because* [Backing] *unless* [Rebuttal].

Using the chart you made of Sherlock Holmes's inferences, write out each inference as a Toulmin argument. Does the Toulmin model present each of Holmes's inferences clearly and effectively?

Rogerian Argumentation

The syllogism and the Toulmin model help you find out what you need to include when writing inferences because they break down an argument into several parts. Rogerian argumentation is a style of arguing that gives you options about how you present your inferences. Rogerian argumentation was worked out in 1970 by Richard Young, Alton Becker, and Kenneth Pike, who based their ideas on the counseling techniques of Carl Rogers, a psychotherapist and communication specialist.

When you think of the word "argument," you probably think of an "I'm right, you're wrong" fight—most people do. This approach, however, is not always the best way to present your position. Instead, consider your purpose: Is your purpose to persuade? If so, then you may want to engage your reader in an adversarial way, especially if you have a strong argument. But if you have another purpose—to explain or describe, for instance—then you might want to take a much less confrontational approach to presenting your inferences. Your reader might be more likely to agree with you if you show that some common ground exists between you and the reader, some room for compromise about the issue. Presenting inferences in this less confrontational way is called *Rogerian argumentation.*

Rogerian argumentation does not attempt to persuade readers to completely change their mind and adopt the arguer's perspective. Rather, it merely attempts to present the readers with information they may not have considered in order to effect a small change. Perhaps the readers will change a part of their own position or look at an issue from a slightly different perspective. If so, the Rogerian argument has been successful.

Rogerian argumentation starts out by establishing common ground between the arguer and the reader. The point here is to approach an issue as if both people are at some level on the same side, rather than opponents. Assume that you are writing a letter to the editor of the local newspaper about what to do with part of the school budget. One option is to spend the money to replace worn out desks, chairs, and other furniture in the school; however, you want the school board to buy new textbooks and library books. If you were to write a Rogerian argument, it might look like this:

> *All of us who are parents want to help our children get the best possible education. The extra money in the school budget is an excellent opportunity to give our students a big step up. Replacing the old desks and chairs and blackboards and such is an excellent idea: The students would be more comfortable and morale, an important contributor to student success, would go up. But I believe a wiser way to spend the money would be to replace the children's textbooks with up-to-date and accurate materials that will have a more direct effect on their learning.*

A Rogerian approach allows the writer to open up a dialogue with the reader, a process of give-and-take that recognizes the authority of both people. If you are presenting inferences about an issue that is controversial, then Rogerian argumentation may help you argue your position more effectively.

EXERCISE 9–14

A shroud is a large piece of cloth wrapped around a corpse before the body is buried. The Shroud of Turin mysteriously bears the image of a person it was allegedly wrapped around. Some people believe the image is that of the historical Jesus, but others disagree. The two articles about the Shroud of Turin that follow provide you with many facts about this controversial object. Using these facts, draw your own inferences about the Shroud. Your purpose here is not to decide whether the Shroud is genuine or not but to understand the information these articles present. After drawing your inferences, present them in a one- to two-page essay using Rogerian argumentation to establish common ground with your reader.

The Case of the Shroud
Joe Nickell

Few issues have offered a better opportunity for science to work cooperatively with religion than has the question of the authenticity of the Shroud of Turin. Yet scarcely has there been such divisiveness between the two spheres, and rarely has science been so abused as it has been in the shroud controversy. FREE INQUIRY has long monitored the debate.[1]

Dubious Beginnings

The "shroud"—one of some 40 cloths alleged to be the very one that wrapped Jesus's body in the tomb—first came to light amid accusations of fraud. It had been at the center of a faith-healing scam, or so it was reported to Pope Clement in 1389 by a bishop who went on to describe how a predecessor, Bishop Henri de Poitiers, had uncovered the artist who had made it. The artist admitted, the report added, that he had "cunningly painted" the shroud, which bore the "twofold image" (i.e., the front and back imprints) of an apparently crucified man.[2]

Continued

Clement had convincing evidence that the shroud was, as he officially concluded, a painted "representation." In addition to the reported forger's confession, there were such commonsense arguments as the cloth's lack of historical record prior to the mid-1350s and that its owner, a man of modest means, refused to say how he had acquired the most holy relic in Christendom. Clement might also have noted the shroud's incompatibility with the Bible, which described multiple burial wrappings, including a separate "napkin" that covered Jesus's face (John 20:5–7).

Even so, the granddaughter of the original owner absconded with the shroud, representing it as authentic despite Clement's official pronouncement. Eventually, although she would be excommunicated for it, she sold it to Duke Louis I of Savoy. Shroud proponents like to say she "gave" it to the Duke; it seems only fair to point out that, in return, he gave her the sum of two castles. Thus the cloth passed to what would become the Italian monarchy, although eventually it was in the actual custody of the Archbishop of Turin. At the death of the exiled King Umberto in 1983, it was finally bequeathed to the Vatican.[3]

Meanwhile, a century ago this year, the shroud's "scientific" period began when the image on the cloth was photographed for the first time. That resulted in the discovery that the darks and lights were reversed, and proponents rushed to proclaim the image a perfect photographic negative. How, they asked, could a medieval artist have accomplished this, long before photography was conceived? In fact, the image was only partially negative, just as an artist who wanted to create the effect of an *imprint* would have produced.[4] With the availability of photographs of the shroud came widespread study of its unique image and the creation of a new discipline, or pseudo-discipline, called "sindonology" or "shroud science."

Scientific Scrutiny
Actual scientific testing of the shroud began in 1969 and occurred in three main phases. Unfortunately, because the "relic" was in the control of

Continued

its religious defenders, who wished it to be proved genuine but feared it might not, there were problems with the way the early tests were conducted, as we shall see. Yet each group produced a major finding:

Fake blood. An official commission conducted extensive tests of the "blood" on the shroud. Although the work was done in secret, and leaks and false denials soon created something of a scandal, one of the results was noteworthy: the "blood" failed all tests, not only the preliminary ones but also such additional analyses as those for speciation and blood groups. The tests included chemical, microscopic, microchemical, and microspectroscopic analyses, as well as thin-layer chromatography and neutron activation analysis. The commission experts did note what they thought were traces of paint. Although Catholics, those conducting the tests on the blood were also internationally known forensic serologists, a fact that underscored the credibility of the results. (Critics had anticipated the negative findings because the shroud bloodstains were unnaturally picture-like and, in contrast to genuine old blood, still bright red.)[5]

Tempera paint. In 1978 the shroud was more extensively sampled by the Shroud of Turin Research Project (STURP), a scientific group that, alas, was composed primarily of religious believers. Its leaders served on the Executive Council of the pro-authenticity Holy Shroud Guild. An exception was Dr. Walter McCrone, an internationally known microanalyst and the only member of STURP with expertise in detecting forgeries and identifying paint pigments. McCrone discovered that the "blood" was actually tempera paint containing red ocher and vermilion pigments. He also found that the entire image area contained red ocher (which was not present on off-image areas), and he believed he detected a tempera binding medium there as well. He concluded the shroud was a medieval painting.[6]

Medieval date. A final blow to the shroud's authenticity was delivered in 1988 when small swatches of the cloth were subjected to radiocarbon testing by accelerator mass spectrometry. Three laboratories—at Oxford,

Continued

Zurich, and the University of Arizona—performed the tests, which yielded dates in the 1260–1390 range, a time fully consistent with the reported forger's confession. The accuracy of the carbon dating was supported by tests on control samples from ancient cloths of known date (such as Cleopatra's mummy wrapping).[7]

For their efforts, the skeptical Commission experts, Dr. McCrone, and the scientists who conducted the radiocarbon dating tests were publicly vilified and subjected to personal abuse from shroud zealots. McCrone, for example, was even held to a secrecy agreement that prevented him from publishing his findings, while authenticity advocates continued to tell the public there was no evidence of forgery. McCrone was eventually "drummed out" of STURP. Two other STURP scientists then claimed they had "identified the presence of blood" on the cloth, but their efforts suffered when it was shown that similar results could be obtained from tempera paint![8]

It became clear that shroud enthusiasts typically begin with the desired answer and work backward to the evidence—challenging those facts that seem incompatible with authenticity and emphasizing those that could be construed to support it. They concocted one rationalization for the contrary biblical description of Jesus's burial (the evangelists could have been in error), another for the lack of historical record (the shroud could have been hidden away), yet another for the forger's confession (the bishop might have misstated the case), and so on, with still other apologetics for the paint and the medieval carbon date.

The results of the carbon dating has been an especially serious problem and one that has not been neglected. For example, some scientists at the University of Texas Health Science Center claimed they had discovered microbial contamination on shroud samples that may have altered the radiocarbon dating, the implication being that the shroud might be genuine after all. However, simple calculations show that for there to be sufficient contamination to raise the date 13 centuries there

Continued

would have to be twice as much debris, by weight, as the entire shroud cloth itself! Besides, both the Vatican and the Archbishop of Turin challenged the sample's authenticity, and Walter McCrone stated unequivocally that the fibers shown in the scientists' photomicrographs "did not come from the 'Shroud' of Turin."[9]

Such embarrassments are common to shroud science. It has often been bad science, pseudoscience, even scientific fraud—as in the case of pollens that were purportedly found on the cloth and that supposedly proved it had once been in Palestine.[10]

In contrast, real science takes pains to be objective. Genuine scientists carefully collect evidence and follow it to the solution—an approach that ultimately prevailed in the shroud controversy. Indeed, overall, the details of scientific and even scholarly evidence were corroborative, that is mutually supportive. For example, there was no historical record prior to the forger's confession because the shroud did not exist until that time. The bright-red "blood" was consistent with tempera paint, the presence of which, in turn, supported an artistic origin. And so on.

The lesson from the shroud controversy is clear. In the case of physical claims—even physical claims in the context of religious belief—it is unfettered science that is the means by which truth can be achieved.

Notes

1. Joe Nickell. "New Evidence: The Shroud of Turin Is a Forgery," FREE INQUIRY 1, no. 3 (1981): pp. 28–30.

2. Joe Nickell, Inquest on the Shroud of Turin (Amherst, N.Y.: Prometheus Books, 1987), pp. 11–17.

3. Ibid., pp. 17–19, 154.

4. Ibid., pp. 77–78, 97–98.

5. Ibid., pp. 109–114, 127–129.

6. Walter McCrone, Judgment Day for the Turin Shroud (Chicago: Microscope Publications, 1996).

Continued

7. P. E. Damon, et al., "Radiocarbon Dating of the Shroud of Turin," *Nature* (1989) 337:611–15.

8. *Inquest on the Shroud of Turin*, pp. 125, 132.

9. CSICOP (Committee for the Scientific Investigation of Claims of the Paranormal), Press release, May 31, 1996; reprinted in *Skeptical Briefs*, June 1996, p. 2.

10. *Judgment Day for the Turin Shroud*, pp. 291, 308.

Archeologist Claims Proof Turin Shroud Wrapped Christ

Reuters

ROME (October 30, 1997 12:34 p.m. EST http://www.nando.net)   A Swiss archeologist said on Thursday she had proved the Turin shroud, one of Christianity's most controversial relics, did wrap the dead body of Christ and was not a medieval fake.

She said new research in Paris had also shown that what appear to be the words "Jesus Nazareth" were written on the cloth shortly after the body was wrapped in it.

"This is the only document on earth that proves the material presence of Christ 2,000 years ago," Maria Grazia Siliato told a news conference in Rome to present her book, "Shroud."

"It is the only real, concrete, archeological relic. Now (its authenticity) is beyond all doubt," she said.

Siliato hopes her book will finally give the lie to carbon-dating tests in 1988 by three laboratories in England, the United States and Switzerland that concluded the fragile linen sheet, which bears the apparently blood-stained image of a crucified man, was a 13th or 14th century forgery.

Continued

In the book, she traces what she says is the history of the Shroud, which many had thought could only be traced to 1357 when crusaders were believed to have brought the 4.4 by 1.4 metre (14.5 by 4.6 feet) cloth to France from the Middle East.

Siliato, who has studied the shroud for 16 years, said the carbon-14 tests were wrong for one simple reason—the fragment tested was a corner of the cloth repaired five times since 1400.

The proof, she said, was that the samples taken weighed 42 miligrammes per square centimeter, whereas the whole Shroud had an average weight of 20-23 miligrammes per square centimeter.

"These are numbers. They can't be discussed on an emotional level," she said. "They prove large scale restoration."

That explained why the scientists in 1988 differed about the shroud's age, dating it from between 1260 and 1390.

The Turin Shroud, which was saved from a fire in Turin Cathedral last April, clearly bears the image of a man with shoulder-length hair and a beard lying flat with his hands crossed, but sceptics down the centuries have dismissed it as a painting and the apparent blood marks as fake.

The image was at one time attributed to master Italian artist Leonardo da Vinci, despite the fact that it was brought to Italy in 1453 when he was just 11 months old.

Siliato said it could not be a print because that would have given it a fluorescent light which it "absolutely" did not have.

Instead, she said the authenticity could be scientifically proven by looking at how another living substance, a leaf for example, reacts with paper, which like linen is a cellulose material.

She said a three-dimensional, heat-resistant living image of the leaf is preserved, and cited perfectly-conserved 17th century examples made by herbalists.

Continued

"There are variables, such as the thickness of the paper or linen, but there is an analogy—the reaction of cellulose on contact with animal or vegetable acids is known," she said.

Siliato said only brief contact was needed—"a few days or hours"—but the image then took 40-50 years to appear fully. "This takes nothing away from believers," she added. Christians believe Christ was resurrected three days after his death.

"It then remains unchanged even several centuries later," she said, citing the example of another shroud, not purportedly that of Christ, which showed the imprint of a body even though the corpse it contained had been reduced to a skeleton.

Siliato said specialized photographs would be taken when the Turin Shroud goes on display next year for the first time since 1978 and computer technology would be used to shed more light on the inscription, which is not visible to the naked eye.

Siliato said the words were written on the cloth to identify it after the top half had been folded over the body.

DRAWING INFERENCES: PROFESSIONAL WRITING

Working out inferences in detective stories and riddles may be interesting as a pastime, but in the field of medicine, inferencing can have serious consequences. A doctor observes the symptoms of a patient (gathers facts) and then makes an inference regarding the cause of the symptoms. This process is also used by a mechanic to diagnose problems with your car and by a coach to pinpoint skills an athlete needs to develop.

The following two articles show doctors inferencing. In the first, "Taking a Stand," the doctor sees evidence of violence and draws an inference that requires her to take action on the child's behalf. In the second article, "The Baby Who Stopped Eating," the doctors must uncover concealed evidence in order to draw the correct inference and properly treat the infant.

Taking a Stand
Pamela Grim

"Medical clearance?" I asked as I paused at the door of Room 7. Inside, a social worker from Child Protective Services was watching over two small children. <u>The boy wore only a man's plaid shirt; the girl was dressed in a filthy white jumper.</u> Someone must have reported these children for suspected child endangerment. They were here in the emergency room for a brief physical exam.

<u>"Is it for neglect or abuse?" I asked.</u>

"Neglect, we think," the social worker replied. "Mom left them at a bus stop. She said she'd come back, but she never did." The worker reached out toward the girl. "Now, here is Tonya. She's four. And this is Raymond. He's two."

Raymond stood gazing up at me, one hand gripping the social worker's pants. He looked as if he would never let go. <u>I pulled his shirt open and examined his chest and back, looking for marks. In the last child abuse case I'd seen, a little girl had come in with circular first- and second-degree burns scattered across her back. Cigarette burns.</u> This kid looked okay, though, just dirty.

I knelt down to look at his sister. "How are you doing, little squirt?" She was a beautiful little girl, open and animated.

"I'm four," she said, showing me three fingers.

"Well, that's very big," I said, smiling, "and for big kids we have a big treat. We have ginger ale. Would you like some?"

She nodded, eyes wide.

"What do you say?" the social worker prompted—an instinctual mother.

The little girl smiled even more and ducked her head in shyness. <u>"Shut up," she said. "Shut up, shut up, shut up."</u>

I looked up at the social worker, my jaw slack in surprise.

First evidence to shape a mental model.

Request for information related to mental model.

Search for familiar information.

Evidence

Continued

"You wouldn't believe some of the stuff that comes out of these kids' mouths," she said.

Evidence

The little girl turned to her brother and gave him a shove. "Shut up, you stupid whore," she said. "Get me a beer."

Child abuse, child neglect. For a doctor one of the most difficult parts of treating abused children is simply making the diagnosis. In the ER this can be even more difficult because a diagnosis must often be made after only a minute or two of observation. One rule of thumb, I've learned, is to be suspicious of any parent who arrives in an ER with an injured child and wants to leave too quickly.

Inference drawn from opening illustration.

Presentation of Mental Model

One summer night it happened just that way. A mother had her son by the arm—he was about five—and she dragged him up to me. "How much longer is it going it be?" she demanded.

It should have been obvious that we were all working as fast as we could. I had just intubated someone who had taken an overdose of antidepressants, and was rushing off to see a woman with heart failure. From where I was standing I could see into the room where the woman lay on her bed struggling to breathe while a burly-looking man sat next to her, holding her hand.

"Ma'am," I said, "it's going to be a little while."

"Well, I don't have a little while. My son is hurt." Something in her tone made me pause for a moment and look at her.

"Dear," I said, "everyone here is very sick tonight."

"Don't you 'dear' me. I'm going to another ER. I've waited over two hours. I want some service."

Ed, the charge nurse, came hustling over. "I put you in that room exactly ten minutes ago." He pointed emphatically at his watch. "So don't tell her you've been waiting for hours." He stopped next to me and whispered in my ear, "I'm worried about this kid."

I knelt down to look at the whimpering child. He had obviously broken his forearm—the radius. There was swelling at the midshaft of the

Continued

Initial evidence and inference.

radius, and the arm beyond canted away at an angle. This was odd. When people fall, they generally fracture the forearm near the wrist. A fracture in the middle of the bone is much rarer and usually occurs from a direct blow. They're called nightstick fractures because people have gotten them from defending themselves against blows from a police officer's nightstick. This kid had such a fracture.

"How did this happen?" I asked the boy.

He looked at his mother and then at me and silently drew away.

"I'm leaving," the mother said, giving the child's other arm a tug. He just stood there, rooted to the floor.

"Wait," I said. "I need to know."

"Don't you 'wait' me. I'm taking my son and I'm leaving."

I looked at her. I had seen a thousand women who were fine mothers and who looked just like her, but looks mean nothing. As I gazed up at her from where I knelt, I was sure—well, pretty sure—that she had hurt her child.

Inference—what is the evidence?

I squatted there a moment, debating this. After all, what proof did I have? Besides, she was going to another ER. She said so. But I was angry. I was angry at her for yanking her child around and for being so damn unreasonable.

"I'm sorry," I said, standing up. I was conscious that I was standing between the woman and the exit. "You can't go anywhere with that child."

She glared at me. "What do you mean?"

"You can't leave," I said. Any parent, child abuser or saint, would be angry with this order, but this wasn't the time for second thoughts. I had taken my stand.

"You mean I can't leave?"

"You can, but the child can't."

"You're crazy." She shook her finger in my face and yanked the boy's arm.

Continued

I got angrier, much angrier—it was as if the scene was lit up by firecrackers.

"The kid stays here," I said.

"You," she repeated emphatically, "are crazy." She yanked again at her son's arms, but this time he pulled away from her, looking in terror at both of us.

"You can't go," I said loudly. "Not until we know what's going on here."

She tried to pass me.

"Call security," I said, turning to Ed. I hadn't noticed he'd left to take care of a drunk with a head wound dripping blood. I was alone in the hall without backup—very poor planning. If I headed for the desk, she would be out the door before I could get help.

"Maggy," I shouted at the desk clerk, "get security."

"This is my boy," the woman shouted. "I can do what I want with him."

The boy was waiting and trying to back away from her. She yanked at his arm again.

"I'm telling you." It took me a moment to realize that I was the one shouting. "I'm telling you, you can't do anything you want. You can't hurt a child, and you can't leave until I know what's going on. If you do, I'm going to have the police after you."

"Police!" she shouted. "You have no idea. So don't you dare threaten me."

She struck out at me and I ducked. At that moment, the firecrackers went out. I was willing to make a scene, but I was not prepared to be attacked. I stepped away, but she came after me, swinging with her free hand and trying to grab my clothes. She kicked me, just catching the side of my knee. As I went down, all I could see were her feet kicking near my face. When I looked up, I saw the burly man who had been sitting with his mother pin the woman to the wall. I got up and began to unpry her

Continued

fingers from the boy's forearm. As I pulled him free, security, like the Texas Rangers, came tearing down the hall.

All I could think was that the child would never forget this, me pulling him away from his mother.

"She's got my baby," the woman screamed. "That bitch has my baby."

"She needs to leave," I shouted at the security guards. "She can't stay here."

"Let's go," said Lenny, one of the guards. "That 'bitch' is the doctor, and what she says goes. You gotta leave."

The woman stood, arms crossed, staring at me. Ed had come running down the hall—he was a big guy and hard to ignore.

"The doctor says you need to leave," he said, looming over her. "I'm escorting you out to the waiting room, and we will talk about what you need to do next."

She allowed Ed to take her by the arm, but then glanced back at me and said, "I'm going to hunt you down, bitch. I'm going to get you for this."

The doors closed. It was a large ER, filled with patients and their families. Everyone stood stunned in silence. After a beat, though, the boy began to wail and the room broke into chatter.

Lenny carried the child back to a cubicle. My ankle was hurt, and I limped after them.

"Are you okay?" Lenny asked me.

"Yeah, fine, fine," I said, but my ankle hurt like hell.

Lenny set the child down on the examining table. He was still waiting.

"Let's get this shirt off him," I said. I thought I had seen marks when I was fighting with the mother.

<u>I had. There were two bruises on the boy's face and bruises on both arms, oval bruises the size of thumbprints. And on his back were dozens of slender, elliptical marks—some were scars,</u>

Evidence and inference— what are the two inferences here?

Continued

but some were fresh and bright red. They were cord marks, abrasions from being hit on the naked back and buttocks with a loop of electrical cord. Unmistakable signs of abuse.

I traced the scars with my fingers, feeling the ridges. The child was just whimpering now. One of the nurses offered him a stuffed doll.

"Sweetie," I said, as I knelt in front of him. "How did you break your arm?"

He stared at me, unblinking.

"Can you tell me? You don't have to be scared. I promise no one will hurt you."

His chin shook. He looked away and said, "D-d-d-d."

"Who?"

"D-d-d-d." He gave up and rubbed his eyes with the wrist of his good arm.

That's all he would say.

The next afternoon the investigating officer, Tiny, dropped by to take a statement from me. Tiny weighs in at a good 350 pounds. I had taken care of his asthma attacks several times.

"What do you think happened?" I asked him.

"I can't comment on an ongoing investigation," he told me. "But between you and me, it may be that the missus has been knocked around a few times by her husband, and I suspect the guy takes more than an occasional swing at the kids, especially this one."

"Why hasn't she filed a domestic violence complaint?"

Tiny shook his head. "He'd lose his job. In fact, he's already been suspended. He's a cop and there's big trouble down at the station. Apparently some people knew about what was going on and never said anything."

"Why is that?"

Tiny frowned. "You protect your own, I guess."

"What's going to happen?"

Continued

"If they charge him—and there's a pretty good chance of that—and if he's convicted, he'll lose his job. That leaves the three kids and Momma...I don't know what will happen to them."

I leaned back in the chair and studied the ceiling. "What good does it do to save the child and destroy the family?" I looked over at Tiny. "How does this happen? Just who does this to children?"

"Well," Tiny said with a shrug, "the kid's dad...he's a good man and all. I knew him in high school. But he drinks, and when he drinks, he gets mean." He paused, then shrugged. "There's lots of other reasons people hit kids, but this is a big one. People will behave like any kind of animal when booze is involved."

Inference of cause based on mental model.

On a hunch, I pulled the medical records for the police officer's wife. Sure enough, there were multiple ER admissions for minor trauma culminating with, about six months before, an admission for multiple facial contusions and a nasal fracture from "a fall down the stairs." Spousal abuse. Clearly. The problem was—though I had no memory

Inference—what's the evidence?

of it—I had seen her. I had read the X-rays correctly; I had sewn up her cuts. But I had missed the diagnosis. Nowhere in my notes did I bring up the possibility of domestic violence. If I had made the diagnosis then, perhaps someone could have intervened before the child got hurt. I had my chance long before the scene in the hallway, and I blew it. I had no one to blame but myself.

As the days and then weeks passed, I tried to find out what happened to the child and the family, but I kept meeting dead ends. Tiny wouldn't give me any information. Nobody I talked to knew the family or admitted that they did.

I wondered if the boy had been farmed out to a relative. What would he remember of the struggle and his broken arm? What about his mother? Was she a victim? She certainly was when I saw her after her "fall," but what was she that day I saw her with her son? Victim or accomplice?

Continued

And what about me? Was I an unwitting accomplice by missing the diagnosis the first time? And in doing what I thought was right for a little boy that afternoon, did I ultimately make things worse? Did I destroy a family? There had to have been a better way, but what was it?

That day, I had acted. I had done what I thought I had to do. But as is so often the case in emergency medicine, I will never really know if I did the right thing.

READING QUESTIONS

1. *Examine the inferences the doctor makes regarding Tonya and Raymond at the beginning of this article. What facts does she use as evidence? What is the inference? What is the warrant that leads her from the facts to the inference? What rebuttals to her inference can you come up with?*
2. *What inference does the doctor make regarding the mother of the boy with the broken arm? What is the doctor's evidence for the inference? What is the warrant? How could you rebut this inference?*
3. *At the end of the story, the doctor checks the medical records of the mother and infers that the woman was abused by her husband. Identify the evidence and the warrant for this inference.*
4. *Explain, in terms of the inferencing process, why you think the doctor did not make the inference of abuse when she first saw the mother's injuries.*

The Baby Who Stopped Eating
Robert Marion

I saved the most interesting case for last," said Molly Wilson, the resident who'd been on call the night before. It was a Saturday morning in early February. Molly and I had spent the last hour touring the Infants' Unit with the interns, stopping to discuss and examine each child who was unlucky enough to be inhabiting the unit that day. I was tired, the day was cold and gray outside, and I'd much rather have been at home in bed. But as the attending physician that month, the most senior doctor on the service,

Continued

it was my job to make sure these children got the best care possible, and so fighting off the urge to daydream, I focused my attention on the resident. "This baby's name is Jarret Fox," Molly continued. "He's a three-month-old who was admitted last night for dehydration. According to his mother, Jarret stopped eating four days ago.

"Stopped eating?" I repeated, quickly coming to full attention. "What do you mean he stopped eating?"

"Just that," Molly replied. "His mom says that Jarret was happy and healthy a week ago. Then, on Tuesday, he seemed to lose interest in nursing. He just stopped sucking, his mother says, and he hasn't eaten anything since."

"That can't be right," I responded. "Three-month-olds don't just suddenly stop nursing and starve themselves until they get dehydrated." "Well, I didn't believe it either at first, but the mother keeps telling the same story: she's been trying to force-feed him since Wednesday but hasn't had any success. Yesterday she brought him to her pediatrician. He said Jarret was about 5 percent dehydrated. He also said the kid was much floppier than he'd been the last time he'd seen him. So he sent him in for rehydration and a full evaluation."

That last part of Molly's report, the part about the increased floppiness, made my heart sink. It suggested a condition I hoped this baby didn't have. "Do you have any ideas about a diagnosis?" I asked.

"The only thing I can think of is spinal muscular atrophy," Molly said.

"That's what I'm thinking, too," I replied. "I hope we're wrong. Let's go see him."

Put simply, a diagnosis of the infantile form of SMA is a death sentence. A relatively rare inherited disease in which the nerves that control movement mysteriously degenerate and disappear, it is the childhood equivalent of the better-known (but no better understood) amyotrophic lateral sclerosis. As the nerves vanish during the first months of life, a child with SMA grows progressively weaker. After initial

Continued

problems with feeding, the infant loses the ability to move its arms and legs. Breathing also becomes difficult. With time, the child becomes more and more hungry for air until finally, by about the first birthday, he or she dies. The cause is usually pneumonia, a common infection in lungs that aren't getting enough air.

As a medical geneticist, I have had the unenviable task of helplessly watching more than a dozen patients live out the nightmarish symptoms of SMA. The only thing I could do was aid families in coping with the loss of their children. As I entered Jarret Fox's hospital room that Saturday morning, the faces of all these children and their families flashed through my mind.

"Ms. Fox," Molly said as we approached Jarret's crib, "this is Dr. Marion. He's our attending pediatrician."

"Sorry we have to meet under these circumstances," I said with a smile as I shook her hand. Barefoot, clad in a peasant blouse and bell-bottom jeans, her long, straight hair parted down the middle, Jarret's mom looked like a long-lost refugee from the Summer of Love. She also looked as if she could use a good night's sleep. "How are you doing?"

"Not too well," she replied. "I'm hoping someone will be able to tell me what's wrong with my son."

"We're going to try to get to the bottom of it," I said. "First, maybe you can tell me the story from the beginning."

Without hesitation, Ms. Fox spilled out the short tale of her son's life. After an uncomplicated pregnancy, Jarret had been born at his parents' home in North Salem, a rural town north of New York City. He was the couple's second child: their daughter, Jessica, now three years old, was "healthy as a horse." Although his birth was attended only by a midwife, Jarret was examined on the first day of life by the family's pediatrician (the only one in the area who practiced homeopathic medicine and made house calls) and declared to be in excellent health. His mother could think

Continued

of nothing unusual about her son's newborn period: in her words, he had been "like my other baby."

The infant had been seen by the pediatrician on a regular schedule, first at two weeks, then at a month, then at two months. He'd received his immunizations and had been growing and developing normally. Ms. Fox explained that her family were strict vegetarians who ate only whole, natural foods. She assured me that Jarret had had nothing but breast milk, adding proudly, "My daughter was exclusively breast-fed for the first 18 months of her life."

But four days ago this idyllic existence had ended. Jarret had simply refused to nurse. "He just wouldn't latch onto my breast," she said sadly. "Nothing I did got him interested. It was like a switch had been turned off in his brain and he wouldn't do it anymore. Just like that."

"Has he been hungry?" I asked, less certain now about the diagnosis.

"At first he was," she said. "That first day, he cried and cried. It was pathetic. But since then, he's just been lifeless, like he just doesn't care anymore."

I could see what Ms. Fox meant. Jarret was a sturdy, beautiful baby, but he lay as limp as a rag doll in his hospital crib, an IV in his left arm and a feeding tube in his left nostril. Although his eyes returned my gaze, Jarret seemed passive and expressionless.

"This doesn't sound like SMA," I said, shaking my head. After finishing my examination, I thanked Ms. Fox and told her that we needed to speak with the neurologist and that we'd be back later. Molly, a few interns, and I assembled in the corridor.

"SMA doesn't start suddenly like this," I began. "The weakness comes on gradually—the first day, the parents notice that the kid's a little floppy, the next day he's a bit more floppy, then a little more floppy the next, until finally they find they can't get him to eat enough to keep himself going. That's when the kid comes to the hospital with dehydration and the

Continued

diagnosis is made. But this story of the weakness coming on suddenly like a switch going off—that's too acute to be SMA!"

"I agree," Molly said. "It sounds almost like the kid was poisoned."

"Poisoned by what?" one of the interns asked. "The kid has had nothing but breast milk. If he was poisoned by something in the breast milk, the mother should have been affected, too."

"Good point," I replied, as a little bell of recognition began ringing in my head. "But Moll's right. It does sound as if he's been poisoned. And I think I know what it was." Without another word, I headed back into Jarret's room with the rest of the ward team trailing behind.

The mother, who had been sitting beside Jarret's hospital crib, rose to her feet.

"Sorry to bother you," I said. "But tell me again, when did you first notice this change in Jarret?"

"Tuesday afternoon," she replied. "When he woke up from his nap. He's usually starving when he wakes up. But that day, I couldn't get him to take my breast for anything."

I nodded. "And your three-year-old. Tell me, how does she get along with Jarret? Does she help you take care of him?"

"Oh, she's crazy about him," Ms. Fox replied with a smile. "She helps change his diapers, and when he spits up, she wipes him with a cloth. She tells me that I'm *her* mother, and she's really Jarret's mother."

I smiled at this also. "Since Jarret's exclusively breast-fed, she hasn't ever fed him, has she?"

"No, we'd never let her. But she always pretends to feed him. She pretends to spoon food into his mouth. It's really cute and they both love it."

"But as far as you know, she's never actually fed him?"

"Definitely not," Ms. Fox replied. "My husband and I are always at the table supervising. We'd never let Jess put anything in the baby's mouth."

Continued

I nodded and continued: "Ms. Fox, what does Jessica have for breakfast?"

The mother, somewhat surprised by the non sequitur, answered without hesitation: "A bowl of hot oatmeal and a glass of milk. Why do you ask?"

"Does Jessica eat the oatmeal plain, or does she put sugar on it?" I asked, already knowing what the answer would be.

As expected, Ms. Fox gave me an angry look. "Dr. Marion, we eat only whole, natural foods—no meat, no processed food, no sugar. Sugar is poison."

"Okay, no sugar," I pushed on. "But does Jessica use anything to sweeten her oatmeal?"

"We allow her to use a teaspoon or two of honey," she replied.

"Ms. Fox, we have to do some tests, but I think Jarret's going to be okay. I'm pretty sure he's got botulism."

It was Ms. Fox's reverence for natural foods that tipped *me* off to the possibility of infant botulism. That, and the suddenness of Jarret's symptoms. While considering the diagnosis as I'd questioned her, I visualized the scenario that had undoubtedly led to the baby's sudden onset of weakness.

Early that Tuesday morning, the Foxes were all in the kitchen. Jarret, sitting happily in his infant seat, had been placed at the table next to his sister, who was enjoying a bowl of oatmeal that had been topped with a few dollops of natural honey, straight from the hive. The children's parents had perhaps stepped away from the table to prepare their own breakfasts. Suddenly, Jessica, pretending to be Jarret's mother, silently offered her brother a spoonful of cereal. The infant eagerly accepted the offer and carefully rolled the strange-textured substance around in his mouth before swallowing.

He smiled with satisfaction as Jessica, still in silence, finished off the bowl.

Continued

Later in the day, Jarret took his usual afternoon nap. When he awoke, his mother found that, mysteriously, he could no longer take her breast.

As Ms. Fox continued to answer my questions, I became more convinced that this scenario (or one like it) had occurred. It had to have. After hearing the story and seeing Jarret, there was no other logical explanation.

Like Ms. Fox, most Americans believe that when applied to foods, terms like "pure" and "natural" are synonymous with "healthy" and "nutritious." This may be accurate for most foods, but not honey. Eating honey—in both natural and processed form—can lead to serious disease or even death in infants. Because of the environment in which it's produced, unprocessed honey often contains spores of *Clostridium botalinum,* the bacterium that causes botulism. The same can be true for processed honey. In most humans, the spores cause no problems: immune cells in the intestinal tracts of older children and adults release proteins that readily bind to and destroy the toxin. But in children under one year of age, infants whose intestinal tracts are still immature, the *C botulinum* survives and starts making toxins. And that spells big trouble. After traveling through the gut's lining and entering the blood stream, the toxins are carried throughout the body, where they bind to peripheral motor nerves, preventing them from carrying messages from the central nervous system to the muscles. Within hours of ingesting even tiny amounts of contaminated honey, previously healthy infants become profoundly floppy and lethargic, unable to smile or cry or suck. If the dose of toxins is large enough, every muscle, including those involved in breathing, becomes paralyzed. If their condition is not recognized quickly, these infants may simply stop breathing and die.

But if the diagnosis is made early, the prognosis for full recovery is good. Although there is no antidote to the toxin, its grip on the nervous system weakens with time. Gradually, the motor neurons create new receptors to replace those blocked by the toxin.

Continued

If the child is supported through this period—if he is tube-fed, provided with oxygen, and placed on a ventilator if breathing becomes difficult—he will eventually return to the state he was in prior to the disorder. The period of paralysis can last weeks or months.

When I told Ms. Fox that I believed Jarret had botulism, she looked at me as if I was crazy. But when the neurologist came by a few minutes later and agreed with the diagnosis, she began to have second thoughts about her initial impression. Later, when an emergency electromyogram (a test of Jarret's muscle and nerve function) revealed abnormal nerve responses consistent with botulism, she, too, became positively convinced of the story I'd invented.

Although we waited three long weeks for the lab reports, the results confirmed the presence of *C. botulinum* toxin not only in Jarret's serum and feces but in a specimen taken from the jar of honey from the Foxes' pantry as well. Because the scenario now seemed so obvious, I urged the Foxes not to confront or blame Jessica; doing so, I argued, would needlessly make the girl feel guilty. Rather, I suggested they have a talk with her, trying to get her to understand that she should never put anything into her little brother's mouth.

As for Jarret, it took him more than five weeks to return to his prepoisoned state, and his recovery was not without complication. On the afternoon of his admission to the hospital, his breathing had become labored, and when a blood-gas analysis revealed signs of respiratory failure, he was transferred to the ICU, where he was intubated and placed on a ventilator. For weeks he remained dependent on machines, unable to breathe, suck or swallow, cry or smile, or move any of his muscles. He continued to be fed milk pumped from his mother's breast (she wouldn't allow him to be fed anything else) through the feeding tube.

Then in early March, his nurse noted what appeared to be a flicker of movement in his left leg. It was so subtle at first that she thought she'd only

Continued

imagined it, but more movement occurred in the following hours. Slowly but surely, Jarret was regaining control of his nervous system.

In the next few days, he was gradually weaned off the ventilator. Soon the feeding tube was removed, and he began eating on his own again, first from a syringe, then from a bottle, and finally, more than a month after he had entered the hospital, directly from his mother's breast. Just about back to his old self, he was discharged in the middle of March.

READING QUESTIONS

1. *The annotations for the first article, "Taking a Stand," show the steps the writer takes in drawing inferences. Annotate "The Baby Who Stopped Eating" to show the steps the author takes to make inferences.*
2. *Examine the way Dr. Marion presents his inferences: does he use a syllogism, an enthymeme, or the Toulmin model?*
3. *Describe the mental model of Dr. Marion at the beginning of the story. What is the usual behavior of infants?*
4. *On what evidence does the doctor base his first diagnosis, that the baby suffers from SMA?*
5. *What evidence makes the doctor reject his first diagnosis and infer that the baby was poisoned?*
6. *When the doctor makes the diagnosis that Jarret suffers from botulism, his inference is presented as a connection. Does the doctor make parallel or sequential connections in reaching his diagnosis? Does the doctor follow those connections up by providing context for his inference?*

DRAWING INFERENCES: STUDENT WRITING

The writing assignment for this chapter is for you to draw and present inferences from two sources for your research project—the assignment is given in detail at the end of the chapter. Here are the drawing inferences papers Tobi and Julie wrote for that assignment.

Which Came First?

Connecting Success and Self-Esteem

Tobi Raney

Though discussing totally different issues, Judy Anderson and Richard Lapchick have produced articles with an interesting connection. In her article, "Confidence's Role in Winning," Anderson explains that personal confidence inevitably leads to success. Lapchick informs his readers that sports are a significant source of confidence in his commentary "Participation Helps Keeps Kids in School, Provide Life Skills." Once we recognize the main points of each article, it is easy to link them and the important process of confidence development becomes more tangible. Clearly, self-confidence and success are circularly related. Without one, the other cannot be sufficiently achieved. Lapchick informs us that sports can be an important tool in the process of building a healthy self-confidence, therefore contributing to personal success.

To understand this connection, we must clearly define success. Does this connection imply that only those who win gold medals and earn straight A's can be truly confident? Certainly not. Success must be defined by each individual, just as personal goals are. It is the degree to which we achieve our personal goals that determines our self-perception (hence the prefix "self"). Our priorities determine our goals. If work is one's priority, and a promotion is a personal goal, then denial of such an advancement will, in most cases, result in lowered confidence. On the other hand, if an employee's family is a priority and he is denied a promotion because he will not work overtime, he will more than likely not feel as discouraged. The improvement of position was not a personal objective.

Lapchick's assertion that sports fit into this cycle raises some interesting questions. Can a nonathletic person possess adequate self-

Continued

confidence? The answer, again, lies in a person's priorities. If sports are an integral part of their life, and they are not successful in that avenue, their athletic failures can lead to a lower self-esteem. Again, though, failure must be defined by the athlete. Not everyone's goal is to simply win. Some participate only to stay in shape, others compete against their own past performances, not their competitors.

Another issue raised in these articles is mentioned primarily by Anderson. She defines two forms of confidence—performance confidence and personal confidence. She insists that both must be present in an individual in order to reach his or her potential. Lapchick indirectly supports this position when he points out how sports have contributed to success in student athletes. By adding the performance dimension to their life, he contends students are closer to reaching their personal capacity. In doing so, they also increase their sense of self-pride, which in turn contributes to future successes, which expand potential—It is a circular process, possessing neither a beginning nor an end.

Where then, does self-esteem originate? From where does success emanate, for that matter? If one powers the other, which should be "jump-started" when a person's self-worth is suffering? In fact, neither area can be placed before the other. Both must be tended to when a person's self-perception is not up to par. We must feel good about ourselves to appreciate, and even to recognize, our own successes. At the same time, we must accomplish something to feel good about ourselves. Regarding sports, a positive self-image alone cannot cause athletic success. Nor can good performance, by itself, raise a person's self-esteem. Athletes, or any of us, must slowly build self-esteem by setting goals and then proceeding to achieve those goals. It is by tending to both the self-esteem and ability areas of an individual that we can ensure a truly successful life. This principle is not unique to the athletic realm. Instead, it is a universal truth, affecting all areas of human life.

Considering the Past
Julie McDowell

In today's sweetener market, aspartame is consumed by more people than any other sweetener. However, just the opposite was true in the 1970s, when the names cyclamate and saccharin dominated and aspartame was in its infancy. A 1974 *Business Week* article, "Sweeteners Await a Cyclamate Decision," addresses the interest of the Searle company—manufacturer of aspartame—in the period pending the consideration to allow resumption of the manufacture of cyclamate (this sweetener had been banned in 1970). Several years later, in 1977 to be exact, *Time* published "A Bitter Reaction to an FDA Ban," which showcased the obsession some Americans had with saccharin.

These articles lead to some question about just how successful aspartame would have been, had cyclamates not been banned and saccharin use had not been limited by the FDA. Especially thought provoking is the knowledge—as reported in *Business Week*—that it took a year following removal of cyclamates for Searle to seriously push for FDA sanction. Had cyclamates never been linked to cancer in rats, would Searle have ever tried to gain approval, and if the manufacturers of cyclamate had succeeded in legalizing the sale of their product again, would the company have pursued it as aggressively?

That question may be hard to answer but is definitely worth examining further. With cyclamate's 1970 ban, saccharin was the only FDA-approved sweetener available to the U.S. consumer. However, as the *Time* article notes, there was already suspicion about its carcinogenic effects. Thus, the timing was perfect for aspartame to appear on the market. Still, the makers of cyclamate were trying to re-introduce their product and had several things in their favor. Particularly of importance was its noticeably lower cost. Though aspartame cost less than sugar at the time, it was greater than 10 times the cost of cyclamate. The two also

Continued

had similar sweetening effects. Because of this, many manufacturers (including Coca-Cola®) would have likely resumed the use of cyclamate.

Additionally, how would American consumers react today to a ban on aspartame? If the proposed saccharin ban's 1977 hysteria is any indication, it would not be very favorable. Following actions by the FDA, consumers, as well as businesses and organizations, expressed their disagreement. *Time* told of saccharin devotees spending hundreds of dollars as they cleaned the shelves of grocery stores. At the time, saccharin was a two billion dollar-plus business, and this public outrage may have helped result in stipulations rather than a ban.

Considering America's ever-increasing interest in health and dieting, it is reasonable to speculate that scenarios similar to those described above would arise if the FDA considered such actions against aspartame. However, this speculation might not even be valid had cyclamate and saccharin not come under scrutiny nearly 30 years ago.

WRITING ASSIGNMENT: DRAWING INFERENCES

For this assignment, you will draw inferences from evidence you have gathered about your research topic and present those inferences in a 300–500 word essay.

1. To draw your inferences, use facts that you have gathered from at least two sources for your research project. The purpose of drawing these inferences is not to decide whether the information is right or wrong, but to develop your individual perspective on the research topic.
2. Analyze your inferences using the Toulmin model. How will you qualify your inferences? Will you need to include your warrants because you think they will be unfamiliar to your audience? Are there rebuttals you will have to deal with in your writing?
3. Be sure to document your sources according to the format assigned by your instructor.

Here are the answers to the riddles: the riddle from "The Motley Fool" refers to Staples. The answer to the first riddle from *The Hobbit* is an egg. The answer to the second one is your teeth.

PART FOUR

Writing to Your Purpose

In Part Four, you are ready to take care of those tasks that will present your paper effectively to your readers. Chapters 10 and 11 address the reference and citation style for your paper. If you are writing a paper in the humanities, you will use MLA style. If you are writing a paper in the social sciences, you will use APA style. As you prepare your working bibliography and cite your sources in your text, you will wish to consult these two chapters.

In Chapter 12, you are introduced to choices regarding the "décor" of your paper: the outline, the title, the introduction, and the conclusion. The importance of the last three components cannot be emphasized enough. A specific, original title prompts the readers' interest; a concrete introduction maintains that interest and sets up your thesis; and the conclusion presents the readers with your major inference from the discussion section of your paper. In fact, all three components are best derived from your discussion, suggesting this order of writing: discussion, conclusion, introduction, and title.

In Chapter 13, annotations of the MLA style paper by Tobi Raney and the APA paper by Julie McDowell illustrate how these two writers applied the techniques discussed in this text. These models should help you in writing your own papers.

Chapter 10   Citing Your Sources—MLA Style

Chapter 11   Citing Your Sources—APA Style

Chapter 12   Arranging Your Presentation

Chapter 13   Managing Your Presentation

CHAPTER 10

Citing Your Sources— MLA Style

In Part II of this book, you were introduced to some basic principles and examples of MLA-style bibliography and citation. This chapter expands on that basic introduction by presenting a larger range of examples; however, this chapter is not an exhaustive guide to MLA-style citation. If you cannot find the kind of bibliographic entry or parenthetical citation for your sources in this chapter, then you should consult the MLA's Web site (http://www.mla.org), *The MLA Handbook for Writers of Research Papers*, or *The MLA Style Manual*.

THE MLA-STYLE WORKS CITED LIST

When you put your list of Works Cited together, keep the following conventions in mind.

1. Number the page the Works Cited list is on in the same sequence and format as the rest of your essay.
2. Use a one-inch margin on all sides of the page.
3. Center the words "Works Cited" at the top of the page; do not underline or place the words in quotation marks.
4. Double space between all lines on the page.
5. Use a "hanging indent": The first line of each entry should be flush with the left-hand margin and all successive lines should be indented one-half inch, five spaces, or one regular tab.
6. Alphabetize all of the entries according to the first word of the entry.

   • Use the last name of the author or first author.
   • For anonymous works, use the first major word of the title, omitting *a, an,* and *the.*

7. Underline or italicize major titles (books, periodicals, Web sites, etc.).
8. Capitalize all words in the title after the first word, except articles (*a, an,* and *the*), coordinating conjunctions, the infinitive to, and prepositions.
9. Space once after marks of punctuation.

Books

The basic format for books is to put:

1. the author's name (last name, a comma, first name, and middle initial or any abbreviations, such as "Jr."), followed by a period;
2. the title of the book, followed by a period;
3. the names of other contributors to the book, such as editors or translators, followed by a period;
4. edition numbers, followed by a period;
5. the place of publication (usually a city name and, if the city is in America, the two-letter state abbreviation; if the city's name is unique and recognizable, such as New York or Los Angeles, then you can omit the state abbreviation), followed by a colon;
6. the publisher (omitting business names such as "Publishers," "Books," and "Press," and abbreviations such as "Inc." and "Co."), followed by a comma;
7. the year of publication followed by a period.

For books published by a university press, there are special abbreviations. If the name of the press is in the same format as "University of Chicago Press," then abbreviate it as "U of Chicago P." If the press's name is like "Harvard University Press," then abbreviate it "Harvard UP."

The following list includes examples of most of the more frequently used types of works cited entries; again, if you cannot find the appropriate entry for your source, then check one of the MLA resources listed or ask your instructor.

One author
Dillard, Annie. *For the Time Being.* New York: Knopf, 1999.

More than one work by the same author
Selzer, Richard. *Down from Troy.* New York: Morrow, 1992.
——. *Mortal Lessons.* New York: Simon and Schuster, 1976.

Two authors
Johanson, Donald and Maitland Edey. *Lucy: The Beginnings of Humankind.* New York: Simon and Schuster, 1981.

Three authors
Lass, Abraham H., David Kiremidjian, and Ruth M. Goldstein. *Dictionary of Classical, Biblical, & Literary Allusions.* New York: Facts on File, 1987.

More than three authors
Turnbull, Ann, et al. *Exceptional Lives: Special Education in Today's Schools.* 2nd ed. Upper Saddle River, NJ: Merrill, 1999.

Works by authors with the same last name
Smith, A. *The Mind.* New York: Viking, 1984.
Smith, C.R. *Learning Disabilities.* 4th ed. Boston: Allyn & Bacon, 1998.

No author listed
Practical Problem Solver. Pleasantville, NY: Reader's Digest, 1991.

Work in several volumes (each volume titled separately)
Hunter, G.K. *English Drama 1586-1642: The Age of Shakespeare.* Vol. VI of *The Oxford History of English Literature.* Oxford: Clarendon, 1997.

Work in several volumes (all volumes with same title)
Graves, Robert. *The Greek Myths.* 2 vols. London: Folio Society, 1996.

Book in a series
Eco, Umberto. *A Theory of Semiotics. Advances in Semiotics.* Bloomington, IN: Indiana UP, 1976.

One selection from an anthology of writings by various authors
Selzer, Richard. "The Knife." *The Art of the Personal Essay.* Ed. Phillip Lopate. New York: Anchor, 1994. 708-714.

More than one selection from an anthology
If you are citing more than one work from a single anthology, then give a full works cited entry for the anthology and cross-referenced entries for each selection. Cross-referenced entries include:

1. the author of the selection (last name, first name, initials or abbreviations), followed by a period;
2. the title of the selection in quotation marks, followed by a period;
3. the last name of the author or editor of the anthology, followed by a period;
4. the page numbers of the selection, followed by a period.

Bender, Robert M., and Charles L. Squier, eds. *The Sonnet: An Anthology.* New York: Washington Square, 1987.
Meredith, George. "By this he knew she wept…" Bender and Squier. 234-5.
Wordsworth, William. "London, 1802." Bender and Squier. 160.

Editor
Lewis, Karron G., ed. *The TA Experience: Preparing for Multiple Roles.* Stillwater, OK: New Forums, 1993.

Work with an editor and an author
Tolkien, J.R.R. *The Silmarillion.* Ed. Christopher Tolkien. Boston:
      Houghton Mifflin, 1977.

Translated work
Kostrovitskaya, Vera S. *100 Lessons in Classical Ballet.* Trans. Oleg
      Briansky. New York: Limelight, 1995.

Introduction, preface, foreword, or afterword
Bishop, Rudine Sims. Foreword. *Reading Across Cultures: Teaching
      Literature in a Diverse Society.* Ed. Teresa Rogers and Anna O.
      Soter. New York: Teachers College, 1997. vii-ix.

Edition
Korbeck, Sharon. *Toys and Prices.* 4th ed. Iola, WI: Krause, 1996.

Reprinted book
Bush, Douglas, ed. *The Portable Milton.* 1949. New York: Penguin, 1977.

Dictionary or encyclopedia entry
"Orc." *Merriam Webster's Encyclopedia of Literature.* 1995 ed.

Authored article in a reference book
Reed, Linda. "Rosa Parks (1913-)." *Black Women in America.* Ed. Darlene
      Clark Hine. New York: Carlson, 1993.

Bible
The New English Bible with the Apocrypha. Eds. Bruce M. Metzger and
      Roland E. Murphy. New York: Oxford UP, 1994.

Unpublished dissertation
Williams, Sean Daniel. *Theorizing a Perspective on World Wide Web
      Argumentation* (Composition, Computers, Internet, Hypertext
      Theory). Diss. U of Washington, 1999.

Articles

Articles are cited with different information than books, although the basic
format is the same. An article's citation includes:

1. the author's name (last name, a comma, first name, middle initial or
   abbreviations), followed by a period;
2. the title of the article in quotation marks, followed by a period (that
   goes inside the quotation marks);
3. the title of the publication, underlined or italicized;
4. if the periodical is a commercial magazine, then record:

   • the date of publication (day, month, year), followed by a colon;
   • the page number(s), followed by a period.

5. if the periodical is a professional journal with sequential page numbers, then record:

   - the volume number;
   - the year of the issue in parentheses, followed by a colon;
   - the page number(s), followed by a period.

6. If the periodical is a professional journal with nonsequential page numbers, then put:

   - the volume and issue number as a decimal (for example, "34.2");
   - the date (month or season and year) of the issue, in parentheses, followed by a colon;
   - the page number(s), followed by a period.

If the article is not signed by an author, then the entry begins with the title of the article. For other variations in article citations, ask your instructor or look in an MLA handbook.

Signed article in a weekly or biweekly magazine
Tharp, Mike. "L.A. Blues: Dirty Cops and Mean Streets." *U.S. News and World Report* 13 March 2000: 20-1.

Signed article in a monthly or bimonthly magazine
Gillies, Mark. "Cooper Star." *Automobile* April 2000: 161-4.

Article in a professional journal—nonconsecutive pagination
Petch-Hogan, Beverly, Jo Anne Dunham-Trautwein, and Howard P. Parette, Jr. "The Branching Strategy for Teaching Mathematics." *LD Forum* 20.2 (1995): 20-4.

Article in a professional journal—consecutive pagination
Ritchie, Joy, and Kathleen Boardman. "Feminism in Composition: Inclusion, Metonymy, and Disruption." *College Composition and Communication* 50 (1999): 585-606.

Article in a daily newspaper
Levins, Harry. "A Bloody History Repeats Itself." *St. Louis Post-Dispatch* 27 June 1999: A12.

"A12" indicates the section of the newspaper and its page. If the section is numbered instead of lettered, then use the following form: sec. 1: 12. If the newspaper is not sectioned, then include only the page number.

If the city of publication is not included in the title of the newspaper, then enclose it in brackets following the newspaper title: *Southeast Missourian* [Cape Girardeau, MO].

If the source is not a news article, then put the appropriate identifier from the following list after the title:

- For an editorial: "Editorial."

- For a letter to the editor: "Letter."
- For a response to a letter to the editor: "Response to letter of John Smith."

Review
Shulman, Polly. "Beyond the Star Show." Rev. of the Hayden Planetarium. *Discover* April 2000: 83-4.

Other Copyrighted Sources
For other sources (of which there are many kinds), do your best to follow the author's name (last name first, first name last); title (usually underlined or italicized); publication information format.

Charts or maps
Irish Family Names Map: Arms and Mediaeval Locations. London: Johnston & Bacon, 1978.

Published interviews
Beck. Interview. *Jane* April 2000: 100-1.

Publications by entities such as corporations or government offices
Department of Health and Human Services. *What You Need to Know About Cancer* (NIH Publication No. 88-1566). Bethesda, MD: National Cancer Institute, 1988.

Pamphlet
Smoking and Women. p-065. Washington, D.C.: The American College of Obstetricians and Gynecologists, April 1986.

Sound recording
Jenkins, Karl. "Elegia." *Adiemus* 2. New York: Sony, 1997.

Videotape or film
Amadeus. Dir. Milos Forman. Burbank, CA: Warner Home Video, 1997.

Television or radio program
60 Minutes. CBS. KFVS, Cape Girardeau, MO. 27 June 1999.

Published letter
Rilke, Rainer Maria. Letter to Franz Xaver Kappus. 17 February 1903. *Letters to a Young Poet.* Trans. Stephen Mitchell. New York: Random House, 1984. 3-12.

Cartoon
Davies, Matt. Cartoon. *Southeast Missourian* 21 March 2000: 10A.

Live performance
As You Like It. By William Shakespeare. Dir. Don Schulte. Forrest H. Rose
Theater, Cape Girardeau, MO. 4 March 2000.

Work of art
Van Gogh, Vincent. "The Starry Night." Museum of Modern Art, New
York.

Noncopyrighted Sources

Noncopyrighted sources are usually primary research. Thus, you need to
provide only the name of the persons or instruments involved, what kind
of source it is, and the date it was created.

Personal interview
Zahner, Russell. Personal interview. 27 June 1999.

Telephone interview
Brooks, Debbie. Telephone interview. 28 June 1999.

Personal survey
Classroom Cheating Questionnaire. Personal survey. 25 June 1999.

Letter
Brooks, Mike. Letter to the author. 23 June 1999.

Electronic Sources

In general, to cite an electronic or online source, you need to provide the
bibliographic entry as you would for a print source, plus the information
identifying the type and location of the electronic source. Specifically, you
need to provide the reader with:

1. the author's name (last name, first name, initials or abbreviations),
   followed by a period;
2. the title of the source, usually in quotation marks, followed by a
   period;
3. the standard publication information about a print version of the
   source (if there is one);
4. online publication information;
5. the date you accessed the source;
6. the electronic location of the source

   - if the source has a URL: put the URL in angle brackets, followed by
     a period;
   - If the electronic source does not have a URL: put the type of source
     (CD-ROM, Online, and so on), followed by a period; the producer
     of the source or the online service from which you retrieved your
     source, followed by a period.

Here are some examples—if you have a different kind of source, look at the MLA's Web page or one of the MLA print guides to find out how to put it in your list of works cited.

Material from a CD-ROM
"History of sports." (1996). *The Academic American Encyclopedia,* 1996 ed. CD-ROM. Danbury, CT: Grolier, 1996.

Online article with a print version (with a URL)
Yang, Dori Jones. "The Empire Strikes Out." *U.S. News & World Report* 15 Nov. 1999: n. pag. 8 Nov. 1999 <http://www.usnews.com/usnews/issue/991115/microsoft.alt.htm>.

Online article with a print version (without a URL)
Stotsky, Sandra. "More Teachers, Smaller Classes: Are These Our First Priority?" *Education Week* 1 April 1998: n. pag. Online. EBSCOHost. 8 Nov. 1999.

Online article without a print version
deForest, Mary. "Female Choruses in Greek Tragedy." *Didaskalia* 4.1 (Spring 1997): n. pag. <http://didaskalia.berkeley.edu/issues/vol4no1/deForest.html>. 21 March 2000.

Electronic text
Lamb, Charles, and Mary Lamb. *Tales from Shakespeare.* Ed. Terry Gray. 25 April 1998. 21 March 2000. <http://daphne.palomar.edu/shakespeare/lambtales/LAMBTALE.HTM>.

Scholarly project
Perseus Project. Ed. Gregory Crane. September 1997. Tufts U. 21 March 2000. <http://www.perseus.tufts.edu/>.

Organizational home page
"Welcome to the ADE Page." *Association of Departments of English.* Modern Language Association of America. 16 November 1999. 21 March 2000. <http://www.ade.org/>.

Personal home page
Reinheimer, David. Home page. 13 June 1999. 8 Nov. 1999 <http://cstl-cla.semo.edu/reinheimer/>.

E-mail
Scates, Carol. "Help." E-mail to Dayna Northington. 20 March 2000.

Online posting

Dimeropoulos, Kosta. "Heteroglossia." Online Posting. 28 June 1999.
    Bakhtin Centre Discussion List. 28 June 1999. <Bakhtin.Centre
    @sheffield.ac.uk>.

MLA-STYLE PARENTHETICAL CITATIONS

Chapter 5 explained how to create and place parenthetical citations. This section provides a more extensive list of examples of the kinds of citations you
might need to use.

1. Citing by Author

    - One author: (Dillard 37).
    - Two authors: (Johanson and Edey 244).
    - Three authors: (Lass, Kiremidjian, and Goldstein 95).
    - More than three authors: (Turnbull, et al. 199).

2. Citing by Title: (*Practical Problem Solver* 244).
3. Citing Multiple Works by One Author: (Selzer, *Mortal* 130).
4. Citing Authors of the Same Last Name:

    - (Deborah Smith 100)
    - (Corrine Smith 125)

5. Citing More than One Source: (Dillard 37; Johanson and Edey 244).
6. Citing a Corporation or Government Office: (Department of Health
   and Human Services 24-5).
7. Citing Sources with Several Volumes: (Graves 2: 10). The number 2
   following the title designates the volume number.
8. Citing Biblical passages: The books of the Bible have standardized abbreviations that can be found either in the Bible or in various bibliographic handbooks. The citations for Biblical passages include the
   book, chapter, and verse. Do not underline the titles of books in the
   Bible: (John 11: 35).
9. Citing Online Sources with No Pages: If an online source gives page
   numbers, then it should be cited in the same manner as print sources.
   If the online source does not give page numbers, then remember to indicate this in the Works Cited list by using the abbreviation "n. pag."
   Then, cite the source by author's name and/or title: (Stotsky).

CHAPTER 11

Citing Your Sources—
APA Style

In Part II, you were introduced to the basic principles of creating APA-style bibliographic entries and parenthetical citations. This chapter expands on the basic examples given in Part II, but it is not an exhaustive list. The examples in this chapter include only the most commonly used formats for APA-style References lists and parenthetical citations. If you don't find the format you need here, then look at the APA Web site (http://www.apa.org) or in the *APA Publication Manual,* or you can ask your instructor.

Some of the examples in this chapter may seem more appropriate to an MLA-style paper in the humanities than to an APA-style paper in the social sciences. The same examples are used in both this chapter and in Chapter 10 to clearly show the differences between MLA and APA style.

THE APA-STYLE REFERENCES LIST

The APA References list is very much like the MLA Works Cited list. The APA Web site requests that writers using the APA style to prepare manuscripts for publication use a tab indent for the first line of each reference entry; however, students submitting manuscripts to their professors are given the option of using the "hanging indent," which is also used in the MLA style. Check with your instructor to find out which format you should use.

Here are some general rules to follow as you put your References list together.

1. Start a new page, numbered in sequence with the rest of the essay. Maintain the same headers and margins as the rest of the essay.
2. Center the section title, "References," but do not underline or place it in quotations.
3. Double space between all lines on the page.

4. Include only "recoverable sources," or sources your reader has access to. Personal communications and other nonrecoverable sources are cited only in parenthetical citations.
5. Place all entries in alphabetical order, according to the first word of the entry.
6. Place dates of publication in parentheses.
7. For more than one work by the same author, place the works in chronological order. For more than one work by the same author in the same year, alphabetize the works.
8. Do not quote or underline short titles (such as articles, essays, short stories, or poems) that would be included in larger works.
9. Underline major titles with a continuous line or italicize the titles.
10. Capitalize only the first word in a title, proper nouns, and the first word following a colon.
11. Space once after marks of punctuation.

Here are examples of the more common entries in an APA-style References list.

Books

To create a Reference entry for a book, put:

1. the author's name (last name, first initial), followed by a period;
2. the year of publication in parentheses, followed by a period;
3. the title, followed by a period;
4. the place of publication, followed by a colon;
5. the publisher's name, followed by a period.

One author
Dillard, A. (1999). *For the time being.* New York: Knopf.

Other works by the same author
Selzer, R. (1976). *Mortal lessons.* New York: Simon and Schuster.
Selzer, R. (1992). *Down from Troy.* New York: Morrow.

Two authors
Johanson, D., & Edey, M. (1981). *Lucy: The beginnings of humankind.* New York: Simon and Schuster.

Three or more authors
Lass, A. H., Kiremidjian, D., & Goldstein, R. M. (1987). *Dictionary of classical, biblical, & literary allusions.* New York: Facts on File.
Choate, J., Bennett, T., Enright, B., Miller, L., Poteet, J., & Rakes, T. (1987). *Assessing and programming basic curriculum skills.* Boston: Allyn & Bacon.

More than one work by the same author published in the same year
Smith, J., and Weiss, L. (1997a). *Hugs for dad: Stories, sayings, and scriptures to encourage and inspire.* West Monroe, LA: Howard.

Smith, J., and Weiss, L. (1997b). *Hugs for mom: Stories, sayings, and scriptures to encourage and inspire.* West Monroe, LA: Howard.

Works by authors with the same last name
Smith, A. (1984). *The mind.* New York: Viking.
Smith, C.R. (1998). *Learning disabilities.* (4th ed.). Boston: Allyn & Bacon.

No author listed
Practical problem solver. (1991). Pleasantville, NY: Reader's Digest.

Work in several volumes (each volume titled separately)
Hunter, G.K. (1997). *The Oxford history of English literature: Vol. VI. English drama 1586-1642: The age of Shakespeare.* Oxford: Clarendon.

Work in several volumes (all volumes with same title)
Graves, R. (1996). *The Greek Myths* (Vols. 1-2). London: Folio Society.

Book in a series
Eco, U. *A theory of semiotics. Advances in semiotics.* Bloomington, IN: Indiana University Press.

One selection from an anthology of writings by various authors
Selzer, R. (1994). The knife. In P. Lopate (Ed.), *The art of the personal essay* (pp. 708-714). New York: Anchor.

Editor
Lewis, K. G. (Ed.). (1993). *The TA experience: Preparing for multiple roles.* Stillwater, OK: New Forums.

Work with an editor and an author
Tolkien, J.R.R. (1977). *The silmarillion.* (C. Tolkien, Ed.). Boston: Houghton Mifflin.

Edition
Korbeck, S. (1996). *Toys and prices.* (4th ed.). Iola, WI: Krause.

Reprinted book
Bush, D. (Ed.). (1977). *The portable Milton.* New York: Penguin. (Original work published 1949).

Dictionary or encyclopedia entry
In APA style, you do not include the title of an article from a dictionary or encyclopedia in the References list. You would mention the title in your text, however.

Merriam-Webster's encyclopedia of literature. (1995). Springfield, MA: Merriam-Webster.

Authored article in a reference book
Reed, L. (1993). Rosa Parks (1913-). In D. C. Clark (Ed.), *Black women in America*. New York: Carlson.

Government publication
Department of Health and Human Services. (1988). *What you need to know about cancer*. Bethesda, MD: National Cancer Institute.

Unpublished dissertation
Williams, S. (1999). *Theorizing a perspective on world wide Web argumentation (composition, computers, Internet, hypertext theory)*. Unpublished doctoral dissertation, University of Washington, Seattle, WA.

Articles

When creating a reference for an article, put:

1. the author's name (last name, first initial), followed by a period;
2. the date of publication (for example, year and month or year, month and day) in parentheses, followed by a period;
3. the title of the article, followed by a period;
4. the title of the periodical, underlined or italicized, followed by a comma:

   - if the periodical is a consumer magazine, then include only the title;
   - if the periodical is a professional or academic journal, then put the title, a comma, and the volume number, underling or italicizing title and volume number;
   - if the source gives an issue number, then include it in parentheses after the volume number, but do not underline or italicize the issue number;

5. the page numbers of the article:

   - if the source is a newspaper, then precede the page numbers with the abbreviation "p." for one-page articles and "pp." for longer articles.

Signed article in a weekly or biweekly magazine
Tharp, M. (2000, March 13). L.A. blues: Dirty cops and mean streets. *U.S. News and World Report*, 20-1.

Signed article in a monthly or bimonthly magazine
Gillies, M. (2000, April). Cooper star. *Automobile*, 161-4.

Article in a professional journal—nonconsecutive pagination
Petch-Hogan, B., Dunham-Trautwein, J., & Parette, H.P., Jr. (1995). The branching strategy for teaching mathematics. LD *Forum*, 20 (2), 20-24.

Article in a professional journal—consecutive pagination
Ritchie, J., & Boardman, K. (1999). Feminism in composition: Inclusion, metonymy, and disruption. *College Composition and Communication,* 50, 585-606.

Article in a daily newspaper
Levins, H. (1999, June 27). A bloody history repeats itself. *St. Louis Post-Dispatch,* p. A12.

Review
Shulman, P. (2000, April). Beyond the star show [Review of Hayden Planetarium]. *Discover,* 83-4.

Other Copyrighted Sources

For copyrighted sources other than books and articles, include the same basic information, and add the type of source in brackets immediately after the title. The only exceptions to this rule are published letters.

Charts or maps
Irish Family Names Map: Arms and Mediaeval Locations [Map]. (1978). London: Johnston & Bacon.

Sound recording
Jenkins, K. (1997). Elegia. *Adiemus* 2. [CD]. New York: Sony.

Videotape or film
Forman, M. (Director). (1997). *Amadeus.* [Videotape]. Burbank, CA: Warner Home Video.

Television or radio program
60 Minutes. [Television program.] CBS. KFVS, Cape Girardeau, MO. 27 June 1999.

Published letter
Rilke, R. (1984). Letter to Franz Xaver Kappus. In S. Mitchell (Trans.), *Letters to a young poet* (pp. 3-12). New York: Random House.

Work of art
Van Gogh, Vincent. *The starry night* [Artwork]. New York: Museum of Modern Art.

Electronic Sources

For electronic sources, put:

1. the author's name (last name, first initial), followed by a period;
2. the publication date, or "last updated date," (year, month, and day) in parentheses, followed by a period;

3. the title, followed by a period;
4. the type of source, in brackets, followed by a period (note that for the APA, the word "on-line" is hyphenated);
5. the date you retrieved the source, in the format: "Retrieved (put the date of retrieval), from (put the service or source here, such as "World Wide Web" or "EBSCOHost"), followed by a colon;
6. the URL of the source (do not follow the URL with a period unless that period is a part of the URL).

For sources not covered here or on the APA Web site, the APA suggests that you consult *Electronic Styles: A Guide to Citing Electronic Information* by Xia Li and Nancy Crane.

Material from a CD-ROM
History of sports. (1996). *The academic American encyclopedia.* [CD-ROM]. Danbury, CT: Grolier.

Online article with a print version
Yang, D. (1999, November 15). The empire strikes out. *U.S. News & World Report*, 15 November 1999. [On-line magazine]. Retrieved November 8, 1999, from the World Wide Web: http://www.usnews.com/usnews/issue/991115/microsoft.alt.htm

Online document without a print version
deForest, M. (1997, Spring). Female choruses in Greek tragedy. [On-line]. *Didaskalia.* Retrieved March 21, 2000, from the World Wide Web: http://didaskalia.Berkeley.edu/issues/vol4no1/deforest.html

APA-STYLE PARENTHETICAL CITATIONS

1. Citing by Author:

   • One author: (Dillard, 1999, p. 37).
   • Two authors: (Johanson and Edey, 1981).
   • Three to five authors: (Lass, Kiremidjian, and Goldstein, 1987).
     ◇ Identify all of the authors when they are first cited. But in subsequent citations, name only the first author, followed by the phrase et al., as in (Lass et al., 1987).
   • Six or more authors: (Choate et al., 1987).

2. Citing by Date: If you use the author's name in the text, then cite only by date of publication and (if the source material is a quotation) by page number: (1999) or (1999, p. 98).

3. Citing by Title: If no author is listed for your resource, then substitute a shortened version of the title for the author's name in the previous citation formats listed: (Practical, 1991).

4. Citing Multiple Works by the Same Author or Authors: If you are using more than one work by an author published in the same year, then alphabetize the works by title in the Reference section and assign

them an alphabetical code according to their sequence: (Smith & Weiss, 1997a).

5. Citing Authors of the Same Last Name:

- (C.R. Smith, 1998)
- (A. Smith, 1984)

6. Citing Multiple Sources: (Dillard, 1999; Johanson and Edey, 1981).

7. Citing a Corporation or Government Office: In the first citation, use the full name of the corporation or office, and include an abbreviation in brackets. Use the abbreviation in subsequent citations: (U.S. Department of Health and Human Services, [USDHHS], 1988).

8. Personal Communications: Letters, interviews, and e-mail messages are not considered "recoverable sources." In other words, your reader cannot access them. Therefore, cite them in your text only, not in the References section:

- Personal Interview: (R. Zahner, personal communication, June 27, 1999).
- Telephone Interview: (D. Brooks, telephone interview, June 28, 1999).
- Personal Survey: (Classroom Cheating Questionnaire, personal survey, June 25, 1999).
- Letter: (M. Brooks, letter to the author, 23 June 1999).

CHAPTER 12

Arranging Your Presentation

All of the work you have done so far has led to this point: you are about to prepare your researched writing project for submission. You have reviewed and used the basic writing principles that are integral to every kind of writing; you have gathered and critiqued source material; you have drawn connections and inferences among pieces of evidence. In this chapter, you will begin to shape the material into a final presentation.

DEFINITION: ARRANGEMENT

> **Arrangement:** Placing the several parts of an essay in an order that most effectively achieves the writer's purpose.

As you have worked through this book, you have drafted significant portions of the body of your researched writing project. Now you must make some decisions about arranging those sections and composing the finished product.

Think of arranging your final researched writing project like unpacking after you move into a new house or apartment. You have validated, connected, critiqued, and inferenced with your evidence, which is like having moved all of your belongings into your new place. But the boxes are just sitting everywhere in random piles. Now, you must take all of the meaning and evidence you have been working with and arrange it to meet your purpose as a writer, which is like unpacking your belongings and arranging them throughout the house.

You will need to create a title, an introduction, and a conclusion. But, before learning about those parts of the project, you need to know the techniques of outlining.

TECHNIQUES: OUTLINING YOUR PROJECT

Your instructor may ask you to include an outline with your final researched writing project. Earlier in the book, outlining provided a way to generate and organize ideas, an activity done before writing a paper. The outline you turn in with your final project, however, should summarize your paper's content, so it is usually done after you have written the paper. Exactly what your outline will look like is again determined by your instructor's preferences. Two of the more common formats for outlines are the *formal outline* and the *sentence outline*.

The Formal Outline

The formal outline follows several rules and conventions. If you are using a word processor, creating a formal outline is fairly easy. Most word processors have an outline function that formats the information for you. However you create your formal outline, keep these expectations in mind: First, put your thesis before the outline in order to unify the information that follows. Second, outline only the body of the essay—do not include your introduction or conclusion in the outline. Here are the other expectations regarding the format of a formal outline:

Division indicators
- ♦ Capital Roman numerals (I, II, III, . . .) indicate major divisions.
- ♦ Capital letters (A, B, C, . . .) indicate major subdivisions.
- ♦ Arabic numerals (1, 2, 3, . . .) indicate minor subdivisions.
- ♦ Lowercase letters (a, b, c, . . .) indicate second-level subdivisions.

Indentations
- ♦ Periods following the Roman numerals should align vertically.
- ♦ All subdivision indicators are indented two spaces after the period of the previous division indicator.
- ♦ Each division must contain at least two entries.
- ♦ Double space between each entry.
- ♦ All entries must be grammatically parallel.
- ♦ Capitalize the first word of each entry.

To see these conventions in action, here is Tobi Raney's formal outline for her researched writing project.

Jumping for Joy

Formal Outline

Tobi Raney

Thesis Topic: Increase in self-esteem of female athletes

   I.   Historical background

       A.   Negative attitudes towards female athletes

       B.   Freedom of movement stifled by modest dress

Continued

II. Parallels of women's sports and the feminist movement

    A. Formation of a women's athletic committee

    B. Dormancy in feminism and changes in female sports

III. Factors contributing to female athletes' self-esteem

    A. The greater the number of athletes, the greater the performance

    B. The roles of participation and competitiveness

    C. The circularity of participation and self-esteem

IV. Sources of self-esteem

    A. Personal definition

    B. Values and personal success

    C. Athletics as a value

        1. High school statistics

        2. College survey

        3. Other research

V. Various benefits

    A. Independence

    B. Confidence

VI. Influence on others

The Sentence Outline

A formal outline is only one way to format your outline. Your instructor may ask you to write an informal outline instead. A common form of the informal outline is called the sentence outline. In this kind of outline, you still use the same kind of divisions and subdivisions as the formal outline. There are three differences, however:

1. instead of a "thesis topic," you unify your outline by giving the "thesis sentence" at the beginning;
2. whereas a formal outline requires at least two entries per division or subdivision, an informal outline can have only one entry in a division or subdivision;
3. because the entries are sentences, they don't need to be grammatically parallel.

Here is Julie McDowell's sentence outline for her researched writing project:

No Sugar-Coated Solution in Aspartame's Immediate Future

Sentence Outline

Julie McDowell

Thesis Sentence: However, this product—aspartame—has an interesting history of both controversy and popularity that has raised much debate but yielded few conclusions.

I.   Aspartame has a fairly simple composition.

    A.   Its three components are aspartic acid, phenylalanine, and methanol.

    B.   It has the same calorie content as sugar, but is much sweeter.

II.   When aspartame was discovered in 1965, two other artificial sweeteners were in use.

    A.   Cyclamate, found to be carcinogenic, was banned in 1970.

    B.   Saccharin, also found to be carcinogenic, was banned in 1977.

III.   FDA approval of aspartame was delayed for several years.

    A.   John Olney and James Turner questioned the safety of aspartame, especially for sufferers of phenylketonuria.

    B.   Further testing confirmed the test results of G.D. Searle, the discoverer of aspartame.

    C.   A three-person panel was appointed to decide the fate of aspartame.

IV.   Aspartame was approved in 1981 and became very successful in the American consumer market.

    A.   Aspartame marketed under the brand names "NutraSweet" and "Equal."

    B.   Aspartame has shown a 40 percent growth rate in yearly sales since 1981.

Continued

> V.   Opponents still question aspartame's safety.
>
>   A.   Attacks on aspartame's safety focus on the ingredient methanol.
>
>   B.   The most common complaint is headaches, but the media focuses on claims of increased incidence of brain tumors.
>
>   C.   Recent studies cast doubt on these attacks.
>
> VI. Despite the large amount of research, no conclusion regarding aspartame's safety has been reached.

EXERCISE 12-1

Select one of the essays from the "Anthology of Student Writing" and create a formal outline for it. Select another essay and create an informal sentence outline for it. After creating the two outlines, briefly respond to these questions:

1. Which outline was easier to create? Why?
2. Which outline gives a more accurate summary of the essay? Why?
3. Compare your outlines with outlines created by a classmate. Which kind of outline is easier to read and understand? Why?

TECHNIQUES: CREATING A TITLE

First impressions are the most important—and your reader's first impression of your paper will be its title. In just a few words, your title needs to tell the reader a lot. It needs to identify the topic of the paper, your perspective on the topic, and your tone, and grab the reader's interest.

Successful titles work in different ways. They can directly state the purpose and topic of a work. Or they can indirectly indicate the topic through metaphorical language or descriptive details. Consider some of the following titles pertaining to science:

The Cambridge Encyclopedia of Astronomy, Simon Mitton

♦ Directly states topic; shows objective tone for reference work

The Riddle of the Dinosaur, John Noble Wilford

♦ Directly states topic

The Grand Tour: A Traveler's Guide to the Solar System, Ron Miller and William K. Hartmann

♦ Directly states topic; uses metaphor for interest

The Three-Pound Universe, Judith and Dick Teresi

♦ Indirectly states topic of the brain through metaphor

The Demon-Haunted World, Carl Sagan
- ♦ Indirectly states topic of superstition through metaphor

Why People Believe Weird Things, Michael Shermer
- ♦ Indirectly states topic of superstition through metaphor

The Panda's Thumb, Stephen Jay Gould.
- ♦ Indirectly states topic of evolution through descriptive detail

Broca's Brain, Carl Sagan
- ♦ Indirectly states topic of the human brain through descriptive detail

In addition to being direct or indirect, titles can also be sentences, phrases, questions, or even single words. Each of these title formats has its own strengths and weaknesses, which are discussed more fully in the following sections.

Sentences and Phrases as Titles

Sentences can work as titles, but phrases tend to be much more successful. Remember the movie *Blade Runner,* starring Harrison Ford and Rutger Hauer? It was based on a novel titled *Do Androids Dream of Electric Sheep?.* The movie producers wisely elected to use the shorter title. Both titles are equally indirect, but the shorter title has greater impact and interest.

If you do choose to use a sentence for your title, do not use your thesis statement. Titles and thesis statements are not interchangable because they have different purposes. A title invites the reader into the work. A thesis sets forth the limited and focused topic and the claim for that topic, letting the reader know directly what will be examined.

Questions as Titles

As titles, questions have the same weaknesses as declarative sentences— they're a little too long and they can give too much information. In addition, questions may immediately provoke an argumentative response that you might not want. Suppose your title is "Should 18-Year-Olds Be Required to Perform Two Years of Public Service Before Entering College or the Work Force Full-Time?" Your reader will naturally answer this question. But, if your reader's answer is not the same as your answer, then it will be much harder for you to achieve your purpose.

Single Words as Titles

Single-word titles will work if they are not so vague or generic as to blur the issue being addressed. *Connections,* the title of a television series by James Burke that explored the connections between historical events, works both ways, directly and indirectly. He literally draws connections, but he also creates a metaphor of how ideas evolve. In contrast, *Galaxies,* the title of a book by Timothy Ferris, directly states the topic.

EXERCISE 12–2

Examine the titles of the essays in the "Anthology of Student Writing."

1. Which titles directly state the essay's topic?
2. Which titles indirectly state the essay's topic through metaphor?
3. Which titles indirectly state the essay's topic through detail?
4. Which titles are the most effective? Why?

Create titles for your final researched writing project.

1. Create a title that directly states your project's topic.
2. Create a title that indirectly states your project's topic through metaphor.
3. Create a title that indirectly states your project's title through detail.
4. Try to use different formats (sentence, phrase, question, single word) as well.

TECHNIQUES: LEADING INTO YOUR THESIS

After you focus your topic and determine your thesis, you're ready to consider how to present that thesis to your reader. Most academic writing places the thesis at the end of the essay's introduction, but what do you do in the introduction? There are several different ways to lead your reader into your thesis.

But first, a general word of advice. William Zinsser, a writing expert, suggests that "the most important sentence in any article is the first one. If it doesn't induce the reader to proceed to the second sentence, your article is dead." Although he mentions only writers of articles, Zinsser's advice is good for *all* writers. Readers of any sort, including your instructor, want to be interested from the get-go.

The lead also gives important information about you, the writer. The first sentence of your paper shows your reader how interested and excited you are about your own work. If you're not interested or excited, the reader will know from the beginning that reading your paper will not be very enjoyable.

Using a Scene as a Lead

Your next rainbow is as close as the nearest garden sprinkler—and as far as the sun. For the rainbow is simply an image of the sun, although a much modified one. Raindrops perform this rearranging of sunlight, and do so by two processes: reflection and refraction.

You can involve your reader in the topic by dramatizing it and putting the reader into the action. The author personalizes the topic—everyone can create a rainbow in the backyard. Then the author increases the interest level by presenting a paradox—how close and yet how distant a rainbow is. The reader easily imagines and participates in this scene. And then the author leads the reader directly into the thesis.

Using an Anecdote as a Lead

The rainbow, at once grand and delicate, appeared in the sky as I sat swaying with my grandmother on her porch glider. Aledo, Tex., is a small town, and there is not much to do there but swing on my grandmother's front porch. As the arc of color took form she turned with a sly look to her grandson, the physicist, and asked me why the rainbow colors appear only in that one arc. Why is the entire sky not filled with colors?

I offered the conventional explanation, comparing the separation of colors in the rainbow to the dispersion of white light by a prism. A particular geometry of scattering, I explained, is needed in order for each of the colors to reach our eyes. Hence the colors are confined to a single arc, a fixed set of directions.

Feeling satisfied with my explanation, and feeling rather smart, I turned back to the sky just as a second rainbow appeared, somewhat higher than the first. One look at my grandmother and I knew I was in trouble. Almost in rhythm with our swing, she asked question after question. Why is the higher bow wider? Why is the sequence of colors reversed in the higher bow? Why is the space between the bows darker than the surrounding sky? What are the faint, narrow arcs just below the first rainbow and just above the second one? And, again, if there can be two rainbows, why not more? Why is the entire sky not covered with rainbows?

Using an anecdote as a lead works along the same principle as using a scene. The story gets the reader involved in the topic. Anecdotes tend to be longer than scenes, though, and therein lies the danger. Leads (like titles) work best when they are short and to the point. You don't want to drag your lead on so much that the reader gets bored or loses the point. Likewise, you need to balance the length of your lead with the length of your essay. Very long leads (like very long quotations) make it look as if you're trying to pad your essay because you don't have much to say yourself.

Using an Allusion as a Lead

The Bible tells us in Genesis that Noah, his family, and all those animals bobbed around on endless waters for 150 days before the Lord finally drained off the flood and allowed them to return to firm land. He promised Noah and his descendants dominion over all nature and never again to visit upon them another flood. And then the Lord set in the sky a mighty bow of brilliant colors. "This is the token of the covenant which I make between me and you and every living creature that is with you, for perpetual generations," He told Noah. "I do set my bow in the cloud, and it shall be a token of a covenant between me and the earth."

Long before Dorothy started her walk down the yellow brick road, rainbows have fascinated mankind. Perhaps no other natural phenomenon has so captured our imaginations as the rainbow. For thousands of years the rainbow has figured in legends and mythologies of nearly every known culture, and artists throughout the ages have celebrated it in painting, poetry, and prose.

In this lead, the writer alludes to the Biblical story of the flood and to *The Wizard of Oz*, perhaps the two most famous rainbow stories in American culture. These allusions work well as a lead because the reader is familiar with them. Because of that familiarity, the reader is willing to "travel" with you from the lead into the less familiar territory of your essay.

Using Description/Definition as a Lead

> *The commonly-observed rainbow consists mainly of a primary and a secondary bow, formed by the strong scattering of direct sunlight by raindrops along a set of directions. The scattering angle of the primary bow is approximately 138 degrees, and for the secondary bow 130 degrees. These main bows are most striking in the sky when the observer is situated between a low altitude sun and a heavy, prolonged rain shower. The distance of the shower from the observer, and its lateral extent, determine the fraction of bows that can be seen. The physical state of the lower atmosphere and the size of the raindrops will additionally influence the clarity and intensity of the primary and secondary bows.*

Instead of creating a scene or using an allusion, this lead opens up with a straightforward, factual description. This kind of lead usually generates interest in the reader by providing the reader with information they do not know. It is especially appropriate for audiences who want a no-frills approach to writing—such as a science teacher who is concerned with your powers of observation, or a busy supervisor who doesn't have a lot of time to spend reading.

Using Connections as a Lead

> *The lovely offspring of showers and sunshine that we call the "rainbow" bears a multitude of other names throughout the world. The French call it the "arch in the sky," the Italians, the "flashing arch." In various dialects of southern Europe it is known as the "arch of St. Martin," the "bridge of the Holy Spirit," the "girdle of God." In Sanskrit it is known as the "bow of Indra," the Annamites call it the "little window in the sky," and the Kabyles of northern Africa the "bride of the rain."*

This kind of lead is closely related to the description lead. Here, however, rather than describing an object, the writer makes connections among many different cultures. The audience is interested by information it probably didn't possess and the several different perspectives on the topic. You can also use contrast as a kind of connection to create an effective lead.

Leads to be Careful About

You should seriously think about some leads before you decide to use them. Many have been in use for a long time, so it's sometimes difficult to generate interest when the reader sees the same old thing at the beginning of the essay. That is not to say that these leads are never effective, but you should think about their downsides before using them.

- *Question leads.* The worst that can be said about a question lead is that you might not like your reader's answer to your question. If you and your reader don't start off on the same foot, then you've made your job as a writer much harder than it needs to be. If you decide to use a question as a lead, be sure to provide a clear answer soon after the question; that way, you and your reader will have some common ground.
- *"Webster" leads.* Like the question lead, starting a paper with a dictionary definition strikes the reader like a very old knock-knock joke. Definitions may be necessary at the beginning of an essay, but you should avoid simply quoting the dictionary.
- *Inverted pyramid.* This kind of lead is a standard—start with a general idea and narrow things down to your thesis. But that definition itself shows the problem. Starting with a general idea often does not generate very much interest because the reader wants to be greeted by concrete information and vivid images.
- *"Cosmic" leads.* This kind of lead begins with "Since the beginning of time . . .," "Throughout history . . .," or a similar phrase. As the writer, you will have to work hard to get from this huge generality to a specific thesis and still have your reader's interest. Start instead with the specific, the concrete, and the memorable.
- *Quotation leads.* Opening with a quotation is as "been there, done that" as questions and dictionary definitions. Not only is this technique old and boring, but you also start off *your* essay with someone else's words. It is better to claim ownership of your writing from the start and construct your lead from your ideas and your words. Think of quotation leads like toupees—the reader will see it and will know it's not yours.

EXERCISE 12–3

Analyze the leads in the essays in the "Anthology of Student Writing."

1. What kind of lead does the writer use?
2. Does the lead grab your attention and interest? Why or why not?
3. Does the lead effectively move you into the essay's thesis? Why or why not?
4. What revisions would you make to the essay's lead?

Draft leads for your final project.

1. Use at least two of the strategies described previously.
2. Which lead do you think is more effective? Why?
3. Show your leads to a classmate. Which lead does your classmate think is more effective? Why?

TECHNIQUES: CONCLUDING YOUR ESSAY

Endings are just about as difficult, if not more so, than beginnings. Pilots in training often say that getting the plane off the ground and flying it are not the problems—landing is the hard part. Hollywood, too, has a problem with endings—there's always a loose end left lying around in case a sequel would make money. But, as a writer, you need to draw your essay to a close.

When you write your conclusion, do not follow the rules of speech writing: "Tell them what you are going to tell them; tell them; and finally, tell them what you have told them." Readers are not listeners. Readers do not want to see the same thing again; they want to see fresh material.

The best advice for writing a conclusion is this: don't think of your conclusion as the end of your essay. Instead, think of it as the last conclusion, the last inference, the final bit of meaning you use to support your thesis. To do this, you need to look carefully at the body of your essay. Reexamine your thesis, assess what you think your reader's perspective now is, and evaluate your purpose. What last little bit do you need to say to make your paper successful? The answer to that question will tell you what to do in your conclusion.

Because your conclusion is so closely related to what you do in the body of a particular paper, you do not want to casually choose one from a list. In general, conclusions rely on the same techniques that are used to develop the body of the paper. Here are these techniques in the conclusions to the rainbow essays that we examined earlier for leads.

Using Definition as a Conclusion

> At any time of year, however, you may be surprised at how often rainbows can be seen, and at their variety. The rainbow may appear with shimmering iridescence near the horizon. Or it may look like a gauzy veil draped across the upper reaches of the sky. But the rainbow is more ethereal than any veil—it has no substance, it is sheerest light.

Reminding us of the diversity in the appearance of rainbows, the writer ends with description and a simile. But the last sentence, a definition of a rainbow as light, defies the concreteness of that simile. Thus, the conclusion reduces the discussion of the article to the single definition, *light*.

Using Summary as a Conclusion

> Not all my grandmother's questions have been answered by this experiment. For example, the faint bows below and above the natural rainbows, which are called supernumerary arcs, have not been explained. Neither has the fading of the rainbow colors as the drops evaporate and shrink. On the other hand, we have seen the delicate colors of more than a dozen rainbows within a single drop of water. What a fabulous sight it would be if all of them were visible in the sky.

This conclusion recalls the lead (the anecdote about a conversation with the writer's grandmother) and how it prompted the experimentation described in the body of the article. It contrasts what has not been answered with what has. The final sentence refers to the grandmother's query about why the sky is not filled with rainbows after a rain shower. In effect, the conclusion summarizes the entire article without merely repeating sentences in the introduction and body.

Using a Question as a Conclusion

> *Few people know that the moon can create rainbows as readily as the sun, so most of us do not look for them on nights when a full moon shines through a light mist. Nocturnal rainbows contain the same colors as the more familiar daytime rainbows but at such low light intensity that the eye does not detect them. However, the careful observer may glimpse these special rainbows— great bands of black and gray arching their way across the nighttime skies. Black rainbows!*
>
> *Goodness! What would Dorothy have said about that?*

This conclusion, consisting of both an allusion and a question, is clearly set up by the previous paragraph, which surprises us with information about rainbows created by the light of a full moon. And the allusion to Dorothy (singing "Somewhere Over the Rainbow" in *The Wizard of Oz*) echoes the allusion to Dorothy in the lead. This conclusion, as well as the previous one, shows that a favorite ploy of writers in creating a conclusion is to circle back to some specific detail of the lead.

Ask questions only sparingly, especially in the last sentence, because ending your paper with a question puts the responsibility for resolving the issue on the reader. The danger therein is that your reader might not answer the question the way you want him or her to. The end of your paper, when you don't have a chance to reinforce your perspective, is the worst time for you and your reader to come up with different answers for a question. Thus, the best question-as-conclusion has the answer implied within it.

Using Results as a Conclusion

> *Thus, chasing rainbows unfortunately does not bring us any closer to them. And for this reason, it still remains impossible to verify the existence of the proverbial pot of gold at the rainbow's end.*

This concluding paragraph is preceded by a discussion of how rainbows are "a product only of the proper angular relationships between the sun, the raindrops, and the observer." The constancy of the angular relationship means that the distance of the observer from the rainbow can never be shortened. So, the conclusion is a result controlled by a natural mathematical ratio.

Using Solutions as a Conclusion

> *It [the science of rainbows] is all very confusing. Maybe it is best to forget the mechanics, and view it with the awe of a small boy witnessing his first rainbow, not knowing then that the beautiful had dawned on his soul for the first time.*

This conclusion follows a paragraph that explains how a double rainbow is formed from both a primary and a secondary rainbow. It offers a solution to understanding the complex physics of rainbow formation.

Using Advice as a Conclusion

So what are the circumstances under which you could expect to see many supernumeraries in a rainbow? Well, if you, too, lacked the effrontery to liberate my long-lost water sprinkler, then watch for a gentle summer rain shower and pay special attention to the top of the rainbow arch.

This conclusion refers to the water sprinkler mentioned in the lead. Having discussed how supernumeraries are produced, the author advises the reader how he or she might observe one.

Using a Quotation as a Conclusion

The average [person] has noticed the rainbow only in its simplest form, yet . . . never fails to thrill at the sight of this gorgeous spectral display. A study of this phenomenon teaches us the details to notice in a rainbow, so that more truly than ever, we may say with Wordsworth:

> My heart leaps up when I behold
> A rainbow in the sky.

This conclusion finishes with a quotation, affirming the point the writer has made about how people feel when they first catch sight of a rainbow.

Conclusions to Be Careful About

As the examples show, conclusions are governed by what comes before them, in both the body and often the introduction. Therefore, you should not randomly choose a conclusion from a list, not even this one. But knowing about the various types of conclusions you can choose from will help you decide how to end your researched paper.

As with leads, however, you should be careful about certain conclusions. Before you use them, make sure they fit your purpose as a writer.

1. *Avoid using a quotation as a conclusion just because it is convenient.* Like the quotation lead, the quotation conclusion surrenders your ownership of the writing. This is your last chance to speak to your audience, your last chance to claim your topic and your writing as your own. Use it.
2. *Avoid using the phrase "In conclusion" or any of its relatives.* When you tell your reader what you are going to do in an essay, you take the focus off your writing and put it on you, the writer. Your reader will know you are ending the paper without having you announce it. Keep the focus where it belongs—on your ideas and your writing.
3. *Avoid restating the thesis.* Readers want fresh material in the conclusion. Simply restating the thesis suggests that you cannot draw meaning out of your discussion. Be aware, too, that summarizing must be handled carefully. A summary isn't a conclusion any more than a thesis statement is. Use a summary, as the previous example shows, to set up your ending.
4. *Don't introduce completely new ideas.* Your readers want *fresh* material, not *new* material. Your conclusion should provide a new perspective

on the "old" information in your essay. If you think that you need to put new information in your conclusion, then take another look at the body of your essay. You probably haven't finished it yet.

5. *Don't apologize for any shortcomings.* If you think that you need to apologize for weaknesses in your essay, then go back and rework the body of your essay. Rather than acknowledging weaknesses, revise them into strengths.

6. *Don't overstate your position.* It's natural to want to sound like you know what you're talking about. But don't sound like your paper offers the last word on your topic. A conclusion should finish off your paper, but it shouldn't finish off the conversation between you and your reader.

EXERCISE 12-4

Analyze the conclusions in the essays in the "Anthology of Student Writing."

1. What technique does the writer use to create the conclusion?
2. Does the author use the conclusion to circle back to the lead? How?
3. Does the conclusion effectively end the essay while leaving room for further discussion on the topic?

TECHNIQUES: INCLUDING GRAPHICS AND APPENDICES

Graphics are an important but often overlooked part of researched writing, especially in the computer age when they are so easy to create and insert into a document. A *graphic* is a visual presentation of information, such as a picture, a table, a chart, and so on.

Graphics offer several advantages over plain text. First, readers can take in the information in a graphic much more quickly than they can by reading a narrative. Second, tables and graphs organize statistical data more clearly than written text. Third, drawings and diagrams allow us to see complex relationships more efficiently than written description. These are good reasons for using graphics in your researched writing.

Presenting Graphics

If you are going to include graphics in your paper, then the first decision you must make is what kind of graphic to use. That decision depends on the kind of information you are trying to present and what your purpose in presenting it is. Here are some of your options:

Tables

- ♦ Present statistical data (such as numbers) in columns and rows.
- ♦ Allow quick comparison of data that would be difficult to read and comprehend.

Graphs and Charts

♦ Show numerical values as pictures; thus, the reader can easily see relationships among numerical evidence.

◇ *Bar Graphs* show relative values of a limited number of data.

◇ *Pie Charts* illustrate how a whole is divided, each slice representing one division.

◇ *Line Charts* show how one set of values changes in relation to another set.

Drawings and Pictures

♦ Offer a visual representation of an object without lengthy description.

◇ *Line Drawings* highlight the interior and/or exterior of complex mechanisms.

◇ *Photographs* present exact visual replicas of exterior surfaces.

Once you have determined what kind of graphic is right for your purposes, you need to connect it to your text. First, identify the graphic by type, number, and title. Use a phrase like "See Chart 1, 'American Birth Rates, 1900–1990'" in your text, and put the same information in a caption under the graphic. Second, briefly explain in your text what the graphic shows and why that information is important. Finally, place the graphic as close to where you mention it in the text as you can. This task is greatly simplified by the "Insert" command in most word processors.

EXERCISE 12-5

Determine which kind of graphic would be most appropriate to present the following information.

1. You are comparing the number of classes a student takes on average in each year of college.
2. You are comparing the number of female police officers to male police officers in your town over the past ten years.
3. You are describing how a car's transmission works.
4. You are breaking down how much money you spend on rent, utilities, food, and entertainment in a typical month.
5. You are describing the appearance of the New York skyline.

Including Appendices

An *appendix* contains supplementary materials that would disrupt the flow of your paper if you included them in the text. Appendices simply give additional information. An appendix might show how you collected information (such as survey instruments, questionnaires, interview questions), photocopies of original sources (such as letters, documents, maps), photographs, spreadsheets, and so on. To decide whether information should go in an appendix, ask yourself this question: if readers ignored the material in the appendix, would they still understand my paper?

If you include an appendix, refer to its number, its title, and its pagination—usually in parentheses—at the appropriate point in your text. For example, (see Appendix C: Smoking Ordinance Survey, p. 11). For another example, look at Tobi Raney's final researched writing project, which is presented in the next chapter. She includes a survey in her essay.

If your paper is following MLA format, then put the appendix at the end of your text but before your list of sources. In a paper using APA format, the appendix goes after the list of References. If you have more than one appendix, start each appendix on its own page, with the title centered at the top of the page. Continue to number pages in the same sequence as the rest of your paper.

CHAPTER 13

Managing Your Presentation

Despite what some soda commercials might try to tell you, when it comes to researched writing, image counts for a lot. The content of your essay is, of course, the most important part of researched writing, but the first impression you make on your reader will come from what your manuscript looks like. You begin to build credibility in the eyes of your reader from the correctness and neatness of your manuscript preparation.

This chapter helps you prepare your manuscript for submission. Some handbooks also discuss manuscript preparation in detail. But no matter what this chapter or your handbook says, you need to find out if your instructor (if you're writing for a class assignment) or your supervisor (if it's on-the-job writing) has any special requirements for your paper or report. For example, an instructor may not want subheadings within a text because they are distracting. On the other hand, a hurried supervisor may want subheadings to access information quickly and easily. The key here is flexibility, the ability to determine expectations and fulfill them.

TECHNIQUES: THE COVER/TITLE PAGE

The purpose of a cover or title page is to identify the paper for the reader. It should include the title, so the reader knows what the paper is about, and your name as the author. Title pages also should identify the class and the professor the paper is written for and the date the paper is submitted. This is the basic required information, but there are different formats. Choice of format, however, will likely be made for you by your instructor or supervisor.

The Cover Page

Your instructor may ask you to put the identifying information for your essay on a separate page. If so, you should center your title on the page and place it four inches from the top of the page. Place the rest of the information near the bottom of the page. Here's what it should look like:

Jumping for Joy

by

Tobi Raney

EN140 Rhetoric and Critical Thinking

Dr. Michael Hogan

December 11, 1998

The Title Page

Another option is to present the identifying information on the same page that the paper itself begins, which is the format suggested by the MLA. In this format, you put your name, the name of the class, the name of your instructor, and the date the paper is submitted in the top left corner of the page. Then skip a line, and center the title on the page. Now skip another line, and begin the text of your essay, double-spaced. Here's what it looks like:

Raney 1

Tobi Raney

EN 140 Rhetoric and Critical Thinking

Dr. Michael Hogan

December 11, 1998

Jumping for Joy

I was in first grade when I first received a flyer, announcing a coed soccer program in my town. I was totally uninterested, but like any dutiful student I took the information home for my parents to read. I would grow to regret my obedience. My parents thought getting me involved in a sport was an excellent idea and informed me that I would be playing soccer in a few short weeks. I protested, but they insisted that I at least give it a try to see if I liked sports. I reluctantly complied but stubbornly decided I would not like it. And I didn't. I dreaded every soccer game. The boys hogged the ball, and there was not one person on the field who couldn't out-kick me. I let three goals slip through my hands as goaltender. The only enjoyable parts of my earliest soccer season were the cartwheels I turned in the grass and the refreshments served after the game. After the last game was played, I heaved a huge sigh of relief. My sports "career" was finally over, or so I thought.

Avoid these typical errors when you put your title or cover page together:

- Do not capitalize all letters of the words in the title.
- Do not underline the title.
- Do not put the title in quotation marks.
- Do double space after the title.
- Do use the same font, style, and size as the rest of your essay.

MANAGING THE PRESENTATION: STUDENT WRITING

Describing what a researched paper should look like is one thing—preparing one is another. To help you manage the presentation of your researched paper, this chapter presents Tobi Raney's researched writing project formatted in MLA style and Julie McDowell's formatted in APA style. Both essays are annotated to show you how these writers managed the presentation of their final researched writing project.

A   Managing the Presentation: For the header, put your last name and the page number, separated by a single space. The header should be one-half inch from the top of the page, and justified on the right-hand margin. *Note:* all margins (left, right, top, and bottom) should be one inch.

B   Managing the Presentation: Your name, the course name, the instructor's name, and the date you submit the paper (*not* the date you write it) are all justified on the left-hand margin, beginning one inch from the top of the page.

C   Arranging the Presentation: Tobi uses a familiar phrase for her title that incorporates alliteration. Although the phrase is almost a cliché, it captures the emphasis she places on the value of athletic competition for females. Titles should be centered on the page. For more information on titles, see Chapter 12.

D   Arranging the Presentation: Tobi chooses to use an anecdote as her lead. By narrating her experience with athletics, she sets up the topic, establishes her ownership of the topic, establishes her authority to speak on the subject, and leads the reader into the thesis statement. As with any anecdote lead, length is a concern: is a two-page lead too long for a ten-page paper? For more information on leads, see Chapter 12.

Jumping for Joy, Tobi Raney

Raney 1   **A**

Tobi Raney

B EN 140 Rhetoric and Critical Thinking

Dr. Michael Hogan

December 11, 1998

C

Jumping for Joy

D

       I was in first grade when I first received a flyer, announcing a coed soccer program in my town. I was totally uninterested, but like any dutiful student I took the information home for my parents to read. I would grow to regret my obedience. My parents thought getting me involved in a sport was an excellent idea and informed me that I would be playing soccer in a few short weeks. I protested, but they insisted that I at least give it a try to see if I liked sports. I reluctantly complied but stubbornly decided I would not like it. And I didn't. I dreaded every soccer game. The boys hogged the ball, and there was not one person on the field who couldn't out-kick me. I let three goals slip through my hands as goaltender. The only enjoyable parts of my earliest soccer season were the cartwheels I turned in the grass and the refreshments served after the game. After the last game was played, I heaved a huge sigh of relief. My sports "career" was finally over, or so I thought.

See notes on opposite page.

Raney 2

figured wrong. They informed me that they wanted me to try soccer until I was in middle school, when I would be permitted to make my own decision about athletics. I made sure they knew what a miserable four years they were causing me to suffer. However, in fifth grade I found myself reluctantly joining the recreational basketball team, though I did have the freedom to decline. I couldn't pass up an activity all my friends were involved in. We couldn't really be classified as athletes (we spent more time at practice worrying about our pony tails than our shooting form), but the sport gave us a common activity to participate in and discuss at the lunch table. Even though I still was not very good at basketball and didn't enjoy it for the sport, I did not want to be left out of this pastime that had become so popular with my friends.

Somewhere between middle school and high school, my perspective on sports evolved. By my freshman year, I was a starter on the volleyball team. Despite the jealousy my position caused with teammates, I had begun to love the sport. I felt I had a place on the court that was mine. As we got older, most of my friends grew tired of sports and quit. In my senior year, I was the only girl in my class to play three sports. I was no longer playing for the social aspect of athletics. The participation was for me. When I was on the track or the court, I felt more confident, as if I were on stage, the fans, my audience. Being an athlete had become a large part of my identity. It is a part of me that has stuck throughout high school and into college. I believe that sports played a crucial

role in shaping my identity and self-esteem. Upon meeting other female athletes

in college, I began to believe that the effect of sports is the same for most

women. The female athlete is rewarded for her participation with a significant

A

increase in self-esteem and the respect of others, among other benefits.

B

    This advantage, a healthier perception of self, may not have always

derived from sports, especially for women. In the ancient Greek Olympics,

women were threatened with death for even observing sporting events (Dyer

120). However, women progressed toward the right to watch and eventually

participate in athletics to a limited degree. In the early 1900s, right after the

emergence of the first Women's Rights Convention, American women were

granted the permission to enjoy a few forms of recreation. They could casually

play croquet, lawn tennis, archery, and some golf. These events, however, were

not competitive. Aggressive women were considered unfeminine, and even

those who did play to win could play only as hard as clothing would allow.

Ridiculously modest dress, covering women from high neck to toe, prevented

virtually all athletic movement. Heavily corseted, they could scarcely bend over

to hit a tennis ball (Talamini 278).

    These standards began to change as society changed. In fact, the evolution of

women's sports follows very closely to the evolution of women in society. A

A   Basic Writing Principles: Tobi places her thesis at the end of her lead and introduction. As readers, we can expect her paper to be structured deductively (see Chapter 9). Tobi's thesis gives us her topic — the female athlete — and her claim — that athletics benefit women. For more information on the thesis statement, see Chapter 1.

B   Connections and Context: Tobi begins the body of her essay with connections and context. She establishes a parallel connection of contrast in the topic sentence of this paragraph, and clarifies that connection by looking at the historical context of females and athletics. Discussing that context is itself a process of sequential connection. For more information on connections and context, see Chapter 7.

Raney 4

study in 1903 revealed the physical merits of exercise for both men and women. Soon, the American Physical Education Association appointed a women's athletics committee (Twin xxiv; Dyer 121). This is one of the first moments in history when the correlation between females and athletics was represented as being positive. As women athletes slowly became more commonplace, the connection became more promising for females interested in sports. However, when feminism in America lay dormant, so did changes in female sports. Then, in the late 1960s the issues were raised again, and the feminist revolution revived athletics as a political issue. When Title IX was passed, equal representation of women's and men's athletics in federally funded institutions was ensured (Twin xxxvi). It is logical that as women gained rights, they were also granted new freedoms on the court, field, and track.

A

An underlying connection also exists. When society began to recognize females as equal to males, women's self-esteem undoubtedly increased. Armed with self-assurance, more women realized it was acceptable to participate in sports. The pool of female athletes expanded, and overall athletic performance began to improve significantly. Old records quickly fell, and being an athlete required more skill than ever before (Dyer 123). Such increased competitiveness now demands that a sportswoman possess self-confidence. As modern studies indicate, the act of participation itself outfits women with an increased self-

B

A   Connections and Context: Tobi ends this section of her essay with the passing of Title IX, major legislation that finally put female athletes on the same level as males. She then states an overall connection between equal rights for women and athletic freedom for women.

B   Connections and Context: Tobi examines another connection. She suggests that public recognition of females is connected to self-esteem. She continues to develop her overall organizational pattern of cause-and-effect.

Raney 5

esteem (Spreitzer 371; Mau 106). It is the first in a series of circular

connections, realized within this issue. Sports increase women's self-esteem,

thereby augmenting their athletic performance. With newfound prowess,

women's self-esteem improves even more. The cycle continues.

[A]   The very development of self-esteem involves the same kind of

connection. Leslie Schenkman Kaplan editorializes that "success is both the   [B]

source of self-esteem as well as the outcome of self-esteem" (342). In order to

have a clear understanding of this relationship, we must first define self-esteem.

[C]   When the National Council of Self-Esteem surveyed hundreds of educators, 27

distinctly different interpretations of self-esteem were obtained (341). Even

definitions in psychology encyclopedias range from the "evaluation an

individual makes of, and applies to himself (Harré and Lamb 561) to "the

evaluative dimension of self-knowledge, referring to how a person appraises

[D]   himself or herself" (Baumeister 83). After comparing and combining these many

definitions, we can broadly explain self-esteem as the way we feel about our

personal qualities, as we have weighed them. Assuming all basic needs for

survival have been met, self-esteem is a central factor in our personality, in our

behaviors, and in how we relate to the world.

The development of self-esteem is more important than the perception

itself. You can think highly of yourself, but not have a truly healthy self-

A   Connections and Context: Tobi takes a step back from the cause-and-effect connection between recognition and self-esteem to examine the cause of self-esteem itself. Not only is she pursuing the sequential connection of cause, but she is also setting up a parallel connection of comparison.

B   Using Sources: Tobi uses the concrete verb "editorializes" here to show Schenkman Kaplan's perspective. The original source, Tobi suggests, was more than just an objective presentation of information. The author also strongly expressed her own opinions. For more information on blending sources, see Chapter 5.

C   Drawing Inferences: Tobi introduces information from several sources to establish a definition of "self-esteem." Because she presents the facts from which she draws her inference, Tobi establishes common ground and common understanding with her audience. For more information on drawing inferences, see Chapter 9.

D   Using Sources: Tobi shows the reader the range of definitions of "self-esteem" and emphasizes the range by blending both sources into one sentence.

Raney 6

perception. You must have built that self-esteem through your personal

successes, or it is a false perception. Self-esteem cannot be given to an

individual. Even compliments and praise cannot enhance your self-perception if

you do not first feel a sense of accomplishment. Note that success is defined by

the person, not society. If the public were to determine who is successful and

who is worthless, only a few of us could possess a healthy self-esteem. Instead,

we must decide the areas of life which we give value to, set goals for, and then

measure our personal successes for those set objectives. This process is how

self-esteem is built and then cultivated.

A   Athletics is becoming a priority in many women's lives. Today one out of

every three high school women plays a team sport (Kunde D1). High school is a

crucial time of finding oneself and building effective self-esteem that will last

throughout life. For at least 33 per cent of the girls going through this

developmental stage, sports are playing some part in their maturation. Both my

personal experience as one of these athletes and research on this topic indicates

that sports are an effective self-esteem builder.

B   My survey of 42 female athletes and non-athletes at Southeast Missouri

State University indicates that sports are a largely positive influence on those

who participate in them (see Appendix, p. 13). In fact, the overall self-esteem

rate of athletes surveyed was higher than that of their counterparts. Regarding

A   Basic Writing Principles: As Tobi moves from one section (context and definition) to another section (primary research and inferences) of the body of her essay, she uses a transitional paragraph to show the importance of athletics for the self-esteem of today's high school females. For more information on transitions, see Chapter 1.

B   Ownership: Tobi uses information from a survey she developed to support her claim that athletic participation is important to self-esteem. By using primary research here, rather than secondary (someone else's survey), Tobi claims more ownership of her project.

Raney 7

which activity made them feel the most self-confident, 59 per cent of all women

surveyed named a sports-related activity, whether they were athletes or not.

Eighty-nine percent of respondents saw a positive correlation between sports

and self-esteem. This number sharply contrasts with the 11 per cent who thought

that sports could affect self-esteem either negatively or positively. No one found

the impact of athletics to be only negative.

A   The results of this survey, while representing only a small number of

women, corresponds to other research and opinions on the relationship between

self-esteem and sports. Robert Mau confirms that "research tends to support the

influence of involvement in sport as an important factor for development of high

self-esteem, self-concept ... in women" (106). The connection can be explained

both biologically and psychologically. It is common knowledge that exercise is

good for our bodies. The physical exertion causes our heartbeat to increase and

blood to flow through the body more quickly than normal. Apparently, activity

also affects our mood. Psychologists Folkins and Sime note that 13 out of 14

studies reported an improvement in mood during and after exercise (Le Unes

and Nation 537).

B   Exercise is an inherent part of athletics, but much more is involved than

simple physical exertion. Teamwork, communication, mental toughness, and

competition are just a few other benefits of organized sports. These components

A   Connections and Context: Now that Tobi has claimed ownership of her project, she makes parallel connections of comparison between her research and secondary research on her topic. She would not have been able to claim as much ownership if she had put the secondary information first.

B   Basic Writing Principles: Tobi again uses a transitional paragraph to move from one section of her essay to the next. She uses the broader term of "exercise" to put athletics and self-esteem into a larger context.

Raney 8

are more than likely responsible for the differences between athletes and non-athletes. Women athletes are found in studies to be more independent than females not involved with sports. They also possess a higher level of personal adjustment, achievement, and dominance and are better adjusted, more popular, and more emotionally stable than their non-athletic counterparts. In a similar study, female high school athletes were discovered to be more energetic, enthusiastic, extroverted, and optimistic (Donovitz 16). All of these qualities are good indicators of a healthy self-esteem. Mau even goes so far as to claim that "research indicates that women athletes may be psychologically healthier than women non-athletes" (108), suggesting that sports participation raises self-esteem and self-concept and lowers depression, tension, and anger in women.

A   Today, female athletes are part of something that is still rising in publicity. The establishment of the Women's National Basketball Association (WNBA) is a perfect example of how women's sports are finally beginning to gain public recognition and, more importantly, respect. Even in eighth and ninth grades, girls involved in sports were found to be more popular and have better leadership qualities than their non-athlete classmates (Donovitz 18). The confidence built by sports and enhanced by peer acceptance can have many implications for a woman's future. Stephanie Streeter, president of a $3.2 billion dollar corporation, explains, "People ask me all the time what career advice I would give to women.

A   Basic Writing Principles: Tobi brings her thesis to completion by confirming the cause-and-effect organization in her claim. This paragraph establishes the benefits (including but not limited to self-esteem) that come from female participation in athletics. For more information on structuring the body of your essay, see Chapter 1.

Raney 9

I say whether you're 5 years old or 25 years old get on a competitive team." She

illustrates that the intensity and concentration that are learned through sports,

along with self-esteem built, are important in any kind of career. Sports

experience also provides women with a common ground with their male

coworkers (Kunde D1).

Obviously, not every well-adjusted woman is so because of sports. Certainly

not all female athletes are successful. However, if a woman values athletics and

sticks to the goals she has set for her athletic experience, she will, more often

than not, experience an improvement in her self-esteem, research indicates. While

the physiological benefits of exercise are always present, the increase in self-

esteem is probably due to the process by which women participate in sports. They

affiliate themselves with a team, work toward a common goal and, in today's

world, earn the respect of their peers and the public.

B

My own career in sports began against my will. Eventually, I was doing it

because of my peers. Then, somehow, it evolved to an activity I did for myself.

And it did benefit me, but my sports participation has also affected those around

me. For every one of us who has a healthy self-esteem, there are many others

who, seeing the joy we exude, are influenced by it. When we realize that our

happiness uplifts others, we have even more pride in ourselves. The profound

connection between a woman's self-esteem and her choice to value sports is

A   Drawing Inferences: By examining the other side of her position, Tobi employs the techniques of Rogerian argumentation. Tobi thus shows the audience that she has approached her topic objectively. This tactic helps establish her credibility as a researcher and a writer. For more information on Rogerian argumentation, see Chapter 9.

B   Arranging the Presentation: In her conclusion, Tobi returns to the personal experience that she described at the beginning of her essay. She once again claims ownership of her topic and shows the reader how her research has changed her perspective. For more information on conclusions, see Chapter 12.

Raney 10

even farther reaching than her body and soul. It travels to others and then returns

to her, renewing with each activity into which she throws herself.

Appendix

Survey: 42 female athletes and nonathletes—Southeast Missouri State

University

1. Do you currently participate in organized sports?

    Yes – 16

    No – 26

2. Did you participate in organized sports in high school?

    Yes – 27

    No – 15

3. Rate your self-esteem (1 being the lowest and 10 being the highest)

    Athletes (high school or college participants)

      average: 8

    Nonathletes

      average: 6

4. What activities make you feel good about yourself:

    Sports-related responses: 25

    Other responses (no sports mentioned): 17

5. What impact do you think involvement in sports has on self-esteem?

    37 – positive impact

    5 – either positive or negative

    0 – negative impact

Raney 12

Works Cited

Baumeister, Roy F. "Self-esteem." Encyclopedia of Human Behavior. 1994 ed.

Donovitz, Jean. "Comparison of Personalities of Eight and Ninth Grade Female

    Athletes and Eighth and Ninth Grade Female Nonathletes." Thes.

    University of Texas, 1971.

Dyer, K.F. Challenging the Men: Women in Sport. New York: U of Queensland

    P, 1982.

Harré, Ron and Roger Lamb. "Self-esteem." The Encyclopedic Dictionary of

    Psychology. 1984 ed.

Kunde, Diana. "Sports Help Prepare a Girls' Career Track." Dallas Morning News

    15 Oct. 1997: D1.

Le Unes, Arnold D. and Jack Nation. Sports Psychology. Chicago: Nelson-Hall,

    1996.

Mau, Robert E. "Differences of Co-dependency and Self-esteem in College Age

    Male and Female Athletes and Nonathletes." Thes. Springfield College,

    1995.

Schenkman Kaplan, Leslie. "Self-esteem Is Not Our National Wonder Drug."

    School Counselor May 1995: 341-3.

Spreitzer, Elmer. "Does Participation in Interscholastic Athletics Affect Adult

    Development?" Youth and Society March 1994: 369-71.

Raney 13

Survey, Southeast Missouri State University students, Oct. 1998.

Talamini, John T. Sport and Society. An Anthology. Boston: Little, Brown,

    1973.

Twin, Stephanie L. Out of the Bleachers. New York: Feminist, 1979.

No Sugar-Coated Solution in Aspartame's Immediate Future, Julie McDowell

No Sugar 1 **A**

No Sugar-Coated Solution in Aspartame's

Immediate Future **B**

Julie E. McDowell

Southeast Missouri State University

A **Managing the Presentation:** APA format asks for *running heads*. A running head consists of the first key word(s) of the title and the page number. Place a running head one inch from the right margin and one-half inch from the top of the page. The title page is the first page. Running heads are placed on all subsequent pages.

B **Managing the Presentation:** In APA format, the title should be placed one inch from the top of the page. Center the title, the author line, and the location. Double-space the lines.

No Sugar 2   **A**

Abstract   **B**

D

Aspartame, a chemical substitute for sugar, satisfies consumers who want a
sugar substitute. Food and beverage manufacturers turned to aspartame after   **C**
saccharine and cyclamate were banned under charges of being carcinogenic.
Gaining FDA approval in 1981, the Searle company marketed aspartame as   **E**
NutraSweet® and Equal®. Over 6000 foods and beverages now contain
aspartame. Like its predecessors, aspartame has critics, who charge that it is
dangerous for persons affected by the genetic disorder of phenylketonuria and   **F**
that it causes memory loss, headaches, brain tumors and even death. But the
National Cancer Institute has been unable to establish a link between aspartame
and brain cancer in children. Though the criticism continues unabated, consumer   **G**
confidence in the safety of aspartame has increased.

A   **Managing the Presentation:** Continue the running head on the abstract page.

B   **Managing the Presentation:** Center the word Abstract.

C   **Arranging the Presentation:** The abstract should be no longer than 120 words.

D   **Arranging the Presentation:** The first sentence identifies the topic.

E   **Arranging the Presentation:** The second, third, and fourth sentences cover the background and success of the product.

F   **Arranging the Presentation:** The conflict over the safety of the product is reviewed in sentences 5 and 6.

G   **Arranging the Presentation:** The abstract concludes with the present situation: consumer confidence.

No Sugar-Coated Solution in Aspartame's

Immediate Future

A Like Pringles® potato chips, it is a product of the Baby-Boom generation. It is something that many have tasted. Although thousands in today's diet-conscious society depend on it, few know its real name. When we hear the phrase "sweetened with NutraSweet®," we may not think of anything other than an ingredient in a diet Coke®, sugar-free Jell-O®, or a pack of chewing gum.
B However, this product—aspartame—has an interesting history of both controversy and popularity that has raised much debate but yielded few conclusions.

C Aspartame (pronounced ah-spar`-tam) has a fairly simple composition, with its three components being aspartic acid, phenylalanine, and methanol (Taylor 1988; Appleton 1996). Chemically, it is known as "the methyl ester of the dipeptide aspartyl-phenylalanine" (Stein, 1997 p. 1112); "N-L-a-aspartyl-L-
D phenylalanine" (Taylor, 1988, p. 155); or "1-methyl-N-1-a-aspartyl-1-phenylalanine" ("Title 21," 1999, n.p). More simply, aspartic acid and phenylalanine are non-essential and essential amino acids, respectively, that combine to form a sweetener 180 to 200 times sweeter than sucrose (table sugar). Although aspartame has about the same calorie content (4 calories per gram) as table sugar, much less is needed to achieve the sweetness of a particular amount of sugar.

A   Arranging the Presentation: Julie establishes reader familiarity with the topic but withholds its identity to create suspense. For more information on leads, see Chapter 12.

B   Basic Writing Principles: In the thesis, Julie identifies the chemical and contrasts its acceptance by consumers with its opposition, making it clear that the issue remains unsettled. For more information on thesis statements, see Chapter 1.

C   Basic Writing Principles: The first paragraph of the body of the paper defines the chemical composition of aspartame, contrasting it with the natural product, sugar. For more information on structuring the body of an essay, see Chapter 1.

D   Using Sources: The abbreviation for page is included in the citation for quoted passages. For more information on APA-style citation, see Chapter 11.

No Sugar 4

A

Background

      When aspartame was first discovered in 1965 by a G.D. Searle scientist,

James M. Schlatter, two other artificial sweeteners—cyclamate and saccharin—   B

were being used in America. Although saccharin was discovered in the last

quarter of the 19th century, and cyclamate in 1937, both gained wide recognition

during the 1950s, as dieting became more common (Sapolsky 1986). More

versatile than saccharin (e.g. solid and liquid forms, heat stability, etc.),

cyclamate provided sweetness without a bitter aftertaste at lower costs. Despite

their vogue, cyclamate and saccharin became targets of controversy in the late

C

1960s and early 1970s.

      Cyclamate was the first to be attacked when Japanese studies found it to

be a carcinogen. In addition, the Food and Drug Administration also linked a

calcium-cyclamate and saccharin mixture to bladder cancer in laboratory rats.

These findings resulted in the removal of cyclamates from foods and beverages

in a ban that was announced on August 27, 1970 ("Bitter Sweetener," 1974).

      Not long after the ban on cyclamate, saccharin also fell under suspicion

when the Wisconsin Alumni Research Foundation, in 1972, "found that

saccharin increased the incidence of bladder tumors in male rats, especially in

the second generation" (Sapolsky, 1986, p. 132). After much anticipation, the

FDA announced on March 9, 1977, an intended ban on saccharin. The public

A   Arranging the Presentation: Underlined headings in the APA paper provide cues to the content that follows.

B   Connections and Context: Julie draws a connection between aspartame and its two predecessors, showing not only that they overlap but also that the search for sugar substitutes was ongoing. For more information on connections and context, see Chapter 7.

C   Connections and Context: Julie notes the controversies about saccharine and cyclamate to set up the context for the next two paragraphs that explain why they came to be banned.

No Sugar 5

hysteria that ensued included saccharin consumers who spent hundreds of

dollars as they cleared the shelves of grocery stores ("Bitter," 1997).

A

Problems

At the same time that saccharin was facing an uncertain future, the

manufacturer of aspartame was taking part in a battle of its own. Though Searle

had begun to prepare for FDA approval in 1971 (one year after the ban on

cyclamate) and had been approved in 1974, one year following its application, it

would be stalled for the next seven years ("Sweeteners," 1974; Sapolsky, 1986).

Preventing full approval were allegations of unreliable testing by Searle, brought

forth by Dr. John Olney and attorney James Turner.

B

Dr. Olney, a Washington University psychology and neuropathology

professor, feared that aspartame might "cause nerve cell and brain damage, and

possibly brain tumor" (Smith, 1981, p. 986). Another concern of Dr. Olney was

the effect of phenylalanine, one of the amino acids that make up aspartame.

This component affects persons with the genetic disorder, phenylketonuria (also

known as PKU) by preventing them from breaking down the amino acid.

Although the FDA's initial approval called for aspartame-containing products to

be labeled with a warning, Dr. Olney felt that the warning did little to protect the

unborn who could potentially carry the gene (Sapolsky 1986). Sources disagree

about the frequency of PKU cases. While some use the figure of one in 10,000

people, others indicate that the figure is only one in 15,000; however, they do

A **Arranging the Presentation:** This heading connects the discussion of aspartame's problems to the previous discussion about saccharine and cyclamate, showing that some people were now leery of accepting any artificial sweetener.

B **Connections and Context:** This paragraph elaborates the reasons for Dr. Olney's caution.

No Sugar 6

agree that it can cause mental retardation if not diagnosed early in one's life

(Hunter & FDA, 1983; Smith, 1981; Sapolsky, 1986).

A

Between 1975 and 1977, further research was conducted to determine the

validity of the conclusions reached by G.D. Searle. An <u>FDA Consumer</u> article

noted that in 1978 the studies were found to be without discrepancies

("Hearing," 1979).

B

The next step in the approval process was the formation of a three-person

board of inquiry, agreed upon by Searle, Dr. Olney, and the FDA. The purpose

of the board was to evaluate the conclusions of these studies and to decide

aspartame's fate. After a selection process, the panel included Walle Nauta,

Vernon Young, and Peter Lampert, a neuroanatomist and a nutritional

biochemist from Massachusetts Institute of Technology, and a neuropathologist

from the University of California-San Diego, respectively (Smith, 1981).

<u>Approval</u>

C

Final debate over approval began in 1980. Following the hearing, the

board ruled that Searle needed to provide more proof that aspartic acid was not

linked to brain tumors in the rats that it had studied. However, after Searle

returned more study findings that did not establish a link, FDA commissioner

Arthur Hayes issued a statement in support of the approval. Consequently, two

of the three board members reversed their opinions, and, in July of 1981, Searle

was at last granted permission to market aspartame.

D

Under the brand names NutraSweet® and Equal®, aspartame could be used,

A   Connections and Context: Julie shows the result of Dr. Olney's protests: more study was conducted, confirming the Searle company's conclusion about the safety of aspartame.

B   Basic Writing Principles: This section contains the chronological account of Searle's quest for approval.

C   Arranging the Presentation: This paragraph concludes the chronological sequence, revealing the continuing debate even in the final stages of approval.

D   Connections and Context: Julie shows the effect of approval for aspartame — its popularity and widespread application in food products.

No Sugar 7

among other things, as a tabletop sweetener, on cereals, and in mixes such as Kool-

Aide®. Because of its instability at high temperatures, FDA withheld approval for

aspartame's use in beverages. However, by 1983, the FDA had also decided that

aspartame could be safely used in carbonated drinks. This decision led to a revolution

in the cola world. In an August 1983 issue of <u>Time</u>, it was reported that "Coke's®

move [to sweeten diet Coke® with aspartame] marks the first time in 30 years that a

major producer has led the market with a new drink" ("How," 1983, p. 44).

Indeed, aspartame has become very successful in the American consumer market.

Sapolsky (1986) observed a 40 percent growth rate in yearly sales since the 1981

approval. The NutraSweet® Web site boasts that the product is found in over 6000

foods and beverages ("All," 1998). And, while a classroom survey indicated that nine

out of fifteen respondents knew what aspartame is, none changed the amount of diet

beverages that they consumed because of their knowledge; four were somewhat

affected; and five were not swayed (refer to Appendix).

A

B

C <u>Opponents</u>

Despite the sales trends, questions pertaining to aspartame's safety still

surface periodically. While aspartame proponents (e.g. the FDA, Nutrasweet®

Corporation, and others.) maintain that aspartame breaks down into its main

components—aspartic acid, phenylalanine, and methanol—and is then absorbed

A   Ownership: Julie includes information from a survey of her classmates, which revealed their indifference to claims about dangers of aspartame.

B   Arranging the Presentation: The parenthetical reference directs us to the Appendix (placed, according to APA-style requirements, after References) where the reader can see the survey questions that Julie prepared and the full results of the survey.

C   Connections and Context: Having examined aspartame's success, Julie shows that success has not reassured those who question its safety.

No Sugar 8

by the body like other foods, opponents argue otherwise ("Everything," 1997).

For example, the Web site www.aspartamekills.com declares that methanol is

reduced further to formaldehyde and formic acid, which then accumulate in the

body ("Aspartame," n.d.). Still others, counter that methanol content is greater

(about four times) in a glass of tomato juice than it is in a soda sweetened with

NutraSweet® (Gorman 1999).

Although the FDA has received over 7000 complaints that aspartame has been the

culprit in ailments and side effects—from memory loss to death—the

most common has been headache (Chase, 1999). Nevertheless, much media

attention has been concentrated on the claim that aspartame's approval has

increased the incidence of brain tumors. Despite the defeat handed him by the

FDA inquiry board in 1981, Dr. John Olney once again made news in a 1996

issue of the <u>Journal of Neuropathology and Experimental Neurology</u> when he

implicated aspartame as the cause for 1985's increase in the number of cases of

brain cancer (Walsh, 1997; Fumento, 1997).

<u>Support</u>

| A |

However, many other publications cast doubt on the findings. In <u>Health</u>

<u>Magazine</u>, Holmes (1997) reported that the greatest increase in brain cancer

rates occurred between 1984 and 1985, after which the rates stabilized despite

the doubling in aspartame use. The FDA has even cited a slight decrease

between 1991 and 1993 ("FDA," 1996). Perhaps most damaging to Dr. Olney's

A   Drawing Inferences: The criticism is contrasted with statistics from credible sources, providing a balanced view of the issue. For more on drawing inferences, see Chapter 9.

No Sugar 9

study are public statements he made in 1987. At that time, he remarked that the effects of NutraSweet® in cancer statistics would not emerge for twenty years (Fumento, 1997). Thus, recalling that the aspartame boom did not begin until 1981, we should not begin to see the effects until around the year 2001.

Within the last five years, more studies have increased confidence in aspartame's safety. For example, the FDA Consumer reported on findings (published in the July 16, 1997 issue of the Journal of the National Cancer Institute) that did not establish a link between aspartame consumption and the occurrence of brain cancer in children. Participating in the study were five United States medical research centers ("Notebook," 1997).

A <u>Discussion</u>

Clearly, aspartame is probably one of the most researched food additives that has still not been proven safe or unsafe. While many mainstream press sources have shown little skepticism in the past few years, other media (especially the Internet) have become grounds for spreading the critics' opinions. Searching the Web, one can find numerous sites by anti-aspartame groups that condemn the use of the sweetener with much loaded language but few well-known and/or well-documented sources. Although there may be truth in arguments from both sides, we are likely a generation or two away from being able to truly study just how much or how little, if at all, our bodies are affected by aspartame and its components.

A   Basic Writing Principles: Having completed her analysis of information from her sources, Julie begins assessing the implications of that information.

A

There is reason, however, to ponder the irony of aspartame. As our nation has expanded its agricultural production to provide an abundance of food, our waistlines have grown too. This girth has led us to search for a "miracle" product that is low in calories but high in taste. Despite our cultural craze to be trim (by watching fat and calorie content and participating in athletic activities), we seem to have ignored *the possibility* that we are compromising our health for chemical "saviors." Rather than relying so heavily on these substitutes as justification for overeating, though, perhaps we should concentrate on reducing the size of our plates.

A   Arranging the Presentation: Julie bases her conclusion on an inference she has about abundant food creating a need and a market for artificial sweeteners. She sees the irony in abundant supplies creating a problem — people who are overweight and need to diet. For more information on conclusions, see Chapter 12.

No Sugar 11

References   **A**

B

All about NutraSweet®. (1998). Monsanto Company. Retrieved June 25, 1999

from the World Wide Web: http://www.nutrasweet.com/html/

his_about.html

Appleton, N. (1996) Lick the sugar habit. Garden City Park, NY: Avery.

Aspartame . . . the BAD news! (n.d.). Aspartame kills. Retrieved June 23, 1999

from the World Wide Web: http://www.aspartamekills.com/

symptoms.htm

Bitter reaction to an FDA ban. (1997, March 21). Time, 60-61.

Bitter sweetener. (1974, August 26). Time, 67.

Chase, M. (1999, June 7). Amid new confusion, here's the truth about

aspartame. Wall Street Journal, p. B1.

Everything you need to know about aspartame. (1997, November). International

Food Information Council. Retrieved June 25, 1999 from the World Wide

Web: http://ificinfo.health.org/brochure/aspartame.htm

FDA statement on aspartame. (1996, November 18). Food and Drug

Administration. Retrieved June 23, 1999 from the World Wide Web:

http://vm.cfsan.fda.gov/~lrd/tpaspart.html

Fumento, M. (1997, January) Sweet nothings. Consumers' Research, 35.

Gorman, C. (1999, February 8). A web of deceit. Time, 76.

Hearing on sweetener. (1979, July-August) FDA Consumer, 2.

A   Managing the Presentation: Center the title heading for the References page.

B   Using Sources: Note that the entries for the APA References are alphabetized and double-spaced just as they are in the MLA Works Cited section. Also, hanging indents are used, as advised on the APA Web site.

No Sugar 12

Hunter, B. T., & FDA. (1983, September). Aspartame: Pro & con. Consumers'
        Research, 11-14.

Holmes, B. (1997, March). Could drinking diet soda give me brain cancer?
        Health, 18.

How sweet it is. (1983, August 29). Time, 44.

Notebook. (1997, November—December). FDA Consumer, 37.

Sapolsky, H. M. (1986). Consuming fears: The politics of product risks. New
        York: Basic Books.

Smith, J. R. (1981, August 28). Aspartame approved despite risks. Science, 217,
        986-87.

Stein, P. J. (1997, September). The sweetness of aspartame. Journal of Chemical
        Education, 74, 1112-13.

Sweeteners await a cyclamate decision. (1974, August 10) Business Week, 47-8.

Taylor, E. J. (Ed.). (1988). Dorland's illustrated medical dictionary (27th ed).
        Philadelphia: WB Saunders.

Title 21—food and drugs. (1999, June 23). Washington, DC: U.S. Government
        Printing Office.

Walsh, J., R.D. (1997, March) Aspartame alert. Parents, 48.

No Sugar 13

A   Appendix

Class Survey (Freshman Composition) Questions and Results (15 responding)

1. Do you consume diet beverages (e.g. Diet Coke®)?

   _6_ Yes

   _9_ No

2. If yes, how often?

   _3_ Nearly every day

   _2_ Once or twice a week

   _1_ Every Few Weeks

   _1_ Seldom

3. If yes, why do you drink them?

   _3_ To cut calories

   _2_ Like the taste better than regular beverages

   _1_ other

4. Do you know what aspartame is?

   _9_ Yes

   _6_ No

5. If yes, does it affect your consumption (or lack of)?

   _0_ Yes

   _4_ Somewhat

   _5_ No

A   Arranging the Presentation: The appendix follows the references section. For more information on appendices, see Chapter 12.

Some Final Words

Tobi's and Julie's final researched writing projects show how they apply the lessons about conducting research from previous chapters. By comparing and contrasting information in various sources, they were able to make the best choices about which sources and which evidence are the most reliable and the most accurate. On occasion, you can see where Julie corroborated information when she listed more than one source in a citation. Dual or triple citations also indicate where the ideas taken from different sources come together to create an original perspective. This is the payoff from work done in *Validating the Sources*.

As the annotations indicate, both *Connections* and *Context* play significant roles in Tobi's and Julie's papers. Less apparent are the judgments they have made about the credibility of their sources. Even so, you can get an idea of their work in *Critiquing the Sources* as you look at Tobi's Works Cited and Julie's Reference pages. The bibliographic information for their sources—authors' names, the sources' titles, and the producers of the sources—shows that they made an effort to select only reputable sources and responsible organizations.

And finally, you can see, especially in their conclusions, how they are *Drawing Inferences*, going beyond the information from their sources and working with the implications of the information that they have brought together.

The papers that Tobi and Julie—and you—wrote prior to the final project prepared them for researched writing by giving them practice in approaching research resources and making those sources work for them. Their preliminary papers helped them understand that sources are more than "banks" of information from which they can make withdrawals. Instead, Tobi and Julie learned that writers must interact with their sources.

In other researched writing required of you, whether in the classroom or on the job, you will use the same techniques you have learned in this course to conduct research and write the final project, whatever it may be. You will not be writing the preliminary essays, but you should still keep a reflective journal. You'll find that recording your interactions with your sources helps you analyze evidence, draw inferences, and create an original perspective in every researched writing project.

An Anthology of Student Writing

DESCRIBE
   Crime on Campus, Matthew Maurer
DEFINE
   Unwanted War, Justin Lankheit
LEARN
   Agricultural Diversity in the Show Me State, Brian Hulshof
EXPLAIN
   The True Predicament in Student Government Elections,
   Amanda Rainey
ANALYZE CAUSE
   Whose Life Is It, Anyway? Mary Stone
RECOMMEND
   *An Assessment of General Studies 101: Problems and
   Suggested Solutions,* Kim Schlosser,
EVALUATE
   Cremation or Burial: What Is Right for You? Melissa Thomas
ASSERT A POSITION
   The Meaning of Education, Andrew Wright
PERSUADE
   A Misinterpretation of Values, Amy Crow

These models of student writing illustrate nine different purposes you may write to. They illustrate the choices you have in fulfilling a writing assignment (when a purpose is not prescribed for you). Sometimes, students narrowly define a researched essay as argument only, but such a definition limits the scope of what they can do. Thus these nine models show the range of choices you have in deciding what you want to do.

An Anthology of Student Writing

This anthology brings together examples of the different purposes for writing defined in Chapter 2. Tobi and Julie, the two student researchers you followed throughout this book, have demonstrated purposeful researched writing. In Chapter 13, Tobi's final researched writing project *defined* self-esteem and *evaluated* the merits of athletic participation for females, and Julie McDowell *learned* what aspartame is chemically and why the Food and Drug Administration studied its potentially harmful effects.

As you read the examples of researched writing here, you will see that some papers clearly have a single purpose, whereas others seem to have more than one purpose. For example, Andrew Wright, searching for an answer to the question "What does it mean to be educated?" uses definition to *assert his position.* But definition is only a means of developing his ideas rather than a rhetorical purpose. Asserting a position predominates as his purpose. Similarly, Brian Hulshof categorizes information, but only as a means of *learning* more about agriculture in his home state, Missouri. His predominant purpose is to *learn* through research, even though he also informs his readers with his writing. So do not think that writing to purpose must have one purpose, excluding all others. But certainly one purpose will predominate.

The introductions to each of the researched papers that follow briefly identify the writers, explain the topics, and indicate the authors' ownership or interest in the topic, as well as their purpose for writing.

DESCRIBE

A criminal justice major, Matthew Maurer selected the issue of campus crime for his research project. He describes university campuses as similar to society at large in terms of incidence of crime and examines the factors involved. His description should inform new students about the nature of their new environment: it is not a 100 percent safe haven.

Crime on Campus

Matthew Maurer

While future students focus on the majors, facilities, and experiences a university offers, they may forget about their personal safety. Presently, students will receive only a booklet that lists crime types and frequencies on the campus. College campuses are not oases where crime is nonexistent. Instead, they have become, in some cases, scary and violent places to live. Therefore, campus police have instituted safeguards such as student escort services and emergency call boxes to combat acts of violence. If students are more educated about campus crime, they can make better decisions about protecting themselves on campus and in the dormitories.

Looking at America's past is essential for understanding our current crime problem. Youthful male workers continuously immigrated to America in search of work. The male population exceeded the female for every year prior to 1946. With this imbalance and the well-known fact that young men are involved in most of the crimes committed, Americans have a built-in tendency towards violence and disorder (Courtwright 3). Various cultural and social influences assured that crime would be a high occurrence in American society. Men often discriminated against other races and were very touchy about honor. Furthermore, the American frontier was considered the most masculine place to be. This fact, coupled with elements like heavy drinking, religious indifference, availability of weapons, and inadequate law enforcement, laid the foundation for crime in America (3).

Despite the decline of crime over the past seven years, it is still an ever-present problem for citizens ("Crime" 8A). Crime and violence are a way of life for many people in America. For instance, one study found that "the United States crime index rates per 100,000 inhabitants went from 1,887.2 in 1960 to 5,897.8 in 1996. By 1996, the crime rate was

Continued

313 percent of the 1960 crime rate" ("Disaster" 1). This same study found that crime in the U.S. accounts for more deaths, injuries, and loss of property than all natural disasters combined (1).

   We know that crime is a very real problem on college campuses despite the fact that reports seldom reflect all the criminal activities. Mary Roark (Board of the Campus Violence Prevention Center) explains, "Like any dysfunctional behavior, violent behavior is caused by an interaction of personality, biology, environments, and social acceptability" (*Campus Violence* 13). The college years are a very vulnerable time for students. Many times, because of the sudden lack of supervision, students commit criminal acts. Furthermore, they belong to "the age group (16-25) that comprises the most frequent offenders and the most frequently offended against" (13).

   Ronald Lauder, a businessman and well-known author on crime, explains that "eighteen-year-old criminals lead all other ages for violent crimes with 685 arrests per 100,000 incidents. Nineteen-year-olds lead arrests for murder. However, eighteen-year-olds are only six arrests behind them. The most violent predators come generally from among men from ages eighteen to twenty-four" (110). Lauder also states that persons eighteen to twenty-one make up only eight percent of the population, yet they account for twenty-three percent of arrests for violent crimes (111). This tendency toward violence coupled with other factors like peer pressure, social hierarchy, sex, substance abuse, and racial prejudice make campuses a perfect environment for crime to breed.

   Surprisingly though, printed incident report handouts attest to low occurrences of crime on every major campus in Missouri ("Facts" 1-5). The Southeast Missouri State University crime awareness booklet offers one criminal incident in 1998 and eight in the past three years. These numbers are similar to those found on most campuses in Missouri. It is difficult to believe these statistics when crimes in the general public number in the hundreds of thousands. However, many colleges have

Continued

hidden crime information behind the Federal Education Rights and Privacy Act (FERPA). Under this law, schools that release a student's educational records without the student's consent can lose their federal funding.

Colleges are able to manipulate FERPA because of the different interpretations of what educational records are and whether FERPA covers disciplinary actions (Paulk 7). For more than two decades, schools have seized on FERPA's Privacy Provisions as a convenient and easy way to cover up the extent of campus crime ("Feds" 10). Carolyn Carlson, a past president of the Society of Professional Journalists, maintains that there is significant evidence that many schools are using secret judicial processes to keep criminal activity out of the public's sight (Stein 11). Executive Director of the Student Press Law Center, Mark Goodman reports that "colleges often deal with serious crimes in secretive disciplinary hearings instead of in the justice system, where information is usually public" (Liveley 1).

Schools across the country may be hiding or fudging their crime statistics to project an image of safety and tranquility at their institutions (Brienza 84). This incident screening makes it impossible to know for sure if a campus is really safe. Few students report to the police when something happens to them, or if they see something happening to someone else (LeShan 137). John Maguire, President of St. Charles Community College, affirms that, "over fifty percent of victims never report their incidents to the police" (Maguire interview). Few report crimes because "People are often afraid that giving information may endanger their own lives. It is sensible to them to insist on reasonable protection before giving information" (Leshan 137).

The hope is, though it remains to be seen, that with the passing of the Higher Education Act many of these problems will be solved. The Higher Education Act states that

> All schools, public and private, that receive federal funding must maintain daily logs of criminal incidents reported to their police

Continued

or security offices. The nature, date, time, location, and

disposition of each complaint must be added to the log within

two business days of the initial report; and information learned

after the initial report must also be disclosed in a log within two

days of its availability. The only exemptions are for information

that would clearly jeopardize ongoing investigations or reveal

the identity of the victims of such crimes as sexual assault.

(Carlson 11)

The various crimes that must be reported include aggravated assault, arson, burglary, manslaughter, motor vehicle theft, murder, robbery, sex offenses, hate crimes, and college disciplinary referrals for alcohol, drugs, and weapons violations (Childs 15). This new approach to crime should lessen the confusion about reporting incidents. At the same time, officials hope it will help campus police keep areas around the campus safer.

Although there is much confusion about campus crime, the effects it has on the student and the universities are irreversible. A victim often experiences "a loss in one's sense of personal control, accompanied by lessening of confidence in one's ability to assess and manage situations" (*Campus Violence* 19). Along with monetary losses, the university's learning environment is jeopardized, ruining its image (24). Whatever the disagreements are about campus crime, these long-term effects cannot be overlooked. Universities are obligated to create a safe learning environment for students. However, sometimes they fall short, so the responsibility is placed on students to make an informed decision about their safety.

Since the establishment of America, crime has been an ever-present problem. Despite a recent decline in crime, it is still a serious problem, even on college campuses. Because some institutions of higher education are extremely concerned with their image to students, they have manipulated crime statistics, creating the appearance of a safe learning

Continued

environment. Fortunately, various groups have uncovered these acts of deception and petitioned our government to clarify regulations for universities regarding crime statistics. With the passing of the Higher Education Act, universities' ability to manipulate the crime reporting process is eliminated. Thus, new students can be better informed about their new educational environment. And the more aware they are of the true nature of that environment, the safer they can be.

Works Cited

Brienza, Julie. "University Must Release Campus Crime Records." *Trial,* Feb. 1998: 84-85.

Campus Violence: Kinds, Causes, and Cures. New York: Haworth, 1993.

Carlson, Carolyn. "Campus Crime Records Progress." *The Quill,* Oct.-Nov. 1998: 11-12.

Childs, Kelvin. "Law Unveils Campus Crime Stats." *Editor and Publisher,* 10 October 1998: 15-16.

Courtwright, David T. *Violent Land.* Cambridge, MA: Harvard UP, 1996.

"Crime Declines for Seventh Year." *Southeast Missourian,* 18 Oct. 1999: 8A.

"Feds Flunk Free Press Test in Campus Crime Cover Up." *Editor and Publisher,* 14 March 1998: 10+.

"Facts and Figures." *Chronicle of Higher Education,* 45 (1999): 1-5. 9 September 1999 <http://chronicle.com/free/v45/i38/stats/mo.htm.>.

"Disaster Center." *United States Crime Statistics.* (1997): 7 October 1999 <http://www.disastercenter.com/crime>.

Lauder, Ronald S. *Fighting Violent Crime in America.* New York: Dodd, Mead, 1985.

LeShan, Eda J. *The Roots of Crime.* New York: Four Winds, 1981.

Continued

Liveley, Kit. "Tighter Reporting Rules for Data on Campus Crime and Aim of a New Bill." *Chronicle of Higher Education,* 21 Feb. 1997: 1-2.

Maguire, John. President of St. Charles Community College. Personal Interview. 10 June 1999.

Paulk, Crystal. "Campus Crime Real Despite What You Read." *The Quill,* September 1997: 48-49.

Stein, M. L. "Campus Crime Info Fight." *Editor and Publisher,* 31 October 1998: 11-12.

DEFINE

Having worked as a "collector" for a pioneering researcher of Lyme disease (Dr. Edwin Masters), Justin Lankheit is well-aware of the increased incidence of Lyme disease passed through tick bites. Justin dragged collecting nets through tree farms owned by Dr. Masters, who himself is a victim of Lyme disease. Justin defines what Lyme disease is and identifies its spread using the metaphor of war.

Unwanted War

Justin Lankheit

Patients of this disease can tell you to the day the last time they felt well. This growing number of patients has suffered debilitating symptoms and numerous losses: jobs, families, relationships, and financial stability. These patients blame not only the disease but also the numerous doctors who didn't listen, wouldn't believe, or passed them along to other physicians when the diagnosis for this epidemic illness was too challenging.

Doctors themselves find it frustrating to tell a patient of doubts about a diagnosis. While many doctors send patients to more specialized physicians, others give their own evaluation. And some, who have themselves been victims of this disease and bombarded with tests, now

Continued

view their colleagues in a different light and speak in terms of having to "fight this war" at any cost (Donnell 351).

This is the war on Lyme disease.

Once considered only a minor irritation in the northeastern United States, Lyme disease has spread to forty-nine states and eighty countries across six continents, and its pathology creates some of the medical profession's worst nightmares regarding diagnosis and treatment. The most commonly reported tick-borne systemic illness, Lyme disease has been called the fastest growing epidemic of the twentieth century, second only to AIDS. Lyme disease is rarely a cause of death, yet misdiagnosis and delay in treatment can lead to permanent disability since the infectious spirochete that causes the disease has a habit for lodging in, and destroying, major systems of the human body, including the central nervous system, where it evades most antibiotics. It has also been known to hide in the cells and conceal its identity, showing symptoms of other diseases.

Lyme disease is therefore frequently referred to as a disease of sickness rather than mortality, but it is more than that. If promptly diagnosed and treated aggressively with antibiotics, Lyme disease, theoretically, can be cured, although no existing test will confirm a cured state. However, because of its widely confusing symptoms, diagnosis and treatment are delayed, and it can become a chronic disease of physical, mental, and social debilitation.

So what is the problem? In this age of modern miracles, why can't physicians evaluate the symptoms, order tests, and begin treatment promptly? The answer, while uncertain, promises to inspire worldwide debate, research, and acknowledgment.

Lyme disease is a tick-borne illness caused by *Borrelia Burgdorferi* in the United States. The suggested carriers of the disease have been mostly ticks of the *Ixodes ricinus* complex. Clinically-diagnosed Lyme disease is relatively common in Missouri. In fact, Missouri was listed as ninth in incidence of Lyme disease by state in 1990 and eighth in number of cases

Continued

for the period 1989-1990 (Feir et al. 475). With increasing frequency, physicians in Missouri have diagnosed and reported cases of Lyme disease that have met the rigorous surveillance criteria of the Centers for Disease Control (CDC). Missouri had previously been considered a nonendemic state, and there has been some controversy over whether or not these cases represent a true borreliosis.

In the United States, Lyme disease has been documented as being spread by the *Ixodes* tick. In the North and Southeast it is commonly the *Ixodes scapularis,* and in the West the *Ixodes pacificus.* In addition, there seems to be growing evidence of infection by the Lone Star tick in the Midwestern and Western states, and even some infections from the American dog tick.

These ticks feed on dozens of mammals, birds, and reptiles, which may then serve as reservoirs to infect other ticks. During the tick's three-stage life cycle, it passes from larva to nymph, to adult. Despite the fact that the tick must be connected to a human for at least twenty-four hours in order to spread infection, its size, coupled with the fact that it injects an anesthetic into the human skin upon both puncturing and withdrawing, makes it difficult to detect easily.

Some researchers maintain that Lyme disease is not necessarily spreading; they say that there is just a greater awareness of it, which has, in turn, caused increasing hysteria, rather than increasing case numbers. Yet, recent epidemiological studies find that not only is the tick vector[1] spreading and the percentage of infected ticks increasing, but that such environmental changes as global warming, resulting in warmer winters, have contributed to the lengthened span of the tick's activity. Despite the indisputable fact that the summer months are prime Lyme season, infection can occur during virtually any month of the year, depending upon one's level of outdoor activity, the weather, and the geographic location.

[1]A vector is any disease-spreading carrier or host.

Continued

While the current trend is moving towards the belief that there is *Borrelia Burgdorferi* in Missouri, some still do not regard this as fact. The reasons for this disbelief are lack of evidence and the possibility of misdiagnosis. Until 1992 *Borrelia Burgdorferi* had not been isolated from humans in Missouri or its neighboring states, in spite of many attempts. Indeed, it had been isolated and grown in culture only a few times. Due to the small number of isolated cases, some people have viewed the reports of Lyme disease in Missouri and neighboring states with skepticism. Yet through a process using an immunofluorescent antibody (IFA), researchers have found this disease in the state of Missouri (Cordes and Granter 955; Johnson, Masters, and Rahn 785). This test was conducted by doing research on ticks collected in rural locations in St. Louis County and many counties that surround Cape Girardeau. After the ticks were collected, they were sent off to a lab where they were tested for the spirochetes that contain the *Borrelia Burgdorferi*. These spirochetes were identified by using the IFA test. Of the ticks collected, two percent carried the disease, confirming that *Borrelia Burgdorferi* is present in the state of Missouri. The doctors and physicians involved in this test are confident in their findings that the disease is present in Missouri, but would like to continue researching in hopes of finding out more about the roles these ticks play.

This topic of Lyme disease has, without a doubt, many unanswered questions and debatable issues. Although these questions are still not answered, the experts in this field are on the edge of having a good grasp of the nature of this disease. In the past decade many ideas about Lyme disease have been disproved, and the idea that *Borrelia Burgdorferi* does not exist in the state of Missouri is drawing to a close. This disease is growing rapidly in various ways. Through ticks, it has spread geographically and now entails many other related diseases and symptoms. From its beginning in 1975, it has needed the attention and care of those involved.

Continued

The first defense in this war against Lyme disease is self-protection. When you enjoy the outdoors, whether in heavily wooded areas or even in your own backyard, you should use an insect spray and wear clothing that you can snug tightly around your ankles to prevent ticks being able to climb up your legs under the clothing. When you go inside, you should promptly remove your clothing and check your body closely for any kind of tick, whether deer ticks (a dark-red beaded shape) or dog ticks (a grayish flat shape). If you spot any crawling ticks, you can simply brush them off into a sink or bathtub and send them down the drain with plenty of hot water. If you find a tick that has embedded itself, using a tweezers, grasp it gently but firmly below its snout next to your skin and pull it gently (do not wrench or tug) to detach it. Then you should disinfect the area (alcohol will do). Save the intact tick (don't crush or smash it) in a closed vial for a week or two until you are sure that no rash develops. If a rash does develop and persist, you and the tick in the vial should visit your doctor.

Thus begins the second defense in this personal war.

Works Cited

Cordes, Paul, M.D. and Scott Granter, M.D. "Physician-Diagnosed Erythma Migrans and Erythma Migran-like Rashes Following Lone Star Tick Bites." *Archives of Dermatology* 134 (1998): 955-60.

Donnell, Denny, M.D., M.P.H. Letter. *Missouri Medicine*. 8 June 1999.

Feir, Dorothy; et al. "Evidence Supporting the Presence of Borrelia Burgdorferi in Missouri." *American Journal of Tropical Medicine and Hygiene* 51 (1994): 475-82.

Johnson, Russell C., Ph.D.; Edwin Masters, M.D.; and Daniel W. Rahn, M.D. "Epidemiologic and Diagnostic Studies of Patients with Suspected Early Lyme Disease." *Journal of Infectious Disease* 173 (1996): 1527.

LEARN

A life-long resident of Southeast Missouri, Brian expects to continue his family's tradition of farming. Familiar with the flat, rich, alluvial soil of the Mississippi delta and the low rolling hills at its north edge, Brian understands that special farming techniques are required. Brian sought to learn more about the influence of topography and climate on Missouri agriculture.

Agricultural Diversity in the Show Me State
Brian Hulshof

Missouri is in the geographic center of the United States. It truly cannot be categorized into any one geographic region. It has traits of a Midwestern state, a Southern state, and a Western state because of its topography. A variety of climate and ground conditions in Missouri has allowed for a very diversified agricultural industry in the state.

Missouri can be divided into three main topographical regions. In the area to the north of the Missouri River lie the Central Lowlands, an area of small valleys and hills, most of which are not very steep. This area generally has very fertile soil. South of the Missouri River, excluding Southeast Missouri, are the Ozark Uplands, an area of steep hills and deep valleys. Consisting of rocky soil, they are remnants of ancient mountains. Much of Southeast Missouri is covered by the Mississippi Alluvial Plain, having the most fertile area in the state. The nearly featureless plain is very level ("Missouri").

The Southeastern part of the state is the most important area agriculturally though it was not even a factor in agriculture until the 1920's. Up until that time, the area was swampland, which was frequently flooded by the Mississippi River. The draining of this swamp uncovered some of the most fertile land in the nation. This area is very similar in its formation to the Nile River valley, being built by annual flooding for millions of years (*Little River* 8). Draining the area was no easy task. More dirt was moved in this project than was moved in the

Continued

construction of the Panama Canal. For decades now, the benefits of this work is reaped every harvest (7).

All the rice production in Missouri is concentrated in this flat, easily irrigatable land. The number of acres planted in rice reached 143,000 acres in 1998, producing 7.4 million hundredweight[1] of rice. Total rice acreage could eventually reach 300,000 acres. Presently, most of the rice is produced in only two counties, Butler and Stoddard, with over half of the rice producers operating in Butler alone (Owen B12).

The lower Mississippi River valley is one of the main rice producing areas in the United States ("Rice"). Lying at the northern boundary of this area, the Bootheel of Southeast Missouri is ideal for rice production. Rice needs to be flooded, and the Bootheel flat land makes flooding easy and economical. Also important is a readily available source of water from the high water table of the area. It would not be profitable to grow rice in any other part of the state because the conditions elsewhere are just not right.

Surprising to most people, Missouri is one of the major cattle producing states in the United States. In fact, Missouri actually ranks second in cattle production behind Texas ("Cattle"). Most of the cattle production is concentrated in the southwestern part of the state where the land is not fertile enough to support row crops because of the thin, rocky soil. Indeed, the Ozark area is fit for little else other than livestock production. The climate is right for the growth of grasses though. Lying in the "Heartland," Missouri is not too far north, and not too far south. The winters are not harsh, and the summers are not too hot, creating an ideal climate for cattle production. The abundant rainfall is good for growing pasture shown by the fact that Missouri ranks second in the United States in hay production ("Facts"). Hay production is spread throughout the state, with the exception of Southeast Missouri ("1997"). The fertility of the soil there makes other crops more profitable than hay

[1] A hundredweight equals 100 pounds.

Continued

production would be. The southwest, where the main cattle production is located, is the main producer of hay, which is used to feed cattle throughout the winter.

The cattle industry is important to the Missouri economy. Livestock accounts for over half of the agricultural receipts for the state. Cattle account for over three-fifths of the livestock sales ("Missouri"). Especially important to the economy of Southwest Missouri, cattle also provide a market for corn produced in other parts of the state, which is fed to cattle to fatten them out. The close proximity of these two resources has a positive effect on the gross agricultural industry in Missouri.

Hogs and poultry are also livestock produced in Missouri. They rely on grain even more than cattle do. Thus, being close to this resource is even more important for hog and poultry producers. Four percent of the hog operations in the United States are in Missouri ("Facts").

The area to the north of the Missouri River, which extends into the Corn Belt, and the Mississippi Alluvial Plain of Southeast Missouri are the main corn producing areas in the state (1998). Very little corn is produced in the southwest part of the state, where the soil is neither fertile enough nor level enough for the production of corn. But the fertile soil and ease of irrigation make the southeast part of the state a prime area for corn. The fertile lands of the Missouri River valley are also good for growing corn.

Corn ranks fifth in the state in sales. It accounts for eleven percent of all agricultural sales in the state ("Farms"). Much of the corn is used within the state by its producers to feed their livestock. If it were all sold, its sales ranking in the state would be higher. Thus, the sales figure underestimates the value of corn in Missouri. Obviously, the production of corn and livestock are very interdependent. One feeds on the other.

Soybeans are the single largest cash crop in Missouri, being grown in most of the state, with the exception of the Southwest, where the land cannot support it ("Facts"). The areas that produce corn are very closely

Continued

paralleled by the areas that produce soybeans. Throughout the state, good corn-producing areas are also good soybean-producing areas. Soybeans are very important to the economy in Missouri. The value of the state's soybean production was over $1.14 billion in 1997 ("1997"). Nearly all soybeans are sold, so this sales figure represents the entire production of the state, a very different situation from that of corn.

Lying on the northern end of the Cotton belt of the South, the Alluvial Plain of Southeast Missouri is a producer of cotton. The Bootheel portion of Missouri is the only place in the state where the climate and soil are right for growing cotton. The climate in the rest of the state is too cool for the growth of cotton.

Missouri is also a producer of winter wheat. Most of this production is concentrated in the southeast and a band running in a northeastern direction just to the north of the Ozark Plateau ("1997").

The areas that produce wheat also produce sorghum ("1997"). Both crops require similar soil and climate conditions. Missouri produces other crops that might surprise many people. For example, the Missouri River valley is a producer of tobacco (1998). And the sandy soil of portions of Southeast Missouri produces potatoes. Missouri is also a major producer of Concord grapes. In fact, the numerous wineries lining the banks of the Missouri River from the middle of the state over to St. Louis have led to the corridor being named "Wein Strasse" (wine street).

Missouri does not produce just one agricultural product, but rather a large variety of products. This diversity provides an economic stability for the agricultural industry of the state. If climatic conditions adversely affect one area or one crop, the other products help to stabilize the economy. Missouri's unique location has over time been a great advantage for its agricultural production, a situation that should carry the state through the 21st century.

Continued

Works Cited

"Cattle." *Encarta,* 1999 ed. CD-ROM. Redmond: Microsoft, 1993-1998.

"Facts for Agriculture." *Missouri Farm Facts.* Missouri Agricultural Statistics
    Service. 2/8/99.
        <www.ext.missouri.edu/agebb/moass/farmfact/farmfact.htm>.

"Farms in Missouri Continue Trends of 1980s and 1990s." Office of
    Social and Economic Data Analysis. University of Missouri System.
    2/14/99. <www.oseda.missouri.edu>.

Little River Drainage District of Southeast Missouri. Little River Drainage
    District. Cape Girardeau, Missouri: 1987.

"Missouri." *Encarta,* 1999 ed. CD-ROM. Redmond: Microsoft, 1993-
    1998.

"1997 Missouri Crops Summary." *Missouri Farm Facts.* Missouri
    Agricultural Statistics Service. 2/14/99.
        <www.ext.missouri.edu/agebb/moass/farmfact/crop/crop.htm>.

1998 Missouri Farm Facts. Missouri Agricultural Statistics Service.
    2/14/99. <www.ext.missouri.edu/agebb/moass/farmfact>.

Owen, Ray B. "Rice Production in U.S. and Bootheel Counties on the
    Grow." *Southeast Missourian,* 26 April 1999: B12.

"Rice." *Encarta,* 1999 ed. CD-ROM. Redmond: Microsoft, 1993-1998.

EXPLAIN

Active in her high school student government, Amanda Rainey was dis-
appointed to discover that university students have little interest in student government. Still interested in university-level student government,
Amanda conducted her research to explain why so few students vote in
Southeast Missouri State University elections.

The True Predicament in
Student Government Elections
Amanda Rainey

Each year in the first few days of April, Southeast Missouri University (SEMO) holds elections for Student Government (SG) and Student Activities Council (SAC). Though these two organizations affect the student life of all on campus, usually around only 7-9 percent of students take the time to vote (Holt; Janey; Fullerton). This situation continues to occur year after year here at Southeast and at many of her sister institutions, those state universities located in Missouri that have a student population similar to SEMO (Maudlin; Saeger).

A survey (see Appendix) conducted among Southeast Missouri State University students during the Spring 1998 semester revealed that an alarming number of students could not even recall when the Student Government/Student Activities Council elections had been held. Out of the 105 students surveyed, only 38 voted in the elections. Only 40 percent of those that did vote could accurately name the new executive board members of either organization.

These numbers may be shocking to some, but not to Elections Committee Chair Emily Holt. "This year actually showed a small increase in voters, with about 9.16 percent of all undergraduates voting," commented Holt about how this year's election results related to those of past years (Personal Interview). The slight increase probably occurred due to the major issues that were addressed in this year's campaigns, such as the proposed construction of a new University Center and new Student Recreation Center that would raise student tuition for many years. Many candidates based their entire campaigns around these issues (Holt; Janey; Fullerton).

This year's election results were tallied as follows:

Continued

Total Number of Eligible Voters	*7,100*
Residence of Eligible Voters	
Group Housing	163
Myers/Cheney	81
Towers	283
Off Campus voters	284
Percentage of students who voted	9.16%

As usual, residents of Towers had the highest number of voting participants with 283. Proximity can give the best explanation for this phenomenon: the voting station for Towers residents stands directly outside the entrance of Towers cafeteria. Anyone who enters the cafeteria between 8 a.m. and 5 p.m. must pass the voting station; therefore, these students are more likely to stop and take the time to vote. Still, more than 800 students reside in Towers, and only 35 percent of them made the effort to vote (Holt; Janey; Fullerton).

Voting stations for group housing seemed to handicap their results. A great number of Greek Housing students mistakenly believed that they could use the Towers voting station instead of the station provided for them in the Greek cafeteria. When these misinformed students were turned away from the Towers station, many did not make the effort again at their appropriate station in Greek cafeteria. This misinformation about the appropriate voting station discouraged many Greeks from voting and could have played a major role in the low voter turnout for Group Housing (Efken).

Off-campus voting statistics followed tradition by being extremely low with only 248 of the great number of commuting students participating. A total number of off-campus students is difficult to estimate due to the large number of people who take only a few courses per semester, though one can be assured that the number of commuters surpasses several thousand students. Voter participation for residents of Cheney and Myers Halls were

Continued

also uncharacteristically low. The University Center hosted the voting station for Cheney and Myers residents in an attempt to make voting easy for many of these residents who regularly dine in the U.C. The station, however, proved to be ineffective since only 81 students from Cheney and Myers Halls voted in the election (Holt; Janey).

To gain a better perspective on student views and participation in the Student Government elections, many students were randomly asked whether they voted in the elections and to give their opinions of the election processes. Eighty residential students were surveyed in elevators of the four towers and in the Towers cafeteria at breakfast and lunch. Their results were grouped by academic class.

	# surveyed	# that voted
On Campus Students	80	33
Freshmen	37	13
Sophomores	24	8
Juniors	11	6
Seniors	8	6

More freshmen were available for survey because freshmen are required to live on campus for two years and are not eligible to live in Myers, thus making them dominate Towers Residence Halls. Students of junior and senior academic status had much higher rates of voter participation. This difference is probably explained by the upperclassmen residing in Towers. Most upperclassmen living in Towers serve as Community Advisors, a position that requires them to understand and be aware of current events at the university and to participate in its many activities. Consequently, these upper class students are often more involved with student life than the average nonresident student of junior or senior status and would, therefore, be more likely to participate in voting. Many of the non-voting students, however, explained their lack of participation in the elections by blaming the Towers voting station,

Continued

claiming that they left for class before the station was set up and returned for the evening after the station had been closed. Many Towers students, regardless of whether or not they voted, clearly communicated that they didn't care what happened in the elections, making student apathy a large contributor.

Twenty-five commuter students were also approached with the verbal survey at the University Center and at Kent Library at various times of day. Those results were grouped by academic status as follows:

Academic Class	# surveyed	# who voted
Off-Campus Students	25	5
Freshmen	7	1
Sophomores	8	2
Juniors	8	2
Seniors	3	0

The prevalence of voting by commuter students lies significantly below that of residential students. One student (who chose to remain anonymous) explained the most probable reason for this particular statistic in his statement that "Commuter students can vote only at Kent Library. Personally, I don't have any classes over there, and I'm not going to trek across campus just to vote." Most commuters responded similarly, saying that the Kent Library voting station was out of their way, and that they would be much more likely to vote if voting could take place at any building. Many of the commuters also stated that they did not feel that issues of SG pertained to them due to their off-campus residence. Therefore, they reasoned, the elections themselves did not pertain to them.

In reality, the issues and decisions of SEMO's Student Government heavily pertain to all Southeast students. SG collaborates with the administration, alumni, and other bodies of the university to discuss and pass important legislation, such as the issue of the new University Center. Student Government also allocates money to any student organization on

Continued

campus that exemplifies a need. The current budget for these handouts is $218,000, all of which comes from student tuition funds (Holt; Janey; Efken; Yaeger).

Southeast Missouri is not the only university experiencing difficulty in obtaining high student participation in SG elections. Susannah Maudlin, SG President at Missouri Western University, reported that only 10 percent of all eligible students voted in their most recent SG election. This rate was an increase from many past years (which usually drew about 5-7 percent of students) due to a bond issue that would raise tuition five dollars per credit hour. "It's pretty obvious that the threat of a higher tuition was the motivating force in getting more people to vote," Maudlin explained. "The ironic aspect is that our Homecoming Queen elections usually run about 12-15 percent of the student body voting," she observed about the problem of voter apathy in relation to student government (E-mail to author).

Andrew Saeger, Vice President of Politics for Student Government Elections at Northwest Missouri University, reports similar trends in low voter turnout. There, only 626 of the approximately 5,500 students voted. Freshmen had the lowest voter participation rate for undergraduates, which, Saeger feels, does not show much promise for the problem to be alleviated anytime in the near future (E-mail to author).

SG leaders at Southeast Missouri and its sister institutions have explored several options about how to encourage higher voter participation among students. Most of these individuals feel that online voting would have the greatest effect on achieving the lofty goal of better voter turnout for student government elections. Such a system would allow Southeast students to log on to the SEMO homepage from any computer on campus and use their student identification number to cast a vote for the candidates of their choice. This system would eliminate the confusion and hassle of separate voting stations by allowing students to vote at their leisure from any university computer. Such a system, though it would

Continued

be highly likely to remedy the low voter participation levels, would be extremely costly for the university to employ. For some students, however, an automated system might prove to be even more confusing than the current system of voting booths and result in alienating some possible voters (Holt; Saeger; Janey; Efken; Yaeger).

Several simpler plans have also been under consideration by SEMO Student Government and student government bodies at other similar institutions. Southeast's Student Government hopes to generate more publicity about SG activities in general throughout the entire school year. SG feels that raising student interest and knowledge about its activities would make more students feel that SG is crucial to Southeast and that SG/SAC elections merit special attention. Enhanced information about the elections in general, including candidate information and election procedures, has also been discussed as a possible step to help solve the low voter turnout predicament (Holt; Saeger; Janey; Efken; Yaeger).

Perhaps the true factor influencing low voter participation in Southeast Missouri State University's SG and SAC elections, as well as in the SG elections at similar universities, lies much deeper than just with confusion of voting stations or lack of publicity. The true problem may be attributed to the American culture and its position toward voting. America ranks near to the bottom on the list of democratic nations in terms of voting in national elections, demonstrating only 55 percent of all United States citizens of legal voting age voting in the 1996 presidential election (Adams et al. 30). Statistics for college-aged voters (those ages 18-24) in national elections show only about 14 percent voting (Exter 67). Various excuses could be made for these poor voting statistics, yet none gives a complete explanation why so many Americans, especially college-age Americans who have just recently gained the opportunity to vote due to their age, neglect their civil duty to vote.

Continued

Though the implementation of an online voting booth and better publicity may somewhat raise Southeast Missouri State University's student voting participation for SG and SAC elections, the low voter participation will probably linger indefinitely. The true problem lies beyond the inefficient placement of voting booths and lack of informative publicity. One Towers resident addressed this dilemma quite clearly when he stated, "Truthfully, I just don't care." This apathy, whether it be from the students or in the American population, has been evident throughout the history of the institution itself. Unfortunately, it is a disease that can be cured only by the individual who suffers from it.

Appendix

These results were obtained through a personally administered verbal survey of Southeast Missouri State University students. Questions asked of the students included the following:

1. Did you vote in the recent SEMO Student Government/Activities Council Elections?
2. Why or why not?
3. What changes do you think could be made that would promote higher vote turnout for these elections?

Works Cited

Adams, Kathleen, et al. "Turning Out the Vote." *Time* 11 Nov. 1996: 30. Online. EBSCOhost. 13 May 1998.

Efken, Tanya. Student Government Senator. Personal Interview. 10 May 1998.

Exter, Thomas G. "One Ad, 1.2 Votes." *American Demographies* Oct. 1992: 67-71. Online. EBSCOhost. 13 May 1998.

Continued

Fullerton, Robyn. Student Government Senator. Personal Interview. 3 May
    1998.

Holt, Emily. Personal Interview. 28 April 1998.

Janey, Danielle. Graduate Assistant to the Student Government Office.
    Telephone Interview. 28 April 1998.

Maudlin, Susannah. E-mail to the author. 29 April 1998.

Saeger, Andrew. E-mail to the author. 28 April 1998.

Yaeger, Amy. Student Government Senator. E-mail to the author. 6 May
    1998.

ANALYZE CAUSE

When Mary Stone was a child, she was struck by polio and had to be placed
in a ventilator (then called an "iron lung") to help her breathe. Now, as an
adult, Mary chose to research how advances in medical technology require
us to consider the ethical issues of using life-support systems in extreme
medical cases.

Whose Life Is It Anyway?

Mary Stone

Throughout recorded history, society has searched for a means to
keep its members alive. It is a natural desire to want a longer life for a
loved one. This desire has sparked advances in life support that were
unheard of two hundred years ago. At that time, cities located on the
rivers were centers of study for resuscitation methods. Deaths from
drowning were common in London, Paris, Venice, and Philadelphia
(Stoller 596). As is so often the case, problems frequently intensify the
search for solutions, and scholars and scientists living in these cities
worked diligently to solve the problem in their own communities. Their
efforts, and those of many others, have produced technology that can not

Continued

only keep accident victims alive during their recovery, but also the technology to keep patients alive longer as they struggle against a terminal disease process.

It is ironic that technology now presents ethical dilemmas that were previously nonexistent. The wisdom of mechanically prolonging life is called into question as society struggles with related issues. The emotional and financial burden placed on the patient, the family, and society is hard to balance with the benefit derived from the technology available. With the caveat that there are no clearly defined answers, perhaps society will find solutions to the problems created by mechanical ventilation.

Ventilator technology has made tremendous advancements over the last century and a half. A patient can be placed on a mechanical ventilator and continue to live for extended periods of time. Death no longer automatically comes when there is a cessation of breathing. A consensus statement on ethical issues acknowledges, "Today's technical ability to extend life using mechanical ventilators often leads to the question of whether it should be done rather than the question of whether it can be done" ("Ethical" 1). Computers have enhanced the ventilator's capacity to minutely adjust airway compliance, responsiveness to the patient's tidal volumes, and sensitivity to the slightest variation in the patient's efforts to breathe (Clinical Therapist). Ventilators truly can take the place of the body's lungs.

This technology is expensive. Typically ventilators are housed in a critical care unit of a hospital where specialists monitor the machines continuously. The average cost of a bed in an Intensive Care Unit (ICU) will run about $1,000 a day. When the charge for the ventilator, intravenous (IV) medications, pulse oximeters, and the like are added in, $2,000 a day is an average figure for hospitals in the Midwest (Case Manager personal interview).

The family of a patient cared for in a nursing home will often suffer severe financial hardship. Private insurance will pay a portion of the

Continued

hospitalization, but very few policies continue to pay for either the amount or the duration needed for ventilator patients (*Your Health* 22). David Broder, writing about reform for the health care system in the United States, declares that "families typically have to bankrupt themselves and turn to Medicaid–essentially a welfare program–in order to pay nursing home costs averaging $40,000 a year" (15).

Finding a nursing home that will take a patient on a ventilator can involve difficulties. Ventilator patients need specialized care by either registered nurses or registered respiratory therapists. A patient will not be discharged to a nursing home without specialization of care being provided (Young and Crocker 350). This same restriction is placed on a patient's receiving home care. At home medical care must be available twenty-four hours a day. Many nursing homes lack the space and staffing to take care of ventilator patients (Clinical Therapist). Because of this shortage, ventilator hospitals have become more common throughout the country. Specialized nursing centers, such as Vencor, provide an intensive care setting for patients on ventilators. Ideally, the Vencor hospital will be able to sufficiently rehabilitate the patient (generally suffering from brain trauma) to allow for release to a long-term nursing facility or to the patient's home. Usually by the time a patient is admitted to a Vencor facility, the money needed to pay for treatment is gone. Medicare will pay for a specified time, but generally the patient has to be bankrupt to qualify for additional coverage. If other family members are financially responsible for the patient, then they will also have to spend their assets before additional help is received (Clinical Therapist).

Realistically, the decision to continue with ventilation is often decided by financial consideration. Families must choose either financial ruin or maintaining the patient on ventilator care. Not all patients lack mental capabilities even though they are on the ventilator. A dysfunction such as chronic obstructive airway disease may make a patient ventilator dependent, but the patient is still cognizant of his surroundings

Continued

("Quality" 3). Rarely does the patient end up on long-term ventilation as a result of a conscious decision making process. Typically, the patient will suffer a hypoxic episode (lack of oxygen) that results in admittance to a hospital and the initiation of ventilator care. The patient will recover enough lung function to be removed from the ventilator, and then be sent home. These episodes become more frequent as the disease progresses towards its inevitable culmination (death). Finally, the patient is unable to be weaned from the ventilator (Clinical Therapist). Certainly, it was never foreseen when ventilators were being developed that cases such as these would occur. But too often, patients, families, hospital personnel and society find themselves facing this terrible dilemma.

Medical ethicists are attempting to define the ethical issues posed and provide some direction for individuals facing these decisions. The responsibility for preserving life still rests with the patient or his surrogate (Kelly 86). Patients or their surrogates can reject medical treatment. If a patient has stated his desire to forgo resuscitative efforts, the doctor and the hospital are obligated to comply (86). Typically there would be a "do not resuscitate" (DNR) order on the patient's chart (90). Unfortunately, not all states recognize this order outside of a hospital. The ambulance personnel responding have to provide resuscitation until hospital personnel can take charge (89).

Realizing that many Americans are afraid of dying a painful death, ethicists stress a patient's right to be free of pain at the end of life. According to the National Hospice report, elderly Americans report that they are uncomfortable talking to their children about the certainty of death and the pain associated with it ("Medical"). Kelly states that "it is always morally right (and always legal) to eliminate physical pain in the entry dying patient" (88). Failure to eliminate pain is sometimes based on the fear of addiction to the painkiller, a fear of causing death to occur faster, or a fear of producing a state of coma in the patient. Kelly categorically dismisses these concerns. If they request it, dying patients

Continued

are entitled to pain relief. It is especially important that pain and suffering are not concerns faced by a patient who wants mechanical ventilation discontinued. The thought of suffocation occurring is enough to prevent most family members and the patient from ever agreeing to the cessation of life support. However, with the assurance that the process of withdrawing the ventilator can be done comfortably, thereby allowing the natural progression of death to occur, decisions can be made based strictly on the wants of the patient, not on the fears (Quill, Lo, and Brock 2102).

Beth-Israel Hospital is at the forefront in providing a hospital setting for dying patients. Explains Dr. Marissa Slavin, head of the hospital's Palliative Care Center, the two biggest concerns patients bring to the center are fear of a painful death, and the fear of dying alone ("Religion"). Patients are encouraged to talk of their fears, and what their hopes are for the possibility of a life beyond the one they're leaving. Dr. Slavin confirms, "A good death is when people can talk about it" ("Religion"). With a facility such as the Palliative Care Center nearby, ventilator patients can be cared for in their own homes, and if they decide to have life support withdrawn, it can be done in a setting such as Beth-Israel Hospital.

The expansion of technology has forced society to grapple with issues that were nonexistent one hundred years ago. Technology has created a method of extending life far beyond anything previously imagined. The ability to prolong life also infers an ability to end life by the withdrawal of mechanical ventilator support.

Although the theoretical issues of ethical care have lagged behind the practical technology of ventilator care, there appears to be hope. Ethical issues are being openly debated especially in the medical community. Choices are being presented, and individuals are being asked to express their wishes for their medical care. Hospitals are taking the lead in providing palliative care for the terminally ill. Beth-Israel Hospital is one

Continued

that provides a place for patients to find solace with others as they face their final days of life. If problems force solutions, then a solution will be found to synthesize the human element with the mechanical.

Works Cited

Broder, David. "Health Care: Searching in the Maze." *The Southeast Missourian* 4 July 1999: 15.

Case Manager. Personal interview (anonymity requested). 27 June 1999.

Clinical Therapist. Personal interview (anonymity requested). 28 June 1999.

"Ethical Issues," Chest. May 1998: 1-2.

Kelly, David. "Ethics of Forgoing Treatment." *RT, The Journal for Respiratory Care Practitioners.* April/May 1999: 85-90.

"Medical News." *KFVS Noon News.* CBS, KFVS, 28 June 1999.

"Quality of Life," *American Lung Association.* May 1999: 1-5.

Quill, Timothy E., Bernard Lo, and Dan W. Brock. "Palliative Options of the Last Resort." *Journal of the American Medical Association* 278.23 (1997): 2099-2104.

Religion and Ethics News Weekly. PBS. WSIU, 11 July 1999.

Stoller, James K. "History of Intubation, Tracheotomy, and Airway Appliances." *Respiratory Care* 44 (1999): 596-605.

Young, Jimmy and Dean Crocker. *Principles and Practice of Respiratory Therapy.* 2nd ed. Chicago: YearBook Medical Publishers, 1976.

Your Health Net Blue Medical Benefits. MedAmerica Health Net Inc. 1997.

RECOMMEND

Southeast Missouri State University requires first-year students to take GS101, a course in critical thinking and an introduction to the university experience. Kim Schlosser wished to research the objectives of the course and survey students to find out what they thought of the course. She used her findings to recommend changes in the way the course is administered and taught.

An Assessment of General Studies 101:

Problems and Suggested Solutions

Kim Schlosser

I was working at the courthouse when Kim, one of the probation officers, came into the office carrying a few books. "I brought you my husband's Bulletin and Handbook from Southeast," she said as she laid them on the desk. "Your Bulletin will be different, but at least you can get an idea about which classes you'd like to take. There is one interesting class all beginning freshmen have to take; it's called 'Creative and Critical Thinking.' Nick [her husband] really enjoyed it."

After Kim left, one of my co-workers walked over to me and said, "My husband had to take that course too; he always complained about what a waste of time it was. I bet you won't like it either." I asked her why she thought her husband and Kim's husband had such different opinions of the class. "I don't know," she replied. "Maybe Nick had a better teacher than my husband."

Maybe. According to Dr. Roseanna Whitlow, a GS101 (General Studies) teacher, students frequently complain about the lack of teaching consistency between GS101 courses (Interview). This lack of consistency is one of the major problems facing GS101. Two other problems are a lack of limitations and students' negative feelings toward the course. GS101 faces three major problems.

Continued

Lack of Teaching Consistency

Dr. John Hinni, Dean of University Studies, contends that a lot of time is spent training GS101 instructors how to teach the nine University Studies objectives (See Appendix). However, he realizes that teachers often use the topics from their own teaching areas to introduce these objectives to their students (Interview). Dr. Hinni's stance is confirmed by Dr. Whitlow, Dr. William Ellis and Mrs. Nancy LeGrand, three GS101 teachers who say that they follow the GS101 guidelines while teaching the class, but like to leave room to introduce their own ideas (Interviews).

Students realize that teachers use methods from their own disciplines to teach GS101. Responding to a questionnaire distributed to thirty students, twenty students said GS101 professors taught according to their profession; seven said the professors used the required text, and three students said their professors used both (student questionnaires). Students feel that there should be some type of standard teaching format for GS101. They are aware the flexibility allowed in teaching GS101 has led to some interesting and beneficial class projects, but they also feel this flexibility has allowed some teachers to get completely off the subject. A common complaint of students is that GS101 teachers spend too much time talking about their personal lives. Dee Beydler, a freshman who completed GS101 last semester, contends, "Instructors should not be allowed to foist their personal crusades on their students, nor should guest speakers try to sell products in the GS101 classes" (Interview).

Although some instructors do not follow GS101 guidelines, others do. Many teachers put a lot of thought and creativity into their GS101 assignments (Critique/Assessment). The 1992 Fall Semester Schedule for GS101 is very detailed and is organized in a way that ensures students will have a thorough introduction to the nine University Studies objectives. The creative assignments and structured schedule indicate that the training GS101 teachers receive is more than adequate. Therefore, some

Continued

instructors are having problems interpreting the information they are given on how to teach GS101. These interpretation problems need to be investigated and changed.

In order for changes to take place in the way GS101 is taught, GS101 teachers should be held accountable for consistency of instruction. A rapport should be established between experienced teachers and newly trained teachers (Whitlow). This sentiment was echoed by Dr. Allen Gathman, professor of biology, who concurs that GS101 classes need to have a more integrated content ("Perceptions").

Lack of Limits

Lack of a standard teaching format and instructors' loose interpretations of how to teach GS101 led students to claim that "GS101 doesn't know what it is" (Hogan). This statement indicates another GS101 flaw: lack of identity. This identity crisis is due to a lack of firm limitations.

When Dr. Fred Janzow, Coordinator of the Freshman Year Experience, was asked why so many of the GS101 assignments duplicated traditional EN100 and EN140 composition assignments, he replied that there is always overlap between the disciplines taught at Southeast (Interview). Though his assessment of overlap may apply to the curricula at any university, course approval requirements do ensure limits to the overlap. Yet, GS101 appears not subject to these limits.

If the English Department decided to teach scientific writing skills to students by appropriating the physics labs and conducting experiments, the Physics Department would be outraged. The Administration would support the Physics Department and would send the English classes back to the English building. However, GS101 classes began appropriating the "Scavenger Hunt" and "Interview" assignments, two traditional EN100 and EN140 projects. Given the University Studies' objective of being able to locate and gather information, it is appropriate that GS101 have

Continued

responsibility for the Library Tour. But when GS101 teachers appropriate the projects used in EN100 and EN140, they are creating an impression of a lack of respect for what others have created for their own use. Also, duplication of this type is unproductive for students and faculty because it wastes their time.

Question of GS101 Benefits

The EN140-02 class conducted twenty-four student interviews and handed out thirty student questionnaires. Overall, the students surveyed attended class on a regular basis, and almost half had a GPA of 3.0 or above. No information was taken on the class standings of the interviewed students, but of the thirty students who filled out the questionnaire, twenty-four were freshmen, five were sophomores and one was a junior. The students who were interviewed gave more negative answers than the students who answered the questionnaires. For instance, two-thirds of the interviewed students said they did not benefit from GS101, while two-thirds of the students who filled out the questionnaires said they learned something useful from GS101. However, when asked how much the material learned in GS101 would benefit them in their personal and professional lives, two-thirds said it would benefit them only to a minor degree or not at all.

The interviews, questionnaires, and critiques of GS101 written by EN140-02 students indicate that students are dissatisfied with GS101.

Proposed Improvements

Orientation is the ideal time to introduce students to GS101. At least an hour of time should be set aside to discuss the course and its goals. Every GS101 teacher should write a one-page description of their class, detailing the structure of the class and the type of assignments given. Students could look through the descriptions and select three or four that appeal to them. This information would prevent a shy student from ending

Continued

up in a GS101 class with a teaching format based on speeches and debates; or an outgoing student from getting stuck in a GS101 lecture class. Students would be much happier with GS101 if they could select a class that was taught according to their own interests.

Dr. Ellis suggested having peer teachers to make the class feel more comfortable (Interview). This is an excellent suggestion, not only because peer teachers have recently gone through the Freshman Year Experience themselves, but also because having a co-teacher may help some professors stay focused on teaching according to GS101 guidelines.

The only way to give GS101 an identity and a set of limitations is to give it a realm of its own, an area that overlaps other disciplines but does not appropriate their materials. This area could be community service. Colleges across the United States are making community service part of their first-year introductory programs. Community service programs, while creating learning opportunities for students, also allow colleges to obtain federal funding and grants ("Community" 10).

Dr. Hinni is enthusiastic about the community service projects the GS101 classes have been involved in and is seeking Federal funding for these projects. My GS101 section did a community service project; not only was it my favorite project, but it was the one I learned the most from. Students can learn some valuable lessons outside the classroom. Lee Knefelkamp amplifies this point: "We must find a way to help them [students] expand their sense of themselves in the context of general education and experiential learning so that they can use experiential and classroom learning as the paired, integrated aspects of the whole that they really are" (50). Community Service projects would be an excellent way for students to combine classroom learning with experiential learning.

The EN140-02 conducted research for this paper in many places on campus, but there is one place we did not go—the GS 101 classroom. The classroom is where the problems are, and the best way to analyze GS101's problems would be to incorporate a system of teacher evaluation

Continued

using classroom observation. The information gathered during the observation would assist GS101 in becoming a more productive, focused class that is beneficial to all students, the University, and the community.

Appendix

University Studies Program

Southeast Missouri State University

Objective No. 1   *Demonstrate the ability to locate and gather information*

This objective addresses the ways to search for, find, and retrieve the ever increasing information available in a technological society.

Objective No. 2   *Demonstrate capabilities for critical thinking, reasoning, and analyzing*

Students today cannot learn all the information that is produced. Therefore, they must be able to evaluate, analyze and synthesize information. They must be able to effectively process large amounts of information.

Objective No. 3   *Demonstrate effective communication skills*

The ability to understand and manipulate verbal and mathematical symbols is a fundamental requirement in any society, especially one that thrives upon the free exchange of ideas and information. Functional literacy is not the goal, rather, students must attain a high level of proficiency in order to be effective and happy citizens.

Objective No. 4   *Demonstrate an understanding of human experiences and the ability to relate them to the present*

The degree to which individuals and societies assimilate the accrued knowledge of previous generations is indicative of the degree to which they will be able to use their creative and intellectual abilities to enrich their lives and the culture of which they are a part.

Continued

Objective No. 5   *Demonstrate an understanding of various cultures and their interrelationships*

Understanding how other people live and think gives one a broader base of experience upon which to draw in the quest to become educated. As we become more proficient in information gathering, critical thinking, communication, and understanding our past, our need to understand other cultures becomes greater.

Objective No. 6   *Demonstrate the ability to integrate the breadth and diversity of knowledge and experience*

This objective deals not merely with the possession of isolated facts and basic concepts, but also the correlation and synthesis of disparate knowledge into a coherent, meaningful whole.

Objective No. 7   *Demonstrate the ability to make informed, intelligent value decisions*

Valuing is the ability to make informed decisions after considering ethical, moral, aesthetic and practical implications. It involves assessing the consequences of one's actions, assuming responsibility for them, and understanding and respecting the value perspective of others.

Objective No. 8   *Demonstrate the ability to make informed, sensitive aesthetic responses*

A concern for beauty is a universal characteristic of human culture. Aesthetics, while usually associated with the fine arts, can be broadly defined to include all areas of human endeavor, for example, science, history, business and sport.

Objective No. 9   *Demonstrate the ability to function in one's natural, social, and political environment*

Students must learn to interact responsibly with their natural, social, and political environments in order to assure continued interrelationships among persons and things. This objective presupposes an educated,

Continued

enlightened citizenry that accepts its responsibility to understand and participate in the political and social process.

Source: *University Studies Handbook 1993-1994*, 6

Works Cited

Beydler, Dee. Interview. 1 April 1994.

"Community Service = University Success." *The Freshman Year Experience Newsletter* Spring 1993: 10.

Critique/Assessment of GS101. EN140-02 Students. 15 April 1994.

Ellis, William. Interview. 6 April 1994.

Hinni, John. Interview. 14 April 1994.

Hogan, Joshua. Interview. 22 March 1994.

Janzow, Frederick. Interview. 11 April 1994.

Knefelkamp, L. Lee. "Discovering, Remembering, Learning: When Our Separate Journeys Converge." *Perspectives on the Freshman Year.* Ed. Dorothy S. Fidler. Columbia: U of South Carolina P, 1991.

LeGrand, Nancy. Interview. 6 April 1994.

Student Interviews. 7 April 1994.

Student Questionnaires. 15 April 1994.

"Perceptions of Existing Relationships Between University Studies and the Major." *Fishbowl Seminar.* Show-Me Center, Southeast Missouri State University. 8 April 1994. School of University Studies. *University Studies Handbook 1993-1994.* Cape Girardeau, MO: Southeast Missouri State University Printing and Duplicating Service, 1993.

Whitlow, Roseanna. Interview. 6 April 1994.

EVALUATE

Melinda Thomas is a health management major from Australia. While she was pondering her topic inventory list, her roommate mentioned that she had investigated funeral costs when writing a paper six years earlier. It was a topic that Melinda had not given any previous thought to, so she decided to add it to her inventory. Ultimately, she chose to evaluate the choices offered by burial and cremation.

Cremation or Burial: What Is Right for You?

Melinda Thomas

In a time of emotional upheaval, such as the death of a loved one, it is hard to make decisions about the disposal of the body. One of the most demanding questions is which method to choose, cremation or burial. Cremation is the process of placing a corpse inside a retort and exposing it to extreme heat from oil or gas flames. This process dehydrates and then incinerates the body to leave only teeth and bone fragments which are then pulverized to the consistency of coarse sand. The process of burial starts with embalming, a preservation technique; the corpse is then placed in a casket chosen by the family and buried underground or in an above-ground tomb. Multiple factors including socioeconomic status, personal values, environmental issues, religion, and wishes of the deceased all play a part in the final decision of body disposal.

The financial resources available to the survivors can have a large impact on the final decision of body disposal. The cost of burial includes different features though many of them can be excluded to cut the final cost. But you have to be aware of the features, or they will be automatically included in the final price. Many services make up the total price. First is the removal of the body from the place of death (cost depending on the distance traveled), the paper work, and death certificate. Refrigeration is necessary if the body is to be held over 48 hours, costing an average of $135 per day (Neptune); next follows

---

Continued

embalming and restoration of the body, costing from $137 to $550 (McManus and Cliff 59) with an average charge of $343 (Davis and Knestout 69). A memorial service at a funeral home will cost between $200 and $400 if it is held on the premises, or a church may hold the service for a free-will offering of around $100 (McManus and Cliff 59). The physical appearance and cosmetology of the corpse for the viewing, including clothes, is approximately $95 (Neptune); and the cost of a three-hour viewing can average out to be between $165 and $220 (McManus and Cliff). Directors may slip in extra fees such as parking fees and charges to use the facilities in preparation for the burial. Actual burial costs include renting a hearse, costing between $160 and $170; a funeral director will cost up to $1,000; a vault or grave liner can be as low as $500; a casket can range from $200 to $5000 for the "top of the line bronze model;" grave diggers run between $450 to $1,200 but more on weekends; the grave site can range between $350 to $2,500 (in a single cemetery); and finally a head stone or monument will cost from $200 for a marker to at least $600 for a headstone ("Burying"). The total cost of burial can amount to well over $4,500.

The cost of a direct cremation, immediate cremation without a ceremony or added extras, involves the delivery charges, paperwork and certificate charges, the cremation itself, and an urn totaling approximately $800 (McManus and Cliff 57). Other optional costs include a special viewing casket, if a viewing is desired, costing from $200 to $17,000. Embalming or refrigeration must take place if a viewing is held or if the body must be held for 48 hours or longer. Embalming costs from $137 to $550 and refrigeration costs around $135 per day. The total cremation process costs between $1,285 and $19,467, which of course would be an extreme.

An individual, when deciding on a body disposal method, may be concerned about the environment and pollution levels. In fact, a study completed by Hansen, found that 19 percent of the subjects chose

Continued

cremation for environmental reasons (4). It is the younger generation who are most conscious of current and future environmental problems, having the attitude that "the dead come back to haunt us in the form of water, soil, and air pollution problems" (Bruning 39). When the body is buried in a coffin and surrounded by a steel vault, it putrefies and does not return to the soil as most people think. Even wood coffins that have been buried without a vault have been found intact 300 years later, raising the question: how long would a fiberglass or a stainless steel coffin last, considering that neither is biodegradable? However, when the body is cremated, the furnace produces high levels of "carcinogenic dioxins, trace metals, hydrochloric and hydrofluoric acid, sulfur dioxide and carbon dioxide" (Kaufman 37). There are also environmental concerns about scattering the cremains and the problems this act may cause (1).

When considering body disposal options in the past, it was feared that when a virus-contaminated body was placed into the ground for burial, the virus would leak out of the coffin and infect people through the ground. The introduction of the steel vault, a steel case around the coffin in the ground, was thought to prevent leakage. With cremation, these fears are put to rest because the body is burned at a high level of heat, destroying almost everything. Before the death and disposal of the body, individuals with such viruses as Hepatitis or Human Immunodeficiency Virus (HIV) experience some type of body degeneration. This degeneration may lead people to feel ashamed or embarrassed of their body; therefore, they choose cremation so that people can remember how they looked before death and not their appearance at death (Hansen 4).

In recent years, the opportunity to live a more mobile lifestyle has increased. The distance between family members has led to a decline in both family and community traditions leading people to re-evaluate even their most basic cultural values. There has been greater movement within the elderly population as they retire to states such as California, Florida, and Nevada. Consequently, these states have experienced an increase in

Continued

the cremation rates. Cremation is an attractive idea for these retirees because it is easier and cheaper to transport their cremains back to their family or final place of rest, compared to transporting a body in a coffin (Szanton 25).

Each person has their own idea about their death and the death of their loved ones. Sometimes people cannot let go of their loved one, wishing to keep them close, even after death. Cremation can be advantageous to these people and their wishes. Cremains are placed in an urn, which the relative can take home with them and do as they please with it. They may keep the urn close by if so desired, or they may scatter the cremains in the deceased's favorite place; achieving the feeling that the deceased is nearby and avoiding the idea of their loved one decaying.

Rituals and traditions influence many people over their choices regarding disposal of the remains. Many options are now available to the public; some of these are purely for burial, some only for cremation, but many of them can be used for either one. More attention has been paid to the psychological results death has on the survivors. It is recommended that a funeral ceremony be carried out for both the burial and the cremation option, allowing the survivors a chance to grieve and adjust to the death. A funeral ceremony is mostly associated with a burial; however, more and more people are having a ceremony before cremation, as a chance for a final farewell. Decisions must be made about the body prior to the final farewell. Decisions about viewing the body may include whether or not a viewing will occur and whether it will be a private or public viewing; embalming will depend on your choice of disposal method and the amount of time before the funeral. The different places available for farewell services for the dead include the funeral home; a church; a chapel; a crematory; graveside; private home services; or a special place requested by the family. Instead of memorial services, others choose to ask for donations to a religious institution, a medical

Continued

institution, a community donation, or for money towards a personal monument or marker, as a remembrance for the deceased (Dawson and Santos 129).

Religion has a major influence in the decision of body disposal. Buddhists believe in cremation because Buddha himself was cremated. The cremation must take place within three days, after which the cremains are collected and kept in an urn ("Buddhist"). The Jewish religion does not allow for cremation because according to Jewish Law "the body was given as a gift from God who expects . . . [people] to take care of themselves and return in the best possible condition" ("Jewish"). Neither do Muslims allow the cremation process to be used as a body disposal method (Akins). Muslims believe that the present life is only a "trial preparation for the next realm of existence" and therefore wish to preserve the body ("How Do Muslims"). But the Christian faith does not give a definitive decision or preference on burial or cremation. Christianity accepts cremation because it is economical, there is no gravesite care, it allows family members to scatter the cremains in a special place, and some people would prefer to have their body disposed of quickly instead of it decaying over a long period of time. In opposition to cremation, there are references to the Bible where burning is used to punish people for criminal acts or improper behavior; in fact, burning was reserved for witches and other heretics. Outside of the Bible, Christians contend that cremation could aid murderers, for "once a body has been cremated, it cannot be exhumed and analyzed for poisons" or fatal injuries (Robinson). Atheists and agnostics tend to rely on other information to make their decisions, such as environmental issues, economical costs, or personal view and medical issues.

The decision of body disposal is complex. On one hand, if you are looking for a low-maintenance, low-cost method, then maybe cremation is the way to go. You do not have to provide for continual upkeep of a burial plot, and a no-frills cremation is relatively cheap. Cremation may

Continued

also be the best choice if you are not happy with your appearance, if you wish to remain physically close to the deceased, or if you live far from your family. On the other hand, burial may be your best choice depending on your religion, if you have concerns about air pollution, or if you feel that you need to provide a special place that your loved ones can visit. Individuals have their own set of beliefs and values; therefore, the decision must be a personal one.

Works Cited

Akins, Can. Personal Interview. December 8 1999.

Bruning, Nancy. "The Ecological Cost of Dying." *Garbage* Jul./Aug. 1992. EBSCOhost. 14 Sept. 1999.

"Buddhist Ceremonies." Ceremonies for the Dead, Buddhist Funeral Rites. 2 Dec. 1999. <http:www.buddhanet/funeral.htm>.

"Burying Business." *The Inquirer* (1998): 9 Sept. 1999. <http:www.philly.com/specials/99/burying/html/gcost02.asp>.

Davis, Kristin, and Brian Knestout. "Paying For the Funeral." *Kiplinger's Personal Finance Magazine* May 1997. EBSCOhost. 14 Sept. 1999.

Dawson, Grace, and John Santos. "Differences in Final Arrangements between Burial and Cremation as the Method of Body Disposition." *OMEGA* 21.2 (1990): 129-146.

Neptune Society. Home page. 01 Nov. 1998. <http://www.cremation.org/calin/prices.htm>.

Hansen, Bruce. "Cremation." *Memphis Business Journal* 27 Sept. 1993. EBSCOhost. 14 Sept. 1999.

"How Do Muslims View The Elderly, Death, And The Afterlife?" *Discover Islam*. 2 Dec. 1999. <http:www.discoverislam.com/22.html>.

"Jewish Mourning." Ahavet Israel-*Jewish Funeral and Mourning Customs*. 1999. 3 Dec. 1999. <http:www.ahavat-israel.com/torat/death.httnl>.

Continued

Kaufman, Martin. "Recycling Yourself." *Earth Island Journal* Summer

   1999: 37.

McManus, K., and J. Cliff. "Keeping Funeral Costs In Line." *Changing*

   Times June 1991.

EBSCOhost. 14 Sept. 1999.

Robinson, B. A. "Cremation vs. Burial: Christian Controversy." Religious

   Tolerance.org. Ontario Consultants on Religious Tolerance. 1997.

   2 Dec. 1999. <http:www.religioustolerance.org/crematio.htm>.

Szanton, Andrew. "Changing Styles Bring Cremation Industry to Life."

   American Demographics Dec. 1992. EBSCOhost. 14 Sept. 1999.

ASSERT A POSITION

Having heard new acquaintances in college complain that they'd prefer to take only courses in their majors, rather than fulfill requirements in subjects that didn't interest them, Andrew Wright researched the question of what it means to be educated. His search began in learning, but his writing clearly shows the product of his learning: a position in which he asserts his understanding of the meaning of education.

The Meaning of Education

Andrew Wright

What does it mean to be educated? That is not an easy question to answer. Why do people seek to be educated? Education has become such a constant in our society that the answer to the question, "Why is school necessary?" seems obvious. It is common knowledge that proper schooling is necessary to have a decent job after both high school and college. So is education simply vocational training? Lee Iacocca, former president and chair of Chrysler Motor Company, seems to support this view when he defines "the purpose of public education . . . [as] training a

Continued

labor force" ("Ted"). However, universities tend to offer a different view of what the purpose of education is. Ohio University, according to its Mission Statement, "holds the intellectual and personal growth of the individual to be a central purpose" (1). Rhodes College offers a similar statement:

> In order to fulfill its purpose, the College must educate students to lead the most meaningful and fulfilling lives of which they are capable; to love learning; to understand and be concerned about justice and freedom, peace and security, and the needs of the world; and to translate that understanding and concern into effective action. (1)

Neither of these mission statements mentions anything about job training. But why else would an individual pay thousands of dollars to a university to earn a post-secondary education? What is worth more: a high-paying job, or intellectual and personal growth? If a high-paying job makes people happy, then that is what education should accomplish. But if intellectual and personal growth makes someone happy, then that is what education should accomplish. The point is, everyone has a different idea of what happiness should be, and no school is going to define that for anyone. If happiness is the overall goal that everyone wants to reach, then education should help to bring that goal within reach. Being educated means having the intellectual freedom to make choices that will provide a greater opportunity for people to achieve happiness in life.

If money equals happiness, then it is possible that job training is an acceptable purpose of education. After all, it is difficult to make money without a job. And it is difficult to get a job without an education. Therefore, it is difficult to make money without an education. The world would be an extremely easy place to live in if it really worked that way. Money is tangible. It has a very specific purpose. It is a medium of

Continued

exchange. Happiness, on the other hand, can mean many different things to many different people. Can something like money, which is so clearly defined, really provide happiness for everyone?

Even though happiness is different for everyone, it is something that everyone wants. It can be argued that the purpose of education is to provide students with the skills to get a decent job after college. But perhaps a step is being missed in this definition. If a college simply taught students the basics for a specific field or vocation, everyone who graduated would be capable of finding a job and become financially secure. For this scheme to work, however, students would have to decide what it is that they want to do before the post-secondary education process begins. The problem is that some students do not know what they want when they start college. Thus, it is more effective for colleges to offer an education that teaches students to think freely, and critically. It is more effective for educators to teach students to grow intellectually. It is advantageous for pupils to soak up as much knowledge as possible, to learn about as many different things as possible. The more knowledge students gain, the greater their chances of finding out what interests them and discovering a career for which they are suited and which challenges them. And therein lies the greatest happiness.

The purpose of education should not just be training individuals for a specific vocation. Training for a vocation should be included in an education, but so should many other goals. Vocational training is a much too narrow meaning for education. Ted Sizer, a leading reformer of education, says that "We must give kids practice in developing habits of thinking about more than just employment" ("Ted"). Employment is important, but there is much more to life than a job. The need for students to think in an informed and flexible manner across a whole range of concerns is what schooling needs to accomplish. Job training is only one of the many goals to be included in those concerns. Nel Noddings, a Phi

Continued

Delta Kappan, suggests that caring for others is "the strong, resilient backbone of human life," and therefore should be on top of the list to be taught to students (368). Social concerns such as caring and respect for others can be advantageous to individuals who wish to find happiness in a job after their schooling is over. In fact, my local survey suggests that most people want education to have a greater meaning and purpose than just vocational training. The survey asked people of a wide range of ages and vocations or professions the question, "What does it mean to be educated?" Of the 53 responses, only nine people suggested that the meaning of education meant job preparation (See Appendix). This survey is evidence that school should have a greater mission than just vocational training.

If a person is truly educated, they know what makes them happy, and they have the tools to achieve that happiness. An education should provide students with those tools. Schools need to be concerned with teaching students to think in a way that allows them to be open to as many choices and possibilities as possible. The more intellectual freedom a student has, the greater the opportunities in life are. The more opportunities a student has, the greater the chance is for finding happiness. In our time, knowledge is changing so rapidly that we cannot be said to be educated simply because we have mastered a course content or a trade. Instead, a truly educated person has learned how to think, how to reason, and how to adjust to new information and situations. Thus, an educated person is flexible and finds contentment in meeting change. To be educated involves an on-going process. A truly educated person is never finished with that process. The quest itself is the ultimate happiness.

Continued

Appendix

Survey: What does it mean to be educated?

Number of respondents: 53 people of various ages and professions surveyed in Cape Girardeau, MO, April, 1996.

Survey Results

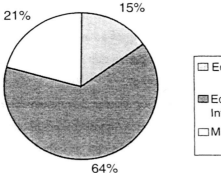

21%   15%

64%

☐ Education Means Job Training

▦ Education Should Mean
   Intellectual Growth of Students

☐ Miscellaneous Responses

Works Cited

Noddings, Nel. "A Morally Defensible Mission for Schools in the 21st
    Century." *Phi Delta Kappan 76* (1995): 365-368.

Ohio University Functional Mission Statement. 11 Apr. 1996.
    <http://www.bor.ohio.gov/fms/fmou.html>.

Rhodes College Mission Statement. 3 Apr. 1996.
    <http://blair.library.rhodes.edu/GenInfohtmls/purpose.html>.

"Ted Sizer on: The Purpose of Education." *Reinventing Our Schools: A
    Conversation with Ted Sizer* 1994. 3 Apr. 1996
    <http://edu/dept/ae-insys-wfed/insys/esd/Sizer/purpose.html>.

PERSUADE

Amy Crow is a sociology major who is interested in family social work. In line with her career interests, she researched the changed demographics of what constitutes a family today. What she learned led her to challenge the concept of traditional family and argue that the definition needs to be changed.

A Misinterpretation of Values

Amy A. Crow

Every day Billy goes to school wearing new bruises, and carrying with him new excuses for how they got there. After school Billy walks home to a small, filthy house where he routinely finds his father passed out on the couch, with a bottle of whiskey in his hand. Billy's mother is usually at the stove cooking dinner. Bruises also mark her body. Billy and his mother are as careful as possible to not make any noise that might awaken the beast that now lies dormant on the couch. Each day the two of them live in fear for their lives.

In this situation divorce seems to be the best answer for everyone involved, especially Billy. To some though, divorce is the destroyer of family values. It is hard to believe, however, that family values can grow and prosper in a setting as dark and distraught as this one. Yet many people are suggesting just that when they contend that marriage should be preserved at all costs.

Tremendous emphasis has recently been put on family values and their effects on society. It is often expressed that family values are withering away and that society is going with them. This concern is generally associated in some way with the government and the increasing divorce rate. Numerous solutions for regaining true family values have been proposed, but little, if any, progress has been made. Perhaps the problem society is facing is a misinterpretation of family values.

Continued

To understand what family values are one must first understand the concept of family. In 1977, E. M. Duvall, author of *Marriage and Family Development,* defined family as "a unit of people related by marriage, birth, or adoption" (LeMone and Burke 37). Over the years this definition has been broadened quite considerably. Today almost any group of people can be considered family, as long as the members care for and about one another. There are not any restrictions, not by race, religion, or even sex. In today's society if you are in a relationship where there is love and commitment, there is family—marriage is no longer a requirement. Many people believe that the family is disappearing, but "the family is bigger than you think" (Enright 30). It is all a matter of who is included when describing family, such as grandparents, aunts and uncles, and neighbors (30). When these people are included, the family picture expands.

Following an understanding of the term *family,* a comprehension of values is also necessary. One of the oldest definitions of values was by sixteenth century philosopher Thomas Hobbes. He asserted that a value is something one takes pleasure from, delights in, and so on (Sullivan 1). If this were all that values are considered today, then there is no doubt that everyone in America has values. Values, in this century, are much more than a mere pleasure. In this day and age, values are often associated, and many times confused, with morals and ethics. Values are learned through love and balance, often in a family situation. Since there is not a specific set of values that everyone must follow, many people have different and unique values.

It is frequently discussed that family values cannot be learned in the diverse families that now exist in society. Many people contend that if a child grows up in any family other than one consisting of a married mother and father, the child will grow up dysfunctional or inadequate. Common beliefs in today's society are that homosexual couples, single parents, and divorcees are not able to properly care for, teach, and love their children. Ironically, it is possible that the people with these views are the cause of the societal break down, not the non-traditional families that customarily are blamed.

Today, over half of all marriages end in divorce, another worrisome concern of society. The majority of the American public is convinced that divorce is destroying the few family values that still exist and, as a result, slaying society. It seems that a hasty connection has been drawn between the increased divorce rate and the decline in the wellness of society. People are assuming that since the two events happened at the same time they must be related. The formula for the situation goes something like this: family values create a healthy society–families produce values–divorce destroys family–therefore, divorce is causing the decay of society. One of Louisiana State's representatives agrees with and supports this rationale, claiming that "our culture has pulled the plug on family values by devaluing the permanence of marriage" (Perkins 294). Yet, it is hard to be convinced that divorce has terminated the family values of our society. With the divorce rates at record highs, the interest of the public is in the success of single-parents. America's concern is with single-parents' ability to instill values in their children, not claiming that remarriage would give the children a better chance to learn values. Studies show that single-parents can be even better than stepfamilies, especially if the stepfamilies "try to impose old nuclear family norms" ("Unrealistic" 2).

Another type of single-parent is the one who was never divorced because she was never married. Between 1970 and 1990, the percentage of single women who have had children almost tripled (Perkins 294). The exact significance of this increase is not clear, though many assert that the increase shows a lack of values in America. This percentage is not just a mere count of teenage girls who became pregnant by accident; it also includes older women who chose to have a baby and raise it on their own, perhaps by artificial insemination. Statistics are not always clearly reported and many times can be deceiving when used to present a particular point.

Continued

The young adults and youth of today's society are regularly accused of not having values or connections with their families. Nevertheless, a national survey held by *Swing* magazine revealed that family, not partying, was on the top of young adults' priority list (Hinds 1). It also seems that Generation X also has a better balance between work and home than most of the members of the baby boom generation preceding it (Hinds 1). It appears that teenagers are also improving in the area of birth rates. Every state in the Union has recorded a drop in teenage birth rates (Meckler 1). The young adults accused of having no family values are also more aware of AIDS. As a result, teenage sexual activity is down and the use of birth control is up (1). All of these factors– family as top priority, fewer teenage births, and drop in sexual activity–show America that young adults do have values, even if no one sees them.

Another solution to the lack of family values is through the government. Many people believe that the government is part of the problem and yet part of the solution. Tony Perkins, a state representative of Louisiana, asserts that the government has decreased the value of "the family through social programs, contorted tax regulations, and permissive divorce laws" (1). In his view, the government appears to be the root of all evil in society and the killer of family. The government once again is becoming a scapegoat for America's problems. Some people assume that the government is also the answer to all of America's problems. Many believe that if the government supported families more in programs and in taxes, families would be more likely to stay together. The House of Representatives Majority Whip, Tom DeLay, and the majority of the house have constructed an agenda designed to support strong family structure. It consists of five parts: reduction of "government burdens" on families, improved education, fighting and winning the war on drugs, protecting "the sanctity of life," and protection for "people of faith" (DeLay 2). A solution to the problem of the breaking down of society would be wonderful, but it is doubtful that DeLay's will be the answer.

Continued

A lot of attention has been turned to the issue of family values, and the conclusion is often that family values are poor or non-existent. It is possible that the problem is not necessarily a lack values, but rather a difference of values. Most likely every American has a set of values that they live by, but they may not correspond to the traditional family values that politicians and others want to regain. The unique values of every individual will probably never be agreed upon or made to be the same as the "norm." Not everyone will ever have the same religion; similarly, not everyone will have the same set of values. Values cannot be given out through government programs nor imposed by those who are convinced that their definition is the only acceptable one. Rather, values are developed in positive relationships with others, whatever the source of those relationships. But until people believe that values have not disappeared, they will continue to place blame, and the search for solutions will go on.

Works Cited

DeLay, Tom. "DeLay on the Family."[online] 5 pages. Available: http://majoritywhip.house.gov/Values/980708DeLayontheFamily .asp [Accessed 03 Dec. 1998].

Enright, Dr. William. "The Family is Bigger Than You Think." *The Saturday Evening Post.* May/June 1996: 30-34.

Hinds, Julie, "Gen Xers have family values after all, national poll says." *The Detroit News.* 12 Apr. 1996: Op-ed page. *The Detroit News Online.* 24 Sept.1998.

LeMone, Priscilla and Karen Burke. *Medical-Surgical Nursing.* California: Addison-Wesley Nursing, 1996.

Meckler, Laura. "Teen birth rates drop nationwide." *The Associated Press.* 01 May 1998: 1.

Continued

Perkins, Tony. "Marriage: The Key to Family Values." *The World & I.*
    Jan. 1998: 294-296.

Sullivan, Morris. "Family Values: Witch-Hunting in the Nineties."[online]
    3 pages. Available: http://mindspring.com/-Ampact-press/articles/
    augsep97/values.htm [Accessed 03 Dec. 1998].

"Unrealistic Family Myths." *USA Today.* Dec. 1998: 1-2.

Troubleshooting Your Writing

1. Troubleshooting Sentences
2. Troubleshooting Grammar
3. Troubleshooting Spelling and Usage
4. Troubleshooting Punctuation
5. Troubleshooting Mechanics
6. Troubleshooting Style
7. False Rules

This appendix offers a quick reference for some of the most common types of editing problems that may show up in your writing. After reviewing this section, you may recognize problems that are specific to your writing and edit them.

APPENDIX

Troubleshooting Your Writing

> Durning the forth grade, I carried a world of small treasures in my personal bank vawlts, my jeans pockets. One held a small lenkth of chain. Silvery and special, to big to be a braclet but to small for any kind of task, the links being only 7 or 8 in length. Some years later I would recognize it as part of a dog chain. But as a farm kid with farm dogs, i never seen a real dog chain. Having only read about walking dogs on a leash, our dog, Lassie coming and going as she pleased, didn't need no leash or chain. But the chain was a treasure tobe carried and played with at school durning class when the teacher was busy. The third grade class occupied the right half of the room. And played with at home. Once, I mindlessly lowered the chain through a hole in the top of my bedroom gas heater. Why I do not know? It was a kid thing to do. And when I pulled it back out, somehow I rotated my hand. Exposing my palm to a very hot length of chain. It hurt something awful. But i did not cry. I carried that brand for about five months before it finally sluffed off. I didn't showed my brand to no one. Not wanting them to know that I was that stuped. But I did keep my treasure. And I kept it out of hot places.

This writer's story is amusing, but hard to read and understand. Readers expect certain conventions in grammar, mechanics, and spelling, conventions that this writer does not consistently follow. So, it's hard to read the story. Troubleshooting this writing will benefit both the reader and the writer. It will benefit the reader, who will have an easier time understanding the story. It will also help the writer because the writing will more likely achieve its purpose.

When you stray from the conventions, your teachers put all of those editing marks in the margins so you will know how to meet your readers' expectations. How serious are those expectations? Once, on a tour of firms in St. Louis, MO, (including Blue Cross and Blue Shield; the NFL Cardinals; McDonnell-Douglas; Pet, Inc.; and the Bureau of Alcohol, Tobacco, Firearms, and Explosives), one of the authors of this book asked the personnel directors how important the conventions of spelling and grammar are on résumés and applications for employment. The directors confirmed that they reject applicants who cannot spell, punctuate, or use correct grammar because they need people who can represent their firms well through their writing.

So, how can you control all of the conventions? Personal computers have made editing an easier task. Spellcheckers find many spelling errors but can miss embarrassing mistakes. Grammar checkers find some mistakes but are less helpful than spellcheckers. Ultimately, you are the one responsible for meeting readers' expectations on the conventions of spelling, grammar, punctuation, and mechanics. Remember that it is *you*—not the computer—that will get the lower grade.

And then there is the matter of style. Editing your writing until it is correct is one thing. Style is how you make your writing your own—it involves the words you choose and the order you put those words in. This chapter shows you some of the elements of style, but you can only develop an individual style through reading other styles and practicing writing yourself.

The first step to troubleshooting your writing is to locate the problem. Every time you get a paper back from your instructor, make a list of the errors. If a problem occurs frequently, you know you need to look for that problem as you edit. If a problem occurs only once or twice, it is probably something you just missed when you were proofreading your paper.

Once you know what problems you need to pay attention to, look in this appendix or in a writing handbook to find out exactly what mistake you are making, how to recognize it, and how to fix it as you edit.

This appendix is not a full list of all the problems a writer may have. If you don't find what you need here, you can consult any one of several handbooks that treat editing issues in great detail. This appendix talks about troubleshooting your sentences, your grammar, your spelling and usage, and your punctuation and mechanics. It ends with a brief discussion of style and some of the "false rules" of English. The place to start is with troubleshooting sentences.

1: TROUBLESHOOTING SENTENCES

Before looking at some common sentence problems, you need to have clear definitions of some important grammatical terms.

1.1: Clauses

A clause is a group of words that contains both a subject and a predicate (main verb). There are several kinds of clauses.

1. **Independent clause:** An independent clause is a clause that stands by itself, presenting a complete statement or concept. It can stand alone

as a sentence, hence the word "independent." Consider the following example:

The recent unusually warm winters have caused some people to worry about global warming.

The sentence contains a subject (*winters*), a predicate (*have caused*), and a direct object (*people*). All other elements in the sentence are modifiers of various words or phrases in the sentence. It contains no other subject-predicate pairs.

2. **Dependent clause:** A dependent clause is a clause that is introduced by a subordinating conjunction, a relative pronoun, or a relative adverb. Although it contains a subject and a predicate, this kind of clause cannot stand alone as a sentence. Dependent clauses "depend" on an independent clause to make a complete sentence. Dependent clauses function either as adjectives, adverbs, or nouns. Here are the different kinds of dependent clauses:

   • An **adjective clause** is introduced by either a relative pronoun (who, whose, which, and that) or a relative adverb (when, where, and why). Adjective clauses modify nouns and pronouns. There are two kinds of adjective clauses.
      ◇ A **restrictive clause** presents information necessary for identifying the noun being described. Look at this sentence:

      The man whose hat fell into the gutter leaped to retrieve it.

      Here the underlined adjective clause identifies one man among many. By itself, the word *man* is general, not specific. Thus, the adjective clause restricts the general word to one individual and is not set off by commas from the rest of the sentence.
      ◇ A **nonrestrictive clause** provides additional information that, although interesting, could be omitted. Therefore, the adjective clause is nonrestrictive and is set off from the rest of the sentence with commas. Take a look at this example:

      Count Dracula, whose coffin served as his bed during the daylight hours, could not risk exposure to the sun's rays.

      Here the noun (Dracula) is specific and does not need the information in the underlined adjective clause for identity or limitation. Therefore, it is set off with commas to show that it could be omitted and not change the essential meaning of the independent clause.

   • An **adverb clause** is introduced by a subordinating conjunction such as *after* (showing time), *because* (showing cause), *so that* (showing result), *if* (showing condition), *although* (showing contrast), *where* (showing location), or *whether* (showing choice). Adverb clauses modify verbs, adverbs, and adjectives. Consider the following adverb clause by itself:

   Because the bank was closed for the holiday yesterday.

The clause contains a subject (bank) and predicate (was closed), but the adverb *because* does not allow the clause to stand by itself. That adverb sets up a condition, promising an effect. Therefore the reader needs more information that will complete the thought, as follows:

Because the bank was closed for the holiday yesterday, my ATM debit will not be dated until Monday.

- A **noun clause** is introduced by some of the same words as are adjective clauses: *who, whose, whom, which, that.* They serve as subjects, direct objects, and objects of prepositions. But because the entire clause functions as a main unit of a clause or phrase, it is never set off by commas.
    - ✧ A noun clause can function as the subject: *Whoever lost a set of keys may retrieve them at the security office.*
    - ✧ A noun clause can function as a direct object: *You may nominate whomever you wish.*
    - ✧ A noun clause can function as an object of a preposition: *You may give your present to whomever you wish.*

We can combine different kinds of clauses to make different kinds of sentences.

1. The **simple sentence** is a single independent clause:

    My brother Joe runs to the store.

    Joe is the **simple subject** of the sentence. *Runs* is the **simple predicate,** or the main verb. These two words make up the essential core of the sentence. *My brother Joe* is the **complete subject.** *Runs to the store* is the **complete predicate.**

2. A **compound sentence** is made up of two or more independent clauses that should be equal in importance and related by idea or logic. The independent clauses can be joined in several ways.

    - The clauses can be joined by a coordinate conjunction (for, and, nor, but, or, yet, so): *Joe runs to the store, and he buys a loaf of bread.*
    - The clauses can be joined by a semicolon: *Joe runs to the store; he buys a loaf of bread.*
    - The clauses can be joined with a semicolon and a conjunctive adverb, such as *however, rather,* and *therefore: Joe ran to the store; however, he did not buy anything.* You can choose from several other conjunctive adverbs to join clauses together.

3. A **complex sentence** consists of an independent clause and one or more dependent clauses. Complex sentences allow us to join related ideas in unequal relationships. Thus, they are more sophisticated than simple sentences or compound sentences: *If you invest just one dollar per day, you can be a millionaire before you reach retirement age.*

4. A **compound-complex sentence** is, as you might be able to guess, the combination of a compound sentence and a complex sentence. To

make a compound-complex sentence, you combine two or more in-dependent clauses with one or more dependent clauses: *If you invest just one dollar a day, you can be a millionaire when you retire, and you will live happily ever after.*

Using these different sentence patterns helps a writer in several ways. First, different sentence patterns provide variety in rhythm and structure. Second, different sentence patterns show the logical relationships among ideas. Finally, different sentence patterns show the reader the relative importance of different ideas.

1.2: Phrases

A **phrase** is a group of related words not containing a subject-predicate pair. Thus, a phrase is always a part of another unit. At the most basic level, a sentence consists of a noun phrase (functioning as the subject of the sentence) and a verb phrase (functioning as the predicate). But usually we think of other groupings as phrases. There are two main types of phrases: *prepositional phrases* and *verbal phrases.*

1. **Prepositional phrases** are phrases introduced by prepositions, a group of words that usually (but not always) indicate location or time. Prepositional phrases can function as adjectives or adverbs. If the prepositional phrase functions as an adjective, then it usually follows the word it modifies:

   Excess salt <u>in our food</u> can make us very thirsty.

   If the prepositional phrase functions as an adverb, then it can be moved around in the sentence.

   I usually jog <u>in the morning</u>.

   <u>In the morning</u>, I usually jog.

2. **Verbal phrases** consist of certain verb forms plus modifiers and objects. Although formed from verbs, verbal phrases do not function as verbs—they function as adjectives, nouns, or adverbs.

   - **Participial phrases** consist of a present or past participle plus modifiers and objects. The *present participle* is formed by adding *-ing* to the present tense of a verb (*climb + ing = climbing*). *Past participles* are formed by adding *-ed* to the regular verb (*type + ed = typed*) or by using the third form of irregular verbs (such as *driven*—from the set *drive, drove, driven*). Participial phrases function as adjectives and can be placed before or after the word they modify:

     <u>Climbing to the top of the observatory tower</u>, the ranger spied a wisp of smoke.

     The supervisor, <u>driven beyond reasonable patience</u>, finally filed a grievance against the employee.

- **Gerund phrases** look exactly like present participle phrases. The difference is that gerund phrases function as nouns, not as adjectives.

  Petting your dog can help reduce stress.

- **Infinitive phrases** are formed by the infinitive (to + the verb) plus any modifiers.
  - ◇ Infinitive phrases can function as nouns: *To sleep for six straight hours is my greatest desire.*
  - ◇ Infinitive phrases can function as adjectives: *I take this opportunity to thank you for your help.*
  - ◇ Infinitive phrases can function as adverbs: *I exercise to maintain muscle tone.*

Now that you are familiar with the different kinds of phrases and clauses that can be used to construct sentences, you can better understand the problems you might have with sentences.

1.3: Sentence Fragments

A **sentence fragment** occurs when a writer punctuates a phrase or a dependent clause as a sentence. Sometimes, the writer is trying to emphasize the information in the phrase or the dependent clause. Other times, writers create sentence fragments when they try to write the way they speak because conversations usually include fragments.

This is not to say that good writers never use fragments. Occasionally, you will encounter fragments in published material, and they work. In this situation, they are called "virtual sentences." But in your college courses and on the job, you are expected to write complete sentences. The following steps will help you revise sentence fragments.

1. If your fragment begins with a subordinate conjunction, then make sure the dependent clause is connected to an independent clause. If it's not, then there are two choices for revision.

   - Delete the subordinate conjunction, making the dependent clause into an independent clause.

     When the tornado damaged the house across the street but not mine.

     Revised: The tornado damaged the house across the street but not mine.

   - Connect the dependent clause to an independent clause.

     When the tornado damaged the house across the street but not mine. I was amazed.

     Revised: When the tornado damaged the house across the street but not mine, I was amazed.

2. If the fragment does not begin with a subordinate conjunction, then ask two questions about your sentence.

- *What is being done?* The action of the sentence should be in a main verb—that is, not a participle, gerund, or infinitive.
- *Who is doing the action?* The subject of the sentence should be the agent or cause of the action.

The answers to both of these questions should be part of your independent clause.

Working long, hard hours at the office. (Working is the action, but who is doing it?)

Revised: She worked long, hard hours at the office.

A series of bad weather, delayed delivery of supplies, and strikes. (This phrase has a possible actor, but what is the action?)

Revised: A series of bad weather, delayed delivery of supplies, and strikes doomed completion of the new school on time.

1.4: Comma Splices

A **comma splice** occurs when two independent clauses are joined by only a comma. One cause of sentence fragments is writing the way we speak. Writing the way we speak can also cause a comma splice. We hear the spoken language as a fluid sound, continuous without vocalizations for breaks or stops. In written communication, however, a comma alone is not enough to separate two sentences clearly. The reader is either confused by the writing or must do the writer's job by editing the comma splice.

There are three major choices for editing comma splices:

1. Replace the comma with another punctuation mark.

    - Replace the comma with a period, making one comma splice into two sentences.

      The car hit me, I fell down.

      Revised: The car hit me. I fell down.

    - Replace the comma with a semicolon. This should be done only if the two independent clauses are relatively short, and if the logical relationship between them is very clear.

      The car hit me, I fell down.

      Revised: The car hit me; I fell down.

2. Add words to the comma splice.

    - Insert a coordinating conjunction after the comma. There are seven coordinating conjunctions (for, and, nor, but, or, yet, so), and each indicates a different logical relationship. Insert the conjunction that expresses the correct relationship:

      The car hit me, I fell down.

Revised: The car hit me, so I fell down.

Not: The car hit me, but I fell down.

- Replace the comma with a semicolon and use a conjunctive adverb to express the relationship between the two clauses. There are many conjunctive adverbs, so you again have to be careful to pick the one that expresses the correct relationship. Also remember that you have to put a comma after the conjunctive adverb:

The car hit me, I fell down.

Revised: The car hit me; therefore, I fell down.

3. Change one clause into a phrase.

The car hit me, I fell down.

Revised: The car hit me, causing me to fall down.

1.5: Run-on or Fused Sentences

Run-on or fused sentences occur when a writer punctuates two sentences as though they were a single sentence. They are like comma splices without the commas:

The car hit me I fell down.

Again, there are several possible causes for this kind of sentence problem. The writer might have the feeling that these sentences are related but might not know how to join them. Or the writer might be writing the sentences as though they were spoken. Regardless of the cause, there are several ways to revise fused sentences.

1. Use a period to separate the two independent clauses.

The car hit me I fell down.

Revised: The car hit me. I fell down.

2. Join the ideas as dependent clause and independent clause.

The car hit me I fell down.

Revised: After the car hit me, I fell down.

3. Join the two clauses in any of the ways suggested for revising comma splices.

The suggested methods of revision should help you write sentences in a way that meets the expectations of your readers. But there's another lesson here as well. As a writer, you have many choices about how to present your ideas. As you write, you connect ideas to each other. You can use different combinations of phrases and clauses to show those connections to your reader.

2: TROUBLESHOOTING GRAMMAR

Grammar problems range from obvious errors such as tense shifts and subject-verb agreement to more subtle usage errors. The obvious problems are usually easy to solve. We can identify them by reading our writing closely or by having a friend do the reading. Usage errors are harder to identify because we have grown up hearing them in conversation and seeing them in print. Therefore, we don't recognize them as errors quite as easily.

Over the years, we have noted some frequently repeated errors in grammar usage. They are listed below alphabetically (not in order of frequency).

2.1: Although/However/Though—Are They Interchangeable?

Take a close look at these sentences:

Although, he never completed his degree.

Though, he never completed his degree.

However, he never completed his degree.

Which of these sentences is correct? Answer: Only the last one.

The first two examples are actually sentence fragments, dependent clauses without an independent clause. They might not look like fragments because the writer has separated the subordinating conjunctions—*although* and *though*—from the rest of the clause.

In contrast, the word *however* is a conjunctive adverb. It provides a transition between sentences by showing that the ideas in those sentences contrast with one another.

2.2: Are:—When a Colon Can't be Used

A colon can be used to introduce a list or series, given certain conditions. Look at this sentence:

The items are: apples, oranges, plums, and mangoes.

This sentence presents one condition under which the colon should *not* be used. Putting a colon after a *to be* verb (*am, is, are, was, were, be, being, been*) is entirely unnecessary and wrong because words that follow either rename the subject or describe the subject. This situation is again solved easily: remove the colon.

Another common misuse of the colon occurs in sentences like this one:

The items include: apples, oranges, plums, and mangoes.

In this sentence, the list now functions as direct objects of the verb. You should never separate a verb and its direct object with any punctuation. Again, simply remove the colon.

You would insert a colon before a list that follows a complete clause. The list simply specifies a general word (in this case *fruit*):

I want to order the following fruit: apples, oranges, plums, and mangoes.

2.3: As or Because—Which Should You Use?

Which of the following sentences is clearer?

As I have only two dollars, I will have to take a bus instead of a cab.

Because I have only two dollars, I will have to take a bus instead of a cab.

If you check a dictionary, you will find that the word *as* can mean "because." But *as* can also mean "at the same time" as well as several other things. The meaning of the first sentence, then, is less clear than the meaning of the second sentence. In cases like this, *because* is a better choice because it is a more precise word.

2.4: Between—Which Case Does It Call for?

Consider this pair of sentences:

Between you and I, the manager made a bad choice.

Between you and me, the manager made a bad choice.

Many people say that the first sentence is correct. They may think that a pronoun near the beginning of a sentence acts as a subject. Or, they may remember when, as a child, their mothers drilled into their heads that it was "my best friend and I" and never "my best friend and me." In this case, however, the pronouns are objects of the preposition *between*. Just as you wouldn't say "the car hit I," you shouldn't write "between you and I."

2.5: Dangling Modifier—Making Connections

Look closely at this sentence—what does it really say?

Walking through the hall, a desk blocked my way.

Exactly! When was the last time you saw a desk walking down the hallway? Who is actually doing the walking? The speaker. But the speaker is only barely present in the sentence (because of the word *my*). Thus, we say that the modifier is dangling because it isn't attached to what it modifies.

Once again, there's a simple fix for this problem—make sure that what a modifier describes is in the sentence. In fact, make sure that the modifier is placed immediately before or after the word it modifies. Here's one way to revise the sample sentence:

Walking through the hall, I had to go around a desk.

2.6: Different From/Different Than—What's the Difference?

Consider these sentences:

Professor Green's teaching style is different than Professor Smith's.

Professor Green's teaching style is different from Professor Smith's.

The difference here seems to be rather minor—and for many of us, non-existent at first glance. But there's an important issue here. Different kinds of writing call for different levels of formality. Informal writing (such as personal letters or journals) can be written informally, and in this case, you could use either of the two examples.

Much college writing, however, requires greater formality. Under those circumstances, you must pay attention to some rules. Do you remember the difference between phrases and clauses? It's important here because, when writing academic essays, you should use *different from* when you are contrasting information in phrases and *different than* when you are contrasting information in clauses.

In formal writing, then, you would want to use the second example. Both "Professor Green's teaching style" and "Professor Smith's" are phrases, so you want to use *different from*. Here's an example of the use of *different than*:

> *Professor Jones's explanation of shading was* different *when he was* explaining *its use in painting* than *when he was explaining its use in movies.*

"When he was explaining its use in painting" and "when he was explaining its use in movies" are both clauses, so we want to use *different than*. Note that "different" comes before the two clauses being contrasted, and the word "than" comes between the two clauses.

2.7: False Coordination—Joining Unequal Forms

When you coordinate words, phrases, or clauses, you join them by using one of the seven coordinate conjunctions (for, and, nor, but, or, yet, so). When you use coordination, your readers expect to see two or more elements that are equal in both emphasis and function. Look at this sentence:

> *The jacket may be light and needed to shield you from the mist.*

In this sample sentence, the adjective *light* and the verb *needed* are joined with the coordinate conjunction and. But adjectives and verbs are not equal in function, so coordinating them does not meet the readers' expectations.

Often, you can revise false coordination by making the coordinated elements equal in function. In this example, however, that's not possible, so revision must eliminate the coordination:

> *A light jacket may be needed to shield you from the mist.*

2.8: Free-Standing Dates or Times—What Do They Modify?

Consider these sentences:

> *My senior year, I finally achieved my big day: graduation.*

> *One o'clock, we went back to work on the excavation.*

Both of these sentences begin with a time expression that is attached to nothing. The reader can see that time is important, but he or she doesn't know how or why. This problem is easily remedied by simply inserting a preposition to create a prepositional phrase of time. Now the entire prepositional phrase modifies the predicate—and provides a time transition into the sentence:

At the end of my senior year, I finally achieved my big day: graduation.

At one o'clock, we went back to work on the excavation.

2.9: Free-Standing Demonstrative Pronouns—What Do They Refer To?

Look at the use of the word *these* in the following passage:

> *Recent discoveries of hominid fossils have caused paleontologists to revise their graphs of the lines of hominid species. These intrigue general readers of popular science articles.*

These what? Species? Lines? Graphs? Paleontologists? Fossils? Discoveries? The use of *these* without a noun creates an ambiguous situation. The reader must stop—if only for a moment—to answer the question, *these what?* As a writer, you never want your reader to have to stop to figure out what you mean. You want the reader to keep moving forward.

As with many of the errors discussed in this section, the solution is fairly simple: always put a noun after *this, that, these,* or *those* every time you use one of those demonstrative pronouns.

> *Recent discoveries of hominid fossils have caused paleontologists to revise their graphs of the number of hominid species. These fossils intrigue general readers of popular science articles.*

2.10: Hopefully—A Cliché

Although *hopefully* is a rather useful adverb, overuse has turned it into a cliché, applied to any situation in which the outcome is in doubt:

> *Hopefully, the rescue of the earthquake victims will not reveal more deaths.*

The problem here is that the reader does not know who is hoping: the rescuers or the reporter. To clear up this confusion, simply state who is hoping, and turn the adverb into a verb.

> *Rescuers hope they will find no more bodies in their search for earthquake victims.*

Even if you know who is doing the hoping, you can still run into problems. Look at this sentence:

> *The family prayed hopefully that their son would be rescued.*

In this case, *prayed hopefully* is redundant, and the sentence would be better off without the adverb:

> *The family prayed that their son would be rescued.*

2.11: Its/It's—Why They Are Not Identical

These sentences show a common error with possessives:

> *The dog bit it's tail.*

> *The dog bit its tail.*

You're naturally used to forming possessives by adding an apostrophe and an "s". But you don't want to do that with pronouns. Think of the possessive forms of *her* (*hers*). Now which of the examples do you think is correct? The second. The first example actually says "The dog bit it is tail."

2.12: Myself/I—Why Aren't These Pronouns Equivalent?

In both written and spoken communication, many people use a reflexive pronoun as the subject of a sentence:

Sally, John, and myself *completed the contract.*

Used as a subject, the reflexive pronoun seems to separate the speaker from him- or herself in a kind of out-of-body experience. In addition, the grammar is incorrect, more indirect, and just plain clunky.

Reflexive pronouns (myself, yourself, himself, herself, itself, themselves) never stand by themselves. Their function is to intensify a noun or pronoun, so they must always be paired with the word they emphasize:

Sally, John, and I myself completed the contract.

If you are not intensifying a noun or pronoun, then omit the reflexive pronoun:

Sally, John, and I completed the contract.

2.13: Only—Where Should It Go?

Examine the following sentences carefully:

Only I have only a penny.

I only have a penny.

I have only a penny.

I have a penny only.

Which of the sentences is correct? Answer: Every single one of them—but they don't all mean the same thing.

The word *only* can move around in a sentence depending on which word it describes. If you mean that you alone in a group are in possession of the coin, then either of the first two sentences is correct. In the first two sentences, the word *only* modifies the pronoun. But if you mean that you are in possession of a single coin and no other money, then either of the last two sentences would be acceptable. In those sentences, the word *only* modifies the amount of money. If you use *only* in a sentence, be sure to place it either just before or just after what *only* describes.

2.14: Subject-Verb Agreement—Keep Them Matched

You will probably not have much trouble making sure that your subjects and verbs agree when the subject and verb are right next to each other. It gets a little more difficult when the complete subject is a phrase, and there are several words between the simple subject and the verb. Locate the simple subject and simple predicate in this sentence (these terms are defined in the preceding section on clauses):

One of the first-year students work as a telemarketer.

The simple subject in this sentence—the noun that controls the verb—is *one*. The confusion arises because *students* sits right next to the verb. But *students* is the object of the preposition, not the subject of the sentence. Regardless of how many words come between the simple subject and the verb, the subject and the verb must agree:

One of the first-year students works as a telemarketer.

2.15: To Try And—No Coordination After *Try*

Here's another writing-the-way-we-speak mistake:

I will try and win the Powerball Lottery.

This sentence is completely acceptable according to the conventions and expectations of spoken communication. But according to the conventions of written communication, this sentence says something the writer might not intend. In written communication, this sentence says that the writer will complete two separate actions: one, the writer will make an attempt to win the lottery, and two, the writer will actually win the lottery. This idea doesn't make a lot of sense—trying does not guarantee winning.

Again, there's a simple fix for this problem: remember that *try* is a verb that should be followed by the infinitive (*to* + the verb):

I will try to win *the Powerball Lottery.*

2.16: Used to/Supposed to—Troubles with a Silent *d.*

The following sentences show other common problems when we forget that writing and speech are not identical:

I use to exercise more before I enrolled in college.

I am suppose to work this afternoon.

The writer has written these sentences in order to re-create how they often sound when spoken aloud. But the sentences are missing an important letter, the *d* that signals the past tense in the first example and the past perfect form of a regular verb following an auxiliary verb in the second example:

I used to exercise more before I enrolled in college.

I am supposed to work this afternoon.

The problem lies in how we pronounce verbs that end in *d* and are followed by the word *to*. When we speak, we often fail to separate these two sounds. So, when we write, we sometimes omit the *d* because it is harder to pronounce without sounding unnatural.

Here is another common example of the same problem:

I should of come home earlier.

Again, the writer is relying on the sound of spoken language in making choices about written language. In spoken language, the contraction *should've* does sound like *should* plus the preposition *of*; however, this sentence should be written one of two ways:

I should've come home earlier.

I should have come home earlier.

Just keep in mind that speaking and writing are different ways to communicate. What is correct when we speak is not always correct when we write.

2.17: Who/Which/That—Which Pronoun Should You Use?

Here's another set of sentences to consider:

The person who refuses to vote has no right to criticize election results.

The person which refuses to vote has no right to criticize election results.

The person that refuses to vote has no right to criticize election results.

Which sentence is correct? Answer: the first one or the third one—but the first one is a better choice.

Here are the rules of thumb for choosing a relative pronoun:

1. *Who* refers only to people, or to animals that are given names.
2. *Which* refers to objects, animals, or ideas. It is used in nonrestrictive clauses (see previous section).
3. *That* refers to objects, animals, or ideas. It is used in restrictive clauses (see previous section).

3: TROUBLESHOOTING SPELLING AND USAGE

Several pairs of words in English look or sound very similar, but each word is spelled differently and has a different meaning and use. Using one word when you intend the other may create the appearance of a spelling error, but the problem really is a usage issue. And usage problems are usually grounded in grammar problems, such as nouns confused with verbs, nouns confused with adjectives, confused verb forms, and the like. When the writer and the writing are confused, the reader is almost certain to be confused.

3.1: Frequently Confused Words

Here is a list of several frequently confused pairs of words—many of which your spellchecker will not catch for you!

1. **Accept/Except:** *Accept* is a verb meaning to receive, as in "I accept your recommendation." *Except* is a preposition meaning to exclude, as in "Everybody voted except John."

2. **Advice/Advise:** *Advice* is a noun meaning counsel: "The board offered the president advice on pay raises." In contrast, *advise* is a verb meaning to give information for considered action: "The board advised the president not to raise salaries."

3. **Affect/Effect:** *Affect* is a verb meaning to influence: "Alcohol affects a person's ability to drive safely"; *effect* is a noun meaning result: "The effect of the decision will be felt in six months."

4. **All ready/Already:** *All ready* is a phrase meaning prepared, as in "We are all ready to party!" *Already* is an adverb meaning previously, as in "We already finished the assignment."

5. **Alot/A lot/Allot:** *Alot* is the nonstandard form for a lot. Do not use it. The proper form, *a lot*, is a two-word phrase meaning many or a large number: "His ad generated a lot of phone calls." Some teachers discourage using this phrase because they find it wordy and awkward. Finally, *allot* is a verb meaning to distribute: "The supervisor will allot six new positions to our department."

6. **Choose/Chose:** *Choose* is the present tense form of an irregular verb. *Chose* is the past tense form. This form is unique to choose, so you must simply memorize it.

7. **Lead/Led:** This pair of words is also a verb form problem. The past tense of the verb *to lead* is spelled "led"; *lead*, pronounced with a short *e*, is a metal, not an action.

8. **Cite/Site/Sight:** *Cite* is a verb meaning to be ordered to appear in court or to refer to an authority. Examples would be "The officer cited the driver for DUI" or "The author cited only the most recognized experts." *Site* is a noun meaning location; for example, "The site afforded a spectacular view of the ocean." Finally, *sight* is a noun meaning vision or a verb meaning to see. Sample sentences would be "Her sight was fully restored with laser surgery" and "Only Big Bird sighted Mr. Snuffle-upagus."

9. **Conscience/Conscious:** *Conscience* is a noun meaning a sense of one's own conduct: "My conscience won't let me steal that candy bar." However, *conscious* is an adjective meaning awareness: "She was not conscious of having caused a problem."

10. **Idea/Ideal:** *Idea* is a noun meaning concept or thought, as in "Her idea saved the corporation a million dollars." *Ideal*, in contrast, is a noun or adjective meaning a standard of perfection or a goal or principle, as in "Michael Jordan was the ideal basketball player."

11. **Light/Lite:** *Light* is a noun indicating a source of illumination; for example, "Please switch on the light." It is also an adjective indicating a lack of weight; an example would be "The feather is very light." *Lite* is the brand name of a beer company and is not an acceptable form of light.

12. **Loose/Lose:** *Loose* is an adjective meaning not attached firmly: "The loose shutter banged against the house when the wind blew." As a transitive verb, *loose* indicates intentional action: "Jill loosed an arrow at the target." In contrast, *lose* is a verb meaning no longer

having possession or knowing location: "You could lose your car in the mall parking lot."

13. **Past/Passed:** *Past* is a noun meaning time before the present time, as in "Accomplishments always lie in the past." *Passed* is a past tense verb meaning an accomplishment, a transfer, or movement, as in "We passed every car on the road."

14. **Quiet/Quite:** *Quiet* is an adjective describing noise level: "The quiet children surprised their parents." *Quite* is an adverb indicating extent or degree: "They put on quite a show."

15. **Than/Then:** *Than* is a conjunctive adverb used to signal comparison, for example, "Jill is older than Jack." *Then,* in contrast, is an adverb indicating past time, as in the sentence, "He was not rich then." Or it can signify result, as in "if-then" complex sentences: "If it rains, then the crops will be saved."

16. **Their/There/They're:** *Their* is the third-person plural possessive pronoun: "The students submitted their papers on time." *There* is an adverb indicating location: "The books lay over there." *They're* is a contraction of *they* and *are:* "They're here!"

17. **Threw/Through/Thru:** *Threw* is the past tense form of the transitive verb throw, as in "She threw the ball to home plate." *Through* is a preposition indicating position, as in "They walked through the door." *Thru* is a nonstandard substitute for the preposition through. Do not use it.

18. **Were/Where:** *Were* is a verb, as in, "They were here yesterday." *Where* is an adverb indicating location: "I wonder where I put my keys."

3.2: Other Usage Problems

1. *Among* is a preposition meaning surrounded by: *Among friends, she was a different person.*

2. *Between* is a preposition meaning from one to another: *Between you and me, I think Joe will win the election.*

3. *Amount* is a noun meaning an uncountable quantity: *I have a huge amount of homework to do.*

4. *Number* is a noun meaning a measurable quantity: *The number of voters will be few.*

5. *Irregardless* is a nonstandard form of regardless—do not use it in formal writing: *Regardless of your reasons, you missed the deadline.*

6. *Is when* is a nonstandard form for a definition, as in the following example: *An uncomfortable adventure is when you wish you were somewhere else.* This sentence implies that an adventure is a time; an adventure, however, is actually an experience. Revise to treat adventure as a noun: *An uncomfortable adventure makes you wish you were somewhere else.*

7. *Is where* is a nonstandard form for identifying location, as in the following example: *The kitchen is where the detective found the body.* A more direct sentence results from removing the *to be* verb: *The detective found the body in the kitchen.*

8. *Lay* is the past form of the intransitive verb *lie*: *Yesterday, the dog lay on the couch.* The verb is intransitive because there is no receiver of the action. *Lay* can also be a transitive verb in the present tense: *Please lay the book on the table.* The verb is transitive here because book receives the action.

9. *Less* is an adjective referring to an uncountable quantity: *There is less water in the ocean now than before.* If the quantity is countable, then use *fewer*: *Fewer people voted in this election than in the last.*

10. *So* does not mean *very*. Take a look at this sentence: *He is so cute.* This construction is incomplete—when *so* is used in this way, a clause beginning with *that* needs to complete the construction: *He is so cute that he makes my knees grow weak.* Your other choice is to write: *He is very cute.*

4: TROUBLESHOOTING PUNCTUATION

Of all the marks of punctuation, the lowly comma give writers the most trouble, but it is also the most useful when used correctly. Many writers are familiar with some minor uses for the comma—in dates, in numbers, after the salutation of a letter, and so on. But there are perhaps five major uses for commas that give writers trouble. Here is a quick review of comma use.

4.1: Using a Comma in Coordination

When you are coordinating two independent clauses, put a comma between the first independent clause and the coordinating conjunction:

My name is George, and I am a mechanic.

Never put the comma *after* the coordinating conjunction.

4.2: Using a Comma after an Introductory Element

An introductory element is a word, phrase, or clause that appears at the beginning of a sentence and describes where, when, or under what conditions the action of the sentence takes place. Separate the introductory element from the main clause with a comma:

Yesterday, a foot of snow fell in New England.

4.3: Using Commas in a Series

You are probably familiar with the journalists' omission of the final comma in a series of three or more items:

We purchased bread, milk, eggs and bacon.

This practice may be acceptable in the limited column space of journalism, but in other kinds of writing, it can lead to confusion of which items go with which if the final comma is omitted. Consider the following sentence:

We ordered bacon and eggs, hot oatmeal and coffee and toast.

Omitting the comma after oatmeal makes it appear that the last three items are one unit. To avoid confusion, you should place a comma after oatmeal to make it clear that three separate orders are made and not just two:

We ordered bacon and eggs, hot oatmeal, and coffee and toast.

4.4: Using Commas with Coordinate Adjectives

Consider this sentence:

There's a bright red fire hydrant in front of my house.

When two or more adjectives (bright and red) appear before a noun (fire hydrant), you must determine whether the adjectives are *coordinate* or *additive*. To do so, ask two questions:

1. Can the adjectives' order be reversed without changing the meaning?
2. Can the word *and* be placed between the adjectives without changing the meaning?

If the answer is "yes" to both of the questions, then the adjectives are coordinate and should be separated by a comma; if the answer to one or both of the questions is "no," then the adjectives are additive and no comma should be used.

For example, a "bright red fire hydrant" is not the same thing as a "red bright fire hydrant," so you already know not to put a comma between *bright* and *red*.

Now, consider this example:

I received fast efficient service at the restaurant.

Does "fast efficient service" mean the same thing as "efficient fast service"? Yes. Does "fast and efficient service" mean the same thing as "fast efficient service"? Yes. So, these are coordinate adjectives and a comma should be added:

I received fast, efficient service at the restaurant.

4.5: Using Commas with Nonrestrictive Clauses

Definitions of restrictive and nonrestrictive dependent clauses appear earlier in the appendix. Just to remind you, a restrictive clause restricts or limits the word it modifies and is not set off with commas:

We want a car that is economical to operate.

A nonrestrictive clause is not important for identifying or qualifying the word it modifies and is set off with commas:

The MR2, which Toyota recently reintroduced, *has a mid-mount engine.*

4.6: Using Commas with Conjunctive Adverbs

You can place commas before and after conjunctive adverbs, or only before, or only after. Confused? Don't worry—placement simply depends on where the conjunctive adverb appears in the clause.

1. If the conjunctive adverb begins the sentence, then you follow it with a comma (it's now an introductory element): *However, I would not be willing to bet the farm.*
2. If the conjunctive adverb ends the sentence, then place a comma before it: *I would not be willing to bet the farm, however.*
3. If the conjunctive adverb interrupts the sentence, then place commas before and after it: *I would not, however, be willing to bet the farm.*

Above all, you must not treat a conjunctive adverb as if it were a coordinating conjunction. If you use a conjunctive adverb (however, therefore, thus, rather, and so on) to join two independent clauses, then you must put a semicolon before the adverb and a comma after it:

The senator voted for the bill; however, his constituents voted him out of office.

4.7: Commas, Periods, and Quotation Marks

Look at the placement of the comma in this sentence:

"Elzie Segar used a lit cigar drawing as a symbol for his name in his cartoons," says Mike Brooks.

Note that the comma is placed inside the closing quotation mark. The same rule holds true for periods:

Mike Brooks reminds us, "Elzie Segar used a lit cigar drawing as a symbol for his name in his cartoons."

4.8: Question Marks and Quotation Marks

Using question marks with quotation marks is not such a simple matter as commas and periods. If the quotation is a question, then you place the punctuation inside the final quotation mark:

"Will you marry me?" he asked.

But if the sentence is a question, then the punctuation is placed outside the final quotation mark:

Did he say, "The weather is perfect today"?

Finally, if both the sentence and the quotation are questions, simply place the question mark within the final quotation mark:

Did she ask, "What is the weather prediction for today?"

5: TROUBLESHOOTING MECHANICS

Mechanics include all of the other marks that show us how to interpret certain parts of the sentence. To a degree, punctuation reflects pauses, stops, and emphases in the spoken language. But nothing in speech marks a capital, a hyphenation, a dash, underlining, or italics. Mechanics are strictly visual devices used in writing according to certain conventions and expectations.

5.1: Capitals

1. Capitalize specific names: *the Supreme Court*
2. Do not capitalize general names: *the court house.*
3. Capitalize all first and last words, all verbs, and other major words in titles: *The Grapes of Wrath.*

5.2: Italics

Italicize if you are using a computer. Underline if you are using a typewriter.

1. Italicize words, letters, or numbers referred to as such without their meaning:

   Ubiquitous *has an interesting etymology.*

2. Italicize major titles, such as books, plays, newspapers, magazines, periodicals, movies, television and radio shows, and musicals.

   Ten Things I Hate About You *is based on Shakespeare's* The Taming of the Shrew.

3. Other titles that would ordinarily be contained within a larger work are enclosed within quotation marks. Such titles would include articles, chapters, essays, poems, short stories, songs, and so forth.

5.3: Abbreviations

1. Abbreviations are usually punctuated with periods.
2. In the case of *A.M./a.m.* you may use either uppercase or lowercase letters to designate the time of day. Whichever you use, be consistent throughout your text.
3. In general, abbreviations are not used alone.

   • Mr. John Smith; Dr. Jones; 1000 B.C.; Joseph Numeral, C.P.A.; 8:15 a.m.; 1972 Michelle Dr.
   • Not *I went to the Dr.*

4. Acronyms are abbreviations for proper nouns, such as government agencies, organizations, or certain medical terms, and are not punctuated with periods.

   • FBI: Federal Bureau of Investigation
   • ZPG: Zero Population Growth
   • MADD: Mothers Against Drunk Driving

   If you think that your readers might not know what the acronym stands for, then write out the full name the first time you use it, followed by the acronym in parentheses. Then in subsequent references, you can use the acronym by itself.

   Although the Negative Population Growth (NPG) and the Zero Population Growth (ZPG) groups appear to have similar goals, they differ in significant ways.

5.4: Numbers

Do not use Arabic numerals to start sentences; instead, spell out the numbers:

Sixteen runners crossed the finish line within four minutes of each other.

Not: 16 runners crossed the finish line within four minutes of each other.

On the other hand, if the spelled-out number is lengthy, then revise the sentence, using figures for economy of expression:

More than 100,000 people attended the concert in Central Park.

Not: One hundred thousand and sixteen people attended the concert in Central Park.

If you use numbers infrequently in your paper, then spell out the numbers that are expressed in one or two words, such as six, thirteen, twenty-nine, and so on. But if you use numbers frequently, spell out the numbers from one to nine; then use Arabic numerals for 10 and above.

When numbers refer to the same kind of category, do not mix Arabic numerals and spelled numerals:

I have 4 pugs and 16 collies.

Not: I have four pugs and 16 collies.

But when the categories referred to are different, vary the form for distinction between the categories:

Our collie gave birth to 16 puppies three days ago.

5.5: Hyphens

A string of modifiers and nouns can often be ambiguous: two adjectives and a noun; an adverb, an adjective, and a noun; an adjective and two nouns. In each of these cases, a hyphen can be used to clear up any ambiguity. A *small-aircraft carrier,* for instance, is a big ship that carries little planes, but a *small aircraft-carrier* is a little ship that carries any size plane.

5.6: Brackets

Use brackets to insert clarifying information or your own words into quotations:

The teacher commented, "Metaphors and similes are two of the most common devices [of figurative language]."

Also use brackets when inserting the word *sic* after an error—it shows that the error is the author's and not yours:

The senator argued, "Regardless of the public's sentiment, we has [sic] to follow the law on this matter."

6: TROUBLESHOOTING STYLE

Besides the conventions in grammar, spelling, punctuation, and mechanics, you are faced with another set of choices, choices that define your writing style. Take a look at the clothes you're wearing. You selected those clothes because you have a certain *style*. When you write, you can choose to "dress" your writing in certain "clothes" that will make your writing clearly and uniquely yours.

The choices that make up style include choices about the words you use (*tyro* instead of *beginner*); figurative language (is the surface *smooth as ice* or *smooth as a baby's bottom*?); and structure (how you put together words, phrases, and clauses). Each successful writer has a unique style. Here are a few choices to think about when you develop your own writing style.

6.1: Parallelism

When the same grammatical structure is repeated (whether in phrases, clauses, or sentences), you are using the stylistic device of parallelism:

> *You will hear more turkeys than you see, and you will see more turkeys than you shoot.*

This sentence illustrates the use of the same structure—a repetition of independent clause and dependent clause. Thus, the clauses are parallel. Parallelism can be used to indicate equal emphasis between the parallel ideas. It can also help to maintain a sense of order in a list whose elements are each long phrases and clauses. Here, the parallelism highlights the difficulty of hunting this wily game.

6.2: Well, Yes, No

> *Well, the committee should resolve its impasse.*

> *Yes, the decision was based on logical judgment.*

> *No, the prescribed medicine always carries warnings about side effects.*

The choices the writer made in these sentences create a conversational style of writing. But conversational writing is very informal writing, and informal writing is rarely appropriate for writing in school or at work. Therefore, in academic or professional writing, do not begin your sentences with *well, yes,* or *no.*

6.3: Contractions

Using contractions is another choice that contributes to an informal style of writing. Some instructors and supervisors will allow you to use contractions, and some will not. You have two options: ask ahead of time if contractions are allowed, or play it safe and do not use any contractions.

6.4: Elevated Language

Sometimes, writers make choices that create a style that is too formal:

> *The closest acquaintances of my heart and I ventured out to attend the social gathering on Saturday evening.*

This writer's choices sound like he or she is trying too hard for formality and come off sounding pompous and ridiculous. The best style for expository writing—whether academic or professional—is simple, clear, and direct:

My friends and I went to a party Saturday night.

6.5: Redundancies

A *redundancy* is an expression that unnecessarily repeats information implied in other words in a sentence. There are many ways for redundancies to show up in your writing. Here are some things to look for:

1. *Redundant nouns and verbs:* The following redundancies are very common, especially in researched writing:

   In the book <u>The Hobbit</u>, *written by the author J.R.R. Tolkien, he tells a story about stealing a dragon's treasure.*

   There are several redundancies in this sentence. The fact that *The Hobbit* is a book is indicated by the italicized or underlined title. The fact that it was written by an author is implied in the fact that it's a book. And there is no need to give both a name and a pronoun here. Stripped of its redundancies, this sentence reads:

   In <u>The Hobbit</u>, *J.R.R. Tolkien tells a story about stealing a dragon's treasure.*

2. *Redundant adjectives:* Largely for reasons of rhythm, speakers often pair adjectives. These pairs, however, often say the same thing. Take a look at these examples:

   Each and every
   First and foremost
   Always and forever

   These are only a few examples of redundant adjective pairs. *First* is *foremost*—and *always* lasts just as long as *forever*. There's no need to include both when you only need one.

3. *Redundant prepositions:* Here are some examples of a different kind of redundancy, redundant prepositions:

   We should <u>*refer back*</u> *to our prerequisites for this course.*

   The professor <u>*continued on*</u> *with her lecture.*

   In both of these sentences, the preposition following the verb repeats the idea of the verb. The *re-* prefix of *refer* means back. *Continue* means "without interruption." Delete the redundant prepositions:

   We should refer to our prerequisites for this course.

   The professor continued with her lecture.

4. *"reason is because"*:

The reason the check bounced is because my account was overdrawn.

Reason implies *because*; revise to use one or the other, but not both:

The reason the check bounced is that my account was overdrawn.

Or: The check bounced because my account was overdrawn.

Similarly, "reason why" is redundant. Change *The reason why the check bounced is that my account was overdrawn* to either of the two examples given previously.

6.6: Clichés

If style is a set of choices to make your writing your own, then clichés have no style. They were created by other people long ago, and they have been used by many people since then. To write with an individual, original style, always use your own words—don't rely on what others have said.

Many handbooks include lists of the most common clichés created from similes (cold as ice, slick as glass, light as a feather, and so on), but there are many other types of clichés. The list in Table A–1 gives just a few of the clichés that appear in student writing. Avoid using these phrases or any other phrase that you didn't come up with yourself unless you are putting a new twist on them as Tobi Raney did in the title of her final researched writing project, "Jumping for Joy."

TABLE A–1

A close-knit family	A feeling of ___ overtook me.
A happy camper	As fate/luck would have it
As I sit here . . .	At that point in time
Back to the drawing board	Believe in yourself.
Blanket of snow	Bogged down in frustration
Bottom line	Bummed out
Burst my bubble	Butterflies in my stomach
Chills up my spine	Chow down
Come back to reality.	Do you get my point?
Don't get me wrong.	Down the drain
Few and far between	Get a handle on it.
Get the point across.	Give them a run for their money.
S/He fell for it hook, line, and sinker.	S/He has it easy.
S/He was always there for me.	S/He'll never give up on me.
I love him/her to death.	I made a total fool out of myself.
I owe it all to him/her.	I was in heaven.
I was on top of the world.	I was sold on the idea.
I will never forget that day.	In one ear and out the other
It came from the heart.	It took my breath away.
It was a breeze.	It's all downhill from there.
Knocked senseless	Like crazy

Continued

TABLE A-1 *continued*

Make a long story short	Make or break
Make the best of it.	My eyes welled up with tears.
My mouth dropped to the floor.	Needless to say
Nerve wracking	No big deal
No skin off my back	Not a care in the world
Once-in-a-lifetime opportunity	Pain in the neck
Pull one over on him/her	Raining cats and dogs
Scared to death	Set my mind to racing
Set your mind to it.	Stick like glue
Sweep me off my feet.	The coast was clear.
The task at hand	This tops the list.
Through thick and thin	Time has flown by.
To say the least	Too good to be true
Up to par	Very time consuming
Weigh all the facts	What the future holds
You can't judge a book by its cover.	

7: FALSE RULES

This troubleshooting guide is not intended to cover every error you might make when you write, although you may think that more than enough has been covered. No one expects you to memorize an entire handbook of grammar and style. To help you manage all of the grammatical information you need to keep in mind, teachers have come up with easy-to-remember rules of thumb.

These rules are written for several reasons. The teacher might be repeating what he or she was taught. The teacher might be trying to keep one part of writing consistent while you work on other parts. Many of these rules are helpful, but others are not even rules. These false rules have been told so many times to so many writers, however, that many people accept them without question. Here are a few examples.

7.1: Do Not Start a Sentence with *and* or *but*

The words *and* and *but* are coordinate conjunctions. Besides simply connecting words, phrases, and clauses, they can show the logical relationships between sentences. For example, *and* can show emphasis, in addition to equality with the previous sentence. And *but* can show strong contrast. You certainly do not want to start every sentence with *and, but,* or another coordinate conjunction, but there is no rule that says you can't do so when it is appropriate.

7.2: Do Not End a Sentence with a Preposition

Winston Churchill, the Prime Minister of England during World War II, dealt with this false rule many decades ago. Consider these examples that Churchill gave to illustrate the point:

> *This is an intolerable situation up with which I will not put.*

> *This is an intolerable situation which I will not put up with.*

Which of these sentences reads more smoothly? The second. The first sentence sounds pretentious and stuffy.

The reason the second sentence is the correct choice here is that the prepositions aren't really prepositions at all. Without objects, the prepositions are in fact adverbs, and you can certainly end a sentence with an adverb.

7.3: Sentences Should Have No Fewer than Ten Words and No More than Twenty-one Words

The shortest verse in the New Testament is two words long: "Jesus wept."

Winston Churchill wrote a sentence about the Russian revolutionary Leon Trotsky that ran on for 84 words. There is no magic number of words that defines a good sentence. What defines a good sentence is that the idea within the sentence is clearly and effectively presented to the reader. How many words belong in a sentence? To adopt an answer from earlier in this book, *as many as it takes!*

Whenever you are presented with a rule about writing, always consider your purpose as a writer. Your writing should clearly communicate a message to your reader. As long as your grammar, punctuation, and mechanics meet the reader's expectations, anything else you do in the sentence is fine, as long as it helps you get your ideas across to your reader.

Credits

INDEX

A

Abbreviations, 471
Ad hominem, 239
Ad ignorantium, 239
Ad misericordiam, 239
Ad populum, 239
although/however/though, 459
Analogies, false, 238
Annotated bibliographies, 103–8
APA bibliography entries, 82–86. *See also* inside back cover
  books, 83
  journal articles, 84
  magazine articles, 83–84
  newspaper articles, 84
  online articles, 84–85
  periodicals, 83–84
  web pages, 85–86
APA style, 82–83
  citing sources, 129–33. *See* APA bibliography entries
  parenthetical citations, 341–42
Appeal to tradition, 239
Appendices, including, 357–58
Arrangement, 343–58
  appendices, 357–58
  concluding, 352–56
  definition, 343
  graphics, 356–57
  outlining, 343–47
  thesis, leading into, 349–52
  title, creating, 347–49
Art, works of. *See* inside back cover
as or because, 460
Audience, 4–5
and purpose, 26, 27

B

Bandwagon appeals, 239–40
Basic writing principles, 3–24
  body, organizing, 11
  editing for grammar, punctuation, mechanics, 13–14
  prewriting activities, 6–8
  professional writing, 16–19
  proofreading, 14–15
  revising, for unity and development, 12–13
  student writing, 19–23
  thesis statement, 9–11
  topic, finding, 15
  topic, limiting, 8–9
  transitions, for coherence, 11–12
because or as, 460
Begging the question, 237
Bible. *See* inside back cover
Bibliographies, 69–108
  annotated, 103–08.
  APA entries, 82–86
  building, 77–108
  defined, 70
  kinds of sources, 71–74
  MLA entries, 77–82
  working, 86–103
Body, organizing, 11
Books, 72. *See also* Sources; inside back cover
Brackets, 472
Brainstorming, 6, 7

C

Capitals, 470
Card stacking, 240
Cartoons. *See* inside back cover
Catalogue of library holdings, 76
Categories, connections and context, 185
Causal analysis
  purpose, 28–29
  student writing, 418–23
CD-ROM material. *See* inside back cover
Charts. *See* inside back cover
Circular arguments, 237
Citing sources, 125–33
  APA style. *See* APA style
  MLA style. *See* MLA style
Clichés, 475–76
Colons, 459
Comma splices, 457–58
Commas
  after introductory elements, 468
  with conjunctive adverbs, 469–70
  with coordinate adjectives, 469
  in coordination, 468
  with nonrestrictive clauses, 469
  and periods and quotation marks, 470
  in series, 468–69
Commenting about sources, 125
Comparisons
  connections and context, 185
  drawing, 56
  false analogies, 238
Conclusions, 352–56
  advice, 355
  definitions, 353
  precautions, 355–56
  questions, 354
  quotations, 355
  results, 354
  solutions, 354
  summaries, 353–54
Connections and context, 183–229
  categories, 185
  comparisons, 185
  connections out of context, 197–209
  contrasts, 185
  definitions, 184
  discovering context, 193–209
  drawing connections, 56–57, 184–93
  leads, 351
  professional writing, 209–18
  student writing, 218–29
Contractions, 473
Contrasts
  connections and context, 185
  drawing, 56
Corporate publications. *See* inside back cover
Cover page, 360
Critiquing sources, 230–83
  accuracy of information, 235
  author's attitude, 235
  fallacies, detecting, 236–49.
  inductive versus deductive presentation, 233
  partitioning of source, 233–34
  professional writing, 250–58
  reading critically, 233–36

significance of source, 235–36
sources' sources, 234–35
student writing, 258–83

D

Dangling modifiers, 460
Dates, free-standing, 461
Definitional purpose, 28
student writing, 401–5
Descriptive purpose, 27
student writing, 395–401
Dewey decimal system, 75
Dictionaries. *See* inside back cover
different from/different than, 460–61
Dilemma, false, 238
Dissertations, unpublished. *See* inside back cover

E

E-mail. *See* inside back cover
Editing, 13–14
Electronic sources. *See* inside back cover
Elevated language, 473
Encyclopedias. *See* inside back cover
Equivocation, 240
Evaluational purpose, 29
student writing, 432–38
Evidence
discrepancies in "factual data," 144–45, 151
false or misleading statements, 151
inferences, 284–323. *See* Inferences
lack of, 152
meaning and, 43–45
omissions of specific detail, 151
reflective journal, keeping, 146–51
variety of sources, consulting, 145–46
Examples, providing, 55–56
Explanational purpose, 28
student writing, 410–18

F

Fallacies, 236–49. *See* specific topics
False analogies, 238
False authority, 240
False dilemma, 238
False sentence rules, 476–77
Films. *See* inside back cover

Formal outline, 344–45
Fragments, 456–57
Freewriting, 6, 7
Fused sentences, 458

G

"Garbage can" thesis, validation paper, 153
Gathering information, 111–12
Generalizations, hasty, 238
Government publications. *See* inside back cover
Grammar troubleshooting, 459–65
although/however/though, 459
colons, 459
dangling modifiers, 460
dates, free-standing, 461
different from/different than, 460–61
false coordination, 461
"hopefully," 462
its/it's, 462–63
myself/I, 463
"only," 463
as or because, 460
pronouns, demonstrative (free-standing), 462
subject-verb agreement, 463–64
time, free-standing, 461–62
"to try," 464
used to/supposed to, 464–65
who/which/that, 465
Graphics, 356–57

H

Hard copy searches, 89–91
Hasty generalizations, 238
"hopefully," 462
however/though/although, 459
Hyphens, 472
Hypothesis contrary to fact, 238

I

I/myself, 463
Illogical thinking, 237–39, 241–49.
Illustrations, providing, 56
Inferences, 284–323
argument, presenting as, 288–89
defined, 284–88
drawing, 288–89

professional writing, 303–19
Rogerian argumentation, 295–96
student writing, 319–23
syllogisms, 290–92
Toulmin Model, 292–95
Inserting sources, 122–25
Interest inventories, 33–37
Internet sources, 73–74. *See also* Sources; inside back cover
at library, 76
locating, 96
online articles. *See* Online articles
web pages. *See* Web pages
Interviews. *See* inside back cover
Introducing sources, 120–22
Italics, 471
its/it's, 462–63

J

Journal articles. *See also* Sources; inside back cover
APA bibliography entries, 84
MLA bibliography entries, 79–80
Journal (reflective), keeping, 146–51

L

Leads, 349–52
allusions, 350–51
anecdotes, 350
connections, 351
"cosmic" leads, 352
definitions, 351
descriptions, 351 ·
precautions, 351–52
question leads, 352
quotation leads, 352
scenes, 349
"Webster" leads, 352
Learning as purpose, 28
student writing, 406–10
Letters. *See* inside back cover
Library, 74–77
catalogues, 76
Dewey decimal system, 75
Library of Congress system, 75
locating sources, 87–88
online sources, 76
periodicals, 76
reference collections, 75

Library of Congress system, 75
Live performances. *See* inside back cover
Loaded language, 240

M

Magazine articles. *See also* Sources; inside back cover
APA bibliography entries, 83–84
MLA bibliography entries, 78–79
Managing, 359–88
cover/title page, 359–62
student writing, 362–88
Maps. *See* inside back cover
Meaning, 42–66
comparisons, drawing, 56
connections, drawing, 56–57
contrasts, drawing, 56
creating, 42, 43, 46–54
evidence and, 43–45
examples, providing, 55–56
illustrations, providing, 56
presenting, 54–60
professional writing, 57–60
sensory perceptions, 55
student writing, 60–65
Mechanics, 470–72
MLA bibliography entries, 77–82. *See also* inside back cover
books, 78
journal articles, 79–80
magazine articles, 78–79
newspaper articles, 79
online articles, 80–81
periodicals, 78–80
Web pages, 81–82
MLA style, 77–78
citing sources, 126–29. *See* MLA bibliography entries
parenthetical citations, 335
Modifiers, dangling, 460
myself/I, 463

N

Newspaper articles. *See also* Sources; inside back cover
APA bibliography entries, 84
MLA bibliography entries, 79
no/well/yes, 473

Non sequiturs, 238
Numbers, 471–72

O

Online articles. *See also* inside back cover
APA bibliography entries, 84–85
MLA bibliography entries, 80–81
Online postings. *See* inside back cover
Online searches, 91–95
Online sources, 73–74. *See also* Sources
at library, 76
locating, 96
"only," 463
Outlining, 343–47
formal outline, 344–45
prewriting activity, 6, 8
sentence outline, 345–47
Ownership, 4–5
topics and, 33, 34

P

Pamphlets. *See* inside back cover
Parallelism, 473
Paraphrasing sources, 116–18
Parenthetical citations. *See* inside back cover
Partitioning sources, 233–34
Periodicals, 72–73. *See also* inside back cover
APA bibliography entries, 83–84
at library, 76
MLA bibliography entries, 78–80
Persuasive purpose, 29–30
student writing, 443–48
Plagiarism, 109–10
Positional purpose, 30
student writing, 438–42
Post hoc, ergo propter hoc, 238
Prewriting activities, 6–8
Project proposal
drafting, 37–38
student writing, 38–41
Pronouns
demonstrative, free-standing, 462
myself/I, 463
Proofreading, 14–15
Punctuation troubleshooting, 468–70
commas. *See* Commas
question marks, 470
quotation marks, 470

Purpose, 4–5
causal analysis, 28–29
choosing, 27–31
defined, 26–27
definitional, 28
descriptive, 27
evaluational, 29
explanational, 28
learning as, 28
persuasive, 29–30
positional, 30
recommendatory, 28
student writing, examples of. *See* Student writing topics and, 33

Q

Question marks, 470
Quotation marks, 470
Quoting sources, 113–16
formats for, 123–24

R

Radio programs. *See* inside back cover
Reading critically, 233–36
Recommendatory purpose, 28
student writing, 424–31
Red herring appeals, 240
Redundancies, 474–75
Reference works, 71. *See also* Sources
at library, 75
Reviews. *See* inside back cover
Revision, for unity and development, 12–13
Rogerian argumentation, 295–96
Run-ons, 458

S

Scholarly projects (electronic). *See* inside back cover
Searches
hard copy, 89–91
online, 91–95
Sensory perceptions, presenting, 55
Sentence ending with preposition, 476
Sentence outline, 345–47
Sentence size, 477
Sentence starting with "and" or "but," 476
Sentence troubleshooting, 452–58
Slippery slope, 238

Sound recordings. *See* inside back cover
Sources. *See also* inside back cover
  accuracy of information, 235
  author's attitude, 235
  bibliographies. *See* Bibliographies
  blending writing and, 119–25
  citing, 125–33. *See* Citing sources
  commentary, 125
  critiquing, 230–83. *See* Critiquing sources
  gathering information, 111–12
  inductive versus deductive presentation, 233
  inserting, 122–25
  introducing, 120–22
  kinds of, 71–74
  number of, 143–44
  paraphrasing, 116–18
  partitioning of, 233–34
  professional writing, 134–37
  quoting, 113–16
  quoting, formats, 123–24
  significance of, 235–36
  sources' sources, 234–35
  summarizing, 118–19
  using in writing, 109–37
  validating, 141–82. *See* Validating sources
  variety of, consulting, 145–46
Spelling and usage, 465–68
Stacking the cards, 240
Stilted language, 473
Straw man distractions, 241
Style troubleshooting, 472–76
  clichés, 475–76
  contractions, 473
  elevated language, 473
  parallelism, 470
  redundancies, 474–75
  well/yes/no, 473
Subject-verb agreement, 463–64
Summarizing sources, 118–19
supposed to/used to, 464–65
Surveys (personal). *See* inside back cover
Syllogisms, 290–92

T
Television programs. *See* inside back cover
that/who/which, 465
Thesis statement
  "clothesline" thesis, validation paper, 153–54
  formulating, 9–10
  "garbage can" thesis, validation paper, 153
  leading into, 349–52. *See* Leads
  supporting, 10–11
  "vehicle reminder" thesis, validation paper, 153
though/although/however, 459
Time, free-standing, 461–62
Title
  creating, 347–49
  question as, 348
  sentences and phrases, 348
  single words, 348
Title page, 360–61
"to try," 464
Topic
  choosing, 31–41
  finding, 15
  general, 33
  interest inventories, 33–37
  limiting, 8–9
  ownership and, 33, 34
  popular, 33
  project proposal, drafting, 37–38
  project proposal, student writing, 38–41
  purpose and, 33
  validation paper, limiting focus of, 153–54
  validation paper, limiting scope of, 153
Toulmin Model, 292–95
Tradition, appeal to, 239
Transitions, for coherence, 11–12
Troubleshooting, 449–77
  abbreviations, 471
  brackets, 472
  capitals, 470
  false rules, 476–77
  grammar, 459–65
  hyphens, 472
  italics, 471
  mechanics, 470–72
  numbers, 471–72
  punctuation, 468–70
  sentences, 452–58
  spelling and usage, 465–68
  style, 472–76

U
Usage and spelling, 465–68
used to/supposed to, 464–65

V
Validating sources, 141–82
  confirming evidence, lack of, 152
  definition of "validation," 143–45
  discrepancies in "factual data," 144–45, 151
  false or misleading statements, 151
  omissions of specific detail, 151
  opposing views, 151
  reflective journal, keeping, 146–51
  variety of sources, consulting, 145–46
Validation paper
  arrangement, 154–55
  citing sources, 155
  inductive or deductive scheme, 154
  professional writing, 156–70
  student writing, 170–82
  writing, 152–55
  "vehicle reminder" thesis, validation paper, 153
Videotapes. *See* inside back cover

W
Web pages. *See also* inside back cover
  APA bibliography entries, 85–86
  MLA bibliography entries, 81–82
Web sources, 73–74. *See also* Sources
  at library, 76
  locating, 96
well/yes/no, 473
who/which/that, 465
Working bibliographies
  building, 86–103
  hard copy searches, 89–91
  library sources, locating, 87–88
  online sources, locating, 96
  student writing, 96–103

Y
yes/no/well, 473

WORKS CITED LIST

Books
One author   328
More than one work by the same author   328
Two authors   328
Three authors   328
More than three authors   329
Works by authors with the same last name   329
No author listed   329
Work in several volumes (each volume titled separately)   329
Work in several volumes (all volumes with same title)   329
Book in a series   329
One selection from an anthology of writings by various authors   329
More than one selection from an anthology   329
Editor   329
Work with an editor and an author   330
Translated work   330
Introduction, preface, foreword, or afterword   330
Edition   330
Reprinted book   330
Dictionary or encyclopedia entry   330
Authored article in a reference book   330
Bible   330
Unpublished dissertation   330

Articles
Signed article in a weekly or biweekly magazine   331
Signed article in a monthly or bimonthly magazine   331
Article in a professional journal—nonconsecutive pagination   331
Article in a professional journal—consecutive pagination   331
Article in a daily newspaper   331
Review   332

Other Copyrighted Sources
Charts or maps   332
Published interviews   332
Publications by entities such as corporations or government offices   332
Pamphlet   332
Sound recording   332
Videotape or film   332
Television or radio program   332
Published letter   332
Cartoon   332
Live performance   333
Work of art   333

Non-Copyrighted Sources
Personal interview   333
Telephone interview   333
Personal survey   333
Letter   333

Electronic Sources
Material from a CD-ROM   334
Online article with a print version (with a URL)   334
Online article with a print version (without a URL)   334
Online article without a print version   334
Electronic text   334
Scholarly project   334
Organizational home page   334
Personal home page   334
E-mail   334
Online posting   335

PARENTHETICAL CITATIONS
Citing by Author: One author   335
Two authors   335
Three authors   335
More than three authors   335

Citing by Title   335
Citing Multiple Works by One Author   335
Citing Authors of the Same Last Name   335
Citing More Than One Source   335
Citing a Corporation or Government Office   335
Citing Sources with Several Volumes   335
Citing Biblical Passages   335
Citing Online Sources with No Pages   335

DIRECTORY TO APA STYLE

REFERENCES LIST

Books

One author   337
Other works by the same author   337
Two authors   337
Three or more authors   337
More than one work by the same author published in the same year   337
Works by authors with the same last name   338
No author listed   338
Work in several volumes (each volume titled separately)   338
Work in several volumes (all volumes with same title)   338
Book in a series   338
One selection from an anthology of writings by various authors   338
Editor   338
Work with an editor and an author   338
Edition   338
Reprinted book   338
Dictionary or encyclopedia entry   338
Authored article in a reference book   339
Government publication   339
Unpublished dissertation   339

Articles

Signed article in a weekly or biweekly magazine   339
Signed article in a monthly or bimonthly magazine   339
Article in a professional journal—nonconsecutive pagination   339
Article in a professional journal—consecutive pagination   340
Article in a daily newspaper   340
Review   340

Other Copyrighted Sources

Charts or maps   340
Sound recording   340
Videotape or film   340
Television or radio program   340
Published letter   340
Work of art   340

Electronic Sources

Material from a CD-ROM   341
Online article with a print version   340
Online document without a print version   340

APA PARENTHETICAL CITATIONS

Citing by Author: One author   341
                    Two authors   341
                    Three to five authors   341
                    Six or more authors   341
Citing by Date   341
Citing by Title   341
Citing Multiple Works by the Same Author or Authors   341
Citing Authors of the Same Last Name   342
Citing Multiple Sources   342
Citing a Corporation or Government Office   342
Personal Communications: Personal interview   342
                           Telephone interview   342
                           Personal survey   342
                           Letter   342